"博物馆、去殖民化、文物返还：全球对话"

专家研讨会
学术文集

国际博物馆协会研究与交流中心
编

MUSEUMS, DECOLONISATION, AND RESTITUTION: A GLOBAL CONVERSATION

图书在版编目(CIP)数据

"博物馆、去殖民化、文物返还：全球对话"专家研讨会学术文集：汉文、英文/国际博物馆协会研究与交流中心编.—上海：上海大学出版社，2024.4
ISBN 978-7-5671-4963-2

Ⅰ.①博… Ⅱ.①国… Ⅲ.①博物馆学-文集-汉、英 Ⅳ.①G260-53

中国国家版本馆CIP数据核字（2024）第078291号

责任编辑　贺俊逸　陈　强
封面设计　缪炎栩
技术编辑　金　鑫　钱宇坤

"博物馆、去殖民化、文物返还：全球对话"专家研讨会学术文集
国际博物馆协会研究与交流中心　编
上海大学出版社出版发行
（上海市上大路99号　邮政编码200444）
（https://www.shupress.cn　发行热线021-66135112）
出版人　戴骏豪

*

南京展望文化发展有限公司排版
上海华业装潢印刷厂有限公司印刷　各地新华书店经销
开本710mm×1000mm　1/16　印张25.25　字数375千
2024年5月第1版　2024年5月第1次印刷
ISBN 978-7-5671-4963-2/G·3617　定价　88.00元

版权所有　侵权必究
如发现本书有印装质量问题请与印刷厂质量科联系
联系电话：021-56475919

CONTENT
目　录

Preface	Emma Nardi	001
序	艾玛·纳迪	
Foreword	Yong Duan	006
前言	段　勇	
Introduction	Carol A. Scott	011
简介	卡罗尔·A. 斯科特	

Decolonising the Museum Paradigm: Unpacking Museum Theory for Anticolonial Practices   001

Bruno Brulon Soares

博物馆去殖民化范式   布鲁诺·布鲁伦·苏亚雷斯

Owning the Past to Create a Better Future—Our On-going Journey of Decolonisation, Hope and Aspiration   034

Dr. Arapata Hakiwai

拥抱过去，创造更美好的未来：正在进行的去殖民化，希望和憧憬   阿若帕塔·哈克瓦

Qaumajuq, A New Model for the Museum in the South   050

Stephen Borys

Qaumajuq：南方博物馆的新模式   斯蒂芬·鲍卫斯

Decolonizing Museum Practices at Saahlinda Naay "Saving Things House"   Sean Young   064

"拯救之家": Saahlinda Naay 的博物馆去殖民化实践   肖恩·杨

Decolonisation as Infra-structure: Can the Museum be Decolonised?   Wayne Modest   077

博物馆知识基础架构的去殖民化   韦恩·莫德斯特

Inclusive Terminology for the Heritage Sector   Carissa Chew   097

文化遗产领域的包容性术语   克利萨·秋

Decolonizing a Regional Museum Service: From Strategy to Community with TWAM   Jo Anderson   Adam Goldwater   Kylea Little   106

地方博物馆服务的去殖民化：从战略到社区   乔·安德森   亚当·戈德华特   凯利·利特尔

Let's Go Round Again—The Museum Carousel and Its "Others"   Roshi Naidoo   120

让我们再绕一圈吧：博物馆的旋转木马与它的"其他部分"   罗希·奈杜

Asia's Difficult Heritage-making between Nationalism and Transnationalism: Colonial Prisons in South Korea, China and Taiwan, China 133

Hyun Kyung Lee

在民族主义和跨国主义之间产生的亚洲黑暗遗产：以中国、韩国和中国台湾地区的三个殖民地监狱改造而成的博物馆为例

李玄卿

Justice, Re-orientation and Empowering African Source Communities by Decolonising Museum Spaces 145

Samba Yonga

博物馆去殖民化视角下非洲原住民社区社会公正、重新定位与赋权

桑巴·杨格

The Role of International Soft Law in Return of Cultural Objects Removed in Colonial Contexts 160

Yunxia Wang

重视国际软法在殖民地文物返还问题上的作用

王云霞

On Coloniality and Restitution from a Latin American Perspective 193

Américo Castilla

论殖民性——拉丁美洲视角下的殖民性与返还问题

亚美利卡·卡斯蒂洛

Examining the Museum Decolonisation and "Semi-colonial"   206

Yong Duan   Ruiqi Zhang   Xi Zheng

博物馆去殖民化与"半殖民地"问题   段 勇   张睿锜   郑 希

Digitally Distributing Authority and Care: Hinemihi o te Ao Tawhito and Her Return   241

Haidy Geismar

以数字方式传播权威和关怀：Hinemihi o te Ao Tawhito 和她的回归

海蒂·盖斯马

How Artist-made Reproductions Can Strengthen Museums and Their Communities: A Case Study   264

Laura Evans

案例研究：艺术家制作的复制品如何作用于博物馆及其社区的发展

劳拉·埃文斯

The Loss, Return and Convergence of Longmen Grottoes Artefacts   281

Jiazhen Shi

龙门石窟文物的流失、回归与聚合

史家珍

Glasgow Museums Repatriation of Objects to the Archaeological Survey of India Duncan Dornan 295
英国格拉斯哥多家博物馆向印度考古调查局归还文物
邓肯·多南

Egypt Fights Against Illicit Trafficking — The Government's Efforts to Preserve Cultural Heritage, Combat Illegal Trafficking in Cultural Property, and Recover What Was Stolen Shaaban AbdelGawad 300
埃及打击非法贩运——政府为保护文化遗产、打击非法贩运文化财产和追索被盗文物所做的努力
沙班·阿卜杜勒·加瓦德

The Repatriation of the Ivorian Talking Drum "Djidji Ayokwe": Challenges and Perspectives Honoré Kouadio Kouassi 322
科特迪瓦 Bidjan 部落的说话鼓 "Djidji Ayokwe" 的归还：观点与挑战
奥纳瑞·卡瓦迪欧·卡瓦西

Repatriation of Ancestral Remains in Australia: Resources for the World Dr. Michael Pickering 347
文物返还经验的全球化共享：以澳大利亚原住民祖先遗骸返还工作为例
迈克尔·皮克林

Preface

Emma Nardi[*]

ICOM is a global organization with approximately 50,000 members spread across 130 countries that provides working tools to museum professionals, encourages the dissemination of good practices, sets quality standards and publishes documents that offer food for thought to be shared. To better address research problems, ICOM signed an agreement with Shanghai University in 2021, creating IMREC (International Museum Research and Exchange Centre) with the following objectives:
- to stimulate a global think tank and an international network;
- to address critical theoretical and practical issues that the international museum community is facing;
- to promote cross-geographical and interdisciplinary collaborations for scientific research on current and emerging issues commonly shared by the museum community;
- to publish data analysis and research reports.

The pandemic limited the work of ICOM–IMREC to one programme — the organisation of a Sustainability Conference in late 2021. As soon as the

---

[*] President of ICOM, President of ICOM-IMREC Governing Board.

sanctions eased, the work of ICOM-IMREC gained momentum.

The organization of the seminar *Museums, decolonisation and restitution: A global conversation* took place on the 20th and 21st March place at Shanghai University. The seminar was streamed online and the keynote speeches are still available on YouTube.

I am particularly grateful for the seminar because it is tightly related to ICOM Strategic Plan on Decolonisation. This is a major interest for ICOM which also created a working group to advise how ICOM, as the global voice of museum professionals and as an international NGO, can address key topics around decolonization and ensure exemplary institutional practice, seeking equity and social inclusion. This important topic, in my view, requires serious research activity.

My entire university life has been dedicated to research. I am therefore aware that research is an indispensable tool to set up the improvement actions that are necessary in a given context. I would like to emphasize that research activity always arises from the awareness of a problem, that is, a critical situation that needs to be solved thanks to a specific intervention. Now a problem is such only if it lends itself to multiple solutions. In fact, there is no problem without alternative solutions and this seminar viewed the twin problems of decolonization and restitution through multiple lenses. Decolonization is a problem because it derives from a complex situation and can be tackled in many different ways. Research can helps show us the different hypotheses we can deal with.

The seminar was dedicated to the interrelated themes of decolonization and restitution, two very important issues for the historical, geographical, economic and ethical aspects that are implied and particularly dear to ICOM. Decolonization is a painful and burning topic not only for the people who have been colonized, but also for the colonizers who in recent times have been confronted with their responsibilities and with a paradigm shift compared to the past. To speak of decolonisation means, among other things, to speak of restitution, with all the problems and possibilities that this entails. What is right to return? When is it right to return? Who decides to whom and how to return? These conversations are an opportunity for connection, personal and professional growth, learning and development across borders and across cultures.

I look at the seminar organized by IMREC with attention and confidence. Experts representing different countries and positions confronted the strength of their ideas to animate a debate whose conclusions are of great interest. The discussion that took place in Shanghai will be a valuable tool for all museums in the world and for ICOM to set up a policy of dialogue, respect and peace.

As President of the Governing Body of IMREC, I could not be more grateful to ICOM-IMREC for organizing this seminar and for sharing the results of the discussion with the global museum community.

序

艾玛·纳迪*

  国际博物馆协会（International Council of Museums, ICOM，以下简称国际博协）是一家覆盖130多个国家、拥有5万多名成员的国际组织，致力于为博物馆专业人士提供实践工具、鼓励宣传优秀举措、制定行业质量标准并发布值得分享的优质资讯。为更好地应对在博物馆研究领域出现的新兴问题，国际博物馆协会与上海大学在2021年签署合作协议，创立了国际博物馆协会国际博物馆研究与交流中心（ICOM-IMREC），中心宗旨如下：

- 发展一家全球性的智库并建立国际合作网络；
- 解决国际博物馆界面临的重要理论与实践问题；
- 针对博物馆界共同面对的当下新问题，推广跨地区跨学科的科研合作；
- 发布数据分析和研究报告。

  受新冠疫情的影响，中心在2021年仅举办了一场学术活动，即2021年年底举办的首届博物馆可持续发展国际学术研讨会。而随着防疫政策的调整，中心的活动也日益丰富。

  "博物馆、去殖民化、文物返还：全球对话"专家研讨会于2023年3月20—21日在上海大学举办。本次研讨会在线上全程直播，其主旨演讲可

---

* 国际博物馆协会主席，国际博物馆协会国际博物馆研究与交流中心管委会主席。

在YouTube视频平台随时观看。

我对本次研讨会尤为重视，因为它紧密结合了国际博协战略规划中的去殖民化议题。国际博协对于这一议题高度关注，并创立了专项工作组为该议题提供建议，以发出国际博协作为博物馆专业人士的全球性平台和国际非政府组织的专业声音，解决围绕去殖民化议题的重要问题并保障优秀的机构实践，同时确保平等与包容的原则。而完成这项重要的任务，在我看来，需要严谨的研究。

我在大学执教的整个职业生涯都奉献给了研究。我也因此意识到研究工作是在各种语境下建设改进方案时必不可少的方式。我希望强调研究工作始于问题意识，即意识到某些情况需要由特定的干预措施来解决。而问题往往也有多种解决方案。事实上，每一个问题都存在多种解法，而本次研讨会提出的去殖民化和文物返还的问题也是如此，需要我们采用多种视角去看待。去殖民化是一个从复杂的情境中诞生的问题，也因而需要多方努力才可能解决。研究则能帮助我们揭示不同的可能适用的假设。

本次研讨会致力于从历史、地理、经济、道德等国际博协尤为关心的角度来讨论去殖民化和文物返还这两个重要的互相关联的主题。去殖民化不仅对被殖民者来说是个痛苦且沉重的话题，对于殖民者而言，近年来也需要负担起他们的历史责任，直面与过去不同的范式转换。而讨论去殖民化时，在许多相关的议题中必然绕不开文物返还及其包含的所有问题和蕴含的可能性。返还哪些文物？何时返还？由谁决定返还的方式和接收的对象？这些对话是极佳的跨越国界与文化去学习与发展、建立联结、获得个人成长与职业发展的机会。

我对于本次国际博协研究与交流中心组织的研讨会充满信心。来自不同国家和岗位的专家学者从各自专长的领域激起了生动的辩论、带来了重要的结论。这次在上海的讨论将为世界上的博物馆和国际博物馆协会提供宝贵的工具来建立一种对话、尊重、和平的政策。

作为中心管理委员会的主席，我很荣幸IMREC能够组织本次研讨会并将讨论的结果分享给全球的博物馆界。

Foreword

Yong Duan*

According to statistics from the United Nations Educational, Scientific and Cultural Organization (UNESCO), the illegal trafficking of cultural heritage ranks as the third largest illicit trade, following drug trafficking and arms smuggling. Its origins can be traced back to the unfair international political and economic order of the colonial era, which led to the illegal loss of cultural artifacts. In the 2023-2028 Strategic Plan of the International Council of Museums (ICOM), decolonisation of museums is listed as one of the six most important issues for the future development of the museum field. This shows the international museum community's reflection and rectification.

Shanghai University aspires to become a hub for international academic research, exchange, and cooperation in the fields of cultural heritage, museums, and cultural restitution. It actively supports the establishment and functioning of think tanks. The International Council of Museums Research and Exchange Centre (ICOM-IMREC), jointly established by the University and the ICOM, focuses on promoting exchanges and cooperation in the international museum

---

* Yong Duan, Vice Chancellor of Shanghai University, the Vice President of ICOM-IMREC Governing Board.

field, organizing international symposiums, and supporting international museum research. The University's Research Centre for Chinese Relics Overseas is dedicated to intercultural dialogue and research on cultural restitution. It conducts transnational research projects, hosted the First China Forum on the International Day against Illicit Trafficking in Cultural Property. Through the joint efforts of the ICOM and Shanghai University, supported with the two research centres, the international symposium on "Museums, Decolonisation and Restitution: a global conversation" was successfully held at Shanghai University in March 2023. The aim was to promote global conversation and the sharing of experiences.

Over 60 museum professionals, experts, and scholars from the United States, Canada, the United Kingdom, Germany, the Netherlands, Brazil, Argentina, Australia, New Zealand, Egypt, Zambia, Côte d'Ivoire, South Korea, and China, participated in the symposium, online or offline. The entire conference was live-streamed globally through multiple platforms, attracting over 140,000 online participants. The symposium featured keynote speeches, thematic salons, and specialized presentations, focusing on the international topics of "Museums and Decolonisation" and "Museums and Restitution". Participants shared and discussed insights and experiences in museum decolonisation within the context of globalisation and diversity.

This symposium proceedings brings outstanding research contributions together from experts and scholars from various countries, covering in-depth discussions on decolonisation of museums and cultural restitution. Under the theme of "Museums and Decolonisation", experts and scholars from different countries and regions discussed the importance, paradigms, practices, and challenges of museum decolonisation. Scholars emphasized that decolonization of museums is a complicated process that requires deconstruction, reconstruction, and redistribution. It involves re-examining history from a modern perspective and providing with new understanding.

Experts also shared their institutional practices and prospects in decolonisation, discussing the roles and responsibilities of museums in community engagement, language, collections, and personnel. The topic of "Cultural Restitution" focused on the relationship between museums and the restitution of cultural objects and their social impact. Experiences in cultural restitution were shared as well, experts emphasized its importance, and highlighted the necessity of combining restitution with the original culture and communities, for protecting and promoting culture and art. For example, innovative platforms and digital display methods for indigenous cultural artifacts were presented, aiming to involve more people in the inheritance of African indigenous culture. These papers provide valuable insights for professionals in the museum field and related areas, offering important guidance for promoting the practices of museum decolonisation and restitution.

Through this symposium, we have become aware of the challenges and opportunities faced by the museum community in decolonisation and restitution. We need to transcend disciplines and geographical boundaries, actively explore principles and attitudes based on historical and cultural frameworks, and encouraging the participation of relevant communities, integrating their voices into the decision-making processes of decolonisation and restitution, to achieve a more equitable and just future.

Finally, I would like to express my sincere gratitude to the ICOM and Shanghai University for their strong supports. I would like to thank all the experts, scholars, and organisations who participated in this symposium for their dedication and sharing. I also appreciate the efforts of Shanghai University Press in publishing this proceedings. It is my hope that this symposium will serve as a starting point for global conversation and further exploration and cooperation in the decolonisation and restitution of the museums. I believe that through our collective efforts, we can shape a more inclusive and diverse museum community and make greater contributions to the inheritance and development of global culture.

前　言

段　勇[*]

据联合国教科文组织统计，文化遗产的非法贩运是仅次于毒品走私和武器走私的第三大非法贸易。其源头可追溯至殖民时代不公平的国际政治经济秩序导致的文物非法流失。在国际博物馆协会的2023—2028战略规划中，博物馆的去殖民化被列为博物馆领域未来发展最重要的六大议题之一，这反映了国际博物馆界的反思与矫正。

上海大学有志于在文化遗产、博物馆和文物返还领域成为国际学术研究、交流和合作的枢纽，积极支持成立并发挥智库作用。上海大学与国际博物馆协会共建的国际博物馆协会研究与交流中心专注于推进国际博物馆界的交流与合作，举办国际研讨会，支持国际博物馆调研；上海大学中国海外文物研究中心致力于推动跨文化对话和文物返还研究，开展跨国课题研究，承办"打击非法贩运文化财产国际日"中国主场活动。在国际博物馆协会和上海大学共同努力下，由上述两个专业智库承办，以"博物馆、去殖民化、文物返还：全球对话"为主题的国际研讨会于2023年3月在上海大学成功举办，旨在促进全球对话和经验分享。

来自美国、加拿大、英国、德国、荷兰、巴西、阿根廷、澳大利亚、新西兰、埃及、赞比亚、科特迪瓦、韩国和东道主中国的60余位博物馆

---

[*] 段勇，上海大学党委副书记，国际博物馆协会研究与交流中心管委会副主席。

相关机构的负责人和专家学者,通过线上线下相结合的方式参加了本次研讨会。会议全程通过多平台向全球同步直播,吸引了线上14余万人参加。研讨会设置了主旨报告、主题沙龙和专题分享等环节,围绕"博物馆去殖民化"(Museums and Decolonisation)和"文物返还"(Museums and Restitution)两大国际议题展开全球对话,共同分享并探讨了在全球化和多元化语境下的博物馆去殖民化的见解和经验。

本次会议的论文集汇集了来自各国专家学者的优秀研究成果,涵盖了博物馆去殖民化和文物返还等议题的深入讨论。在"博物馆去殖民化"议题下,来自不同国家和地区的专家学者就博物馆去殖民化的重要性、范式、实践和挑战等方面进行了深入研讨。学者们强调,博物馆的去殖民化是一个复杂的过程,需要进行解构、重构和再分配,从现代化的视角重新审视历史,为我们提供全新的认知窗口。同时,专家们也分享了各自机构在去殖民化方面的实践经验和展望,探讨了博物馆在社区参与、语言、藏品和人员等方面的角色和责任。"文物返还"议题聚焦于博物馆与文物返还之间的关系和社会影响力。专家们分享了本国在文物返还方面的经验,讨论了文物返还的重要性,强调了将文物返还与原文化和社群相结合的必要性,以保护和弘扬文化和艺术。以原住民文物为例,有专家分享了创新的原住民文物平台和数字化展示方式,旨在让更多人了解和参与到非洲原住民文化的传承中。这些论文将为博物馆界和相关领域的从业者提供宝贵的启示,对于推动博物馆去殖民化和文物返还的实践具有重要的指导意义。

通过本次研讨会,我们意识到了博物馆界在去殖民化和文物返还方面面临的挑战和机遇。我们需要跨越专业和地域的界限,以历史和文化框架为基础,积极探索多元和平等的原则和态度。重要的是,我们要鼓励相关社群的参与,将他们的声音融入去殖民化和文物返还的决策过程中,以实现更加公平正义的未来。

最后,我要衷心感谢国际博物馆协会和上海大学的鼎力支持;感谢所有参与本次会议的专家、学者和组织机构,感谢他们的奉献和分享;感谢上海大学出版社为本论文集的出版付出的努力。也希望本次会议能够成为一个全球对话的起点,推动博物馆界在去殖民化和文物返还方面的进一步探索与合作。我相信,通过我们的共同努力,能够塑造一个更加包容和多元的博物馆领域,为全球文化的传承和发展作出更大的贡献。

Introduction

Carol A. Scott*

At the ICOM Triennial Conference held in Kyoto during September 2019, there were two panels on decolonisation and repatriation which aimed to explore and examine '... how the sector is leading and responding to the decolonisation movement.' These well-attended sessions sparked lively discussion and debate. Four years have passed, and we find that the conversation on decolonisation and restitution has gained momentum.

The 2019 Savoy-Sarr report on the restitution of cultural material to sub-Saharan Africa, the subsequent return of Benin Bronzes to Nigeria from museums in France, Germany, the UK and the US, the Black Lives Matter movement, many conferences and an increase in critical literature have put decolonisation and restitution at the centre of a new museology. Importantly, the issues of decolonisation and restitution are now discussed within frameworks of social justice and ethical practice. It is considered 'right' that source communities have access to the cultural material which signifies their identity and heritage and that museums should engage with these same communities as intellectual

---

* Carol A. Scott, Chair of Academic and Programming Board, ICOM-IMREC.

equals.

Not surprisingly, when ICOM (the International Council of Museums) began to develop its new Strategic Plan for 2022–28, decolonisation featured prominently as one of the most pressing issues facing museums today. Of several strategies adopted by ICOM to address decolonisation one is to lead 'a global conversation to clarify what is encompassed within the concept and practice of decolonisation in museums.' The conversation, which is the subject of these papers, was developed through a new International Museum Research and Exchange Centre (ICOM–IMREC) which is a partnership between ICOM and Shanghai University. '*Museums, decolonisation and restitution: a global conversation*' took place on the 20th and 21st March 2023 at the University of Shanghai.

From the outset, the Working Group planning this seminar established that a 'global' conversation would be both internationally representative[1] and intellectually comprehensive. The subjects of decolonisation and restitution in these papers are explored across theory and practice, through examples of restitution within countries as well as between them and by recognising that colonisation and its aftermath are not phenomena confined to an historical period involving the actions of the global north towards the global south but are part of the histories of other countries around the world.

Over two days, a picture emerged of an evolving theoretical discourse and its practical implementation. Also exposed was the extent of systemic, institutional change yet to be achieved if decolonisation is to be realised and the many gaps in policy and legal frameworks that continue to impede efforts for successful restitution. The following twenty-one papers challenge and inspire us to continue the work that has begun in this critical area of museum work.

---

[1] 30 speakers and moderators from 21 different countries participated.

Decolonisation

Decolonising involves creatively reimagining the way museums work, who they work with and what they value. It covers all areas of practice and creates a framework to better support people and institutions. Decolonising is a collective activity, which can be messy, thoughtful, imaginative, and emotional.

It is driven by the desire for justice and equity in that it aims to rebalance power and representation away from the coloniser narrative of history and society. This work is intersectional, as it challenges structural inequalities across the board to redress forms of historic and ongoing harm.[1]

Decolonisation is, as keynote Wayne Modest describes it, a 'capacious' term embracing systemic institutional change, repatriation and social justice. It involves addressing the wrongs of the colonial past and its continuing legacy of global social and economic inequity in the present. In this first set of papers, we take the pulse of the museums and decolonisation across the world.

The gauntlet is laid down with the first paper in this volume by Bruno Brulon Soares, a museologist and anthropologist from Brazil now lecturing at the University of St Andrews in Scotland. He argues that museums are agents of the colonial legacy, using spatial and intellectual borders to separate source communities from their material culture and perpetuating a 'them' and 'us' mentality. Brulon challenges us to disrupt these borders by *deconstructing* the intellectual frameworks through which museums interpret difference, *reconstructing* them by embracing non-Western systems of knowledge

---

[1] https://www.museumsassociation.org/campaigns/decolonising-museums/supporting-decolonisation-in-museums/ introduction/#

and *redistributing* power and curatorial authority by engaging the source communities from whom objects were removed.

In the following three papers, a national museum, a provincial art gallery and a local museum demonstrate how museums can be re-imagined when intellectual and spatial borders are eliminated.

At Te Papa Tongarewa (the National Museum of New Zealand), Arapata Hakiwai, Maori co-leader describes how the adoption of authentic biculturalism has enabled the museum to implement a model of governance that shares leadership and cultural authority between Maori and non-Maori, interpret New Zealand's history through multiple lenses and bring Maori into the museum as equal co-producers.

For Stephen Borys, Director and CEO of the Winnipeg Art Gallery in Manitoba Canada, collaboration is the mechanism through which the Inuit community in the northern part of the province have become co-producers of Qaumajuq, a new, multi-purpose Inuit art centre which is fostering dialogue between indigenous and nonindigenous communities and between the Canadian urban south and its remote north.

Community- embeddedness at Saahlinda Naay on Haida Gwaii off the west coast of Canada, enables this *Keeping Things Place* to re-imagine the museum from a First Nations perspective. Sean Young, Collections Manager describes how Haida values inform decisions, how Haida knowledge systems inform interpretation and how collections of 'belongings' (objects) are regularly taken out of store to be used by the community for ritual purposes.

Although these three papers illustrate active attempts to decolonise, in the opinion of Wayne Modest, Director of Content at the National Museum of World Cultures in Rotterdam, attempts to decolonise museums have generally failed. He attributes this failure to a reluctance to embrace the systemic changes required. He contends that museums tend to deflect, conceal and subsume decolonisation within other frameworks such as multiculturalism and diversity while reinforcing and leaving intact the very structures which perpetuate a colonial afterlife. Failure to grasp the fundamental social justice principle underlying decolonisation means museums risk remaining part of the colonial legacy of global social and economic inequality. What might decolonisation look like, he asks. And what might it inaugurate? The next three papers consider these questions.

In the first instance, decolonisation requires a new language. The language used in exhibition interpretation can misrepresent identities and perpetuate colonial world views. Carissa Chew, a recent PhD graduate from the University of Hawai'i at Mānoa, led the Cultural Heritage Terminology Network (CHTNUK) and the development of the Inclusive Terminology Glossary at the National Library of Scotland (2020–2021). The glossaries which have been generated from these projects provide critical guidance for museums' use of terminology.

Active decolonisation interrogates the intellectual concepts and practices underlying the structural basis of museums. Jo Anderson, Adam Goldwater and Kylea Little from Tyne and Wear Archive and Museums (TWAM) in the UK describe 'stepping out' of the normal comfort zone and 'stepping back' to consider what museums do, why they do it and what factors influence current practice. This process of 'distancing' has enabled TWAM to establish an interdependent approach that is delivering decolonisation practice across the institution.

A decolonised workplace requires new set of skills, attitudes and knowledge among its staff and leadership. The professional development side of decolonisation is the work of Roshi Nadoo, the Decolonising Programme Officer at the Museums Association in the UK. But Nadoo cautions that authentic commitment to change must confront questions of power-sharing and authority. In the absence of willingness to address these fundamental issues, decolonisation programmes risk becoming little more than tinkering at the edges.

With Hyun Kyung Lee's paper, we are reminded that colonisation is neither a phenomenon confined to the global north/south axis nor specific to any period of time. Lee, Assistant Professor in the Critical Global Studies Institute (CGSI) at Sogang University in Seoul looks at the complexities of heritage interpretation within three Asian countries colonised by Japanese occupation prior to and during the second World War II. The challenges of interpreting the past within current geo-political events and relationships is cogently described.

Restitution

The terms, *restitution* and *repatriation* are often used interchangeably in discussions about the return of objects removed from source communities during colonisation. *Repatriation* tends to focus on 'the act ... of restoring or returning someone or something to the country of origin, allegiance, or citizenship'[1] and is more frequently applied in cases where the return of objects is between countries and involves diplomacy. *Restitution* directs attention to loss or theft as the reason behind object removal and the subsequent return of objects to communities as an act of restorative justice. Both terms are used by the authors of these papers and are applied in this introduction.

Samba Yonga, founder of Ku-Atenga Media and co-founder of the Zambian Museum of Women's History looks at the impact on both museums and source communities when objects are separated, dislocated and de-contextualised from local knowledge and systems of meanings. Drawing on a current case study that uses a digital interface to connect objects held in European museums with the communities where they originated, she demonstrates a process of collaboration which can recover cultural memory, restore important original knowledge and

---

[1] https://www.merriam-webster.com/dictionary/repatriation

correct misrepresentations.

The international policy and legal framework within which restitution operates is the subject of the next three papers. Yunxia Wang, who currently holds the UNESCO Chair on Cultural Heritage Law at Remin University, comprehensively describes this framework and exposes its many gaps. She argues for greater clarity in the scope of restitution efforts including the categorisation of material and revisiting statutes of limitations. She contends that a more unified and united international effort in the development of legal and policy instruments is required to improve the current situation.

From Argentina, Americo Castilla, the Academic Director of TyPA Lab on Museum Management, argues that law and policy are only the beginning of efforts to return objects. Of equal importance is redefining social behaviour so that the public actively support the voluntary return of objects as acts of equity and justice.

It is not only during periods of direct colonisation that cultural heritage is appropriated or lost. Yong Duan, Vice-Chancellor of Shanghai University notes that the pre-colonial Qing Dynasty when social, political and economic instability fragmented the country, left it vulnerable to object removal by foreign powers. Duan sees a positive shift towards negotiating the return of objects and makes the case for greater international co-operation and agreements between countries to build on this development.

Every new development encourages innovation. Repatriation and restitution have stimulated similar creative responses. Two next papers provide examples of digital and artistic innovation.

In the example provided by Haidy Geismar, Professor of Anthropology and Co-director of the Digital Anthropology Programme at University College London the digital space provided a forum for resolving a contested case for the return of a Maori meeting house situated on a National Trust property. The result is a consensus-decision for repatriation of the house to New Zealand.

In the next example Laura Evans, Distinguished Teaching Professor in Visual Arts and Design at the University of North Texas describes the role of artists in creating high-quality replacement replicas for museum objects being returned to source communities and the influential role that the public can play in supporting museums to resolve repatriation claims.

Five case studies complete this publication. Each one takes a critical look at the process of restitution and the factors which have contributed to a successful (or unsuccessful) outcome.

The Longmen Grottoes was a casualty of the unstable Qing Dynasty, losing many items to overseas collections. In more recent years, a 'Longmen model' has secured the physical and virtual return of an increasing number of objects. Jiazhen Shi, the President of the Longmen Grottoes Research Institute in China, describes this model and the way it is introducing a new era for cultural heritage recovery.

Duncan Dornan, the Head of Museums and Collections at Glasgow Life in Scotland describes how institutional policy on repatriation can evolve. Although an initial request for return of a Ghost Shirt by the Wounded Knee Survivors Association (WKSA) of the Lakota Sioux Nation in the US was refused, the request was eventually granted when other stakeholders including the local Council and the public supported a change of policy.

On a national level, Chaàbane Abdeljaouad, the Director General of the Egyptian Repatriation Antiquities Department describes an integrated approach combining legislation, policy, policing, community engagement, co-operation with international auction houses, museums and the governments of other countries which has resulted in the recovery of 29000 objects in the last decade.

Repatriation requests are not always positive. Although French President Emmanuel Macron publicly supports the repatriation of African cultural objects, the universe of actors involved in the repatriation process can halt progress at any of the many steps along the way. This is the subject of a case study outlined by Honoré Kouadio Kouassi, Deputy Director-General of the National Higher

Institute of Arts in the Republic of Cote d'Ivoire which has been actively pursuing the return of 'Djidji Ayokwe', a talking drum of great significance to Ivorian collective memory and identity,

The final paper by Michael Pickering, Honorary Associate Professor in the Department of Heritage and Museum Studies at the Australian National University ends with a positive note. He presents a further digital initiative '*Return, Reconcile, Renew*' to demonstrate that meaningful restitution can be a positive force to reconcile past hurts, create new relationships and foreground community knowledge, meaning systems and ritual practices.

Conclusion

What have we learned from this global conversation about decolonisation and restitution?

First and foremost, decolonisation does not exist in a vacuum—it is part of a wider system of inequality and injustice. For museums to play their part in rectifying the legacy of colonialism requires profound systemic change that takes museums out of their comfort zone. The journey involves confronting assumptions of intellectual superiority and admitting other knowledge systems as equals. The structural foundations of museum require interrogation. Intellectual and spatial borders need to be removed so that source communities can share the museum space as partners.

Secondly, objects do not exist in a vacuum—they are essential components of community memory, knowledge and ritual practice. Their removal interrupts these systems, making cultural activation and reactivation an essential part of the restitution process.

Thirdly, though the legal and policy framework for repatriation and restitution remains incomplete, support is developing in other directions. There is growing co-operation between nation states to return objects amid calls for greater global co-operation. Digital is supporting repatriation through identifying the location of removed objects, foregrounding the knowledge of source communities and correcting misrepresentations of objects held in museums where interpretation has been confined to Western intellectual systems.

Finally, new relationships are being built through the repatriation and restitution process. These are developing between other global actors, across nations, with source communities and with the public whose role as a positive influence on restitution and repatriation decisions is only just emerging. And this seminar also built relationships and a commitment to continue the conversation.

简　介

卡罗尔·A. 斯科特*

　　2019年9月，国际博物馆协会在日本京都召开了第25届大会。在这场三年一届的国际博协大会上，有两场关于去殖民化和文物返还的小组讨论会，旨在探究和考察"博物馆各部门应如何领导和应对去殖民化运动"。这些会议吸引了众多与会者，并引发了热烈讨论。而四年过后的今天，我们发现有关去殖民化和文物返还问题的讨论依旧热度不减，且势头越发强劲。

　　2019年，关于向撒哈拉以南非洲地区返还物质文化资源（cultural material）的《萨瓦—萨尔报告》（Savoy-Sarr Report）[①]出台后，法国、德国、英国和美国的博物馆随即向尼日利亚归还贝宁青铜器。黑人平权运动（Black Lives Matter Movement）也逐渐发展起来。许多会议和不断增多的重要文献也逐渐将去殖民化和文物返还的问题置于新博物馆学研究的核心地位。重要的是，现在去殖民化和文物返还问题正被放在社会公正和伦理实践的背景下进行讨论。人们也意识到，作为文物来源的原住民社区理当接触到这些能够代表其身份和遗产的物质文化材料，博物馆应该与这些社区在知识层面展开平等交流。

---

* 卡罗尔·A. 斯科特，国际博物馆协会研究与交流中心学术委员会主席。
① 萨瓦—萨尔报告是指法国的Bénédicte Savoy和塞内加尔的Felwine Sarr两位学者一同撰写的一份报告，这份报告为文物（物质文化资源）归还计划做了规划。延伸阅读：https://itsartlaw.org/2019/01/31/the-sarr-savoy-report-restituting-colonial-artifacts/。

因此毫无意外地，当国际博协开始制定其2022—2028年的新战略计划时，去殖民化作为当今博物馆面临的最紧迫的问题之一，自然占据了显著位置。在国际博协为解决去殖民化问题而采取的几项战略中，其中一项是举办"一场全球对话，以厘清博物馆去殖民化概念和实践所包含的内容"。这次以参会论文为议题的对话，将借助国际博协与上海大学合作建立的新的国际博物馆协会研究与交流中心来展开。2023年3月20—21日，"博物馆、去殖民化、文物返还：全球对话"专家研讨会在上海大学如期举行。

从一开始，筹划本次研讨会的工作组就确定，"全球"对话既要具有国际代表性[①]，又要在思想理念上具有全面性。这些论文所探讨的去殖民化和文物返还的问题涵盖了理论和实践两方面，既有境内文物返还的案例，也有国际间返还的案例。同时，与会论文也意识到殖民及其后续影响并不仅仅是一种局限在北半球国家对南半球国家开展殖民掠夺的现象，还影响了其他国家的部分历史时期。

经过这两天的会议，我们逐渐形成了一幅有关去殖民化和文物返还问题的发展蓝图，有关这一议题的理论辨析及其工作实践都在不断发展。不过，在发展的同时也暴露出现存的问题，即目前我们的政策和法律框架对去殖民化和文物返还方面的内容关注还不够，而政策法律中的空白正持续影响着文物返还工作的成功推进。所以，想要实现去殖民化的目标，我们还需要进行系统性、制度性的变革。下面21篇与会论文积极应对当前挑战，并激励我们继续在博物馆工作的重要领域开展工作。

博物馆的去殖民化

博物馆"去殖民化"需要博物馆创造性地去重新设想自身的工作方式、工作对象和价值意义。"去殖民化"这一趋势涉及博物馆所有的工作领域，并创建了一个框架来为人们和机构提供更好的支持。去

---

① 此次会议共有来自21个不同国家的30位演讲者和主持人参与其中。——作者注

殖民化是一项大规模多主体参与的集体工作，它可能是混乱无形的，也可能是深思熟虑的、富有想象力的，也可以是感性的。

博物馆去殖民化工作的动力来自对公平和正义的渴望，旨在重新构建起权力与代表性之间的平衡，摆脱殖民者权力话语下对历史和社会的叙述。这项工作向结构性不平等问题提出了全面挑战，需要多部门的协作，以补救、修正各种形式的历史性伤害以及后来的持续性创伤。①

就如我们主旨发言人韦恩·莫德斯特（Wayne Modest）所描述的那样，去殖民化是一个含义十分"宽泛"的术语，包含着系统性、机构性变革、文物返还和社会正义等多个方面的内容。它涉及要去修正在过去殖民历史中存在的错误，并要解决殖民历史在当今全球社会和经济不平等的大环境下对殖民地国家和地区造成的持续性的遗留问题。第一组论文将带领我们深入了解世界各地的博物馆和去殖民化工作情况。

本场开篇的第一篇论文作者是布鲁诺·布鲁伦·苏亚雷斯（Bruno Brulon Soares），他是一位来自巴西的博物馆学家和人类学家，目前在苏格兰的圣安德鲁斯大学任教。他认为，博物馆是殖民遗产的代理人，使用空间和认知门槛将本土社区与他们的物质文化资源隔离开来，并使"他们"（原住民及其社区）和"我们"（博物馆）这一存在隔阂的心态永久烙印在人们心中。布鲁伦对"我们"发起挑战，他希望去打破这些隔阂，他通过接纳非西方的知识体系来重新解构博物馆诠释差异的知识框架，并通过与遭遇文物流失的本土社区的接触来重新分配权力和策展的话语权。

下面三篇论文中，三个不同的机构（一个国家级博物馆、一个省级美术馆和一个地方性博物馆）将会展示当没有知识和空间的界限时，博物馆将会是什么情况。

新西兰国家博物馆（Te Papa Tongarewa，蒂帕帕国家博物馆）：毛利人共同领导人阿若帕塔·哈克瓦（Arapata Hakiwai）向我们展示了，在真

---

① https://www.museumsassociation.org/campaigns/decolonising-museums/supporting-decolonisation-in-museums/introduction/#. ——作者注

的需要采用双文化叙事的情况下，他们是如何使博物馆能够实施一种可以在毛利人和非毛利人之间共享主导权和文化权力的管理模式，并能通过多元视角诠释新西兰的历史，让同样作为历史创造者的毛利人平等地进入博物馆。

加拿大曼尼托巴省（Manitoba）温尼伯美术馆（Winnipeg Art Gallery）：馆长兼首席执行官斯蒂芬·鲍卫斯（Stephen Borys）说道，通过合作机制，该省北部的因纽特人①社区（Inuit community）也成了"Qaumajuq"的共同缔造者。"Qaumajuq"是一个新的多功能的因纽特人艺术中心，它促进了原住民和非原住民社区之间以及加拿大南部城市和北部偏远地区之间的交流与对话。

加拿大西海岸海达瓜依岛的嵌入式社区"Saahlinda Naay"：一个从原住民视角将"保留事物的地方"重新规划成博物馆的地方。该机构的藏品经理肖恩·杨（Sean Young）介绍了海达人的价值观在博物馆决策中发挥的作用，以及海达人知识体系对博物馆阐释的影响，并介绍了博物馆如何定期从库房中取出馆藏资源供原住民社区在其仪式中使用。

尽管这三篇论文展示了博物馆去殖民化的积极尝试，但位于鹿特丹的荷兰国立世界文化博物馆（National Museum of World Cultures）的内容总监韦恩·莫德斯特提出，其实博物馆去殖民化的尝试普遍面临着失败的困境。他将这一失败归咎于博物馆不愿接受目前所需的系统性变革。他认为，博物馆倾向于转移、掩盖去殖民化的本质，将其归入多元文化和多样性等其他框架内，而同时又完整保留并强化了使殖民主义后续影响持续延续的这些结构。如果不能把握好博物馆去殖民化本质上所追求的社会公正原则，博物馆就有可能继续成为全球社会和经济发展不平等背景下的一部分殖民遗产。他提出了"去殖民化应该是什么样子？又会带来什么？"的问题，而接下来的三篇论文也将探讨这些问题。

首先，博物馆去殖民化需要一种全新的语言。展览诠释中使用的语言可能会歪曲身份，固化殖民世界观。克利萨·秋（Carissa Chew）最近

---

① 因纽特人（Inuit），生活在北极地区，黄种人，分布在从西伯利亚、阿拉斯加到格陵兰的北极圈内外，分别居住在格陵兰、美国、加拿大和俄罗斯。

刚从夏威夷大学马诺阿分校（University of Hawaii at Mānoa）博士毕业，她创建了文化遗产术语网络（CHTNUK）并完成了苏格兰国家图书馆（National Library of Scotland）包容性术语词汇表的开发工作（2020—2021年）。这些项目产生的词汇为博物馆去殖民化工作中所需的专用术语提供了重要指导。

当前活跃的去殖民化项目对博物馆原有的结构基础、知识理念与实践提出质疑。英国泰恩威尔郡档案馆和博物馆（TWAM）的乔·安德森（Jo Anderson）、亚当·戈德华特（Adam Goldwater）和凯利·利特尔（Kylea Little）认为博物馆应该"走出"正常的舒适区，"后退一步"去反思一下博物馆自己在做什么、为什么要这么做以及哪些因素影响了博物馆当前的去殖民化实践。这种"拉开距离"的过程使英国泰恩威尔郡档案馆和博物馆提出了一种能够在整个机构内开展去殖民化实践、各个部门相互合作的工作方法。

英国博物馆协会（Museums Association in the UK）中致力于"去殖民化"专业发展的去殖民化项目官员罗希·奈杜（Roshi Nadoo）认为，博物馆去殖民化的工作场景需要工作人员和领导层具备新的技能、态度和知识。但奈杜也提到，真正想要对变革做出承诺，就必须要面对权力的共享和话语权的问题。如果没有解决这些根本问题的意愿，去殖民化的计划就有可能变成只是在边缘对这一议题修修补补而已。

而首尔西江大学（Sogang University）全球批判性研究院（Critical Global Studies Institute，CGSI）的助理教授李玄卿（Hyun Kyung Lee）的论文提醒我们，殖民化既不是一种局限于全球南北轴线的现象，也不是任何时期的特有现象。李玄卿探究了第二次世界大战前和战争期间被日本占领的三个亚洲殖民地遗产阐释的复杂性。她着力讲述了在当前地缘政治事件和关系中阐释历史过往所面临的挑战。

文物返还

在讨论归还殖民时期从原住民社区拿走的文物时，"返还"（restitution）

和"遣返"（repatriation）这两个词经常交替使用。"遣返"往往强调的是"将某人或某物归还或送回其原生地、效忠地或国籍所属地的行为"[①]，经常用于国与国之间文物归还和涉及外交的情况。"返还"一词则更强调文物流失的原因（如丢失或被盗等），随后将文物返还到原社区，是一种修复正义的行为。与会论文中作者们使用了这两个术语，我也在此次的导言中加以运用。

Ku-Atenga传媒的创始人、赞比亚妇女历史博物馆的联合创始人之一桑巴·杨格（Samba Yonga）探讨了当文物与原住民知识及其价值观念体系分离、错位和去语境化时，对博物馆和文物本土社区带来的影响。目前，一项研究案例利用数字技术平台将欧洲博物馆收藏的文物与文物本土社区联系起来，她通过这项研究展示了这样一种合作方式，这一方式可以帮助修复文化记忆、恢复重要的原始知识，并纠正当前对原住民社区及其知识、价值观念的错误表达。

接下来的三篇论文主要关注的是文物返还工作中所依据的国际政策和法律框架。目前在中国人民大学任教，并担任联合国教科文组织文化遗产法教席教授的王云霞全面介绍了有关文物返还的法律框架，并揭示了其中存在的许多空白。她主张进一步明确文物返还工作的范围，包括材料的分类和重新审视条例的局限性。她认为，为改善当前状况，需要国际社会在制定法律和政策文书方面做出更加统一和团结的努力。

阿根廷艺术理论与实践基金会（TyPA — Theory & Practice of the Arts）实验中心博物馆管理研究院的学术主管亚美利卡·卡斯蒂洛（Americo Castilla）认为，法律和政策只是文物返还工作的开端。与之同样重要的是重新定义这项社会行为，使社会公众能够意识到文物返还是一项公平、正义的行为，使其可以积极支持并自愿参与到文物返还的工作中来。

还有十分重要的一点，即文物流失或被侵占的现象并非只在当时的所谓直接殖民的时期才有。上海大学党委副书记段勇指出，清朝末期的半封建半殖民地时期，由于社会、政治和经济的不稳定，国家四分五裂，文物

[①] https://www.merriam-webster.com/dictionary/repatriation.——作者注

很容易被外国列强掠夺。段勇认为，目前涉及文物返还的谈判已经出现了积极的转变，他还主张在此基础上加强国际合作，强化各国之间的协议。

每一次新的发展都会积极鼓励创新，文物遣返和返还也激发了这样的创造性成果。接下来的两篇论文就提供了数字和艺术创新的案例。

伦敦大学学院（University College London）人类学教授，数字人类学计划的联合指导人海蒂·盖斯马（Haidy Geismar）提供了一个案例。即数字空间提供了一个论坛，解决了关于归还国家信托基金财产中的毛利会堂（Maori Meeting House）的这一争议案件。最终，各方通过这一论坛达成共识，决定将该房屋归还新西兰。

在第二个案例中，北得克萨斯大学（University of North Texas）视觉艺术与设计学院的接触教学教授劳拉·埃文斯（Laura Evans）介绍了在为博物馆归还文物给本土社区时，艺术家在制作高质量的具有可替代性的复制品方面有重要作用，并提到公众在支持博物馆解决文物归还索求方面能够带来的影响及作用。

接下来的与会论文中还有五个案例。每个案例都对文物返还过程以及促成成功（或导致失败）结果的因素展开了批判性审视。

龙门石窟就是清朝动荡时期的牺牲品，许多文物流失海外，成为海外的收藏。近年来，"龙门模式"确保了越来越多的文物以实体和数字化的形式回归。中国龙门石窟研究院院长史家珍介绍了这一模式，并展示了这一模式是如何将文化遗产的恢复引入一个新时代的。

苏格兰格拉斯哥生活博物馆（Glasgow Life）的藏品负责人邓肯·多南（Duncan Dornan）介绍了机构的文物返还政策是如何演进的。比如之前美国拉科塔苏族人[①]的膝伤幸存者联盟（Wounded Knee Survivors Association，WKSA）最初提出的归还一件"幽灵衬衫"（Ghost Shirt）的请求遭到了拒绝，但在包括当地议会和公众在内的许多其他利益相关者支持改变政策的情况下，该请求最终得到了批准。

在国家层面，埃及文旅部文物返还办公室主任沙班·阿卜杜勒·加瓦

---

① 拉科塔（Lakota）部落是美国西部地区的一个印第安人（美洲原住民）部落，苏族（Sioux）是美国印第安人中的一个民族。

简 介

德（Shaaban Abdel Gawad）介绍了一种将立法、政策、治安管理、社区参与与国际拍卖行、博物馆和其他国家政府合作联合起来的综合方法。凭借这一方式他们在过去的10年中成功追返了29 000件文物。

不过，文物返还的请求也并不总是正向的。尽管法国总统埃马纽埃尔·马克龙（Emmanuel Macron）公开支持非洲的文物返还工作，但这一过程中涉及的众多参与者都有可能会在诸多步骤中的任何一个环节上阻碍工作的推进。科特迪瓦共和国国家高等艺术学院副总干事奥纳瑞·卡瓦迪欧·卡瓦西（Honoré Kouadio Kouassi）概述了这一案例研究的主题，该学院也一直在积极争取"Djidji Ayokwe"的返还，这是一件对科特迪瓦集体记忆和身份认同具有重要意义的"会说话"的鼓。

最后，澳大利亚国立大学（Australian National University）文化遗产与博物馆研究系名誉副教授迈克尔·皮克林（Michael Pickering）以一篇积极、正向的论文为我们这次研讨会画上了句号。他介绍了未来"返还、调和、更新"的数字倡议，以证明有意义的文物返还可以形成一种积极的力量，调和过去的伤害，建立新的关系，并强调本土社区的知识与价值观体系及其礼仪习俗。

结语

我们从这场有关博物馆去殖民化和文物返还的全球对话中能够明白什么呢？

首先，博物馆去殖民化并非存在于真空之中——它是一个更广泛的不平等和不公正体系中的一部分。博物馆想要修正殖民主义所带来的遗留问题，在这一方面发挥自身的作用，就必须进行深刻的系统改革，使博物馆走出自己的舒适区。在这个过程中，博物馆需要正确看待所谓知识优越性的假设，平等地接纳其他知识体系。博物馆也需要重新审视自身的结构基础，需要消除知识和空间的边界与隔阂，使原住民社区能够成为合作伙伴，平等地共享博物馆空间。

其次，文物也并非是存在于真空之中的——它们是社区记忆、知识和礼仪习俗的重要组成部分。文物流失会破坏这些系统，因此，文化的激活和恢复也是文物返还工作的重要组成部分。

第三，尽管有关文物遣返和返还的法律和政策框架还不完善，但其他方面的支持正在不断加强。在加强全球合作的呼声中，各民族和国家之间在文物遣返方面的合作日益增多。数字技术也在通过确定流失文物的位置、强调文物原生社区的知识体系来支持文物返还工作，并意识到博物馆诠释一直局限在西方知识体系中的这一片面性问题，积极去纠正博物馆中对文物的错误描述。

最后，通过文物遣返和返还工作，我们正在建立新的联系。这些联系是在全球其他行动者之间、各个国家之间、与文物本土社区以及公众之间建立起来的。公众对文物返还和遣返方面的决策有着重要的积极影响，而这一作用目前才刚刚显现。此次研讨会，我们建立了紧密联系，未来，相信我们将会继续展开更多对话。

Decolonising the Museum Paradigm: Unpacking Museum Theory for Anticolonial Practices

Bruno Brulon Soares[*]

Abstract: The presentation approaches the modern/colonial paradigm that defines the history of museums in the so-called West and determine museum practice until present time. By looking at the modern museum from its borders, i.e. from the perspective of its subaltern subjects, excluded from the narrative of major institutions, I intend to provoke an exercise of reflexivity. As part or such an exercise I propose to critically consider the "post-colonial" museum in its persistent reproduction of coloniality, notably in the context of European national institutions. I will argue that the recent discourse of "decolonisation" adopted by these museums and some museum scholars allow new ways for institutions to continue acquiring and exhibiting non-European materials, thus preserving coloniality as part of a national project grounded in modernity. I will, therefore, propose an introduction to anticolonial museum practice, based on a threefold and interrelated process that encompasses *deconstructing*, *reconstructing*, and *redistributing*. Going beyond the decolonial conception of the borders and the persistence of the divisions between *them* and *us* inherited from colonialism and that are no longer useful to understand relations of exchange and appropriation, this presentation seeks to theorise on the practical ways to tackle the margins and to disrupt the borders used to subjugate and

---

[*] Bruno Brulon Soares, professor of Cultural Heritage at University of St Andrews.

dehumanise. Thus, I will argue that there should be no "decolonised" museum, because museums as we know them were an important part of colonialism. But museums can be part of the process of decolonisation, as anticolonial institutions that can be used to denounce the persistence of coloniality and to critically address our colonial heritage.

Starting from the borders

I would like to start my speech from the borders of the modern museum. I invite you to take this position, an unusual one for museum professionals, which places us as the "outsiders". This is the position of the Others, the outcasts of museum's dominant narratives that have been reproducing coloniality much beyond the end of colonialism.

From the outside, the contemporary architecture of certain museums is the result of a historic and spatial dissimulation. Asymmetrical lines and the overlapping of materials and colours construct the disfigured temple as an attempt to hide its modern origin and tradition without losing its grandeur. As I cross the street at the quai Branly, I am invited to escape old Paris for a moment. Even from a distance, I can already feel the force of a call emanating from the museum's façade and the indistinguishable building that I can see just ahead covered by a glass wall. There is mystery and drama before I even reach the entrance of the Musée du quai Branly—Jacques Chirac, located in the middle of the French capital.

By leaving behind the "classical" city to enter the "exotic" environment created by the museum's architecture, locals or tourists are invited to embrace the position of a foreigner, or of the "explorer". The museum performance is the enactment of an imaginary displacement, and, once inside, the long journey to reach its permanent collections is just one of the parts of a border that mimics the colonial encounter as national entertainment for the twenty-first century.

The plunge into the unknown is announced by the translucent wall that only allows one to see the exoticism of the museum's garden. The latter proclaims a rupture with rationality and classical aesthetics by establishing a scenario of asymmetry and controlled disorder. When entering its unmistakable premises, no visitor is unaware of the fact that they are crossing a frontier. Finally, we are convinced to temporarily leave the clarity of what is already known in the "City of light". As the visitor travels between worlds and radical aesthetics, the light in the exhibitions becomes dimmer. In this environment, the materials of others are displayed without revealing the museum's founding ambiguity. I refer here to the paradoxical principle according to which colonial history must be forgotten to enable the aesthetic appreciation of the works of colonised people.

Even though conceived in the 1990s and inaugurated on 20 June 2006 as a new reading of non-European collections in the French capital, the Musée du quai Branly is today the main inheritor of France's colonial materials. Gathering the ethnographic collections of the Musée de l'Homme and the Musée national des arts d'Afrique et d'Océanie — former Musée de la France d'Outre-mer, belonging to the Ministry of the Colonies until 1960[1] — the new museum intended to "liberate" the so-called "primitive arts" from their colonial past.

According to French president Jacques Chirac, who was described in the *Le Figaro* newspaper as "l'avocat des oubliés" ("the lawyer of the forgotten")[2],

---

[1] Originally created on the occasion of the colonial exhibition of 1931 as the "permanent museum of the colonies", it was renamed in 1935 as the museum of the French overseas territories (Musée de la France d'Outre-mer), and then again by André Malraux in 1960, when it was renamed the museum of the arts of Africa and Oceania. In 1990 it became part of the departments of French museums, and was turned into the national museum of the arts of Africa and Oceania. After losing its collection to the Musée du Quai Branly, it ceased to exist in the Palais de la Porte Dorée, giving way to the Cité nationale de l'histoire de l'immigration (National City of Immigration History), inaugurated in 2007.

[2] In the words of François Fillon, in hommage to Chirac, in November 2011. *Le Figaro*, 24 November 2011. Available at: www.lefigaro.fr. Access in: 23 December 2011.

the institution entirely dedicated to the arts and civilisations of Africa, Asia, Oceania and the Americas stems from a political will to "do justice to the so-called extra-European cultures" (Chirac, 2007), recognising their place in the European cultural heritage. However, the criticism of most analysts of the museum concerns the fact that the universalism intended by Chirac applies only to cultures that have disappeared or are situated outside of the "official" history, and without any type of relationship with those of the present (Amselle, 2010: 62). Stated as "decidedly post-colonial" and a place of "reconciliation and sharing" (Musée du quai Branly, 2000: 23, 34 quoted from Ruiz-Gómez, 2006: 421), this museum with an ambiguous discourse is not only presenting colonial objects as art, but it is reinforcing modern separations that were inflicted on humanity through colonialism.

My aim in this talk is to reconsider the debate on decolonisation in museological literature to propose the deconstruction of the museum and its decolonial discourse in the present. With this purpose, I'm obliged to acknowledge the shifting usages and some contradictions in the discourse of decolonisation in the current debate on museums and cultural heritage, with no ambition of being exhaustive, yet considering its multiple genealogies in museology.

One of my main arguments in this speech is that the modern museum and its decolonial recreations operate similarly to the way the immune system functions for the human organism, as well as in the legal immunization of social systems, inspired by the analogy proposed by Roberto Esposito (2011). This analogy stems from the fact that some self-declared "decolonial museums" contain an element of the same substance they are intended to defend against—which can be known as coloniality.

Following this approach, as a presidential project to stand as Chirac's monument to his role in history, the quai Branly museum that took on his name after 2016 is also a political response to the issue of identity and the community claims for social justice and cultural representation in the France. Such claims are not new in the context of this country, as demonstrate some of the recent studies by European scholars that, for the first time, recognise the historical background of the repatriation debate beyond Europe (Sarr & Savoy, 2018; Savoy, 2022). In fact, the neutralisation of conflict or the mere suppression of indigenous voices had proven easier to be conquered in the past than they are now.

Looking at some of the basis of museum theory, I will stress that the decolonisation of museums and that of museology is dependent on a threefold and interrelated process that encompasses *deconstructing, reconstructing*, and *redistributing*, necessarily in that order. The problem with today's discourse on the decolonisation of museums has to do with its restricted focus on the last part of this complex and difficult process, disregarding its more fundamental procedures. I will argue that this is a flaw with political consequences, because if you redistribute heritage without rethinking the regimes of value and knowledge in which heritage is produced and preserved — which are marked by coloniality, rationality and violence — these regimes will essentially and pragmatically stay unchanged.

The Modernity/Coloniality paradigm

Since the last decades of the twentieth century, museum theory has had to deal with critical studies that have put the museum under scrutiny by questioning its colonial roots. These reflexive analyses, marked by a strong influence from critical anthropologists (Balandier, 1951; Stocking, 1985; Clifford, 1997), have denounced our "colonial legacies" (L'Estoile, 2008) in their urgent need for reinterpretation and renegotiation in the present. The influence of critical thinking and postcolonial studies on museum theory have also provoked the recognition of museums' central role in decolonising the past preserved in their collections.

Notably, these analyses have questioned the assumption that there is an essence of colonialism that overlooks the actual diversity of colonial projects and interactions, as well as the idea that the inhabitants of a post-colonial world are necessarily passive recipients of this legacy. As Benoît de L'Estoile has noted, these analyses have helped to draw a distinction between *colonial relations* in a generic sense and *colonisation* as a restricted historical occurrence. Based on this distinction, the museum can be perceived as an institution determined in time and space—it is modern and founded in Europe, disseminated as part of the Westernisation of the world. But it is also politically determined as an instrument of colonialism, embedded in coloniality.

Among Latin American authors, a *decolonial* approach was defined between the 1970s and the 1990s, based on the concept of coloniality of power and knowledge forged by Peruvian sociologist Aníbal Quijano. By evoking the idea that modernity and coloniality are two sides of the same coin, notably in the constitution of the Americas, decolonial thinkers point to how relations of power established during the colonial period and the expansion of Europe have shaped the modern world and have been transformed into other forms of oppression and violence reproduced through global capitalism.

"Coloniality" serves these authors as a frame to criticise the European paradigm of rationality/modernity that states that coloniality of power is linked to coloniality of knowledge. From the 1970s on, then, in Latin America, "decoloniality" opened up the path for the reconstruction and restitution of silenced histories, repressed subjectivities, subalternised knowledges and languages (Mignolo, 2007: 451). However, they are currently criticised for insisting on some barriers of their own, by recurring to a separation between "them" and "us", colonisers and colonised, thus ignoring the very agency and creativity of dominated individuals in the construction of modernity.

In parallel to the decolonial school, *postcolonial* currents based on the post-structuralism of Michel Foucault, Jacques Lacan and Jacques Derrida were also serving to deconstruct the colonial heritage in the social sciences and denouncing relations based on domination and hierarchisation — in the works of Edward Said, Gayatri Spivak and Hommi Bhabha, for instance. In its various ramifications in different parts of the world, postcolonial studies examine the effects of and reactions to European colonialism, analysing its processes from the sixteenth century up to and including the neo-colonialism of the present day.

By acknowledging the recent philosophical criticisms to the monolithic discourse of decolonisation, I will consider modernity not only as part of the problem here enunciated, but also as part of the solution. This way, I will not ignore that in the recent decolonial literature, the same thinkers that pursue dismantling modern thinking and reason are using modern tools and knowledge produced in the West to decolonise. The same paradox applies to the "decolonial" museums. As I have been arguing, the museum, as a Western institution embedded in modernity cannot be part of the result of decolonisation — there will be no "decolonised" museum, because museums as we know them were an important part of colonialism. But museums can be part of the process: as anticolonial institutions they can be used to denounce the persistence of coloniality and to critically address our colonial heritage. Thus, one of the founding questions for our analysis can be posed: how can these museums fight the very coloniality that historically and philosophically constitutes them?

On showcases

As part of their known function, showcases, the *vitrines* where artefacts are placed, serve to classify and display selected elements of the world, which means that they give meaning to the world through the work of museologists and curators. As one of museum's founding borders, showcases are also a trace of modernity. Lines and glass surfaces, in their rectilinear divisions, rationally break down the world in its fragments for the knowledge of modern men.

In the past, by establishing new hierarchical relations between artifacts, showcases served to create a "cultural geography of power" (Costa, Poulot, & Volait, 2016: 11) by the spatial and symbolic separation between a centre and its peripheries. In its physical and political sense, the showcase exerts the principle of the prison, as elaborated by Foucault in his description of disciplinary power. Discipline, in the Foucauldian conception, is responsible for organising an analytical space (1995: 143). The distribution of bodies in the disciplinary cell inflicts a distribution of posts and the creation of a certain hierarchy of power according to a classification. Ordinance, in prison as well as in the showcase, is a way to regulate bodies in space and hence to establish disciplinary control. Compulsory visibility, as an important part of disciplinary power, is what subjects the objects of observation to their own objectification, in prison as well as in museums.

Even though museums have changed and so have their architecture and exhibition spaces, the principle of the showcase has remained as an insurmountable element in their modern structure. Perceived, in museums, but also in its commercial use, as a Western technology designed to maintain a neutral point of view (the one of the Western subject), the showcase has been used to represent colonised subjects as objects, therefore reshaping their subjectivities. The Others, in museums showcases, are explored in their element of "thingness" that emanates from every form of corporeality. Like other forms of colonial technology, the showcase works against the very *work of life*, in the sense proposed by Achille Mbembe (2017: 143), which consists in "sparing the body from degenerating into absolute thingness, in preventing the body from becoming a simple object."

In the case of Western museums showing non-European objects, what is displayed is the result of a complex and collective exercise of power, one that involves several stages of cultural appropriation. The collections that belong to the Musée du quai Branly are the result of a vast history of extraction of materials from the colonies, one that involved the necessary separation of cultural creators from their productions. These objects have progressively made up the reserves of ethnographic institutions with important scientific collections for the study of French scholars. These were the fruit of explorers and adventurers, and later scientists and ethnologists, including all kinds of materials, from important apprehensions from the French mission to Greenland in the 1930s to famous and "spectacular" objects that belonged to ethnologists such as Claude Lévi-Strauss. These objects, further, no longer belong to the ethnographic institutions that helped to explain them in the past. They have been introduced into yet another performance in which the scientific showcases have been replaced by a new and refined dramatic effect created by light, shadows and glass for the presentation of primitive art.

By framing social reality in the classification of its fragmented parts, colonial museums are narrating the past in a way that preserves certain inherited separations between things and persons, culture and society, primitive and civilised, etc. These divisions draw back from the history of the collections presented in the quai Branly. What is today on display in the Musée du quai Branly are works of art without artists, creations from another world that, once deprived of any historical context, serve to merely stir the colonial interest of European audiences. Such an attempt at cultural appropriation can be perceived as the ultimate act of dehumanisation of those populations, some of which are no longer alive to reclaim their self-representation.

Decolonising as a verb

Going beyond the analyses whose focus remains on the repatriation of cultural goods without the proper reparation of past injustices, I seek to demonstrate how an *anticolonial turn* in the museum sector is yet to be achieved. Such a turn depends, from a theoretical perspective, on a deeper recognition of museums' founded coloniality, and, from a practical stance, on placing community engagement in the centre of museum's mission as a driving-force to contest the colonial narratives and restore the social fluxes of material culture.

Since the 1990s, when the anthropologist James Clifford proposed to apply the notion of "contact zone" to the museum context in the influential chapter "Museums as contact-zones" (1997), certain institutions and professionals changed their discourse to present themselves to society in a different manner, opening their doors to multiple communities, albeit with a condescending and pacifying approach. Inspired by such a conception, some museums engaged in contact relations with source-communities in order to redress social and historical inequalities. This contemporary — yet, still modern — conception of the museum was corroborated by other relatable notions such as the "integral museum", proposed in 1972 in the Round Table of Santiago de Chile, a referential event for Latin American museology organised by ICOM and UNESCO; and it was also sustained by the provocative notion of the museum as "forum" presented in the widespread article by Canadian museologist Duncan Cameron (1971). Thus, at the end of the last century museums were already struggling to decolonise, even though back then "decolonisation" as a concept had even less consensus than it has today.

More recently, some authors have been calling attention to the fact that the notion of the "contact-zone" has been taken up as a "neocolonial genre", or a way of re-inventing the museum as "a site in and for the center ..." that maintains inherited asymmetries and preserves its colonial anatomy (Boast, 2011). In this perspective, we can observe today that most central institutions continue to ignore the experimental museologies of marginalised communities, such as those resulting from social engagement in indigenous museums, racial minorities' heritage associations, or LGBTQI+ grassroots organisations that struggle to safeguard and transmit their own cultural references. Meanwhile, the practices and methods that attend heteronormativity, whiteness and coloniality remain largely unchallenged (Sandell, & Frost, 2010; Nguyen, 2018; Brulon Soares, 2020).

Following the notion of the "contact zone" or the museum-forum, museums in central places engaged in new methods as a salvation recipe to decolonise, as if the resolution of past injustices was finally going to lead them towards a postcolonial future. In this perspective, several textbooks in some parts of the world started using "decolonisation" as a noun, referring to various conceptions for museum democratising methods or, more strictly, to formal restitution or repatriation.

Other works will use a number of adjectives referring to specific trends in the museum field, also dealing with decolonisation even though not always using the term: either through community engagement and experimental practices, such as in Brazilian *social museology* (Chagas, & Gouveia, 2014; Chagas, Primo, Assunção, & Storino, 2018), or in a critical reading of museums' exhibitions and historical discourse, according to Hispanic *critical museology* (Lorente, 2006; Navarro, 2012), or referring to a deeper revision of museum performativity, in the different interpretations of *reflexive museology* (Teather, 1991; Butler, 2015; Brulon Soares, 2015). Even though with distinct approaches to similar museum issues, these adjectives and trends refer to specific attempts to change the established order, seeking to cast a critical look on colonial violence entrenched in the structure of the canonical museum.

In an alternative sense, when used as a verb in its more dynamic conceptions, "to decolonise" refers to open practices and "bottom-up" approaches that allow community members to change museums' authorised narratives in a critical appropriation of cultural heritage. Assuming decolonisation as a verb, or as a continuous museum action that is necessary for institutions who wish to undertake an anticolonial attitude, I prefer to take into account the proposal of Achille Mbembe (2015), moving away from an instrumentalist approach of the term to explore a postcolonial critique of authorised discourses:

> Decolonization is not about design, tinkering with the margins. It is about reshaping, turning human beings once again into craftsmen and craftswomen who, in reshaping matters and forms, need not to look at the pre-existing models and need not use them as paradigms.

In short, I will defend that *to decolonise*, as a museum action, requires acknowledging the multiple ways museums can be driven by communities and shaped together with their various audiences to achieve the contestation of history and their own unrestrained transformation in this process. I propose to look at museums from the perspective of their multiple actors and their agency to perceive decolonisation not as something that can be apprehended in museum manuals but as a movement towards liberation.

Based on the analysis of museums in their current transformation, I would propose that "movement" is the key word in this general statement. While "liberation" can be relative and rarely fully accomplished, "movement" is the only constant that drives museums and societies into their future. In all the observed waves of decolonisation throughout the contemporary history of museums, movement is always a proclaimed aim to achieve political and social change. Decolonising, thus, encompasses all movement and agency that defines the museum structure, from the perspective of its curators and directors but also in the engagement with their audiences and source-communities. Rather than a forum with a defined agenda, museums in their stable presence inherited from previous centuries can serve as barricades, protecting the most vulnerable and allowing their fight to continue until its ultimate accomplishment: the conquering of the museum itself for whatever purpose and use.

The colonial divide: destitution, appropriation, restitution

On 12 June 2020, the forged order in the quai Branly plateau of collections was disturbed, this time by an external act of activism when five members of the panafrican movement Les Marrons Unis Dignes et Courageux attempted to seize a Bari funeral artifact from the museum's long-term exhibition. The manifestation of African activists was a form of protest amid the Black Lives Matter movement in the French capital, but one that also aimed for reopening the debate on repatriation of African objects, never really put in practice by the museum. The physical attempt of repatriation of the Bari pole was documented in a 30-minute video and spread around the world via social media and the online press. In this contemporary document, the activists stated that "their heritage" should be taken back to where it belonged, because "most of the works were taken during colonialism and we want justice" (Solomon, 2020). The protesters were stopped by a museum security guard, who was also a black man. The video ends when the two non-European descendants face each other before engaging in what appeared to be a physical dispute for the stolen object.

This radical scene, captured in film by the activists themselves, was probably the closest that the quai Branly museum has ever been to exposing coloniality in its exhibition space. But the trespassing of the museum border was only momentary. The five protestors accused of stealing the African funeral pole from the museum faced French court in the following months, with the case hinging on whether the act was theft or a political action against colonialism (*The Art Newspaper*, 2020). The Congolese activist Emery Mwazulu Diyabanza, who led the protest group, was fined € 1,000, and the activists were banned from the museum premises.

The Musée du quai Branly—Jacques Chirac, a national project aiming for the decolonisation of France's colonial collections, was born with the promise to provide its visitors with the unique opportunity to see the "chefs-d'œuvre de l'humanité" ("humanity's masterpieces", as recalls Dias, 2002: 17). Nonetheless, what it accomplishes in reality is the dehumanisation of peoples from the different contexts of the world represented in its highly aesthetic exhibition. It is worth noting that when French national heritage was constituted, after the French Revolution, the criteria evoked for the preservation of national heritage were primarily aesthetic ones. The monuments and collections under the newly inaugurated modern state were to be preserved as a response to the complaints of artists, art dealers and collectors against revolutionary vandalism and aiming for the safeguarding of the chefs-d'œuvre.① In the case of colonial materials, even when treated as ethnographic objects during the twentieth century, their exoticism was progressively being interpreted as "beautiful". As noted by James Clifford (1988: 228), this progressive assimilation of cultural objects into an "art-culture system" explains why in the mid-nineteenth century some indigenous objects were "grotesques" or "antiquity" and by 1920 they were considered cultural witnesses and aesthetic masterpieces.

As Mbembe argues, this renewal of an anticolonial critique within European aesthetics and politics, "shaped the reevaluation of Africa's contribution to the project of a humanity to come" (2017: 41). In this sense, the surrealist movement and the proponents of primitivism in the 1920s, and later again in the configuration of the quai Branly ideology, in the 1990s, were key contributors to this inclusion of alternative aesthetics in Western art through the exclusion of the creators. What has changed, then, in the representation of the Others in French collections? Who defines the criteria to value their works

---

① The concept began to be used to justify the preservation of works of French heritage that were in the process of being destroyed from the end of the 18th century, particularly by artists, especially sculptors. (See Fiori, 2011, p. 136).

today? Who profits from these criteria in the post-colonial world?

The colonial divide that was once inflicted between peoples and their cultures is still an open wound that marks the sector of cultural heritage in France and in many other former metropolises. To call attention to it, to affirm that the ownership of certain objects must be questioned, and to act for restitution in the post-colonial era still means to defy the structures of power raised as a result of the combination of colonialism, modernity and the expansion of the West.

The reaction to anticolonial activism in a (post-)colonial institution, in the case of the quai Branly, helps to denounce how discipline in the museum continues to be prioritised over human experience and the social bounds that constitute our heritage. Meanwhile, the classification of "African artifacts" expropriated from Africans and incorporated into a national French collection continues to reproduce the imperial epistemology according to which some museums' frontiers cannot be trespassed.

The Anticolonial Museum: dismantling decolonisation

"The colonial world is a compartmentalized world," says Fanon (2004/1961: 3) on *The Wretched of the Earth*. In his own observation, colonisation inflicts a dividing line between the "native" existence and that of the European. "The border", as Fanon puts it, "is represented by the barracks and the police stations" spread throughout the colonies and still a symbol of colonial violence, but also of institutionalised racism and apartheid in the post-colonial world.

If we agree with its main critics, coming from different perspectives and academic backgrounds, colonisation had as one of its most lasting effects the demarcation of borders — political, epistemic, racial, territorial, or others. Contemporary museums have inherited some of these borders, incorporated, during the past few centuries, in their systems of classification, in their curatorial criteria and in their performativity when presenting collections to an audience. Throughout this speech, I intended to demonstrate how the discourse of "decolonisation" and the label of a "post-colonial museum" can be used in favour of these very colonial borders, operating for their sedimentation and reinforcement in the present. The reason for this apparent contradiction lies in the fact that some modern museums have continued, much beyond the end of colonialism, to reproduce symbolically and materially the hegemony of the colonising subject of the West and its counterpart as "a site of savage exteriority" (Mbembe, 2017: 27–28).

Based on Fanon and some of his readers in decolonial and postcolonial studies, we can say that borders are actually an important element for the functioning of the centre. But Fanon will also consider the border as a potential site of invasion from where an anticolonial intrusion, through an act of violence, may generate a change in the entire system. This has to do with the fact that for Fanon, Mbembe and others, "the only way for the colonized to restore themselves to life was to use violence to impose a redefinition of the mechanisms through which death was distributed" (2017: 164). In this new order that involves the disorder of the established system, our colonial heritage can be contested through an act of violation and, finally, shared based on the plurality of social experiences and the re-humanisation of the dehumanised.

What is at stake with this act of anticolonial invasion is the risk of tampering with a defined line between who is in and who is out, one that has been explained by Esposito in his biopolitical analysis of immune systems. In his perspective, whether the danger is a disease threatening the individual body or a violent intrusion into the body politic, it ultimately has to do with "trespassing or violating borders" (2011: 2). In this analogy, what remains constant is the location of this strange body, always on the border between the inside and the outside, the self and the other, the individual and the common.

However, the penetration by the stranger corrupts and ends up altering the collective body from within. In the process of its assimilation, the stranger becomes something else, an *antibody* that is now part of the protection of the collective body. It is an intrusion kept to generate a memory that will prevent the body politic from any reinfection. A memory that creates immunisation.

In the case of post-colonial museums, the very elements of the Other incorporated in their collections will allow them to decolonise, a contradiction that we have tried to expose in this speech. In the terms of Esposito, the dialectical figure that emerges is that of "exclusionary inclusion or exclusion by inclusion" (2011: 8). The Other not only is preserved as part of the self, but it also constitutes the condition for its self-definition. At the same time, after it penetrates the collective system, paradoxically its life depends on a wound that cannot heal, "because the wound is created by life itself."

What is implied in this conception is the idea that real anticolonial agency cannot emanate from the centre towards its margins, in a movement that replicates the one of colonisation. The premise of a supposed "rupture" from traditional museology (and its colonial legacy) that took shape in the old claims for decolonising the museum, can be explained by the postcolonial critique of Gayatri Spivak (1993: 66–67), who stated that a radical revision coming out of the West is usually the result of a desire "to conserve the subject of the West, or the West as Subject". In other words, some decolonial devices can also serve to allow the dominant subject of the West to continue its discourse on behalf of its subaltern others in a condescending and colonising way.

From this perspective, the issue of decolonising museum collections is not solemnly related to ownership, or a mere matter of provenance. Even though repatriation is disputed in the legal arena, involving nation states and their representatives, real reparation is not only a matter of attributing who owns cultural heritage and who should profit from it. Repairing past injustices is dealing with the open wounds that make colonisation and modernity parts of an irreversible process of dehumanisation. Reparation, thus, is "a process of reassembling amputated parts, repairing broken links, relaunching the forms of reciprocity without which there can be no progress for humanity" (Mbembe, 2017: 182).

Following the anticolonial approach, we must *dismember* first, in order to *re-member* later. What Fanon defined as "counter-violence" has to do with a necessary intrusion that perforate the borders and disturbs the order of things holding within. From this invasion, an antibody is created, as a body that was once a threat to the collective body, which is a menace of distress and devastation. It also informs the invaded body of its potential power of destruction. Therefore, the antibody is responsible for creating a resistance from within, a tolerance to the strange presence that will never be completely expurgated nor completely accepted as its indistinct part.

What I'm envisioning here is a museum that puts into question its own centrality and coloniality, by becoming itself the necessary antibody for the permanent fight against colonialism and neocolonialism. This way, the anticolonial museum may serve us to open new windows onto the past, fostering empathy and mutual understanding, allowing colonised and colonisers to deal with the open wounds left by the very history that separated us. As a border bending over the centre, the museum is also a space of conflict and violence where modernity is pervaded and its walls are shredded through the agency of the subalterns who, holding on to their scattered fragments, are coming back to life.

References

Amselle, J. L. (2010). *Rétrovolutions*. Essais sur les primitivismes contemporains. Paris: Éditions Stock.

Balandier, G. (1951). La situation coloniale: Approche théorique. In *Cahiers internationaux de sociologie*, *11*, 44–79.

Boast, R. (2011). Neocolonial Collaboration: Museum as Contact Zone Revisited. *Museum Anthropology,* 34 (1), 56–70.

Brulon Soares, B. (2020). Descolonizar o pensamento museológico: Reintegrando a matéria para re-pensar os museus. *Anais Do Museu Paulista: História E Cultura Material,* 28, 1–30.

Brulon Soares, B. (2015). The Museum Performance: Reflecting on a Reflexive Museology. *Complutum,* 26(2), 49–57.

Butler, S. R. (2015). Reflexive Museology: lost and found. In A. Witcomb, & K. Message (eds.), *The International Handbooks of Museum Studies: Museum Theory* (pp. 159–182). Chichester. West Sussex: John Wiley & Sons.

Cameron, D. (1971). The museum, a temple or the forum, *Curator,* XIV (1), 11–24.

Chagas, M., & Gouveia I. (2014). Museologia social: reflexões e práticas (à guisa de apresentação). *Cadernos do CEOM,* 27, 41, –22.

Chagas, M., Primo, J., Assunção, P., & Storino, C. (2018). A museologia e a construção de sua dimensão social: olhares e caminhos. *Cadernos de Sociomuseologia,* 11 (55), 73–102.

Chirac, J. (2007). In *Musée du Quai Branly.* Le guide du musée. Paris.

Clifford, J. (1997). *Routes: Travel and translation in the late twentieth century.* Harvard University Press.

Clifford, J. (1988). *The Predicament of Culture. Twentieth-Century Ethnography, Literature, and Art.* Cambridge, Massachusetts and London: Harvard University Press.

Costa, S., Poulot, D., & Volait, M. (2016). Introduzione/Introduction. In S. Costa, D. Poulot, & M. Volait (Eds.), *The Period Rooms:* Allestimenti storici tra arte, collezionismo e museologia (pp. 7–17). Bologna: Bononia University Press.

de L'Estoile, B. (2008). The past as it lives now: An anthropology of colonial legacies. *Social Anthropology/Anthropologie Sociale,* 16(3), 267–279.

de L'Estoile, B. (2007). *Le goût des Autres. De l'exposition coloniale aux arts premiers.* Paris: Flammarion.

de Royer, S. (2011). François Fillon loue Jacques Chirac, «l'avocat des oubliés». *Le Figaro,* Paris, 24 November 2011. Available at: https://www.lefigaro.fr/politique/2011/11/24/01002-20111124ARTFIG00756-francois-fillon-loue-jacques-chirac-l-avocat-des-oublies.php.

Esposito, R. (2011). *Immunitas. The Protection and Negation of Life.* Polity Press: Cambridge.

Fanon, F. (2004 [1961]). *The Wretched of the Earth.* New York: Grove Press.

Fiori, R. (2011). *Paris déplacé. Du XVIII siècle à nos jours.* Paris : Parigramme/ Compagnie Parisienne du Livre.

Foucault, M. (1995). *Discipline and Punish. The Birth of Prison.* New York: Vintage Books.

Lorente, J. P. (2006). Nuevas tendencias em teoria museológica: A vueltas con la museologia crítica, *Museos.es*, 2, 231–243.

Mbembe, A. (2017). *Critique of Black Reason.* Durham and London: Duke University Press.

Mbembe, A. (2015). *Decolonizing knowledge and the question of the archive.* Lecture delivered at the Wits Institute for Social and Economic Research. https:// africaisacountry.atavist.com/decolonizing-knowledge-and-the-question-of-the-archive.

Mignolo, W. D. (2007). Delinking: The rhetoric of modernity, logic of coloniality, grammar of decoloniality. *Cultural Studies*, 21(2), 449–514. https://dx.doi.org/10.1080/09502380601162647

Navarro, Ó. (2012). History and education as bases for museum legitimacy in Latin American museums: Some comments for a discussion from critical museology point of view, *Museologica Brunensia*, 1 (1), 28–33.

Nguyen, T. (2018). Co-existence and collaboration: Australian AIDS quilts in public museums and community collections. *Museum & Society,* 16(1), 41–55.

Quijano, A. (1992). Colonialidad y modernidad-racionalidad. In H. Bonilla (Ed.), *Los conquistadores,* (pp. 437–447). Tercer Mundo.

Ruiz-Gómez, N. (2006). The (Jean) Nouvel Other: Primitivism and the Musée du Quai Branly. *Modern & Contemporary France*, vol. 14, n. 4, November 2006, pp. 417–432.

Sandell, R. & Frost, S. (2010). A Persistent Prejudice. In: F. Cameron and L. Kelly (eds.), *Hot Topics, Public Culture, Museums* (pp. 150–174). London: Cambridge Scholars Publishing.

Sarr, F. & Savoy, B. (2018). *Rapport sur la restitution du patrimoine culturel africain: Vers une nouvelle éthique relationnelle.* http://restitutionreport2018.com/.

Savoy, B. (2022). *Africa's Struggle for its Art. History of a Postcolonial Defeat.* Princeton and Oxford: Princeton University Press.

Solomon, T. (2020). Activists face trial after attempt to seize African artifact from Paris's Quai Branly Museum as protest. *ARTnews*. Retrieved from https://www.artnews.com/art-news/news/quai-branly-protest-african-artifact-seized-activists-1202691064/. [Accessed on 17 April 2021].

Spivak, G. C. (1993). Can the subaltern speak? In P. Williams and L. Chrisman (Eds.), *Colonial discourse* and *post-colonial theory* (pp. 66–111). Columbia.

Stocking, G. W. (Ed). (1985). *Objects and Others: Essays on Museums and Material Culture* (pp. 146–166). Madison: University of Wisconsin Press.

Teather, L. (1991). Museum studies. Reflecting on reflective practice, *Museum Management and Curatorship*, 10, 403–417.

The Art Newspaper (2020). Trial of Quai Branly protestors in Paris centres on 'political' aspect of activist action. Available at: https://www.theartnewspaper.com/2020/10/02/trial-of-quai-branly-protestors-in-paris-centres-on-political-aspect-of-activist-action. Accessed in: 22 December 2022.

博物馆去殖民化范式

布鲁诺·布鲁伦·苏亚雷斯*

大家好！所有人上午好！下午好！晚上好！我非常高兴参加这次会议，也非常荣幸由我来开启讨论环节，为为期两天的活动拉开帷幕，这真令人兴奋。首先，我想感谢我的朋友和同事卡罗尔·斯科特（Carol Scott）和安来顺，感谢组织者组办了这个非常有启发性的项目，项目中的许多主题都契合了当今世界正探讨的去殖民化问题。同时要感谢这个项目背后的工作人员，他们有的来自上海大学，有的来自国际博物馆协会秘书处。由于本人有其他安排而未能来到现场，对此深表遗憾。但我很高兴能通过线上的方式与大家相聚一堂，希望在接下来的两天里为您们的讨论贡献绵薄之力！

我想先解释下，对于本次演讲来说，我将关注的是博物馆的边界，在这里我把它定义为我们的现代性意义上的分界线，它一直将自我与所谓的他者分隔开来，有时甚至将我们与我们自身的其他部分分隔开来，这些部分无法用理性来解释，或者无法通过现代性来理解。所以我会讨论边界的存在，也会讨论一些越过这些边界的去殖民做法。

从边界讲起

首先，从博物馆的边界开始讲起，这些边界是这个现代机构自殖民化以来造成世界分裂的部分原因。所以我会邀请您们站在这一立场，这对博物馆专业人士和策展人来说可能是一个非同寻常的角度，即作为博物馆的局外人，纵观全局。这是他者的立场，即在由博物馆主导的叙事中，他们

---

* 布鲁诺·布鲁伦·苏亚雷斯，苏格兰圣安德鲁斯大学文化遗产学教授。

被排斥在外。在殖民主义时代,这些叙事不断被复制,哪怕殖民主义结束,其影响力也不可小觑。如果看看一些至今还收藏了殖民地藏品的当代博物馆外观,您就会发现这一点。某些博物馆的当代建筑是历史和空间异化的结果,因为对称的线条以及材料和颜色的重叠构建了被毁坏的寺庙,试图隐藏其现代起源和传统而又不失去其根基。当我穿过巴黎的街道时,已然感受到巴黎老城的魅力,即使在远处,也可以感受到从博物馆外墙发出的召唤力量,以及我可以看到前方被玻璃幕墙覆盖的难以辨认的建筑。在我到达位于巴黎城中心的凯布朗利·雅克·希拉克博物馆(Museo Quai Branly Jacques Chirac)的入口前,就已经感受到了它的神秘和戏剧性。它把优雅的城市甩在身后,进入博物馆后所带来的异域环境使得当地人或游客可以化身为外国人或探险家。博物馆的展陈犹如一场梦幻的表演,一旦进入这个漫长的观展旅程,观赏的常设展览只是一个更广泛边界的一部分,它把殖民地遭遇模拟作21世纪的国家娱乐。透过半透明的墙寓意着进入一个未知的世界,在这里人们只被允许看到博物馆花园里的异国情调。后者通过建立一个不对称和受控的无序场景,来彰显与理性和古典美学的断裂。当进入其明确无误的空间时,所有的参观者都知道他们正在跨越边界。当参观者穿梭在不同的世界和激进的美学之间时,展览中的光线变得暗淡。在这种环境下,他者的物质文化会隐藏起博物馆创建时的模糊性。我在这里指的是一个自相矛盾的原则,即必须忘记殖民历史,才能对被殖民者的作品进行审美欣赏。尽管构思于20世纪90年代并于2006年6月20日落成,但作为法国首都对欧洲以外藏品的新的解读,凯布朗利博物馆如今是法国殖民时期文物的主要继承者,它收集了在1960年之前属于法国殖民部的各个博物馆的藏品。

新博物馆旨在将所谓的原始艺术从其殖民历史中解救出来。

根据法国总统雅克·希拉克的说法,《利菲·加图》(Liffey Gatto)杂志称他是为被遗忘者辩护的律师,建立这个专门收藏研究非洲、亚洲、大洋洲和美洲艺术和文明的博物馆是出于政治意愿,即为所谓的欧洲以外的文化主持公道,承认它们在欧洲文化遗产中的地位。然而,博物馆的大多数分析家对此批评道,希拉克所意图的普适主义只适用于已经消失的文化,或者是被官方的历史排除在外且与现在的文化没有任何关系的文化。可以说，在已经和解并供分享的方面，这个博物馆是明显的后殖民主义。这个有着模糊话语的博物馆不仅把殖民主义的物品作为艺术品来展示，而且还在通过殖民主义强化施加在人类身上的现代剥离。

我这次演讲的目的是针对博物馆学文献中关于去殖民化的争论，以提出博物馆的解构及其在当下的去殖民化的话语权。基于此目的，我得承认，在目前关于博物馆和文化遗产的争论中，去殖民化的话语本身存在着使用上的变化和矛盾，当然还有野心，但要考虑博物馆学中的多种谱系。

这并不是要对凯布朗利博物馆进行批判，尽管在过去的15年里，已经有好几位学者这样做了。这些批评确实充实了博物馆研究文献，但我更希望把这个博物馆的边界和外观用于生动地隐喻殖民主义遗产，因为迄今为止，博物馆一般都被殖民主义色彩笼罩着。这里，我说的不仅仅是欧洲的博物馆，也指博物馆作为一种殖民手段，遍布着整个殖民世界和当代世界。

因此，我在这次演讲中的一个主要论点是，现代博物馆及其去殖民化的再现，其运作方式类似于免疫系统对人类机体的功能，以及在类比中所启发的社会系统的法律免疫中也是如此。这个类比源于这样一个事实，即一些自行宣布为去殖民化的博物馆也包含了它们所要抵御的相同物质的元素——殖民性。按照这种方式，作为一个总统的项目，作为纪念希拉克总统在历史中的角色的建筑物，2016年后以他的名字命名的凯布朗利博物馆也是对其身份问题的政治回应，以及对法国社会正义和文化代表的社区诉求。这种诉求在这个国家的背景下并不新鲜，正如欧洲学者最近的一些研究表明，这些研究首次认识到针对文物返还辩论的历史背景远远超出了时代框架。

事实证明，冲突的自然化或原住民诉求的中立化，甚至仅仅是压制他们的声音，在过去都比现在更容易发生。如果我们看一下博物馆理论中的一些基本原则或基本文献，我会强调博物馆的去殖民化以及博物馆学的去殖民化取决于一个三层的、相互关联的过程——解构、重构和重新分配，必然是按照这个顺序。

今天关于博物馆去殖民化的讨论，与它关注这一复杂而艰难过程的最后部分有关，而这种关注受到限制，无视其更基本的机制。我将论证这是一个具有政治后果的缺陷，因为如果你重新分配文化遗产，而不重新思考生产和保存遗产的价值和知识体系，这些以殖民性、理性和暴力为标志的制度在本质上和实践上将保持不变。

现代性/殖民性范式

自20世纪最后几十年以来，正如大家在这些示例中看到的，博物馆理论不得不应对批判性研究，这些研究通过质疑其殖民根源来对博物馆进行审视。这种反思性的分析标志着受到批判性人类学家的强烈影响，这些批判大多受到弗朗兹·法农（Franz Fanon）的奠基性著作《全世界受苦的人》的启发。他们谴责我们的殖民遗产，因为他们现在迫切需要重新解释和重新谈判。

有一些分析有助于区分一般意义上的殖民关系和作为受限历史事件的殖民化。基于这种区别，博物馆可以被视作是这样一个机构，即对它在时间和空间上进行了定义。它是现代的，起源于欧洲的，是对世界西化的一项举措，而四处传播。但在政治上，它是植根于殖民主义的工具。批判性思维和后殖民研究对博物馆理论的影响，也促使人们认识到博物馆在对其藏品中保存的过去进行去殖民化方面的核心作用。

因此，我们今天有非常多的关于博物馆理论的文献，把博物馆放在去殖民化或后殖民主义的背景下，与拉丁美洲作者中的后殖民主义理论的发展平行，在20世纪70年代和90年代之间，基于权力的殖民性概念以及秘鲁社会学家阿尼巴尔·奎杰罗（Aníbal Quijano）的认识，提出现代性和殖民性是同一个硬币的两面的想法，主要是在美洲的语境中，定义了一种去殖民化方法。这位去殖民化思想家指出，在殖民时期和欧洲扩张期间建立的权力关系如何塑造了现代世界，并通过全球资本主义和其他几种形式的新殖民主义转化为其他形式的压迫和暴力再现。于是，殖民性成为这些作者批判欧洲理性范式与现代性的框架，指出权力的殖民性与知识的殖民性相关。然而，他们目前因坚持己见而饱受诟病，例如，反复出现他们与我们、殖民者与被殖民者之间的隔阂，从而忽视了现代性构成中被统治个人的能动性和创造力。

通过承认最近对去殖民化的单一话语的哲学批评，我将考虑现代性不仅是这里阐述的问题的一部分，似乎这个问题可以简单地通过承认殖民性或非殖民性的实践来解决。但这里我将现代性视为解决方案的一部分。这与博物馆有很大关系。这样一来就不会忽视在最近的去殖民化文献中，那些追求这种精神上的现代思维和理性的思想家也在使用西方生产的现代工具和知识来进行去殖民化。

同样的悖论也适用于所谓的去殖民化博物馆。作为植根于现代性的西方机构，博物馆不能成为去殖民化结果的一部分，不会有去殖民化的博物馆，我们也无法用任何实际的术语来描述去殖民化的博物馆会是什么样子，因为我们所知道的西方博物馆，是殖民主义的重要组成部分。但是博物馆可以参与去殖民化过程，即使它们不能成为解决方案的一部分或是成为解决方案，但它们可以作为反殖民机构发挥作用，可以用来谴责殖民主义的持续存在并批判性地解决我们的殖民遗产问题。这是我们要分析的基础问题之一，即可以根据对博物馆作为去殖民化进程的一部分的这种看法来提出问题。

这些博物馆如何与历史上和哲学上构成它们的殖民性作斗争？我的回答不会是客观的，或显而易见的，但我想说，这与我们所说的博物馆反思性或反思性博物馆学有很大关系。通过它，我们可以真正把自己和我们的机构置于批评之中，如同我们把殖民主义的历史置于同样的批评之中一样。

陈列柜

基于此目的，我想首先提出博物馆最明显的边界之一，那就是博物馆的陈列柜，作为其已知功能的一部分——陈列柜，玻璃橱窗用于放置文物，起到了分类并向世界展示特定元素的作用，这意味着它们给予了博物馆学家和策展人的工作世界意义。作为博物馆的最原始的边界之一，展示柜也是现代性的一个痕迹。它们是通过一种理性概念来实现的，这种理性将主体和客体、线条和玻璃表面以直线划分，合理地分解了世界的碎片，为现代人在过去的知识中建立了新的文物之间的等级关系。展示柜通过中心和外围的空间和象征性的分离来创造一种权力的文化地理。在这里，这种分离将我们带回到的"地理大发现"的迷思中，根据这个迷思，欧洲以外的人民需要被征服，这样欧洲才能重新发现它们在现代历史中的地位，同时也发现它的边缘，正如阿根廷哲学家杜塞尔所主张的那样，现代性并非欧洲独有的现象，而是在与非欧洲选择的辩证关系中构成的。在其物理和政治意义上，展示柜发挥了福柯在描述纪律权力时阐述的监狱原则。福柯观点中的纪律负责组织分析空间，纪律单元中的主体分布造成职位分布和一定权力等级的产生。根据分类，监狱中的法令，以及陈列室中的法令，都是在空间中规范主体的一种方式，以加强建立纪律控制。因此，作为纪律权力的一个重要部分，强制的可见性是观察对象在监狱和博物馆中被物化的原因。

尽管博物馆发生了变化，它们的建筑和展览空间也发生了变化，但陈列柜的原则仍然是现代结构中不可逾越的元素，在博物馆是这样的；而且在其商业用途中，作为一种旨在保持中立的西方技术也是这样。从西方主体的角度来看，陈列柜用来展示被殖民的主体即客体，因此，在某种意义上重塑他们的主体性，即是在物性元素中探索博物馆陈列柜中的其他藏品，而这种元素则以各种形式散发出来。像其他形式的殖民方式一样，展示柜的机制与生命的原则相反，将人变成物，如同阿契尔·班贝提出的。这在于防止主体退化为绝对物体，防止主体成为一个简单的客体。这就是生命的作用，而根据此作者的说法，博物馆的作用是与这一过程相违背的。

在西方博物馆展示非欧洲的文物时，所展示的东西是一种复杂的、集体行使权力的结果，其中包括几个阶段的文化占有。凯布朗利博物馆的藏品是从殖民地攫取众多文物的一个缩影，其历史涉及文化创作从其生产中的剥离。这些文物逐渐为民族学机构提供储备，为法国学者的研究提供了重要的科学收藏价值。这些文物包括了各种材料，是探险家和冒险家以及后来的科学家和民族学家的成果，涉及从20世纪30年代法国对格陵兰探险中的斩获，到属于著名探险家带回的文物。这些文物甚至不再属于过去曾探索其奥秘的民族学机构。现在已经将它们置入另一种展示中，在这样的环境中，科学陈列柜被一种由光影和玻璃产生的新的、精致的戏剧效果所取代，以便更好地展示原始艺术。

作为动词的"去殖民化"

除了重点关注返还文化产品的分析之外，没有对过去的不公正行为进行适当的赔偿，我试图证明我们在博物馆领域所讨论的这种反殖民转向如何仍然有待实现。从理论上看，这种转向取决于对根植于殖民性的博物馆的更深层次的认识，从实践上看，它取决于将社区参与置于博物馆使命的中心，作为对殖民主义叙事的质疑和恢复物质文化的社会流动的推动力。

自20世纪90年代以来，人类学家詹姆斯·克利福德提出了博物馆作为交互地带，其概念应用于博物馆环境。一些机构和专业人士改变了他们的话语，以不同的方式向社会展示自己，以一种居高临下和安抚的方式向外界的多个社区开放。在这种观念的启发下，一些博物馆与来源社区建立了联系，以纠正社会和历史上的不平等。这种当代但仍然现代的博物馆概念得到了其他相关概念的佐证，例如1972年在智利圣地亚哥举行的著名的圆桌会议上提出的整体博物馆，这是由国际博物馆协会和联合国教科文组织组织的拉丁美洲博物馆学会议。这次会议就是这样一个案例，但它也得到一些启发性概念的支持，包括加拿大博物馆学家邓肯·卡梅隆在很多文章中提出把博物馆作为论坛的概念。

因此，在20世纪末，博物馆已经在为去殖民化而抗争，博物馆学已经面临着去殖民化，这成为博物馆的一种新的可能性。尽管当时去殖民化作为一个概念比今天更缺乏共识。根据交互地带或博物馆论坛的概念，中心地区的博物馆采用新方法去殖民化，好像过去不公正的解决方案最终将引领他们走向后殖民时代。从这个角度来看，世界某些地区的一些教科书开始将去殖民化作为名词来使用，以代指博物馆民主化方法的各种概念，或者更严格地说是正式的返还和返还文物，好像去殖民化可以被视为一个孤立的事件。另外，去殖民化作为动词使用时，在其更动态的概念中，指的是开放的实践和自下而上的方法，允许社区成员在文化遗产的批判性挪用中改变博物馆的授权叙述。这种方法考虑到了阿契尔·班贝的提议，摆脱了工具主义的概念，将去殖民化在重塑和重塑人性的层面上予以探索，这意味着将人类再次变成手工匠人。

殖民分裂：贫困，侵占，归还

但是，博物馆如何才能在去殖民化的同时，将过去殖民时期的一些边界作为我们殖民遗产的一部分保留下来。我现在要从实际的角度，多谈谈殖民主义的分歧。例如，2020年6月12日，凯布朗利博物馆唯一收藏的高原藏品的展示台遭遇了骚乱。这是由于激进主义的外部行为造成的。当五名泛非洲主义运动的成员，在利马大厅，以独特、尊严、平等的方式试图从强大的博物馆常设展览中夺取一个葬礼文物，这也是非洲活动家在法国首都进行的"黑人平权运动"的抗议形式之一。其目的也旨在重启关于返还非洲文物的辩论，尽管博物馆从未将返还真正付诸实践。一段30分钟的视频记录了试图将葬礼柱送回原处的过程，该视频通过社交媒体和在线媒体传播到世界各地。在这份当代文件中，活动家们表示，他们的遗产应该被带回属于它的地方。因为大部分文物都是在殖民主义时期被拿走的，他们要伸张正义，但是抗议者被一名博物馆保安拦住了。他也是一名黑人。视频结束时，这两个非欧洲后裔面对面，为争夺被盗物品似乎发生了肢体上的冲突。这个由活动家自己拍摄的激进场景，可能是这个只有立方体的博物馆在其展览空间中最接近于暴露其隐藏的殖民性的一次。但对博物馆边界的侵犯只是瞬间的事。在接下来的几个月里，五名抗议者被指控从博物馆偷盗非洲葬礼柱，站上了法国法庭，案件的关键在于该行为是偷盗，还是反对殖民主义的政治行动。

凯布朗利博物馆实际上有一个旨在将法国的殖民地藏品去殖民化的国家项目，它承诺为游客提供独特的机会，让他们看到人类文明的文化结晶。事实上，它所做到的则是对来自世界不同背景的人们的非人化，并在它高度审美化的展览中呈现。在这里，美的标准也是一种掩饰殖民历史的策略。就殖民的物质文化而言，即使在20世纪被当作民族学藏品，其异国情调也逐渐被解释为美丽。正如詹姆斯·克利福德所指出的，这种将文化物品逐步同化为艺术，纳入艺术文化体系的做法，解释了为什么在19世纪中期，一些原住民物品是怪诞的或古老的，而到了1920年，它们被认为是文化的见证和美学的杰作。

正如我们今天所知，20世纪20年代的超现实主义运动和原始主义的支持者们。再后来，我们在20世纪90年代构成了凯布朗利博物馆的理念，通过对创作者的排斥，将这种另类美学纳入西方艺术。那么，在法国藏品中，其他藏品的表现发生了什么变化？今天谁来定义评价他们的话语标准？在所谓的后殖民世界中，谁从这一标准中获益？曾经在各国人民及其文化之间造成的殖民分裂仍然是法国和许多其他前大都市文化遗产领域的一个未愈合的伤口，提醒着大家某些文物的所有权应当受到质疑。最后，要在后殖民时代采取返还行动，仍然意味着要界定因殖民主义、现代性和西方扩张的结合而产生的权力结构。

与此同时，为非洲人征用并纳入法国国家收藏的非洲文物的分类继续再现内部认识论，根据这一认识论，一些博物馆的边界不能被侵犯。

反殖民博物馆：消除去殖民化

殖民世界是一个分隔的世界，弗朗兹·法农在其著名的《全世界受苦的人》中指出，在他观察中，殖民化在本土与欧洲之间划出了一条分界线。正如法农所说，边界的代表是遍布殖民地的军营和警察局，它仍然是殖民主义暴力的象征，也是制度化的种族主义和种族隔离的象征。如果我们同意来自不同视角和学术背景的主要批评者的观点，那么殖民化最持久的影响之一就是划定边界，包括政治、认识、种族、领土或其他方面的边界。当代博物馆继承了过去几个世纪在分类系统、策展标准以及向观众展示藏品时的表现力中所包含的一些边界。

在这篇演讲中，我试图展示去殖民化的话语和后殖民博物馆的标签是如何被用来支持这种殖民边界的，并在当下对其进行沉淀和强化。造成这种明显矛盾的原因在于，有些人利用现代博物馆在殖民主义结束后，仍继续以象征性和物质性的形式再现西方殖民主体的霸权，并将博物馆作为野蛮外部场所的对应物。

根据法农和他在殖民和后殖民研究中的读物，我们可以说，边界实际上是中心运作的一个重要因素。但法农也将考虑把边界作为一个潜在的入侵地点，从那里通过暴力行为进行的反殖民主义入侵可能会在整个系统中产生变化。这是法农、班贝和其他人会赞同的一个观察，即被殖民者恢复自己的生活的唯一途径是使用暴力来强行重新定义机制，即分配机制。这种反殖民入侵行为的风险在于篡改了谁是谁非的界限，埃斯波西托在《免疫共同体》中解释了这一点。在他看来，无论这种危险是威胁个人身体的疾病，还是对政治身体的暴力入侵，最终都与侵入和侵犯边界有关。在这个类比中，保持不变的是这个异化的主体始终位于内部与外部、自我与他者、个体与公共之间的边界上。然而，外来物的渗透会腐蚀并最终从内部改变集体的主体。在同化的过程中，外来物变成了另一种东西，成了抗体，现在是保护主体的集体的一部分。它是一种入侵，保持这种入侵是为了产生一种记忆，这种记忆将防止政治体受到任何再感染，这种记忆创造了免疫。

但是，甚至在这种纳入他人的去殖民化行为之前，凯布朗利博物馆就已经在定义自己，并自我宣称是一个后殖民主义博物馆。这个后殖民时代的博物馆在2021年向贝宁共和国返还了26件非洲文物，这对其在当代世界的政治地位来说是一个非常重要和具有象征意义的行为。但是，这仍然是国家间的交易。这是两个民族国家之间的交易，仍然位于现代结构。这些法国博物馆不涉及社区参与，更不用说与社区成员长期建立联系了。因此，就后殖民博物馆而言，将他者的元素纳入他们的藏品中，我在这次演讲用埃斯波西托的术语揭示了其去殖民化中的矛盾，用这位哲学家的话说，其辩证的形象是一种通过包容而达成的排他性。他者不仅作为自我的一部分被保存下来，而且还构成了自我定义的条件。这一概念所暗示的是，真正的反殖民机制不能从中心向边缘发散因为这只是在复制殖民性。从这个角度来看，尽管返还在法律领域存在争议，涉及民族国家及其代表，博物馆藏品去殖民化的问题并不仅仅与所有权或藏品出处有关。

真正的赔偿不仅是一个归属谁、谁拥有文化遗产，以及谁应该从中获利的问题。修复过去的不公正即处理开放的伤口，这些伤口使殖民化和现代性成为新的可逆转的非人化过程的一部分。我再次引用班贝的论述，文物返还是一个重新组装和引导部分的过程，修复断开的链接，重新观察互惠的形式，没有这些，人类就不可能进步。我们中的一些人可能会问自己，博物馆如何能做到这一点？博物馆如何参与到更为复杂和长期的赔偿过程中？例如，这里我带来的里约热内卢印第安博物馆的作品，这是一个自20世纪50年代以来一直与原住民合作的博物馆。我要说的是，自21世纪以来，尤其是这些博物馆一直在与当地原住民建立牢固的伙伴关系，不仅是为了获得文物或返还文物，而且是真正向这些原住民学习如何照顾这些属于他们的文物。所以这种长期的合作，则要复杂得多，它不是个孤立的返还案例，而是有着更多的互相理解。而且，它确实涉及更深层次的修复过程。从反殖民主义的角度来看，我可以说，当我们谈论重新组装部件时，我们必须首先拆解，以便以后记住，这在某种程度上就是原住民对博物馆的诉求。今天，我们可以看到，在公众场合，原住民群体对涉及博物馆和文化遗产的博物馆有许许多多的诉求。在这个意义上，法农所定义的反暴力与必要的入侵有关，这种入侵穿透了边界，扰乱了事物内部的秩序。因为诉求实际上会以不同的方式传达给博物馆。今天的一些博物馆已经被这些诉求所触动，或是说被击穿和侵入，并将本土艺术的激进主义和反殖民主义主张纳入其展览中，例如里约热内卢艺术博物馆的这次展览，这就是艺术策展人与原住民之间合作的重要案例，特别是在这种情况下，展览实际代表了该博物馆的政治主张，而不是美学主张。因此，从这种入侵来看，我们可以说，抗体是作为曾经对主体构成威胁而生的产物，它的存在是令人烦恼的，并具有破坏性的威胁，它还将其政治潜力及其破坏力告知被入侵的主体。因此，抗体负责从内部产生抵抗，是对外来异物的不容忍，这种存在永远不会被完全清除，也不会被完全接受，被视为不可分割的部分。所以博物馆可以选择是否模拟这一机制，从内部做出改变，或是选择让异物作为一个可以帮助他们抵御任何其他形式高压的元素。

我的演讲即将结束，我的本意是给你们带来一些思考的契机，而非解决方案。但我想以这张照片作为结尾，这是巴西原住民的活动家和艺术家的作品，他的照片在去年的一个特定展览中被一个主要的博物馆机构审查，同时还有其他五张谴责巴西土地纠纷的照片，这家自称去殖民化的博物馆拒绝将这些照片纳入展览，恰恰是通过拒绝一些原住民艺术家和策展人的反殖民主义主张来维护自己的边界。因此，这是一个反殖民主义主张没有被重要的博物馆机构认可的例子。

我们可以问问自己，那么什么是反殖民主义博物馆？我想避免对此进行定义，我不打算在这个演讲中提出定义。这个演讲不是关于定义的，不是为了创造界限、创造边界的，恰恰相反，它真的是要启发我们思考，任何博物馆如何能够超越其边界采取行动，真正为那些试图在所谓的后殖民世界中生存的人的生活带来具体的改变。

在这个例子中，我们可以清楚地看到在巴西的土地争端中边界是多么重要，而在博物馆中，尤其是在艺术机构中，边界又是那么的不起眼。因此，我这里设想的是这样一个博物馆，它质疑自己的中心地位和殖民性，成为反对殖民主义和新殖民主义的斗士。这样一来。反殖民主义博物馆可以为我们打开了解过去的新窗口。培养同情心和相互理解，让殖民者和被殖民者处理两者截然不同的历史所留下的开放性伤口，同时也理解这种塑造历史的机制。

博物馆也是一个冲突和暴力的空间，这里弥漫着现代性，从属者的历史、人文、艺术价值也将从博物馆中弥散出来，赋予藏品新的生命。

非常感谢！谢谢！

Owning the Past to Create a Better Future — Our On-going Journey of Decolonisation, Hope and Aspiration

Dr. Arapata Hakiwai*

Tēnā koutou kei ngā mana, kei ngā reo, kei ngā ihi, kei ngā whakamataku. Mai i te whenua o Aotearoa he mihi ake ki te whenua me ngā iwi o Haina, heoi anō rā, kei ngā maunga, kei ngā awa, kei ngā mana o ngā iwi maha o te ao. Tēnā Koutou.

Greetings from Aotearoa, New Zealand. Can I first acknowledge all the museums, universities, and thought leaders present as part of this important seminar global conversation on *'Museums, Decolonisation and Restitution: A Global Conversation'*. I greet the International Museum Research and Exchange Centre (IMREC), in partnership between ICOM and the Shanghai University, in organizing and hosting this significant event. Firstly, can I greet the people and whenua of China, along with the many people, cultures, mountains and rivers present and online. I greet you all from Aotearoa, New Zealand. Tēnā koutou katoa.

It's both an honour and privilege to be here today to share some insights on New Zealand's National Museum — the Museum of New Zealand Te Papa Tongarewa (Te Papa). My name is Dr Arapata Hakiwai, and I've worked at Te Papa for over 25 years. I'm the Kaihautū or Māori co-leader of Te Papa and, along with the Tumu Whakarae (CEO) Courtney Johnston, I share the bicultural leadership of

---

* Dr. Arapata Hakiwai, Kaihautū (Māori co-leader), Museum of New Zealand Te Papa Tongarewa (Te Papa).

our national museum. This unique shared leadership structure was an intentional directive and tangible expression of the 'bicultural' museum aspiration that formed the creation of our new national museum that opened on the 14 February 1998.

I accepted the invitation to speak here today because I love my indigenous language and culture and I want this to continue for my children, their children, and those generations yet unborn. We know that museums can play an important role in the maintenance and revitalization of culture and identity and to say that we museums are at the crossroads is an understatement. There are real challenges ahead of us and we need to have courage and commitment to do acknowledge that and do something about it. The impact and legacy of colonisation and western imperialism is real and in front of us. Our museums have thousands of cultural treasures that remain connected to their source communities but distanced and alienated from them. Museums are being challenged by their own fraternity and by the peoples and communities they serve. Some are meeting the challenges of our contemporary society becoming more relevant, more engaged, and more meaningful but many still do not want to change. They are content to perpetuate dinosaurian museum traditions and practices that are racist and privilege class and western culture.

Museums must be more than passive repositories that hold vast collections of objects and treasures of cultures and peoples throughout the world. The responsibilities and indeed obligations of museums with respect to the collections they hold and the voices and knowledge systems they present require a new consciousness, a new paradigm, an openness, and courage to own their past to embrace themselves for a better future. This symposium is very timely, and I'm honored to be able to share the experiences that we've gone through and continue to go through, as New Zealand's national museum. For us who care for the cultural treasures, curate exhibitions, and carry out research and events we need to critically reflect and look at ourselves and our museum practices.

Re-imagining the museum has been the focus of many museums in recent times. Why? Because we know that many museums have not served the interests of their communities and cultures well. They have denied the vitality of life and agency to the very communities whose treasures they care for. They have not acknowledged or recognised the continuing living relationships regarding the treasures and their people's and cultures. They have not been open and honest in acknowledging the impact and legacy of their colonial histories and stifling museum practices and traditions.

We know that museums have not served Indigenous and First Nation peoples well. They have denied agency, involvement, and participation. For the most part we have been *'on the outside looking in'*. Like many other museums in New Zealand our national museum was strongly colonial in its history and operation. It's no surprise that many of our large museums in New Zealand were formed during the time of the New Zealand wars in the 1840−70's. Museums like our national museum were colonial constructs of the highest magnitude where directors and staff actively contributed to the taking of our taonga (treasures) and actively involved in the exchange and trade of our ancestral remains. The colonial context also initiated what some termed salvage anthropology with Pākehā, or non-Māori, in control of our cultural heritage. Our national museum missed a great opportunity to play an important role in enhancing our nations sense of history, identity and belonging. It was this context that created the desire for the new national museum.

Dating back to 1865 our old national museum did not serve the interests of its communities in Aotearoa, New Zealand, very well. The buildings were old, run down and too small. Its museum practices were outdated, western oriented and elitist. It was colonial in its look and colonial in its operation and management. Being formed with a colonial natural history focus Māori were often presented as exotic and primitive exotic peoples. The building and collection storage areas were sub-standard. The Māori taonga or treasures were stored in appalling conditions and although there did exist some relationships with Māori, by and large the national museum did not engage, collaborate or partner actively with Māori to any great extent. It was stifling museum practice at its worst. The nation didn't want a blueprint of the old and Māori certainly wanted something very different. Te Papa was a deliberate disruption.

Right from the start there were issues regarding the sharing of power and decision making, of recognizing mana and authority, of giving voice and empowerment to our communities whose treasures we hold. Creating and sustaining enduring meaningful relationships was essential to our bicultural ethos. Building trust and respect with Māori takes time and is borne out of showing mutual respect and doing the right things. In mapping a vision for the future there was a strong resolve and determination to create a unique museum practice informed and shaped by the Māori world. This journey was radically different from any other museum in the world and today continues to evoke awe and respect from the international museum community. Arguably, however, it was Māori indigenous agency that inspired and activated change and creative innovation challenging accepted museum practice and reinventing the national museum as a place of meaning and belonging — '*Te Papa — Our Place*'.

Dare to dream; Dare to challenge; Dare to change

To understand the dramatic change and transformation that our national museum went through is to understand the history that led to Te Papa's founding vision and concept. Our museum grew largely out of what was happening in the 1980's as this was an important time in our country's history. Some of these events included the following: —The Treaty of Waitangi Act 1975 established the Waitangi Tribunal as a commission of inquiry to hear Māori grievances against the Crown concerning breaches of the Treaty; From 1985 the Waitangi Tribunal was empowered to investigate Treaty claims dating back to 1840; The Māori Language Act came into force in 1987; The Kōhanga Reo National

Trust for early Māori education is established in 1982 along with the first two Kōhanga Reo or Māori language nest programs; the first Māori university is established and Te Karere Māori news program airs on television. There was a new and vibrant period of political rights for language and land rights. Te Papa had to dream and challenge itself to reimagine something far better than what it was. Te Papa reflected on its historical past and challenged itself over and over again on what it was doing and what it should be doing. It critiqued itself and pursued a pathway that it knew was unique in its indigenous positioning and transformational with its community empowerment. We also looked overseas at what other great museums were doing to help shape and inform ours as well as having a powerful group of international museum directors to assist our process.

The Te Māori exhibition 1984−1987, that travelled to the Metropolitan Museum of Art in New York, the Saint Louis Art Museum, the de Young Museum, San Francisco, and the Field Museum of Natural History, Chicago, then back to the main centres of New Zealand, was a landmark and seminal event in our nation's history. A Māori exhibition comprising 174 treasures, Te Māori signalled to the world that our treasures were still connected to our Māori people and culture. This exhibition was the first time where Māori had real involvement in the exhibition and its success was noted by our politicians, officials and Māori people. The Te Māori exhibition shook up our museum sector as it questioned museum-iwi relationships and issues around interpretation, governance, power, and control. Te Māori was transformational, and it awoke the spirit of our ancestors in distant shores and stirred the imagination and minds of those working in museums. Its influence and legacy were profound. It changed the lives of people and museums, it involved our people in ways never before undertaken, and it said to the world *'Here are our taonga and we are its people'*. It was described as a journey and voyage of rediscovery.

The exhibition challenged those who managed and controlled our taonga and in a highly visible way highlighted the inadequacies of museum-Māori relations.

Te Māori signaled a "turning point", no turning back, a time for museums to examine and change the way they do things, the way they operate. This is why Te Papa was created, this is why our national museum had to transform itself, this is why our nation wanted something far better than a museum that did little in the lives of our peoples. The success of this exhibition was an important impetus for a new national museum based on active community engagement, participation and recognition of living relationships and cultural knowledge.

Te Papa—A journey of decolonisation, hope, and aspiration

Te Papa was built as a site of decolonisation, hope and aspiration. It knew that our former national museum had privileged class and western culture, and denied agency, representation, and meaningful relationships with Māori. To this end the Karanga Aotearoa Repatriation Program was created in 2003 where a dedicated team was formed with both Government and Māori mandated support to negotiate and undertake the return of Māori and Moriori ancestral remains held in overseas museums and cultural institutions. Addressing our dark colonial past was important for our new national museum and the establishment of the Karanga Aotearoa Repatriation programme in 2003 was a direct response to owning and addressing the colonial history and actively working towards healing the future. Māori knew that our ancestors were traded, sold, and exchanged throughout the world and in the early consultations Māori tribes wanted the Government to do something about it.

Re-imagining the museum was deliberate and Māori were involved in creating this transformation and difference. Māori tribes carried their carvings from the old museum to the new museum before Te Papa opened and the symbolism was powerful — away with the old and the welcoming in of the new. As a site of decolonisation, we knew that we had to do a lot of things to rebalance, reset and reimagine. Honouring and recognizing the mana of indigenous knowledge not as the exotic other or primitive people but as a valid and knowledge tradition with mana and integrity was deliberate in our planning. Te Papa in its exhibitions, research and events has always recognised and promoted Māori indigenous knowledge. Not having Māori involved in the decision-making process also led to new structures and policies that gave mana to our national museum.

Te Papa was very deliberate in its critical examination of itself and its operations. As Amy Lonetree reminds us, *'critical self-analysis is an important dimension of a site for decolonisation'* [1]. Te Papa has always done this critical self-reflection, and we continue this today, as we know museum practice is ever changing. There were many tribal gatherings, meetings, and reflections during this time. The principles and pillars that were required for the new national museum challenged the old museology and gave confidence for the future. How do we recognise and give affirmation to Te Tiriti o Waitangi—Tiriti o Waitangi, our nation's founding document? How can we involve our communities in everything we do? How can Te Papa be a bicultural museum with active Māori participation? How can we recognise the Māori world and knowledge traditions? Returning ancestral remains and taonga (prized treasures) to their descendant kin communities is both addressing the injustices of the past and supporting the vitality of contemporary cultures. There was courage and commitment to go where we haven't gone before.

Te Papa is well-known for its bicultural mandate, its scholarship, its innovation and fun, and the success of this has been built on relationships and actively working with our many communities. Perpetuating the past and blindly following policies and practices that do little for the maintenance and revitalization of Māori culture serves no meaningful purpose. In fact, it's a

---

[1] Lonetree, Amy. Decolonizing Museums: Representing Native America in National and Tribal Museums. The University of North Carolina Press, 2012.

modern form of recolonisation that further disenfranchises and alienates. If we put our communities and peoples at the center, we know that we can focus on things that matter.

Vision—What we can become, rather than what we are now

Having innovative strategies and practices that speak uniquely about who we are, what we do, why we do it and how we do it is important. We must think more about what we can become, rather than what we are now. The process of imagination is powerful because it allows us to step outside the boundaries we know so well and are familiar with, to think about what museums could become. Te Papa's vision was about what we could become rather than except what we were.

The change and difference of this planned new museum was poignantly stated in many of the guiding documents. To provide a new opportunity to care for and look after Māori taonga (treasures). Biculturalism at Te Papa is a reflection of the partnership between Tangata Whenua and Tangata Tiriti. Biculturalism at Te Papa is the foundation on which we celebrate the natural and cultural diversity of Aotearoa, New Zealand. Biculturalism at Te Papa acknowledges the unique position of Māori in Aotearoa, and ensures integral Māori participation in the governance, management, and operation of Te Papa. Statements like this were further reinforced with the Museums Bicultural Policy, which set guiding principles that affirmed the right for Māori to manage their taonga in the most appropriate way. Te Papa's Concept also stated that we will honour the principles of the Treaty of Waitangi. The bicultural partnership is based on the three key Treaty principles pf partnership, participation, and protection. The partnership is also founded on three key Māori concepts Rangatiratanga, Kāwanatanga and Kaitiakitanga that help define the nature of our relationships within Te Papa, and with our external communities.

Decolonisation is putting something right that should have been done many years ago. Museums can and should have courage to do the right thing. But what is the right thing? Why should we put up with the way things are? Why shouldn't we decolonise our museums? Why shouldn't we reconnect the treasures we hold to their source communities? There are no valid reasons why we shouldn't. Culture and identity are at the center of most, if not all, of the Treaty of Waitangi claims in New Zealand and this immediately puts into focus museums. Why? Because they house our treasures, and we know that our taonga continue to form the very foundations of Māori tribal identity and history. There is an undeniable responsibility for museums to be something far greater and meaningful to the living contemporary cultures than just accumulating and amassing vast quantities of treasures. The questions we need to ask is how important are these treasures to their people, cultures, and land? Many argue that the contemporary role of museums is to recognize the vitality of living indigenous cultures and to be a platform for their future maintenance, development, and revitalization. I totally agree. This transformational agency has been described by Stephen Weil as being a shift "from being *about* something to being *for* somebody"[①]. Museums should democratize themselves and their collections. Museums should be dynamic centers for cultural revitalization and revival. Museums can play more of an active role and not a passive duty of care. As the national museum, we have to address our past so that we can play more of an active role in the lives of our communities and contemporary society both now and into the future.

Tēnā koutou katoa. Greetings to you all.

---

① Weil, Stephen. *Making Museums Matter*. Washington D.C. Smithsonian Institution Press, 2002, 29.

拥抱过去，创造更美好的未来：
正在进行的去殖民化，希望和憧憬

阿若帕塔·哈克瓦*

  我谨代表奥特亚罗瓦①（新西兰）向出席此次"博物馆、去殖民化、文物返还"全球重要对话的所有博物馆、高校和专家学者致以诚挚的问候与感谢。

  在线上线下各种多元文化背景的人们与山川河流的见证下，感谢国际博物馆协会与上海大学合作建设的国际博协研究与交流中心举办这场重要会议。

  我在奥特亚罗瓦（新西兰）向各位问好。作为新西兰（国家博物馆）的代表，很高兴能够向大家介绍新西兰蒂帕帕国家博物馆（Te Papa Tongarewa）。我是阿若帕塔·哈克瓦博士，在蒂帕帕工作已经超过25年了。我是蒂帕帕博物馆领导团队的毛利共建人和联合馆长之一，与首席执行官和双文化重要领导人科特尼·约翰斯顿·巴什尔一起领导我们的博物馆。这样的独特的共同领导结构是我们双重文化愿景的体现，这种愿景是蒂帕帕博物馆在1998年2月14日开放后不断形成的。

  今天，我受邀发言，是因为我热爱我的文化，热爱我的语言，并且希望这种热爱可以延续到我的孩子和还未出生的后代们身上。我们知道，博物馆在文化和身份认同的维持和振兴发展中扮演着重要的角色。其实，博物馆不仅处在选择的十字路口，也正面临着真正的挑战。我们需要有勇气并且承诺去解决这些问题。殖民主义和西方帝国主义的影响和遗留问题是

---

* 阿若帕塔·哈克瓦，新西兰蒂帕帕国家博物馆毛利共建人、联合馆长。
① 在新西兰对原住民权益及自身特色历史愈发重视的情况下，"奥特亚罗瓦"一名亦得到越来越广泛的应用。Aotearoa成为"新西兰"在毛利语中最广为接受的名称。

真实存在的，而且就摆在我们面前。现在，博物馆拥有数千件来自原住民的来源社区的文化珍品，但却与它们相距甚远。博物馆正受到来自行业内以及所服务的人民和社区的挑战。一些博物馆正在应对我们当代社会的挑战，变得更具相关性、参与性，更有意义，但也有许多博物馆不想改变。他们仍在传统和实践中坚持过时的做法，这些做法是种族主义、特权、阶级和西方中心的体现。

博物馆不仅仅是被动的仓库，更是拥有遍布世界各地文化和民族宝藏的机构。博物馆对其所持藏品的责任和义务，以及其所呈现的声音和知识体系，需要一种新的意识和范式，并要以开放和勇气去接受过去，为美好的未来而拥抱自己。这次研讨会非常及时，我很荣幸能够分享作为新西兰国家博物馆，我们所经历的与社区合作的经验。

为了我们的藏品保护、展览评估、研究与活动的开展，我们需要批判性地反思和看待自己博物馆的实践。为什么重构博物馆成为近来许多博物馆关注的重点？因为我们知道许多博物馆并没有很好地服务于社区和文化权益，他们否认了他们所关心的珍宝所属的社区的生命力和代理能力，他们没有承认或意识到藏品和它们所属的人与文化之间所延续的生动关系，他们没有开诚布公地承认他们的殖民历史和压抑的博物馆惯例传统及实践所带来的影响和遗留问题。我们知道，博物馆并没有很好地为原住民和第一民族群体服务。博物馆拒绝了这些群体的能动性、存在和参与。大多数情况下，我们一直处于局外人的位置。像新西兰的许多其他博物馆一样，我们的国家博物馆在历史和运营管理上都具有十分强烈的殖民主义色彩。这并不奇怪，因为我们许多大型的博物馆是在19世纪40年代至70年代的新西兰战争期间成立的。像我们国家博物馆这样的博物馆，有着规模化的殖民结构，领导和工作人员对我们民族的成就和遗产通过交换与贸易不断地进行掠夺。这种由白人和非毛利人控制我们文化遗产的背景意味着我们需要抢救性的人类学。我们国家博物馆错失了一个能够在增强我们国家历史、身份认同和归属感方面发挥重要作用的良机，这导致了我们对建立新国家博物馆的渴望。

回溯到1865年，那时我们旧的国家博物馆并没有很好地服务于它的社区和奥特亚罗瓦的利益。博物馆的建筑又旧又破旧，十分狭小，博物馆的做法也很过时，且当时是以西方为导向和精英主义，是具有殖民色彩的，并且在运营和管理上受殖民命运和历史的束缚。由于以带有殖民色彩的自然历史为重点而形成博物馆，毛利人通常被视为是带有异国情调和原始的人。当时的建筑和藏品库区也不符合标准。毛利人的语言或藏品也保护得十分糟糕。尽管国家博物馆与毛利人存在一些关系，但总体上并没有真正参与到毛利人中来，没有与毛利人达成合作或建立伙伴关系。博物馆这种令人窒息的做法最糟糕的体现，就是国家不想要一个以毛利人为核心的蓝图。毛利人也不想和这样冷漠的机构打交道。而蒂帕帕则是为了改变这一现状而出现的。

从一开始，权力和决策的共享就是问题的关键，包括共建方式、话语权和赋予社区权力方面。创建和维持持久有意义的联系对我们的双重文化精神至关重要。与毛利人建立信任和尊重需要时间，这需要建立在相互尊重、做正确的事情和规划好未来愿景的基础上。我们有强烈的决心去创造一个独特的、由毛利人和毛利文化去形塑的博物馆实践。这段经历与世界上任何其他博物馆都有很大的不同，且在今天仍然得到国际博物馆界的尊重。然而，可以说是毛利的原住民能动性激发和激活了变革和创新，挑战已有博物馆实践，将国家博物馆重新塑造为充满意义和归属感的地方——蒂帕帕，我们的地方。

敢于梦想，敢于挑战，敢于变化

要理解我们国家博物馆经历的巨大变化和转型，就要了解导致蒂帕帕成立的愿景和概念的相关历史。我们的博物馆主要是在20世纪80年代发生的事情中发展起来的，可以说这是我们国家历史上的重要时期。其中一些事件包括：《怀唐伊条约》的签订促使成立了怀唐伊法庭，以调查委员会的身份听取毛利人对英国王室违反条约的不满。从1985年开始，怀唐伊仲裁法庭开始有权向1840年起违反条约的行为进行索赔。1987年，《毛利语法》生效，并为发展毛利人的教育成立了Kōhanga Reo国家信托基金。伴随着毛利语首个规范模式的出现，以这些项目为突破口的大学建立起来，并且电视上出现了一档以毛利语进行报道的新闻节目。对于语言、土地的政治权利，这是一个新时期。蒂帕帕有一个梦想，去梦想和挑战自己，重新想象自己的未来，反思自己的历史，一遍又一遍地挑战自己正在做的事情以及应该做的事情。博物馆会批评自己，并追求一条符合原住民独特定位的、具有变革性的、赋权于社区的转型道路。我们还看到了海外其他伟大的博物馆正在做什么，以此帮助塑造和启发我们的博物馆，同时还得到了许多卓越的国际博物馆馆长协助我们博物馆的发展。

  1984—1987年关于毛利人的巡展，去到了纽约、圣路易斯、旧金山和芝加哥巡回展出，最后到新西兰的中心，这是我们国家历史上的一个里程碑和开创性的事件。这次展览展出了174件文物，并向世界表明我们的宝藏仍与我们的毛利人和文化联系在一起。这是毛利人第一次真正参与到展览中。这次展览所取得的成功得到了我们政府的注意。这场关于毛利人的展览震撼了我们国家整个博物馆界。博物馆与毛利人社区的关系，以及围绕诠释、治理、权力和针对毛利人所有权等议题提出的问题是博物馆走上转型道路的开端，这唤起了我们对祖先精神的追求，并将不同内容融入博物馆工作人员的想象和思维中。它的影响和产物是深远的。它改变了博物馆中人们的生活。它以前所未有的方式让我们的人民参与其中，在世界上获得一席之位。"这里是我们生活的城镇，我们是这里的人民。"这些叙事构成了我们重新发现自己，并成为领导者的旅途。

  对于我们来说，这是自然而然的事情。这个展览挑战了那些以高度可见的方式管理和控制我们的人，体现出博物馆与毛利人关系中存在的不公。毛利人展览是一个转折点，没有回头，这是博物馆审视和改变他们做事方式、操作方式的时候。这也是为什么我们创建了蒂帕帕，也是我们国家博物馆不得不自我转型的原因，这就是为什么我们的国家想要的是比一个沉默的博物馆更好的东西，因为后者对我们人民的生活影响很小。这个展览的成功，对于一个以积极的社区参与，参与和认可我们的生活关系和文化知识为目标宗旨的新的国家博物馆的建立，是一个重要的推动力。

蒂帕帕：一场去殖民化、带有希望和愿望的旅行

蒂帕帕是作为去殖民化、带有希望和愿望的目的而建立的，它知道我们以前的国家博物馆在特权阶级和西方文化方面享有特权，并抑制了毛利人的主动性、代表权，以及与毛利人建立有意义的联系。鉴于此，2003年我们创建了目前的奥特亚罗瓦文物返还计划。在政府和毛利人的授权支持下，我们成立了一个专门的团队负责协商谈判，并承担起与海外有关博物馆和机构洽谈归还其所保存的毛利人和莫里奥里人祖先遗骸的任务。解决我们黑暗的殖民历史，对于我们的新国家博物馆的建立以及当前的奥特亚罗瓦文物返还计划的推行是很重要的。2003年的改革是对殖民历史的直接回应，旨在积极修复毛利人祖先在全世界被贩卖、出售和交换的历史，让未来毛利人的后代可以了解这些历史。

在早期的谈判阶段中，毛利部落希望政府采取行动能够为毛利人做些事情。重塑博物馆是有意为之的，毛利人参与了这种转型和变革。毛利部落在旧博物馆关闭前将雕刻品从旧博物馆运到新博物馆，这象征着摆脱旧事物，去迎接新的变化。在去殖民化的过程中，我们知道我们必须做很多事情，以尊重和承认本土认知的方式，不是作为异国情调或原始族群，而是作为一种有效的、合法和有尊严的知识传统，来重新平衡、重置和重新构想。蒂帕帕的展前研究和调查活动一直被认为是本土知识的宣传者。现在毛利人参与决策过程也带来了新的结构和政策。

这些给了我们国家博物馆具体的方式，审慎地、有目的性地去发展运营蒂帕帕。正如埃米·隆特里（Amy Lonetree）所提醒我们的，"批判性自我分析是去殖民化的一个重要维度"。我们在蒂帕帕一直在做这件事。因为我们知道，博物馆的实践是一直在变的。在此期间，会有许多部落会议、常规会议和深刻反思。新的国家博物馆所需的原则和基础挑战了旧的博物馆理念，并为未来打下了坚实的基础。我们如何认识和肯定《怀唐伊条约》这一我们国家的奠基性文件所带来的觉醒？我们如何让我们的社区参与我们所做的一切？我们如何创建一个有着毛利人主动参与的双重文化

博物馆？我们如何认识毛利人的世界和知识传统？将祖先遗骸和有价值的藏品返还给后代社区，既能纠正过去的不公，又能支持当代文化的活力。我们有勇气承诺去到探索前人未曾到达的地方。

蒂帕帕以其文化管理、学术、创新和乐趣而闻名。这种成功是建立在联系和积极与我们众多社区合作的基础之上的。他们过去尝试过的盲目的政策和做法，对维护和振兴毛利文化没有什么作用，也根本没有任何意义。事实上，这是一种现代意义上的再殖民化。这进一步使人失去权力、变得疏远。如果我们把我们的社区和人民放在中心，我们知道我们可以专注于非常重要的事情。

愿景：我们能成为什么，而不是我们现在是什么

拥有独特的创新策略和实践，能够清晰地展现我们是谁，我们做什么，为什么这么做以及我们如何去做，这是很重要的。我们认为，我们必须更多地考虑我们可以成为什么，而不是我们现在是什么。想象的过程是强大的，因为它让我们走出我们已有的限制，思考博物馆可能变成什么样子。现实的愿景是关于我们的未来，而不是仅仅接受我们的过去。

这个计划中新博物馆的变化，最初在许多指导文件中被表述为提供一个新的机会来照顾和保护毛利人的语言或藏品。蒂帕帕的双重文化主义成了我们庆祝奥特亚罗瓦（新西兰）自然和文化多样性的基础，双重文化主义承认毛利和奥特亚罗瓦在推进公共治理、管理和运营中的独特地位。像这样的声明进一步强化了博物馆的双重文化政策，其中的指导原则肯定了毛利人以最合适的方式管理这种文化遗产的权力。这个概念还声明，我们将尊重《怀唐伊条约》的原则。双重文化伙伴关系基于条约的三个关键原则：伙伴关系、参与和保护。这个伙伴关系还创建了三个关键的毛利概念，这些概念分别是 Rangatiratanga, Kāwanatanga 和 Kaitiaki tanga，以帮助确定我们在文件内部和外部社区之间关系的本质。

去殖民化是在纠正过去的错误，即那些应该在很多年前就完成的事情，博物馆有能力、有责任，也应该有勇气做正确的事情。但什么是正确

的事情？我们为什么要忍受现状？我们为什么不能推进我们博物馆的去殖民化？我们为什么不能重新将我们拥有的藏品与来源社区联系起来？没有任何合理的理由说我们为什么不能这样做。文化和身份认同是新西兰《怀唐伊条约》中所有索赔的核心，并且这将迅速让博物馆的价值和重要性受到重点关注。为什么呢？我们的城镇将如何继续在毛利人部落身份和历史的基础上形成呢？博物馆有一种不可推卸的责任，即在积累和收集大量藏品以外，更重要的是成为对生活、文化有意义的机构。我们需要问的问题是这些藏品对人们、文化和土地有多重要？许多人认为博物馆的当代角色是要认识到目前活态的原住民文化中的活力，并视其为未来维护、发展和振兴的平台。我完全同意这种观点。这种转型被史蒂芬·威尔（Stephen Weil）描述为"从对物的关注转变为对人的服务"。博物馆应该使自己和馆内收藏变得民主化。博物馆应该是文化振兴的动态中心，并且博物馆可以扮演更积极的角色，而不是被动地承担责任。作为国家博物馆，我们必须解决我们过去遗留的问题，并在社区和当代社会的生活中扮演更积极的角色。

很高兴今天能与大家分享这些观点。

Qaumajuq, A New Model for the Museum in the South

Stephen Borys[*]

Qaumajuq, Canada's new Inuit art centre at the Winnipeg Art Gallery in Winnipeg, Canada has given us the opportunity to shift our nation's eyes to the north. The WAG houses the world's largest collection of contemporary Inuit art, comprising carvings, drawings, prints, textiles, photography, and new media. Supported by an unparalleled record of exhibitions, publications, and research, this collection represents Inuit identity, culture and history. To celebrate the art and to honour the people who created these works, the WAG built Qaumajuq. This is a centre for exhibitions, research and learning, studio practice and artmaking. It is a bridge, enabling peoples from the North and South to learn and work together. It is a gathering place—a community hub for exploration and advancement—with art serving as a lens on the Arctic.

In developing plans for Qaumajuq, the new Inuit art centre, I have often thought about the idea of the new museum model; not just what it looks like, but how it feels, communicates, and functions. The words that best describe this model are catchwords and phrases like "northness," "the new future," "shared values," "letting the objects (and artists) lead," "crafting the value proposition to the outside world," "finding the a-ha! moment," and "the museum as a physical manifestation of many conversations". Along this journey to Qaumajuq, all of these words have impacted on the project. But one phrase that has become

---

[*] Stephen Borys, Director and CEO, Winnipeg Art Gallery.

crystal-clear as a validation of the forward-looking path: this new museum is the physical manifestation of many conversations.

With these many conversations, I think of the coloured pencil drawing entitled Drum Dance by the Baker Lake artist Luke Anguhadluq, produced in 1970. The artist's graphic works are often organized around a central focal point, and this drawing is no exception. In this elegant drum dance composition, the people radiate from the central yellow drum, and their faces—some frontal, some in profile—form a ring around the edge of the drum. The image of the drum dance in the drawing by Angughadluq seemed perfectly aligned with the way in which the constituents and stakeholders around the Inuit art centre project came together with respect, understanding, and common purpose.

Throughout program and stakeholder development, the architectural design by Michael Maltzan Architecture of Los Angeles, the building phase, and the capital campaign, I have been inspired and challenged to reconsider the template for the museum in the twenty-first century. "The new museum" is still a building, but its function and mandate far exceed those of a physical structure housing collections, exhibitions, and research spaces. The new museum is about dialogue, exploration, and reconciliation, alongside the still-vital tasks of collecting, preserving, and exhibiting. Learning and advancement contribute to this enterprise, augmented by enrichment, enjoyment, and the overall pursuit of health and wellbeing through art and culture.

The museum reflects, responds to, and is the community. It is a place where the acts of invitation, welcome, and engagement thrive, enabling the museum to be relevant, impactful, and sustainable. The value proposition begins with the art and the artmakers, but it is expanded to reflect multiple voices in the sectors that have come to define contemporary cultural thought.

The great Canadian 20th— century communicator Marshall McLuhan said that "Art at its most significant is a distant early warning system that can always be relied on to tell the old culture what is beginning to happen." Art is one of our oldest universal languages, one of the first and last ways we communicate with each other. Before letters and words, before the assemblage of vocabularies and dialects, there has been a visual means in which thoughts, emotions, and ideas are documented. And while not always easily defined or understood, these forms, colours, gestures and physical expressions are a way of speaking. For centuries art has been the cultural expression of humankind.

Art is a living force, capable of imparting, responding to, and shaping ideas and perspectives. Art needs more places in our city where it can flourish —be seen, enjoyed, studied, and shared, leading to the prospect of opening people's minds to new ideas and new ways of thinking. With its exhibitions and programs, Qaumajuq is transforming the public experience of art, establishing new pathways to understanding and appreciation.

Qaumajuq is where the story of Indigenous art can be revealed and become revelatory: where viewers launch their own expeditions to the Arctic. Inuit art can inform and motivate children and youth, deepening their understanding of our relationship with the North and its peoples. Increased opportunities for virtual connectivity bring students face-to-face through new learning streams. Innovative teaching and training initiatives ensure that Indigenous cultural workers have a place to study and apprentice in the field.

The new museum is a creative and evolving conversation led by the values and stories that honour and reflect the full community of stakeholders and constituents. This exercise is at the heart of the museum today: fostering new voices and narratives to ensure the Winnipeg Art Gallery and Qaumajuq remain meaningful and relevant in purpose and plan.

Qaumajuq is a transformative place led by the images and stories from the art, people and land. Linking northern and southern Canada is at the heart of the centre's mission where art is a vehicle for artistic, educational and economic development. Through regional, national, and international partnerships, the new centre has become a forum for innovation and exploration, helping shift the public experience through art, establishing new pathways to understanding and respect.

The development of the new centre is grounded in strong partnerships with Indigenous and non-Indigenous stakeholders in Manitoba, across Canada and the Arctic. The Centre is at the forefront of a cultural renaissance as Canadians progressively recognize the importance of Indigenous art and its power to bridge past and future. Together we are responding to Canada's Truth and Reconciliation Commission's calls to actions for museums. Indigenous leaders and perspectives are helping guide all areas of operations within the Centre and the WAG. This process has been led by an Indigenous Advisory Circle, including members from all four regions of Inuit Nunangat as well as First Nations and Métis representatives. The WAG has engaged Inuit birthright organizations, governments, associations, arts organization to ensure the centre is a place where Inuit feel welcomed and inspired.

I recall a conversation a couple years ago had with the editor in chief of Canadian Art magazine. He had three questions about the new museum—or the museums for the 21st century. What should our museums look like in the future? How will we get there? And what is standing in the way?

What does the new museum look like? — well, it's an evolving conversation. How do we get there?—through respectful dialogue led by the values and stories that honor and reflect the full community of stakeholders and constituents. What's in our way—only the traditions and templates that we have used for decades to define and guide us in the museum sector. This is what must change in order to foster new voices and ideas—if we want to be meaningful, present, and around for the next century.

The WAG holds in trust the world's largest collection of contemporary Inuit art: close to 14,000 Inuit artworks, over 175 exhibitions, and 60 publications. This is an unprecedented international record. But that's not enough to build an Inuit art centre. To celebrate the art and to honor the people who have created these works, the WAG embarked on a dialogue with the North and the people connected to the North, and it was named Qaumajuq.

This new museum is still a building, but its infrastructure is much greater than any form or edifice. Advancing beyond but not neglecting the age-old tasks of collecting, preserving and exhibiting, Qaumajuq is about exploration and reconciliation. Learning and advancement contribute to this enterprise but these are augmented by enrichment, enjoyment and the overall pursuit of health and wellbeing through art and culture. This museum reflects, responds to —and is the community.

Qaumajuq is a collection of objects, ideas, and people reflecting cultures and stories that look back and ahead. It is a place where the acts of invitation, welcome, and engagement thrive, enabling the museum to be relevant, impactful, and sustainable. The value proposition may begin with the art and the artmakers, but it has expanded to reflect multiple voices and agendas in the sectors that have come to define and celebrate contemporary cultural thought. Art is a living and dynamic force in the world capable of imparting, responding to and shaping ideas and perspectives. And in this vibrant, global exchange we call cultural democracy, the museum is the forum.

Qaumajuq is a centre for exhibitions, research and learning, studio practice and artmaking. It is a bridge, enabling peoples from the North and South to meet, learn, and work together. And it is a gathering place defined by Indigenous principles and voices with the art serving as a lens on Canada's Arctic. This is a transformative place led by the images and stories from the art, people, and land.

Northern engagement has been critical to developing the new centre, its exhibitions and its programming. The all-Inuit Guest Curatorial Team for the inaugural exhibition INUA was led by curator and academic Dr. Heather Igloliorte. This team represents all regions of Inuit Nunangat, including the Inuvialuit region of the western Arctic; the territory of Nunavut; Nunavik, Quebec; and Nunatsiavut, Labrador.

Art commissions, artist residencies, cultural-worker training programs and internships are being developed in partnership with the Government of Nunavut, Arctic College, and the Inuit Heritage Trust. The Community Gallery in Qaumajuq is dedicated to different communities throughout the year to highlight their art. Beyond exhibitions, the programming at Qauamuq is guided by the national Indigenous Advisory Circle, with Inuit representatives involved in economic development, arts and education.

The WAG continues to build relationships in all Inuit regions, as well as the rest of Canada, to ensure the WAG is serving national interests. We are working with governments, birthright organizations, arts associations, educational institutions and private sector to develop programs, exhibitions and programming that will elevate Inuit art and spur economic development.

The WAG is a partner in major Social Sciences and Humanities Research Council of Canada (SSHRC) grant, in conjunction with University of Winnipeg and Concordia University, to build a blueprint to bring more Inuit into careers as arts workers. This seven-year project is focused on creating and facilitating training and employment opportunities in the North and South. Training takes place at the WAG and in participants's home communities.

The Nunavut and WAG collections are being used as a tool to train young people and cultural workers, in partnership with Government of Nunavut and the Inuit Heritage Trust. The program was piloted in 2017 and continues to bring young people from Northern communities to the WAG to learn from the collection as well as their Elders. The WAG commissions work by emerging and established artists to provide exposure. Artist residencies allow southerners to witness work being created so they can understand its value. These residencies also provide valuable experience and retail training for artists.

With more than 50 percent of the population in the three northern territories of Canada under the age of 24, the engagement of young audiences is critical. The WAG, with Cisco and TakingITGlobal, hosts virtual field trip for schools across the North. A cultural-worker training program for Inuit youth is being developed for the North, in partnership with the Government of Nunavut. Formal gallery-operations internships to those of Inuit descent so they gain hands-on work experience. This program is being developed with Arctic College, the Government of Nunavut and the Inuit Heritage Trust.

The WAG is a conduit for trade opportunities between Manitoba and Nunavut, with the Kivalliq and Baffinland Regional Chamber of Commerce Trade Shows taking place at the new centre in Winnipeg. This is a joint business initiative to enhance regional trade. The WAG Gallery Shop provides new retail opportunities for Inuit artists. The WAG also participates in various international, national and regional conferences, trades shows, symposia that support and highlight Northern and Inuit art and culture.

Qaumajuq provides opportunities to promote Inuit culture, through the following: Inuktitut and multi-lingual interpretation, didactics and signage; Elders-in-residency program to connect Inuit elders with their art, and with the larger community; Multi-lingual publishing projects using the collection; and maintaining a relationship with Arctic College on the publication and broad distribution of Inuit materials.

Among the Indigenous Advisory Circle's first recommendations to the WAG was the formal naming of the Inuit art centre. The naming initiative was in direct response to the 2007 United Nations Declaration on the Rights of Indigenous Peoples Article 13, and the 2015 Truth and Reconciliation Commission's Call to Action 14. This step was significant, as it was the first instance of the implementation of such an initiative within a major arts organization in Canada. With the support of the Indigenous Advisory Circle, language keepers and Elders came together in a powerful moment of cross-cultural reflection and relationship-building to establish permanent names for the centre and its public spaces. The assembled group represented all four regions of Inuit Nunangat, including Inuvialuit Settlement Region, Nunavut,

Nunavik, and Nunatsiavut. Recognizing that WAG buildings are located on Treaty 1 territory—the unceded territory of the Dakota people and the homeland of the Métis Nation—it was also important to include Anishinaabemowin and Cree speakers, as well as Michif and Dakota speakers.

The circle gifted us the name Qaumajuq, which means "it is bright, it is lit" in Inuktitut. The name was chosen to signify the hope that has always been present amongst Indigenous peoples and cultures. The name stands as steps along our path to integrating and honouring Indigenous knowledge, and they reflect an important journey for the gallery. The naming initiative is also another step towards decolonization, and ensuring that Qaumajuq will be an accessible and inclusive place for everyone.

The new Inuit centre connects people to each other through art: it builds bridges between people as they create together and speak with each other. Throughout the development of the centre, we have declared loudly that art is a voice. It reflects and shapes our experiences; it opens our hearts and minds to new ideas. It forms and shifts our perspectives. Art heals and inspires, and it fuels understanding. Qaumajuq is a welcome to all of these possibilities: it is bright, it is lit. Thank you.

Qaumajuq：南方博物馆的新模式

斯蒂芬·鲍卫斯 *

大家好，我是斯蒂芬·鲍卫斯（Stephen Borys）。

现在我们将关注点放在加拿大北部地区。我是温尼伯艺术馆的馆长和首席执行官，Qaumajuq是温尼伯艺术馆内的加拿大新因纽特艺术中心。温尼伯艺术馆拥有世界上规模最大的当代因纽特艺术收藏，里面包括雕刻、版画、素描、纺织品、摄影和新媒体艺术品。这些藏品也在展览历史、活动项目、展览研究方面得到了空前的支持。为了艺术，也为了向创作这些作品的人致敬，温尼伯艺术馆建立了Qaumajuq博物馆。Qaumajuq博物馆是一个集展览、研究、学习于一身的艺术中心，也是一个艺术工作室，兼具艺术创作与实践的功能。同时它也是一个连接南北的桥梁，让来自这两个地区的人群能够在一起学习、工作。它是一个聚会场所，一个探索和进步的社区活动中心，以艺术作为展示北极地区的视角。

在为这个因纽特艺术中心——Qaumajuq博物馆制定发展计划时，我经常会思考新的博物馆模式，不仅仅是它的建筑外观，还有它带给观众的感觉、与观众交流的方式和博物馆应具备的功能。最能描述这种模式的词是一些流行语，比如"北极特性""全新的未来""共同的价值观""以物为导向""为外部世界打造价值主张""寻找的瞬间"，这些都是关于新博物馆模式各种讨论的具象化，这些词都逐渐证明了这条前瞻性道路的有效性：这座新博物馆是加拿大、北美和北极圈许多对话的具体体现。

在这许多对话中，我想到了贝克湖艺术家卢克·安古哈德鲁克（Luke Anguhadluq）的彩色铅笔画《鼓之舞》，它是在1970年完成的。在这个优

---

* 斯蒂芬·鲍卫斯，加拿大温尼伯美术馆馆长与首席执行官。

雅的作品《鼓之舞》中，人们呈放射状围绕着黄色的鼓面，他们的脸围绕着鼓面的边缘形成一个圈。安古哈德鲁克在这里创造的形象恰好象征着因纽特艺术中心的参与者和关联方们带着尊重、理解和共同目标走到一起的方式。

在整个项目和参与方招纳，建筑由洛杉矶迈克尔·马尔赞建筑公司设计，建造过程以及资本运作中，我受到了启发和挑战，并重新思考了21世纪新博物馆的模式。"新博物馆"，仍然是一个建筑，但它的功能和任务，远远超过任何物理结构、展厅、藏品、展览和项目。这个新博物馆实际上是关于对话，是关于探索、和解，以及仍然非常重要的收集、保存和展示的功能。学习和进步有助于这项通过艺术和文化来丰富、享受和全面追求健康和幸福的事业。

博物馆反映、回应着社区的声音与需求，并且也是社区的代表。在这里，层出不穷的邀请和欢迎共建的行为，使我们具有联系性、影响力和可持续性。价值主张始于艺术和艺术创作者，但它的扩展反映了定义当代文化思想的各个领域的多种声音。

伟大的20世纪加拿大沟通者马歇尔·麦克卢汉说："艺术最重要的一点是：它是一个远古的预警系统，可以用来告诉人们旧文化将发生什么。"艺术是人类最古老的通用语言之一，是我们第一种也是最终的彼此沟通的方式。在文字与书写之前，甚至在词汇和语言出现之前，就已经有了记录思想、情感和观念的视觉手段。几个世纪以来，艺术一直是人类的文化表达方式。

艺术是一种有活力的力量，能够回应、塑造思想与观点。在我们的城市、我们的国家，艺术需要更多的空间来蓬勃发展，能被看到、被研究、被分享，从而拓展人们的思想，接受新的想法和新的思维方式。通过展览和项目，Qaumajuq博物馆正在改变公众的艺术体验，作为展示本土艺术故事的空间，Qaumajuq是建立理解和欣赏的新途径。

博物馆的评论家发起了北极探险活动，寻找可以启发并激励儿童和青少年的因纽特艺术，这加深了他们对我们与北极地区、与北极人民之间关系的了解。线上的联结给学生带来了更多面对面接触的新的学习机会，以及创新的教学和培训计划。

新的博物馆是一个创造性的、不断发展的对话，几乎就像一张地图，并由界定加拿大北极地区社区中的价值观念及其故事所引导。这项工作是当下运营博物馆的核心，是培养艺术思维的新声音、新表达，以确保温尼伯艺术中心和Qaumajuq的宗旨和规划能够持续保持联系性并产生价值与意义。

Qaumajuq是一个关于由这片土地上的人们所主导的变革的图像和艺术的故事。连接加拿大北部和南部的艺术创作，这是我们艺术中心的核心使命。通过地区、国家和国际合作，这个新中心已经成功反映了北极地区正在发生的事情，响应了他们所讨论的、所热爱的、所受到的启发。

新中心的发展建立在与本土和非本土利益关联方强有力的伙伴关系之上。这个艺术中心是加拿大文化复兴的先锋，在这里我们看到并认识到本土艺术和文化的重要性。本土文化就像是一座连接过去和未来的桥梁。我们正在共同响应加拿大真相与和解委员会的号召，特别是呼吁博物馆采取具体行动。当地原住民的领导人以及基于原住民文化的观点正在帮助指导我们在艺术中心各个方面的运作。这一过程由一个本土咨询团引领，成员包括来自因纽特努南加特所有四个地区的成员以及第一民族和Métis代表。温尼伯艺术中心参与了因纽特的出生权利组织、政府协会和艺术组织，以此确保我们的艺术中心是一个让因纽特人感到宾至如归并欢欣鼓舞的地方。

我想起了几年前与加拿大艺术杂志主编的采访谈话，他问了三个关于Qaumajuq博物馆的问题。在未来，这个博物馆应该是什么样子的？我们怎样能够完成这样的目标？我们的阻碍是什么？

它应该是什么样子的？这是一个不断发展的对话。我们如何完成这样的目标？通过价值观和故事引导的相互尊重的对话来建设它的新中心，尊重所有参与其中的人所有利益相关者。是什么阻碍了我们？实际上只有传统和固有的模式阻碍了我们，也许这些东西在过去就禁锢住了我们前进的道路。将这些僵化的模式改变，是培养艺术界新声音与新想法的先决条件。

温尼伯艺术馆拥有世界上最多的当代因纽特艺术品，将近14 000件。我们举办了超过175个展览，出版了60多本相关书籍。这是一个史无前例的伟大记录。但是对于建造一座因纽特艺术中心来说，我们目前所做的还远远不够。为了艺术并向创造这些作品的人致敬，温尼伯艺术馆开始了与北极人民的对话，以确保Qaumajuq博物馆能够反映并体现他们的精神与文化。

新博物馆仍然是一座建筑，但它的基础设施建设要比任何一种形式或建筑都要完善齐全得多。在这里我要再一次提到卢克·安古哈德鲁克的作品，这个作品向我们展现了人们是如何聚集在一起，环绕成圆，以平等的姿态表达多元的声音。通过这样的方式，我们保护并庆祝因纽特文化的艺术成就。因此，我们创建了这个艺术中心，以此对外展示并纪念这些伟大的艺术作品。这是一个艺术与文化的探索之地，也是一个和解之地。

Qaumajuq是藏品、思想与观者的集合，也是许多人的个人旅程，对我和我的家人也是这样，对温尼伯美术馆的所有工作人员和董事会成员来说也是如此。在这里，"邀请""欢迎"和"参与"的概念生根发芽，蓬勃发展。价值主张可能始于艺术作品和艺术创作者本人，但它现在包括了许多声音、观点和议程，它们已经开始定义当代艺术是什么。艺术是一种有生命的力量。它是动态的，它所到之处能够传递、回应和塑造新的思想和观点。而在这个充满活力的全球交流中，我们称之为文化民主，Qaumajuq处于中心位置。

Qaumajuq是一个展览、研究、学习和工作的实践中心。它是一座桥梁，使来自北极和南方的人们能够相遇，共同学习和工作。这是一个由本土原则和本土观点定义的集会场所。

北极人群及其文化的参与对于新的艺术中心建设及其展览和项目的发展至关重要。全员因纽特专家的策展团队在Qaumajuq领导了INUA的首届展览。这里是四位策展人，右边是首席策展人希瑟·伊格洛奥尔特博士（Dr. Heather Igloliorte）。这个团队代表了因纽特努南加特的所有地区，包括因纽维奥特地区、努纳武特地区、努纳维克地区和努纳提阿武特地区。

Qaumajuq开发了艺术委员会、艺术家和驻地、文化工作者培训计划和实习机会，这些都是基于我们与努纳武特政府、北极学院和因纽特遗产信托基金合作的成果。Qaumajuq的社区画廊全年都致力于服务不同的社区，这样他们就可以突出他们的工作。

温尼伯艺术馆继续在所有因纽特地区以及加拿大其他地区建立合作关系，以确保它能为国家利益服务。我们正在与政府、本地组织，以及各个协会、机构、学校，同时也与私人运营的部门合作，以开发新的项目、展览和研究，使我们能够宣传因纽特艺术，提升其影响力。

温尼伯艺术馆是与温尼伯大学在康科迪亚大学联合进行的加拿大社会科学人文研究委员会主要拨款的合作伙伴，在那里我们正在构建一个蓝图，让更多因纽特人加入并从事艺术工作。这个项目的重点是在北极和南方创造和促进培训和就业机会。培训是在温尼伯艺术馆和Qaumajuq中与参与者一起进行的。

与政府和遗产信托机构合作，Nunavut和温尼伯艺术馆的收藏也用于培训年轻人和文化工作者。这一2017年的试点项目继续将来自北极的年轻人带到温尼伯艺术馆，让他们从这些藏品中学习因纽特文化。同时，他们还可以从长者那里学习到相关文化与艺术知识。温尼伯艺术馆委托艺术家创作新的作品并与之开展合作。

加拿大北部三省超过50%的人口年龄在24岁以下。所以年轻观众的参与是至关重要的。温尼伯艺术馆与思科以及TalkingITGlobal合作，把因纽特艺术推向全球，我们为全国各地和加拿大北部地区的学校举办虚拟田野考察的实践项目。北极地区为因纽特青年制定了文化工作者培训计划。所有因纽特人后裔都有正式进入艺术馆并参与运营实习的机会，以便他们获得实践经验。这个项目正在与北极学院、其他中学、政府和因纽特遗产信托共同开发。

温尼伯艺术馆开展的合作项目为马尼托巴省和努纳武特省之间提供了贸易、生产、艺术委托等机会的渠道。在我们与北极开展合作的过程中，存在着非常多的商业合作机会。温尼伯艺术馆的画廊商店也提供了新的零售机会。我们随时都在委托艺术家创作新的艺术品。同时温尼伯艺术馆参与支持和强调北极与因纽特艺术和文化的国际、国家和地区会议、贸易展览和研讨会。Qaumajuq提供多样的机会来推广因纽特文化，包括：多语言翻译教学和标识系统，长者驻留计划在因纽特艺术家与老年人群之间建立联系，利用藏品出版多语言读物，与所有北极学校和大学保持关系，以确保其出版物能够得到学校的支持并且分发到位。

原住民咨询团向温尼伯艺术馆提出的第一个建议是赋予因纽特艺术中心一个新的名字。这一命名的倡议行动是对2007年《联合国土著人民权利宣言》第13条，以及加拿大真相与和解委员会第14号行动呼吁的直接回应。这一行为意义重大，因为这是加拿大的主要艺术组织首次实施此类举措。在原住民咨询团、语言保护者和长者的支持下，我们一起为该中心及其公共空间确定了永久名称。聚集在一起的团体代表了因纽特努南加特所有的四个地区，以及第一民族和马尼托巴的Métis代表。

他们把这个名字Qaumajuq赠予给我们，意为"明亮的、被点亮的"，选择这个名字是为了点燃一直存在于原住民及其文化中的希望。这个名字代表了我们在融合并尊重原住民知识的道路上迈出的重要一步，同时也是温尼伯艺术馆在发展过程中的宝贵经历。这个命名倡议也是朝着去殖民化迈出的另一步，并确保Qaumajuq将成为一个对所有人都开放和包容的地方。

新的因纽特文化中心将通过艺术把人们彼此联系起来，在人们之间架起桥梁，让人们一起创作，互相交流。在Qaumajuq艺术中心的发展过程中，我们大声宣布，艺术是一种声音，它反映并塑造了我们的人生经历。艺术能让人感受到治愈、鼓舞，能够让人们感受到自己是被理解的。Qaumajuq欢迎所有这些可能性。它是明亮的，它是被点亮的。

谢谢，再见！

Decolonizing Museum Practices at Saahlinda Naay "Saving Things House"

Sean Young*

Good morning. My name is Gid yahk'ii, Sean Young. I'm a proud member of the Haida nation. I am from the Gaag'yals Kii'Gawaay, Raven clan of K'uuna Llnagaay (Skedans). Currently, I am the manager curator of collections and the lab of archaeology at Saahlinda Naay Saving Things House Haida Gwaii Museum at Kay Llnagaay. I am also an educated and trained archaeologist. I've worked as a professional consulting archaeologist in the field on Haida Gwaii since 1997. I've also worked as an instructor and guest lecturer for the Haida Gwaii Institute's natural resource and marine conservation semesters. For up to three months, every summer since 2004, I've worked for the Haida Gwaii watchman program as a cultural ambassador and caretaker, living in ancient Haida villages (as well as cultural sites), and the Skagway ilna Guy instance UNESCO World Heritage Site, all of which are located within waii Haanas National Park Reserve's Haida Heritage Site.

Saahlinda Naay (saving things house) the Haida Gwaii Museum is the results of one of the earliest, if not the earliest steps towards decolonization and reconciliation also known as tl'lyahda, ("making things right") in the world of indigenous peoples and museums. A vision of both haidas and settlers residing on Haida Gwaii, our museum Society was formed in 1971, which at that time was called the Queen Charlotte Islands museum society. And the original Queen

---

* Sean Young, Collections Manager Saahlinda Naay, Haida Gwaii, Canada.

Charlotte Island Museum was opened in 1976. Saahlinda Naay is a place for transmitting our traditional ways of Being or Laws of Yahguudang (Respect) and "ad kyanang tlaagang" (to ask first) upholding Xaayda Kil and Xaad Kil (the Haida language), as well as our intangible cultural heritage, and stimulating creativity and community development, in addition to caring for and exhibiting our Haida belongings. Saahlinda Naay was the name given to our museum by elders, community members, and this (Skidegate) Haida immersion program.

The museum is governed by the longest standing all-Island board on Haida Gwaii. This board is represented by all communities on Haida Gwaii, both Haida and non Haida. Today, along with the Skidegate band Council, and Quay Harness Parks Canada. We are proud partners in the award winning Haida heritage site at Kay Llnagaay. Our museum's mandate is to promote understanding for all that Haida Gwaii is, with a primary focus on all aspects of historic and contemporary Haida culture. We are also dedicated to supporting and presenting Haida Gwaii's settlers history, and natural history, and to building capacity in the fields of arts and heritage. Almost 50 years ago, Saahlinda Naay began with a small collection of Haida and setller works generously donated by local families. Today we are internationally recognized facility with an ever growing collection of ancestral and contemporary belongings, including impressive representations of the island's natural world, an archive rich with history of Haida Gwaii, and an existing annual schedule of art exhibitions and educational programs. Our museum exists today because of the vision, dedication and hard work of the people of Haida Gwaii. People who know that by working together, good things happen. The Haida Gwaii Museum is located within the Haida Heritage Center at Kay Llnagaay, which was a dream of the height of people for decades. During the 1990s and early 2000s, framework groups led by the Haida Gwaii museum staff, Parks Canada, Skidegate band Council, elders, chiefs and community members from Island communities met and helped design and create the new center before any groundbreaking or disturbance of the development site, we were informed and directed by the Haida people to be cautious.

The new Haida Heritage Center and Haida Gwaii museum are located at Kay Llnagaay or sea lion town, an ancient site home to the Kay Llaanas Kayahlaanas eagle clan, a large and strong family group with a Hereditary Chief (Gahlaay), matriarch (GwaaGanad), and many Elders. We house a unique and comprehensive collection of historical and post-contact belongings and archival materials that is made accessible to the public within a setting that evokes the community identities of both Haida and settler communities on Haida Gwaii. Our collection includes ancestral and contemporary Haida works, both utilitarian and ceremonial, settler pieces, audio recordings of Haida songs, histories and stories as given by Haida elders in both Haida and English languages, and a plethora of photographs. Addressing contemporary social issues concerning the politics of land, the environment, and interdependent ecologies, as well as presenting Haida oral histories and politics of cultural heritage and memory within the context of the contemporary. They are a critical part of the mandate of the Haida Gwaii museum. We tell ancient Haida histories of creation and natural history and environmental change and the recent retellings of the stories that are just in the last few years being told by scientific findings.

The Haida Gwaii museum speaks with the Haida voice first, by sharing our culture and worldview, and putting forward multiple ways of knowing that empower our once nearly silenced voices. Dominant Western narratives are challenged by including Haida knowledge holders, and community scholarly voices, and by exploring community centered ways of knowing. Throughout the museum labeling and interpretation is done in Xaayda Kil and Xaad Kil (Haida Language from Skidegate and Old Massett) first and then English. Elders and fluent in Haida and hud'kil speakers from the Skidegate Haida immersion program are consulted and provide us with the proper spelling and the interpretation for the museum. Our Haida clans and families are also consulted if the culture belongings is noted and recorded to be originating from their specific ancestors clan or town.

In our museum, Haida belongings serve many important uses in addition to the usual museum functions of exhibition, research, educational programs and conservation. For example, some pieces in our collection, whether they are on display, or are safely stored in the vault are used within Haida ceremonies, feasts and other significant events such as marriages, belongings, such as masks, coppers, box drums, and bent wood boxes are carefully removed from display and storage and made available to our people. We work hard to make these pieces available to our clans and people for special uses such as pot lashes, while maintaining our responsibility to care for these belongings and maintain their security. This is a very delicate and serious matter of balancing our responsibility, to conserve and preserve the belongings to the standards followed by all museums around the world and following our cultural practices and wishes of our clans, elders, and people. The underlying message of the museum encourages a holistic informal learning experience by cutting across traditional museum boundaries that separate our experiences of the natural and cultural worlds. Haida knowledge, scientific information, natural specimens, oral histories and art, all blend in a fluid and constantly changing exhibit context. Underlying it all is the understanding of our inseparable relationship to the land, sea and the super-naturals. that which gives Haida Gwaii its incomparable natural and cultural character.

In Haida, this is gina 'waadluxan gud ad kwaagid" (everything depends on everything else, or everything is connected). We have created relationships, and I've worked with museums from around the world. That great example of our decolonizing work we have done is with the Humboldt forum in Berlin, Germany on the "Ts'uu — of cedar and people" Exhibit and the revitalization of the Northwest Hall, where the Haida and other indigenous nations showcased their creativity, scholarship and histories of living cultures. With a Sue of cedar and people exhibit, we were involved over the entire process of the exhibits creation. This included co-curating, text and label creating, and editing and design. At home a great example of decolonizing an exhibit is our Supernatural Exhibit, also known as our oral history exhibit. This exhibit starts with the Haida history, about the creation of Haida Gwaii and its people. People come from the supernatural beings that came out of the ocean. Our world began thousands and thousands of years ago, Haida oral histories tell of these beginnings and the many events are followed, including the affairs of the notorious Nang Kilsdlaas (Raven). This island was nothing but saltwater, they say, raven flew around, he looked for a place to land in the water. By and by he flew to a reef lying on the south end of the island to sit on it. But the great mass of supernatural beings had their necks resting on one another on it, like sea cucumbers. It was both light and dark they say.

This original story was recorded by John Swanton in 1905, as told to him by Haida historian. Within our oral history exhibits, we bring together two ways of knowing Haida Gwaii's ancient past, Haida oral histories, and recent discoveries in geology, geography, climate studies and archaeology. Many supernatural beings referred to in the Haida histories are connected to natural events that occurred tens of thousands of years ago. This exhibit area highlights three histories that enrich our experience and knowledge of Haida Gwaii's past. These include Nang Kilsdlaas (Raven), Kalga Jaad (ice woman), SGuuluu Jaad (Foam Woman), and Jiila Kuns (Creek Woman). The ancestral beings provide testimony to how far back Haida knowledge of the islands extends into Haida Gwaii's ancient past. Kalga Jaad talks to the last ice age when the late Wisconsin Cordelian ice sheet was at its height from 20000 to 23000 years ago, and began slowly receding about 15600 years ago.

By 13000 years ago, the west Coast mainland the Hecate Strait and Haida Gwaii were still largely ice free, sea levels are known to have been around 150 meters lower than levels found today. Kalga Jaad, a supernatural being and Haida ancestors is said to have led the Haida to lands and territories that were free from the advancing glaciers and provided resources to live by. References to Kalga Jaad are shrouded in mystery, but the name is preserved and it still is used today in Skidegate. by many clans, including the Gak'yaals KiiGwawaay Raven Clan of K'uuna Llnagaay. Beginning in the 1980s and 1990s, archaeologists began piecing together evidence of very old habitation Sites, found in intertidal areas. From an era when sea levels were considerably lower than today, SGuuluu Jaad (Foam Woman) stories speaks of a time when the sea levels were lower, and then started to swiftly rise, forcing our ancestors to move away farther in land from the rising sea. Science tells us this started around 15000 years ago when the glaciers are receding within a secondary level of exhibits (backdrop to the 3 story modules).

The sequence of science, archeology and natural history of human history on Haida Gwaii are revealed through stone, bone, wood, technology, the changes into technology over time, and rare petrified caribou and walrus specimens. Yahguudangang "to pay respect". Also repatriation. All our ancestors are our relatives, and we have a deep connection to them. We are who we are today because of them. We believe that as long as the remains of our ancestors are stored in museums, and other unnatural locations far from home, that their souls of these people are wandering and unhappy. Once they are returned to their homeland of Haida Gwaii and are laid to rest with honor, the souls can rest, and the communities may heal a bit more.

The Haida repatriation committee, HRC, started around 1995, is a group of volunteers who have taken on the responsibility and are dedicated to the repatriation of the remains of Haida ancestors, cultural belongings, and intangible heritage from global museums and institutions from around the world. The HRC is made up of two official branches, the Skidegate repatriation and cultural committee, (located in the village of Skidegate and administered through the Haida Gwaii Museum) and The Old Massett

Repatriation & Cultural Committee (located in the village of Old Massett and administered through the Haida Heritage Society). Individually, each committee works on behalf of their community, and together we work on behalf of the Haida nation. The task of the HRC are to research and identify where Haida ancestors and culture belongings are located in Canada, the United States, Europe and around the world, to contact, to form relationships and negotiate with institutions for the return of remains and funerary materials and to see that remains of the ancestors are cared for with proper respect, and brought home in safety for burial on Haida Gwaii.

We have been working on repatriation of Haida ancestors over the past 30 years. Repatriation is a long and complex process that involves many people. The Repatriation Committees of Skidegate and Old Massett are authorized to do this work on behalf of our nation by the Hereditary leaders of Haida Gwaii, the Council of the Haida Nation, the Skidegate Band Council and the Old Massett Village Council. Regular consultation and planning meetings are held with our Hereditary Chiefs Council, Elders and the rest of the Haida communities, and every part of the process is guided by the wishes of the Haida community. Today, the remains of over 500 ancestors have been returned home. This has been our first priority. When this work is complete, we will turn our attention to the work of repatriating other Haida belongings and culture materials.

Repatriation is a long and complex process that involves many people. The repatriation committee of Skidegate and Old Massett are authorized to do this work on behalf of our nation by the hereditary leaders of Haida Gwaii, the Council of the Haida nation, the Skidegate band Council and Old Massett Village Council. Regular consultation and planning meetings are held with our hereditary chiefs Council, elders and the rest of the Haida communities. And every part of the process is guided by the wishes of the Haida community.

Thank you for listening and I look forward to answering any questions you may have.

"拯救之家"：Saahlinda Naay 的博物馆去殖民化实践

肖恩·杨*

早上好，我是 Gid yahk'ii（Sean Young，肖恩·杨）。我为自己是一名（加拿大）海达族人而自豪。我来自 Gaag'yals Kii'Gawaay，K'uuna Llnagaay（斯凯丹斯）①村落的鸦族。目前，我在 Kay Llnagaay 的海达瓜依博物馆"拯救之家"工作，是海达瓜依博物馆藏品部和考古学实验室的负责人。同时，我也是一名受过专业教育和培训的考古学家。自1997年开始，我以考古学家的身份担任了海达瓜依地区的专业顾问。我也是海达瓜依研究院自然资源与海洋保护课程的讲师。自2004年开始，每年夏天中的三个月，我都会以文化大使和看护人的身份参与海达瓜依守望者项目的工作。在项目工作期间，我会住在海达的古村落中，这里的文化遗址和世界遗产"Skagway ilna Guy"都在瓜伊哈纳斯国家公园保护地（Gwaii Haanas National Park Reserve）的海达遗址（Haida Heritage Site）之中。

Saahlinda Naay 拯救之家隶属于海达瓜依博物馆（Haida Gwaii Museum），是最早开始去殖民化的博物馆之一。对原住民和博物馆来说，也可以理解为"弥补过去的错误"（tl'l yahda）。在海达瓜依族民和定居者的共同愿景下，我们的博物馆协会于1971年成立，当时被称为夏洛特女王群岛博物馆协会（Queen Charlotte Islands Museum Society）。随后，最初的夏洛特女王岛博物馆于1976年开放。Saahlinda Naay 是一个传达我们（海

---

* 肖恩·杨，加拿大海达瓜依博物馆 Saahlinda Naay 藏品部主任。
① K'uuna Llnagaay（Skedans）位于加拿大 Louise Island 的东北角。参考资料：K'uuna Llnagaay (Skedans)—Gwaii Haanas National Park Reserve, National Marine Conservation Area Reserve, and Haida Heritage Site (canada.ca)。

达族)传统生存方式或法律的地方,即尊重(Yahguudang)和好问(ad kyanang tlaagang),维护Xaayda Kil和Xaad Kil(即海达语),以及我们的非物质文化遗产,并在展示和保护海达遗产的基础上激发创造力和促进社区发展。Saahlinda Naay是长老、社区成员和海达沉浸式项目给博物馆所取的名字。

该博物馆由海达瓜依岛上历史最悠久的全岛委员会管理,这个委员会由海达瓜依社区的所有成员组成,包括海达族人和非海达族人。如今,我们和斯基德盖特部落委员会、格瓦伊哈纳斯国家公园一起,成了一同在Kay Llnagaay获奖的海达遗产地的合作伙伴。我们博物馆的任务是促进对海达瓜依岛的全面了解,主要关注历史上和当代的海达文化的全部领域。我们还致力于支持和呈现海达瓜依岛居民的自然与人文历史,并构建在艺术和遗产领域的能力。大约50年前,Saahlinda Naay依靠着当地家庭慷慨捐赠的少量海达藏品和定居者的作品建馆开放。现在,我们是一个国际上公认的,无论是历史还是现当代藏品都在不断丰富的机构,如关于岛上自然景观代表性标本,丰富的海达瓜依历史档案,以及现有的艺术展览和教育项目的年度规划。今天,我们博物馆的存在正是源于海达瓜依人民的期待、奉献和辛勤工作,人们(海达人)相信通过共同努力,创造美好。海达瓜依博物馆位于Kay Llnagaay的海达遗产中心内。这是海达人几十年来的一个梦想。20世纪90年代到21世纪初,由海达瓜依博物馆工作人员、加拿大公园局、斯基德盖特部落委员会,长老、酋长和来自全岛社区的社区成员所领导的工作组开会交流,帮助海达当地设计和创建新的中心区。在博物馆建设项目开工以及干扰地区发展问题出现之前,海达人就告诉我们要小心谨慎。

新的海达遗产中心和海达瓜依博物馆位于Kay Llnagaay,或称"海狮镇",这是一个古老的村庄遗址,是Kay Llaanas Kayahlaanas鹰族的家园,是一个庞大而强大的家族团体,有一个世袭酋长(Gahlaay)、族长(Gwaa Ganad)和许多长老。我们收藏了独特且全面的历史性及后接触的藏品和档案材料,这使得观众能够接触到一个可以重视起海达和定居者他们社区身份的环境。我们的藏品包括海达人祖先和当代海达人的作品,涵盖了生产生活物品和礼器，还有定居者的作品，海达人歌曲的录音，海达人长者用海达语和英语讲述的历史和故事，以及大量的照片。解决有关土地政策、环境和相互依存生活形态等的当代社会问题，以及当代海达人的口述史的展示和文化遗产与记忆保存的政策制定，都是海达瓜依博物馆重要任务。我们讲述古代海达人的创世史、自然史以及环境变化史，并且近年来随着科学的新发现进行更新和修正。

海达瓜依博物馆最先要代表海达人发言，分享我们的文化和世界观，并提出多元的认知方式，放大我们曾经几乎被压制的声音。通过海达文化的保有者和社区学者的声音，和探索以社区为中心的认知方式，我们挑战了西方主导的叙事话语。在博物馆中，我们首先用 Xaayda Kil 和 Xaad Kil（来自 Skidegate 和 Old Massett 的海达语）进行标注和解释，然后是英语。我们咨询了海达族的长老和讲流利海达语的人以及 Skidegate 海达沉浸式项目，他们为我们提供了博物馆中正确的拼写和解释。同时，当文化所属被指出并记录为源于特定的祖先宗族或城镇时，我们还会咨询涉及的海达部族以及一些家庭。

在我们的博物馆里，除展览、研究、教育项目和保护等博物馆常规功能之外，海达人的物品有着许多重要用途。例如，一些收藏品，无论是被展示还是被安全地储存在我们的保险库中，都可以被用于海达人的仪式、宴会和其他婚礼之类的重大事件之中。诸如面具、铜器、箱形鼓和弯曲的木箱等物品被小心翼翼地从展示或储存中取出，供我们海达的居民使用。我们努力让我们的部族和人民在特殊情况下如冬季赠礼节中使用这些物品，同时我们还要肩负起保护这些物品，维护其安全的责任。这是一个非常微妙且严肃的问题，因为我们需要平衡好博物馆的责任，我们既要按照全世界所有博物馆的标准来保护和保存这些物品，又要遵循我们的文化习俗和我们部族、长老和人民的愿景。博物馆通过跨越传统博物馆的限制，将我们对自然世界和文化世界的体验进行区分，鼓励全面的非正式学习体验。在博物馆中，海达的知识、科学信息、自然标本、口述历史和艺术都融合在一个流动和不断变化的展览之中。博物馆的所有工作都是基于对我们与土地、海洋和超自然密切关系的理解。这使得海达瓜依具有无可比拟的自然和文化特征。

在海达语中,这就是gina 'waadluxan gud ad kwaagid(一切都取决于其他的一切,或一切都有联系)。我们海达瓜依博物馆已经与世界各地的博物馆建立了联系,并展开了合作。在我们所做的去殖民化的工作中,一个非常成功的案例是与洪堡论坛在德国柏林合作举办的"Ts'uu——雪松与人民"展览和"西北厅"的赋活(改造)。在那里,海达族和其他土著民族展示了他们自己的创造力、学术研究和活的文化历史。在"Ts'uu——雪松与人民"展览中,海达瓜依博物馆参与了展览的整个创作过程。这包括共同策展、文本和标签的创建和编辑、设计的工作。在我们的馆里,也有一个非常好的去殖民化案例,就是我们的超自然展览,也就是我们的口述历史展览。这个展览从海达人的历史开始,讲述了海达瓜依岛的创建和岛上居民的来历。海达的居民是来自海洋的超自然生物。海达瓜依的世界始于千年前,海达人的口述史讲述了这些故事,包括臭名昭著的Nang Kilsdlaas(乌鸦)的事情。他们说,这个岛除了盐水什么都没有。乌鸦飞来飞去,在水中寻找一个可以降落的地方。渐渐地,乌鸦飞到了漂在岛南端的一块礁石上,想坐上去。但是大量的超自然生物让它们的脖子在上面互相靠着,就像海参一样……他们认为,这既是光明的,又是黑暗的。

这最初的故事是由约翰·斯旺顿在1905年记录的,是一位海达族历史学家告诉他的。在我们的口述历史展览中,我们提供了学习海达瓜依岛古老历史的两种方式,一方面是海达人的口述历史,另一方面是最近地质学、地理学、气候学和考古学方面有关海达的发现。海达族历史中提到的许多超自然生物都与数万年前发生的自然事件有关。这个展区突出了三个历史故事,丰富了我们对海达瓜依岛过去经验和知识的认识。这些故事包括Nang Kilsdlaas(乌鸦)、Kalga Jaad(冰女)、SGuuluu Jaad(泡沫女)和Jiila Kuns(溪女)。这些祖先遗物所提供的证据表明,海达人对岛屿的了解可以延伸到海达瓜依岛的远古时代。Kalga Jaad提到,最后一个冰河时期,晚期的威斯康星州科迪勒兰冰原在20 000—23 000年前处于高峰期,大约在15 600年前冰原开始慢慢消退。

到13 000年前,美洲西海岸大陆、赫卡特海峡和海达瓜依岛基本还是上没有冰，当时已知的海平面比今天的大约低150米。Kalga Jaad是一位超自然的海达族女祖先，据说是她带领海达人来到了一个领土地区并提供了生活资源。这个地方不受冰川推进的影响，并能够提供他们生活下去的资源。关于Kalga Jaad的记载虽然被蒙上了一层神秘的面纱，但这个名字被保留了下来，并在Skidegate地区沿用至今，Skidegate的许多部族，包括K'uuna Llnagaay的Gak'yaals KiiGwawaay鸦族都在沿用这一名字。从20世纪八九十年代开始，考古学家开始拼合在潮间带所发现的有关古老聚落遗迹的物证，考古学家分析发现当时的海平面比今天低得多。泡沫女的故事中提到，当时这些海平面较低，然后开始迅速上升，这迫使我们的祖先不得不搬走，去离海平面更远的陆地上生存。科学告诉我们，海平面的上升大约始于15 000年前冰川消退时，这展现在展览的第二单元中（3个故事模块的背景）。

通过石、骨、木和技术，以及它们随时间的演变，罕见的驯鹿和海象石化标本，展览向我们揭示了海达瓜依岛人类历史的科学序列、考古学和自然知识。Yahguudangang"为表敬意"，特请返还先祖遗物。我们的祖先是我们的亲族，我们与他们有着深厚的联系。我们相信，正是因为他们，我们才能够成为现在的自己。我们认为当我们祖先的遗骸被存放在博物馆和其他远离家乡的非自然地点，他们的灵魂是流浪漂泊的，并不快乐。而当他们被送回故乡的海达瓜依岛，并被体面地安放，灵魂就可以得到安息，我们的社区也会得到治愈和安慰。

海达遗物返还委员会（HRC）大约于1995年成立，是一个由志愿者组成的团体，HRC承担起"致力于与全球博物馆和世界各地机构建立联系从而返还海达祖先的遗骸、文物和非物质遗产"等工作的责任。HRC由两个官方分支机构组成。一个是Skidegate文物返还和文化委员会，位于Skidegate，通过海达瓜依博物馆进行管理；另一个是Old Massett文物返还和文化委员会，位于Old Massett，通过海达遗产协会进行管理。每个委员会都代表他们所在的社群进行工作，我们共同代表海达民族展开工作。HRC的任务是研究确定海达先祖的遗骸和文物在加拿大、美国、欧洲以及世界各地的具体情况，并与各机构沟通，建立联系，就海达先祖遗骸的返还和丧葬事宜进行谈判，并确保我们先祖遗骸得到适当的保护，且能被安全地带回到他们的故乡——海达瓜依岛进行安葬。

30多年来，我们一直致力于海达祖先的归国工作。这是一个涉及许多人的漫长而复杂的过程。海达瓜依世袭领导人、海达民族理事会、Skidegate Band理事会和Old Massett Village理事会授权Skidegate以及Old Massett文物返还和文化委员会代表我们民族开展这项工作。我们与世袭酋长委员会、长老和其他海达社区定期举行磋商和规划会议，每一项工作都以海达社区的意愿为指导。目前，已有五百多位海达先祖的遗骸被送回故乡。这一直是我们的首要任务。当这项工作完成后，我们将转向其他海达族遗物和物质文化的返还工作上。

文物返还工作是一个漫长复杂而且涉及多方利益的过程。Skidegate和Old Massett的返还委员会由海达瓜依的世袭领袖、海达民族理事会、Skidegate部落理事会和Old Massett村理事会授权，代表我们海达民族进行工作。我们与世袭酋长理事会、海达族长老和其他海达社区会定期举行协商与规划会议，工作的过程中充分尊重海达社区的意愿，以社区的愿景来展开工作。

感谢大家的聆听，非常期待大家的提问。

Decolonisation as Infra-structure: Can the Museum be Decolonised?

Wayne Modest*

I want to thank you for inviting me, I must admit that I've done this probably six times already. Because I find it very hard to record a talk. Um, and that said, you know, I would have loved to have been there with you all. But my agenda just could not allow me to travel at this point. Also, because it would help me to engage in a conversation rather than talking to a screen, which I find enormously difficult. I want to also thank the organizers for inviting me to be a part of this, and inviting me at this point for this kind of discussion, because I think that it is such an urgent thing that we are struggling with other institutions right now.

For me, institutions, museums inhabit a very uncertain space. It is an uncertainty that one sees in the rising criticism about our role within society. And I, what I, you know, see to the lens of a scholar with whom I think, sometimes Stuart Hall and what you would call the conjuncture, this political moment, and what this moment itself offer, as threats, what are the opportunities? So in a way, one of the things that I'd like to think with you today is, what threats do decolonization bring? What opportunities, it also bring for us to inaugurate a different kind of institution for the future. So I want to congratulate the organizers for this already.

What I'll do is I'll read a little what I'll also just talk through some of my

---

* Wayne Modest, Director of Content, Wereldmuseum Rotterdam.

experiences. And forgive me if I ramble. My rambling is, it's yeah, it's part of, I think, I'll start off with the two quotations that I think are important for us to think with. One is from Tuck and Yang, from an article of about 2011, I think, which is called Decolonization is not a Metaphor. And the other is from a publication by Saidiya Hartman called Lose Your Mother, I think, where she was trying to come through slavery and its afterlife in the present. And I think both open up for us are thinking about what animates by interest, the why are we in this place? Why the demand for decolonization? And especially after about 30 years of diversity initiative and diversity policies, after the new museology movement, one could say that started already now what the 1980s Why are we still here demanding a certain kind of decolonization? My suggestion is that the long history of shifts and change that has been happening in the news changes that hadn't been happening in the museum have not necessarily fully addressed the infrastructure, the systemic ways in which race coloniality inequality is embedded in the institution. Rather, it has been at that top level of change, that actually resuscitates the system that we got that the museum is or has been.

So first Tuck and Yang yet they say this kind of inclusion is a form of enclosure, dangerous in how it domesticates decolonization it is also a foreclosure, limiting in how it recapitulates dominant theories of social change. When metaphor they say invades decolonization, it kills the very possibility of decolonization. It recenters whiteness, it resettles theory. It extends in a sense to the settler. It entertains a settler future. And second, from Saidiya Hartman, if slavery persists as an issue in the political life. It is not because of an antiquarian, antiquarian obsession with bygone days, or the burden of a too long memory. But because black lives are Still impairment and devalued by a racial calculus and a political arithmetic that were entrenched centuries ago. This is the afterlife of slavery, she says. Skewed chance live chances, limited access to health and education to museums even I would say. Premature death in conservation, impoverishment. So this paper is invested in also thinking about the museum, as a part of that political arithmetic and ratio calculus that was entrenched centuries ago. It is about how we, as institution, are conscripted in a politics of diversity, or even of a happy decolonization I will explain that later, that extend this inner sense of the settler, and that continues to entertain a settler future.

As we are all aware, decolonize as a term, as a concept, has reemerged recently to describe demands, the diverse demands for and practices of institutional change. While institutions like many of us here, but definitely my institution, have tried to claim the term as our own. We must admit that it is grassroots in activists initiatives, grassroots mobilization, including decolonize, this place in the US, or decolonize, the museum in the Netherlands, or even Berlin, decolonial in Germany, while other initiatives across Europe and America that have led to the demand for decolonizing, the museum's for decolonize, universities and archives, as well as curriculum methodologies, and even disciplines. For many of these activist mobilization decolonization has or was an answer to the failure of diversity policies implemented by institutions that, as feminist scholar Yvonne Benschop suggests, have failed in their attempts to confront issues of social justice. Benschop argues here, that the challenge of diversity is much more than a change in terminology from categories like gender, ethnicity, age and class, to the more encompassing and concealing term diversity. And I want to emphasize that diversity as a concealing term, she continues, in contrast to gender, or other categories of identity, which are often represented as sources of social inequality in organization, diversity does not so powerfully appeal to our senses of social justice. And I want to remind us, actually, that within many of the political spaces across Europe anyway, and in America, I must say that my talk here reflects what my own location position location from the Netherlands, that we often dismiss claims, based around marginalization of marginalized groups around question of gender, ethnicity, age or class, and especially around questions of racialized belonging as identity politics, which I think is an easy for closure of the possibility of the discussion of what how access is denied to practices of racialization or gendered practices. Indeed, if diversity was the language and policy framework through which more equitable unjust institutions or societies were to be formed, for many activists calling for decolonization, these initiatives had fallen trap to the exercise of kickboxing. Diversity on these columns had been conscripted to a neoliberal reductive multicultural politics that served to govern difference rather, not while centralizing white male cisgender norms as fulcrums around which all difference was to be measured. Diversity for these activists had failed. We needed to decolonize.

It is not my intention in this brief presentation to review the long history of diversity politics, policies. Including in the Netherlands, many of you would have already known about this. Many of you in the audience would also have already known of the criticism of the many diversity policies that have emerged over the years. I wanted to within the Netherlands, for example, we could trace back these questions of diversity policy, at least to the 1990s, coinciding with many of the discussion around the questions of multiculturalism, and the multicultural society, and the ways in which there were a discussion around that around social cohesion, inclusion with in which museums are also a part. And the ways in which actually, much of this discussion on multiculturalism was pronounced dead by many polities across Europe, that the plural, the possibility of a plural society was unknown instead, whether or not it is through politicians in England or Germany, or in the Netherlands. For many in the museums and heritage sector in the Netherlands, for example, these questions were tied to the code of cultural diversity that emerged in the 2000s. And the ways in which we would measure ourselves by as institutions as to whether we're diverse enough by looking at what we call the four Ps, you know, our personnel, or programming, our partners, and I need to remember the other one, but it's not coming to me right now. My interest is not in rehearsing this history. My interest is rather in for grounding, the question of failure, and how these policies have seemed to fail us, or at least in the ways in which we have actually been able to structure institutions that are more inclusive, or have changed to be more welcoming to others. Hints of this failure was what I wanted to address in the opening chords that I gave.

However, if one were to want to rehearse this, one could go back to the work for example of Sara Achmed. And her wonderful critique of the question of being included over and over again, or the ways in which diversity to talk works to ground, particular frameworks of thinking of particular normative understandings of institutions, or the work of, for example, the amazing work of Sumaya Kassim, in that article that circulated over five years or so ago, thinking about the impossibility of decolonization in institutions, as well as the work that she had done with the museum in Birmingham. My ultimate aim, however, in this talk, is to think through what might decolonization look like in relationship to earlier policies, and how decolonization may be able to inaugurate a different kind of institution that does not settle settler futures, what actually inaugurate futures have greater equity and justice for all peoples. And not only some.

I want to suggest that the earlier politics of diversity was one that often abstracted from the very politics around which it hovered a colonial politics or racial politics, a politics of a of normative understanding of how societies are a culture a colonizing politics, that tried to push against a certain kind of or tried to establish what I call a happy multiculturalism, a hockey multiculturalism that does not undo ongoing structures, but rather one that would like to decolonize with a hug.

Before I go there, though, I want to open up two things. One, there are many, of course, who asked the question around the term decolonization and what it might mean. And for the audience that we are here today, I realize that some people might say all but decolonization is not for me, it is for places that had settler colonial projects such as the US Imperial colonial projects, such as in

Europe, and there are other places which did not have colonialism in the same way. My understanding of decolonization, as imagined through the different activist projects that have happened was that it was a much more capacious category, one that did not see coloniality as simply emergent out of an imperial colonial formation, but rather, one that saw coloniality as the afterlife of an of imperialism that has settled in the ways in which we understand the way we live today. And therefore, if one were to, for example, take decolonize this place and the project of decolonize this place, as they imagine their activities formation in New York, then one would see how it ties questions of coloniality to questions of race, gender, climate justice, but even questions of gentrification, as it was mapped onto an unequal distribution of resources and live chances for marginalized very often precarious, peoples who were regarded as different from a white settler nor decolonization in this framework, then, is not just about thinking, the moment of colonization into emancipation and the decolonization movement that happened, for example, from the 1940s onward, but rather, the embedded structure of colonial understandings, including the ways in which that the colonial understanding that structure the world in which we live, even, as in all the formations such as first and third world, overdeveloped underdeveloped, developing world, so it was a category of thinking about equity, and justice for all. That's one thing.

The second part of what I'd like to do before I go into a few examples, for us to think with, and what I mean is, is to think about the question, why, why I want to think through the question of decolonization and infrastructure. Now, for those of you in the social sciences, and humanities, and who are academics, much more than me, who is a museum person, you will know about what has been called the infrastructural turn in the social sciences and humanities, and the ways in which certain scholars, for example, in urban anthropology or geography, have been thinking about infrastructure, the way how to think infrastructure, in the distribution, on equal distribution of inequality. By infrastructure there, they were more interested in, as I understand it, erodes social technical assistance, some people would call it roads and bridges and colleagues and whatever. And whole, one could understand or use those structures infrastructures, as a way of understanding the world we live in, and how those help us to distribute life chances. While that is important for me, as I'm interested as well, in thinking about the museum as an infrastructure, as a part of a social technical system that animates the ways we hold a whole life chances are distributed, I wanted to take infrastructure in another way. I wanted to understand it as the both the intellectual as well as the practical, systemic modes through which we organize museums, whether in conservation, or in exhibition or even in the the question of the intellectual infrastructure on which the museum is based, so in this is an ethnographic museum, or this is an art museum, or this is a history museum, and how those different disciplinary frameworks around which the museum is this continues to divide the world into those one side of the world as whether or not it is those people who are primitive or primitive craft, art, whatever, and the other side of the world, those people who have art history that cannot be that. For me is perhaps the most important in terms of thinking about the infrastructure, as we in my museum anyway, continue to ask, what does it mean, to be ethnographic? As opposed to be contemporary art? What does it mean, to be ethnographic as opposed to be historical? In that sense, I want you to just think through a set of examples, and you might as ways of thinking how we think infrastructure, what might it mean, to think conservation, its norms and practices, its modes of care, its modes of imagining preservation, as part of an infrastructure of inequality, Or, conversely, is it possible to think, conservation, as a rather, an infrastructure to facilitate the redistribution of care, not only for collections, but also for communities. As well as thinking through the ways in which for example, and I've heard this by others, I've said it myself, that conservation itself can be a stumbling block for restitution, and therefore, a stumbling block, or a way of keeping the current museological form of who can care for and who must be cared for, in terms of objects and collections. It is that, that I'm interested in. Now, many of you, I would have said this to some of you before, so you would have heard it before. But many of you would have heard the example that I've given where I reflect on an earlier idea of my work in the Caribbean, and the ways in which within the Caribbean, and in Jamaica, where I work, we were always so invested in trying to keep the norms of conservation. Because these norms come down to us when I used to live there, in the certain rules and regulation, a certain forms and structures that we needed to live by, that we needed to uphold. If we were actually to accede to that we were actually to live up to the call that was being made by ikon, for example. And so, the for several years while working in along with other thinkers around conservation in Jamaica, if I remember the ongoing struggle that I felt in trying to stick to the norms of what is the right temperature? How do I keep those temperature and relative humidity? How do we ensure that objects live forever, in that context, have a Caribbean that is always human, and that is always hot, but one that always also was not as well enough to be able to implement the systems that we were capable of we were we felt that we were required to keep up. No, I know that this might be an old fashioned way of thinking conservation. Because at the time when we were thinking this that was already in the 2000s. We were already aware that there had been much changes in the thinking around what conservation could be or could become. And yet, I want to still ask the question, how many of us still place that norms of preservation as a kind of requirement for who can care for objects and where objects can be cared for best.

One of the things that animated our discussions while I was in junior, anyway, was a series of returns of objects that people they're wanting, I will not call out names of which object it was, I've written about it other ways, but that those objects could never be returned, because of the possible failing, of us being able to achieve those conditions. But in this sense, that is only a pragmatic notion of the infrastructure. I am also interested in just the very notion of what is to be preserved. And the idea of preservation, what objects are allowed, or should be allowed to live forever, or what objects should die should disappear.

And here again, I want to give you another example. When I was in Jamaica, I was part of a project working on a masquerade tradition called Junkanoo. And I remember, was trying to acquire an object, it was a mask that you dance, and you dance it on your head. And at the end of the dance, the group that dances the object, it should be destroyed. It's a natural parts of the process of stitch structure. And I remember us in the museum wanting to preserve it. Also, because there was a similar object in the American Museum of Natural History that was preserved. It has been there for since 1919, collected by this political Martha Beckwith, and it's in a terrible condition, I must tell you what, the one in Jamaica was new, we had commissioned it, and we wanted to keep it. And therefore, we actually paid the community to stop that process where it should have been destroyed. And eventually, what happened was, there was a lot of unsettling in the community, there was a lot of criticism of us. Eventually, the objects died a natural death when it was eaten by insects. But what interests me here is the ways in which this desire for preservation also, we had that desire for preservation, that would suggest that we stop the lifecycle of the objects in an attempt to keep it forever, as record. It is that I'm interested in. What happens when conservation not only as a practice, but also as a way of thinking is part of the structuring, of who keeps who is allowed to preserve what is returned. I am interested in that. And it is there that I'm thinking through the question of the infrastructure on which our institutions are based.

My second example, would be a legal infrastructure. And the question of what we often use is also in the restitution conversation about it was the law at the time. And here I am drawing on a large project that we're working on, you can look at it online called pressing matter where we are interested together with colleagues such as water for heart and wonderful, amazing student, as a taker, who is we've been thinking about the question about what legal framework have been put in place to be able to govern? Who keeps what object? And what where, when we say it was the law at the time, what does that mean? But hold that legal framework is also a part of sometimes the foreclosure have a possibility of return and restitution sometimes. So one of the things that we've been tying with in this or thinking within this was one important thing is the legal infrastructure around which are the legal frameworks around which our conversation around it was the law the time not similar to the legal framework, that was embedded in the colonial project. And therefore, that was also embedded in the racialized project of creating are the racial categories are owned within the colonial hierarchies, so how do we unpack on hinge the category of international law and heritage law that would make it or made it possible for objects to come to us, for objects to be in our collections, for objects to be taken in times of war, but also the legal frameworks around questions of, of, of illicit trafficking? Who do those legal instruments continue? Or how did they shape the ways in which objects, now so many objects are in European museums, in relationship to other places, such as the Caribbean or Africa? And what might it mean? To see these as the infrastructure of any of immobility of objects, actually, if you were to think about it is also the same infrastructure, of immobility of people's, because in many cases, the same people from whom objects are here in the in Europe and European museums are very often the same people who need visas to travel to Europe, when we don't, kind of we don't need visas to travel to these countries.

So what is that legal entity intellectual framework on which the idea of international law is based? And how does that perpetuate a certain kind of coloniality of ownership, the coloniality of the rights to preserve, but also the coloniality of the distribution of heritage in certain spaces, and not other spaces, made thinking through the legal infrastructure, help us to inaugurate a different kind of heritage distribution, and make thinking that in relationship to the racialized history of law, and international legal framework, also help us to think again, about questions of restitution, and redistribution. My colleague Water Volhard and L. Spitz suggest that one of the caution that they want to place within the question of restitution today is that one of the things that we do is that we say that this discussion must be more ethical discussion, and not legal discussion. And by excluding the law, what we might do is exclude the very nature in which the law has been the infrastructure on which we have been able to take, but also to keep objects within our museums. And my final thinking around infrastructure, is what I alluded to in the beginning. Because if there is anything, and this is what I think of as the epistemic intellectual framing, system systemics, on which the museum is friend is it works.

I'm interested in whole institutions like ours emerged around issues of ethnography, art, history, and the ways in which ethnography was a category for thinking about those people in a particular place. That was not Europe that was not white. And the ways in which that same conversation around an ethnographic museum in the present continuous these modes of thinking about a divided world. For us in my museum that has immense consequences, it is the consequence of where those contemporary art happen. What is the temporality of the contemporary in relationship to modern and tradition? But it is also embedded in the collections policies that we try to create in our institutions. When we think about what is art? What is design? What is craft? What, who, which places has art or design or, or fashion and which places are textile dress and craft. For me, a part of the decolonial project is also embedded in the very categories of the institutions that we inhabit today that seems to perpetuate the kind of divided world, which creates a hierarchy of making, a hierarchy of doing, but also creates temporal distancing between who is contemporary, when is the contemporary, when is tradition. And one of the things that we're interested in where a colleague of mine and many others have been doing a book that is coming out, hopefully this year, about temporality that it is actually.

Within the this, the infrastructure, intellectual infrastructure, that we struggle, or this intellectual infrastructure, that we struggle with ideas of why we still make the distinction between those people who are traditional, and almost feel that tradition cannot live in the present, that tradition must be past. So embedded in this infrastructure is also a temporal idea about developed under developed, over developed or who is contemporary, that kind. It is that what I mean by taking decolonization, not just in a politics of recognition, that would include others, that will include me in a European institution, where some would say, I am also other, but rather a kind of politics of real capacious thinking about the very foundations on which the institution is based, so that we can unravel these foundations to create an institution where diversity can flourish, where plurality is a possibility, rather than thinking that there is a west of us that knows and an other that must be a certain that we must help or educate. In many ways, one could suggest that the restitution debate, still frump had still has its foundation in that kind of this discussion. A decolonial project would take the political recognition and the politics of redistribution together to unravel an institution that would create a future we share with the each other and, and also think about the planet, but also a future that is more equitable.

And just this is what I want to share with you today. That decolonization most be a systemic exploration of the institution to create a systemic solution for racism that is systemic, for the inequalities that are systemic, but for and inequalities that are systemic to the institution that colonialism created, but that coloniality continues to feed in the present.

Thank you. I probably talk too much. Thanks.

博物馆知识基础架构的去殖民化

韦恩·莫德斯特[*]

感谢大会对我的邀请,我必须承认,我大概已经录了六遍了,因为我发现录制视频真的很难。话虽如此,我其实很想和大家共聚现场,但由于行程原因,我正在出差而无法到达现场。另外,现场发言也有助于我参与讨论,而不是对着屏幕说话,我觉得这非常困难。我还想感谢主办方对我的邀请,并在这个时候邀请我参加这个话题的讨论。我们现在正在与其他机构一起努力,所以我认为这个话题非常紧迫。

对我来说,机构,也就是博物馆,目前所处的状态充满了不确定性。可以从越来越多的关于我们的社会角色的批评声中看到这种不确定性。从一个学者的角度来看,以及有时从斯图尔特·霍尔以及所谓形势的角度来看,我看到我们目前所处的政治时刻,以及这个时刻所带来的威胁和机遇。因此,在某种程度上,我今天想和大家一起思考一个主题,就是去殖民化带来了什么威胁?同时,这为我们在未来建设不同类型的机构带来了什么机遇?另外我对大会的成功举办表示祝贺。

接下来我将谈谈我的个人见解和一些经验。如果我扯远了,请大家见谅。这也是我本次分享的一部分,首先我要从两段引文开始,我认为这对我们思考这一话题至关重要。第一段是引用了塔克和杨在2011年左右发表的一篇文章,叫作《去殖民化并非隐喻》。另一段来自赛迪亚·哈特曼的一本名为《失去你的母亲》的出版物,她在书中介绍了自己试图从奴隶制和其后续影响中走出来的历程。我认为这两本书都为我们打开了思考的大门,我们为什么会在这个地方?为什么要求去殖民化?尤其是在多元化倡

---

[*] 韦恩·莫德斯特,荷兰世界文化博物馆内容主管。

议和多元化政策出台了约30年之后。新博物馆学运动已经于20世纪80年代开始，为什么我们仍在这里呼吁去殖民化？我认为，博物馆领域长期以来发生的转变和变化并未完全涵盖，也并未彻底解决更为基础层面的系统性问题，即在机构中根深蒂固的种族、殖民性和不平等问题。相反，正是因为变革仅存在于高层，才一直维持着博物馆现有的或旧有的体系。

  首先谈谈塔克和杨，他们说这种包容性是封闭的，是危险的，对于去殖民化的驯化，它也是一种排斥，是限制社会变革的主导理论的重述方式。他们说当去殖民化这一概念被视为隐喻时，就被扼杀了去殖民化的可能性。它再次肯定了白人中心论，重新定义了理论，它服务于殖民者的未来。其次，赛迪亚·哈特曼指出，奴隶制始终是政治生活中的一大问题。这不是因为对过去岁月的痴迷，或者是记忆太长的负担，而是因为黑人的生命价值仍然被几个世纪前就根深蒂固的种族思维和政治算计所抑制和贬值。这就是奴隶制的延续，不公平的生存概率，有限地获得健康、教育和接触博物馆的机会，在保护和贫困中过早死亡。因此，本文也致力于思考博物馆作为几个世纪前根深蒂固的政治算计和种族思维的一部分，也就是关于博物馆作为机构如何被征召参与多元化政治，甚至是快乐的去殖民化政治。这点我将在稍后解释，这会增强殖民者的内在意识，并继续为殖民者的未来服务。

  众所周知，"去殖民化"这一术语和概念近期再次活跃于大众视野中，用以描述对机构变革实践的各种需求。虽然我们这里的许多机构，我所在的机构肯定包括在内，都试图把这个词作为我们自己的术语。但我们必须承认，这其实是起源于基层活动家倡议、基层动员，包括在美国、荷兰、德国柏林的去殖民化运动。而欧洲和美洲的其他倡议导致了博物馆、大学、档案馆、课程甚至学科的去殖民化需求。对于这些动员运动中的许多人来说，去殖民化已经或曾经是对机构实施的多元化政策的失败回应。正如女权主义学者伊冯娜·本肖普所说，这些政策在应对社会公正问题时失败了。本肖普在这里认为，多元化的挑战远不止是术语的变化，是从性别、种族、年龄和阶级等类别，到更具包容性和隐蔽性的术语多元化。我想强调，她还认为，多元化作为一个隐藏的术语，与性别或其他类别的身份形成鲜明对比，后者往往被明确指向组织中社会不平等的根源，但多元化却不会强烈地煽动社会正义。我想提醒大家，无论如何，在欧洲和美国的许多政治领域里，我必须说这反映了我们自己在荷兰的情况，尤其是围绕身份政治的种族化归属问题时，我们经常驳回边缘化群体在性别、种族、年龄或阶级方面被边缘化的说法，这也因而很容易忽略从种族或性别的角度讨论的可能性。事实上，如果多元化能形成更公平公正的机构或社会的语言和政策框架，那么对于许多呼吁去殖民化的活动家来说，这些举措已经落入了踢皮球陷阱。这些类别的多元化已经被征用到新自由主义的归纳性多元文化政治中，以白人男性的性别规范作为标尺来衡量所有差异，以此来管控差异。对于这些活动家而言多元化是失败的。我们需要去殖民化。

在这次简短的演讲中，我无意回顾多元化政治和政策的悠久历史。包括在荷兰，许多人应该已经知道了这一点，也已经知道多年来出现的对不少多元化政策的批评。例如，在荷兰我们可以将这些多元化政策问题追溯到20世纪90年代，恰逢围绕多元文化主义和多元文化社会问题的许多讨论，以及围绕社会凝聚力和包容性进行讨论的方式，博物馆也是其中的一部分。事实上，这场关于多元文化的讨论在很大程度上被欧洲各地的许多政体宣布停止，无论是英国、德国还是荷兰的政治家都表示，多元社会的可能性被宣告死亡。例如，对于荷兰博物馆和遗产行业的许多从业者来说，这些问题与21世纪初出现的文化多元化准则有关。我们作为机构衡量自己是否足够多样化的方式，我们称之为四个P，也就是人员（personnel）、项目（programming）、合作伙伴（partners），还有一个我现在还没有想到。我的目的不是复述这段历史，而是找到失败的原因。这些政策是让我们失望的原因，或者至少能帮助我们打造更具包容性的机构，或者已经变革得对他者更为友好。这种在失败中发现的问题就是我在开头所说的想解决的问题。

如果要追溯历史，我们可以看萨拉·阿赫梅德的作品中对反复出现的问题的精彩批判，或者她关于多元化的讨论方式、关于机构的特定规范理解的特定思维框架的批判，或者对苏玛亚·卡西姆等人的伟大作品的批判。

她在五年多前广为流传的文章中,思考了机构中实现去殖民化的不可能性,以及论述了她在伯明翰博物馆所做的工作。然而,在这次演讲中,我的最终目的是思考去殖民化与早期政策的关系,以及去殖民化如何能够开创一种不同类型的制度,这种制度并非要确定殖民者的未来,而是为所有人,而不仅仅是某些人,提供更公平和正义的未来。

早期的多元化政治往往是从它所围绕的政治中抽象出来的,也就是殖民政治或种族政治,或是对社会发展文化的规范性理解,或是某种试图建立我所说的快乐多元文化主义的、殖民者的政治。这种类似曲棍球的多元文化主义不会破坏目前的框架,而是通过调和来实现去殖民化。

但在这之前我想谈两件事。有很多人围绕"去殖民化"一词及其潜在含义提出了问题。我们今天在场的听众里,有些人可能会说去殖民化不适合我们,它适合有殖民者定居的地方,比如美洲的定居殖民者,或是欧洲的帝国主义殖民者,但其他没有殖民主义的地方并不适合。我对去殖民化的理解是,正如通过已经发生的各类运动所体现的那样,它是一个更广泛的类别,它不认为殖民主义只是从帝国主义的殖民形成中产生的,而是将殖民主义视为帝国主义的残余,以我们理解的当下的方式延续下来。因此当我们观察例如纽约的去殖民化运动的组成时,我们会发现这些活动家将殖民性的问题与种族、性别以及气候正义等问题联系起来。甚至是城市士绅化问题,因为它映射出资源的分配不公和被边缘化群体的生存机会问题,而这仅仅因为他们偏离了白人殖民者所倡导的规范。在这样的框架下理解去殖民化,就不仅是要思考从殖民化到解放的历程和从20世纪40年代开始的去殖民化运动,而是嵌入式认识殖民的结构,包括构建我们生活的世界的认识殖民的方式,就像在第一和第三世界、过度发达、欠发达、发展中世界等所有形态中一样,这是一种面向全体公平正义的思考。这是第一点。

第二点是,在讨论例子前,我想请大家思考这个问题,为什么我们要思考去殖民化和基础设施问题?人文社科从业者比我更像学者,还有博物馆领域的从业者,你们知道所谓的人文社科的基础设施转向,如城市人类学或地理学等领域的学者,思考基础设施在分配不公中运作的方式。据我所知，他们对基础设施中的社会技术援助更感兴趣，有些人会称之为道路、桥梁等等。总的来说，人们可以通过这些结构和基础设施来理解我们生活的世界，以及理解这些结构如何帮助我们分配生存机会。这对我来说很重要，因为我也很有兴趣把博物馆视为一项基础设施和社会技术系统的一部分，一种盘活机会的分配方式。但我想从另一个角度看待基础设施，无论是在保护、展览还是博物馆知识的认知基础方面，都把它理解为我们组织博物馆的知识和实践的系统模式，例如这是一个民族志博物馆，或者这是一座艺术博物馆，一座历史博物馆。博物馆围绕不同学科框架划分世界，将人们划分为这一边是拥有原始工艺、原始艺术的人，另一边是拥有艺术史的人。而对我而言，最重要的关于基础设施的问题，就是一直在问，民族志是什么？是与当代艺术相对立的吗？民族志和历史是相反的概念吗？从这个角度来说，我希望你们思考一系列的例子，来思考我们是如何看待基础设施的。例如在思考遗产保护时，将保护的规范和实践、保护模式、关于保护的设想与不平等的基础设施的结合意味着什么？或者相反，是否有可能针对藏品和社区，以保护来促进重新分配基础设施。又或者，例如我从其他人那里听到过，我自己也说过的，也就是思考保护本身可能是文物返还的绊脚石，以一种维系当前博物馆学形式的方式来决定谁可以保护藏品，谁又是被保护的藏品，这点是我比较感兴趣的。我之前对许多人说过这句话，所以你们以前可能也听到过。在座许多人可能都听过我举的例子，我在其中回顾了我早期在加勒比地区工作的想法，以及在牙买加工作的经验，当时我们致力于维护保护规范。这些规范最终变成了我们的规则和规定，我们需要遵守和坚持的某些形式和结构。例如，我们需要加入某些组织，就需要履行国际博协发出的呼吁。因此，在牙买加与其他思考者一起从事保护工作的几年里，我还记得我在努力遵守正确温度的规范时所经历的挣扎。如何保持馆内的温度和相对湿度？在这种情况下，我们如何确保物体的永续存在？加勒比地区的环境常年总是潮湿、炎热的，不能支持我们实施我们有能力实施的系统，但我们觉得必须严格按照标准执行。我知道这可能是一种老式的保护思维。因为在我们思考这个问题的时候，已经是21世纪初了。我们已经意识到，关于保护可能是什么或可能成为什么的想法发生了很大变化。然而，我仍然想问一个问题，我们中有多少人仍然把保存规范作为一种要求？要求谁可以照顾物品，在哪里可以最好地照顾物品。

我上大三时，有件事激发了我们的讨论，当时人们想要一系列物品返还原主。我不会说物品名称，之前已经用其他方式说过，但这些物品永远不会返还，因为我们可能无法实现这些条件。但从这个意义上说，这只是一个实用的基础设施概念。我对什么东西应该被保存这一概念也很感兴趣。对于保存的想法，哪些物品可以被永久保存，哪些应该摧毁，哪些应该消失。

在这里，我想再举一个例子。我在牙买加的时候参与了一个名为Junkanoo的化装舞会传统项目。我记得当时我想要一个东西，是一个跳舞用的面具，你可以把它戴在头上跳舞。这些面具应该在舞会结束时被销毁。这在这个过程中是一个很自然的步骤。我记得我们想在博物馆里保存这件物品。此外，因为美国自然历史博物馆里也保存了一件类似的物品，它自1919年以来一直在那里，是由政治家玛莎·贝克维斯收藏的，现在状况很糟糕。我告诉大家牙买加的那件是新的，我们已经发出了委托，想保留它。由于这件物品本应该被销毁，因此，我们向社区付费要求他们停止销毁的程序。后来这件事引发了社区内的许多风言风语，也有很多对我们的批评。这批物体最终因虫害而受损了。但我在这里想说的是这种对保存的渴望，正是出于这种对保存的欲望，我们试图暂停物体的生命周期，试图将其永远保存下来，作为记录。这就是我感兴趣的点。当保护不仅是一种实践，而且作为一种思维方式成为结构的一部分时，会发生什么？也就是思考由谁保存？什么物品可以保存？什么物品可以被归还？我对此很感兴趣。我认为这是博物馆机构所面对的基础建设问题。

我的第二个例子是法律基础建设。我们在文物返还的讨论中也经常用到这一工具，也就是当时的法律。这是我们正在做的一个大型项目，大家可以在网上看一下，叫作"pressing matter"，是我们与志同道合的同事以及优秀出色的学生一起做的。我们一直在思考这样一个问题，即建立了什么样的法律框架才能进行治理？什么物品由谁保存？什么时候什么地点最为合适？我们说当时的法律是什么意思呢？但法律框架有时也会排斥文物返还的可能性。因此，我们一直在关注或思考一件至关重要的事，就是法律基础建设，以及围绕其展开的法律框架和讨论。当我们讨论"当时的法律"时，并没有考虑到嵌入殖民进程中的法律框架，因此，那些法律框架也是种族化项目中的一部分，以及维持着殖民等级制度下的种族分类。那么我们如何解释国际法和遗产法，使物品能够，或有可能流向我们，成为我们的收藏，还有如何对待那些战争时期流失的文物，如何围绕非法贩运问题打造法律框架？这些法律文书由谁续写？它们如何影响现在馆藏于欧洲的那么多藏品与加勒比地区或非洲等的关系？这可能意味着什么？将这些视为藏品移动受限的基础设施意味着什么？事实上，仔细一想这也是人类移动受限的基础设施。因为在很多情况下，在欧洲和欧洲博物馆收藏的文物所来源的社区中生活的人往往需要签证才能前往欧洲，而欧洲人却不需要，我们不需要签证就可以去这些国家旅行。

那么，国际法理念所基于的法律实体知识框架是什么呢？它如何在藏品所有权、保存权利、地域分配等方面延续了殖民性，决定遗产可被分配于某处空间，而非另一处空间？这使我们通过法律基础建设进行思考，帮助我们开启遗产分配的新模式，并使我们思考与种族化的法律历史以及国际法律框架有关的问题，也有助于我们重新思考文物返还和再分配问题。我的同事沃特·沃尔哈德和斯皮茨在归还问题中提出了一个建议，即我们开展的讨论必须更多地聚焦道德，而非法律。通过排除法律，我们可以排除创造了这些法律基础的本质，而那也是我们掠夺并将藏品保留在馆内的基础。我对基础设施的最终想法是我在开始时提到的，也就是我所认为的作为博物馆运作基础的认知论的、系统性的知识框架。

我对围绕民族志、艺术、历史等主题出现的机构很感兴趣，我也很有兴致研究民族志，民族志是一种研究特定地方的人群的类别。无关欧洲，无关白人。并且，当前围绕民族志博物馆的讨论方式延续到关于世界分裂的思考模式。对本博物馆而言，它有着重要的意义，这意味着当代艺术在何处发生。在现代和传统的关系中，当代的时间性是什么？但它也嵌入我们的藏品政策中。什么是艺术？什么是设计？什么是工艺？来自何处、出自何人，什么样的东西算是艺术和设计，哪些又算是纺织品和手工艺？对我来说，去殖民化项目的一部分也嵌入了我们今天所处的这类机构中，这些机构似乎维持着世界的分裂，创造了一种创作和行为的等级制度，也造成了时间上的距离。当代是什么？当代的时间范围是什么？传统的时间范围是什么？我的同事和其他作者在写一本书，有望在今年出版，这本书是关于时间性的。

在知识基础设施中，我们正在努力思考为什么我们仍然要划分群体，比如这些是传统群体，认为传统就不能活在当下，而是必须成为过去。因此，这个基础设施中还包括关于发达、欠发达、过渡发达或当代定义的时间性。这就是我所说的去殖民化，不仅仅是在政治中认可他者，比如在欧洲机构中认可我这样的人。有些人会说，我也是他者。这是一种对机构根基进行广泛思考的政治，这样我们就可以打破这些基础，创建一个多元化可以蓬勃发展、充满前景的机构，而不是存在着一个文明、富有知识的西方，和一个必须被帮助或被教育的他者。在许多方面，人们可以认为关于归还问题的争论仍然基于这样一类基础。一个去殖民化项目将结合政治承认和再分配政治，来帮助机构创造一个彼此共享的未来，并将地球环境因素纳入考量，这也有助于创造更公平的未来。

这就是我今天要与大家分享的内容。去殖民化应当是对制度的系统性探索，为系统性的种族主义、系统性的不平等创造系统性的解决方案。但殖民主义创造的制度中，不平等是系统性的，并且这种殖民主义仍在持续滋长。

我可能说得太多了，感谢各位的聆听。

Inclusive Terminology for the Heritage Sector

Carissa Chew[*]

The heritage sector can use language as a tool to create and curate socially conscious catalogues, collections, displays, and learning resources for the future. This paper offers a brief introduction to two major inclusive language projects created by the author in conjunction with work completed at the National Library of Scotland. The first of these is the Inclusive Terminology Glossary, which is a collaborative project that provides specific language guidance on the historic and contemporary usage of terms relate to race, ethnicity, gender, sexuality, religion, and disability. The second is the Cultural Heritage Terminology Network, which is a virtual space that promotes practice sharing and cross-institutional collaboration on inclusive description issues. Both projects can be accessed through the website: www.culturalheritageterminology.co.uk.

Rationale

There is power in textual representation and when a text paints a derogatory and dehumanising image of an entire group of people, it can serve to legitimise hatred towards them. Language choices can enact forms of non-physical violence — such as psychological, bureaucratic, and symbolic violence. And words can, of course, also encourage and provide legitimation

---

[*] Carissa Chew, University of Hawaiʻi at Mānoa.

for hate crimes and physical acts of violence. Consciously or not, descriptions, displays, and subject headings written and used by heritage professionals often reproduce colonial discourses of power. And when heritage institutions replicate racist, sexist, homophobic, or ableist, fallacies today, they not only contribute to the circulation of *misinformation*, but they perpetuate the violence of *misrepresentation*.

When we apply "essentialized, ahistorical categories and labels" to entire groups of people, we risk the creation of *distorted* information and the reproduction of harmful stereotypes. And when our language is homogenising, we cause additional harm by erasing diversity and dishonouring people's self-identities. To quote Colleen McGloin and Bronwyn L. Carlson in their study of the politics of language, written text has the "capacity [...] to construct reality; produce ideas, beliefs, and stereotypical representations, represent, misrepresent, and imbue readers and viewers with particular views about the world."[①]

The decolonisation of language is therefore an incredibly important aspect of broader decolonisation work. From a practical perspective, moreover, using the most appropriate terminology available enhances the quality of collections information and improves the discoverability of materials, complementing the accurate curation of the historic record.

Inclusive Terminology Glossary

It is therefore important that the heritage sector is held accountable for the language that they choose to use and the context that they choose to provide. This can be a daunting task, however. The language that people use and the identities that they choose, after all, have shifted over time and place.

When I was working as the Equalities, Diversity, and Inclusion intern at

---

[①] Colleen McGloin and Bronwyn L. Carlson, "Indigenous studies and the politics of language," *Journal of University Teaching and Learning Practice* 10. 1 (2013), 4.

the National Library of Scotland, I began to make a list of the historic terms that had been used to discriminate against groups with protected characteristics in the past. This list continued to expand, however, as I realised that I also needed to educate myself about the preferred terminology of marginalised groups today, and how these terminology preferences have changed over time.

I found that there were some existing guidelines out there — but these did not relate to all areas of inequality, and these were mostly produced in the USA, Australia, and the Netherlands which has left an enormous gap in knowledge about the language legacies of the British Empire. Additionally, I realised that I needed not only an understanding of different communities and their self-identities around the world, but also knowledge of the language of race, diaspora, disability, and LGBTQIA+ issues in Britain and its former colonies, as well as specific local and regional languages and terminologies within the UK.

To facilitate the identification of harmful terms and to provide guidance on more appropriate terminology, I created the Inclusive Terminology Glossary, which now exists on Google Drive as a collaborative online project. It is a work-in-progress, and anybody can contribute to it to improve the quality of information that it contains.

This "live" glossary is unique because I created it with cultural heritage professionals in mind, and its more ambitious in its scope than any other project that exists. It includes notes on time periods in which particular terms were used and contains archaic spellings and misspellings to help with the task of identifying discriminatory language and harmful materials across catalogues and collections. For ease of navigation, the Glossary is split into numerous sections, reflecting different areas of history and protected characteristics.

This glossary is useful whether you are working to identify harmful records, adding advisory notices to your catalogues, or actively making amendments to your metadata. It shows a list of terms related to different protected characteristics along with a contextual note on the appropriate use of terminology, and any preferred or alternative terms that exist. These linguistic dilemmas are often very complex, and the glossary aims to provide guidance so that heritage professionals can make better informed decisions when it comes to language choices. It is an educational tool rather than a "quick fix" guide. A lot of the terms that come up are not necessarily offensive in their own right but can be harmful when misapplied to people or places.

What I'd eventually like to see is the Glossary project to get funding behind it so that we can hire a series of editors and community groups who can periodically review the guidance so that there is the remunerated involvement of the communities that are represented in the Glossary, to make it truly "Inclusive".

Cultural Heritage Terminology Network

The second resource to introduce is the Cultural Heritage Terminology Network, which builds off the foundations of the Glossary project. The premise for both projects is that it is essential to promote cross-institutional collaboration when it comes to inclusive description work because it is a universal problem facing the heritage sector, the scope of the task is enormous, and there's a huge amount at stake. Commitment to social justice in the heritage sector needs to extend beyond the boundaries of thinking of just our own individual institutions: how can we share resources and work together to achieve real change?

Lack of access to knowledge and resources is often used as an excuse not to prioritise equalities work, hence why I've been actively trying to share my work as widely as possible. And by creating this online network, I am encouraging others to do the same, because inclusive description resources are of benefit to the entire sector. By creating a collaborative glossary and a shared network space that is free and accessible, heritage professionals can incorporate inclusive description practices into their work even in the face of underfunding and under resourcing issues.

The Cultural Heritage Terminology Network is a virtual space that promotes practice sharing and cross-institutional collaboration on all kinds of inclusive description issues. Through the Forum, you can engage in discussions about descriptive practice relating to a whole range of issues from the creation of advisory notices and the revision of controlled international vocabularies, to ideas about the future development of the Glossary as a funded project and an online database. On the Resources page you will find over 200 EDI resources for heritage professionals that I have collated over the course of two years. This is an amazing reservoir of knowledge for anybody working in the heritage sector, and it will be kept up to date to encourage the use of existing resources.

文化遗产领域的包容性术语

克利萨·秋[*]

大家好，我是克利萨·秋。我是夏威夷大学马诺阿分校的历史学博士生和助教。我在英国遗产领域从事平等工作已两年有余。2021年，我在苏格兰国家图书馆完成了为期九个月的有关平等性、多元性和包容性内容的实习。近期，我与格拉斯哥艺术学院图书馆和帝国战争博物馆合作，开展了两个独立的包容性编目项目，这两大项目都是由我创建的，我将在这里做简要分享。

第一个项目是创建包容性术语词汇表，这是一个合作项目。该项目针对种族、民族、性别、性向、宗教和残障等有关术语及其历史和现代用法提供具体的语言指导。第二个项目是搭建文化遗产术语网络，即搭建一个虚拟空间，促进描述包容性问题上的实践经验分享和跨机构合作。目前，你可以通过网站（culturalheritageterminology.co.uk）访问这两个项目。

在正式开始之前，我想提醒大家，我参考和分享的内容中确实涉及歧视性语言和不良图像，但这仅作为示例。

基本原理

我想先提供一些背景信息，我的工作基于这样一个基本原理，即遗产领域可以将语言作为工具，来为未来创造和策划可形成社会意识的目录、收藏品、展览和学习资源。文本表述是有力量的。当一份文本对某个群体的形象加以贬低，予以非人化描述时，便可使人们对该群体的仇恨合法

---

[*] 克利萨·秋，美国夏威夷大学马诺阿分校历史学博士、助教。

化。语言的印迹能以非身体暴力的形式显露出来，如心理、官僚和符号暴力。话语也可能滋生仇恨犯罪和身体暴力行为，并为其提供合法性。话语的暴力既可能是有意为之，也可能是下意识这么做。遗产专业人员撰写和使用的描述、展览和主题词往往会重现殖民时期的权力话语。而如今，当遗产机构重复种族主义、性别歧视、恐同言论或残障歧视等谬论时，它们不仅促使了错误信息的传播，还让由不实描述引发的暴力得以延续。

当我们对某个群体冠以一个集中的类别和标签而忽略历史背景时，我们很有可能会创造出歪曲的信息，再次产生糟糕的刻板印象。语言的同质化，意味着我们抹杀了多元性、损害了他人的自我身份，从而造成额外的伤害。科琳·麦克格洛因（Colleen McGloin）和布朗温·卡尔森（Bronwyn L. Carlson）在《语言政治研究》中写道，"书面文字具有构建现实，形成想法、信念和刻板印象的能力，也能传递错误信息，将特定的世界观灌输给读者和受众"。

因此，作为非殖民化工作的一部分，语言的非殖民化也尤为重要。如果从这一点出发，使用最合适的术语就显得十分实用，这不仅可以提高馆藏信息的质量，还有助于他人找到相关材料，也使得历史记录的策展更为准确。

包容性术语词汇表

因此，遗产领域要对他们选择使用的语言和提供的背景负责，这点尤为重要。但在实践中，难度不可估量，我们不得不从世界各地悠久而纷繁的历史中做出取舍。人们使用的语言和他们选择的身份，随着时间和地点的变化而转移。

因此，当我在苏格兰国家图书馆开展我的第一个包容性编目项目时，我尝试列出过去用于歧视"受保护特征"群体的历史术语。这个列表越列越长，而我也意识到，我还需要不断学习，了解如今边缘化群体的首选术语，以及这些术语的选择偏好是如何随时间变化的。

我的确找到一些既有的准则，但未涉及所有的不平等领域。而且这些准则大多由美国、澳大利亚和荷兰编撰。可见，人们对大英帝国的语言遗留问题的认识尚浅。我还意识到，我不仅需要了解世界各地的不同社区和当地的自我身份，还需要了解英国及其前殖民地的种族、流散、残障和性少数群体等问题的语言，以及英国境内特定的地方和区域术语。

为帮助大家识别有害术语，提供更合适的术语或指导意见，我创建了包容性术语词汇表，作为在线合作项目，大家可在谷歌云端网盘上访问这个表格。该项工作远未完工，仍在进行中，任何人都可以助一臂之力，提高其中的信息质量。

因为该表的创建对象是文化遗产专业人员，而且其涵盖范围较其他现有项目都大，所以这个"实时"词汇表也算得上独树一帜。该表中纳入了特定术语的使用时期说明，还纳入了术语的原始拼写和错误拼写，以帮助大家在目录和藏品中识别歧视性语言和有害材料。

无论是需要识别有害记录、在你的目录中添加忠告性通知，还是想要主动修正元数据，该词汇表都会很有帮助。该词汇表列出了各种受保护特征的相关术语、如何适当使用该术语的背景说明，及其相应的首选或替代术语。相近术语的选择往往非常复杂。该词汇表旨在提供指导说明，以便遗产专业人员在选择用语时能做出更明智的决定。它更像是教育工具，而不是一个"快速定位"指南。很多术语本身并不一定具有攻击性，但如果用错对象或地方，就会造成伤害。

人们常常问我，词汇表未来要如何发展。我已经与苏格兰国家图书馆和其他英国的合作伙伴开展讨论，准备将其发展为一个更复杂的数据库。我希望，这个自发组织的项目最终能得到资金支持，这样我们就可以雇用许多编辑和社区团体，由他们负责定期审查指导说明。如此一来，参与词汇表创建的社区能够获得报酬，也真正彰显了其"包容性"。

文化遗产术语网络

此外，我今天想分享的第二个资源是文化遗产术语网络。可以说，没有第一个词汇表项目，就不会有这个项目。两个项目有一个相同的前提，即在涉及包容性描述工作时，必须寻求跨机构合作。遗产领域普遍会面临这个问题。任务广泛，涉及资料浩如烟海，问题非常繁杂。在社会公正和遗产领域，我们需要群策群力，不能只局限于单个机构的思维界限。我们如何才能共享资源，共同实现真正的改变？

我们通常拿缺乏获得知识和资源的途径作为借口，借此将平等问题的工作一拖再拖。因此，我一直在积极尝试，尽可能地向更多人分享我的工作。通过创建这个在线网络，我鼓励其他人也加入进来，因为包容性描述资源的建立对整个遗产领域都有好处。通过创建合作词汇表和免费的共享网络空间，即使面对资金不足和资源不足的问题，遗产专业人员仍可以将包容性描述的实践纳入他们的工作中。这意味着，在这个时代，恐怕再无借口说缺乏描述性实践。

文化遗产术语网络就是搭建一个虚拟空间，促进各种包容性描述问题上的实践经验分享和跨机构合作。在论坛中，你可以参与描述性实践的讨论，这其中会涉及一系列主题。从忠告性通告的编写和受控国际词表的修订，到词汇表未来成为受资助项目和在线数据库的发展畅想。在资源页面上，你会发现我在两年时间里为遗产专业人员整理的200多个EDI资源。对任何在遗产领域工作的人来说，这都是极为珍贵的知识宝库。我将持续更新资源，鼓励大家使用现有的资源，并在现有的工作基础上继续加以发展。

我建立了一个博客，用来分享有关良好实践的想法。目前，你可以在博客中找到我总结的有关包容性描述工作的10个关键原则。今天就不详细展开了。我们也创建了Twitter和Instagram等社交媒体账号。此外，我们建立了电子简报，供大家注册使用，你将每月收到新资源的更新，也将了解遗产领域即将发生的大小事件。可以说，在这里，你能了解所有与包容性描述相关的内容。我真心希望任何对包容性描述工作感兴趣的人参与进来，并参与我所创建的这些项目。

我的演讲结束，感谢您的聆听。欢迎大家分享自己的观点或提问。

Decolonizing a Regional Museum Service: From Strategy to Community with TWAM

Jo Anderson   Adam Goldwater   Kylea Little[*]

Just by way of introduction, my name is Adam Goldwater and I'm museum manager of the Great North museum Hancock. And joining me later on will be Kylie Little & Joanne Anderson.

Just a snapshot of our museums and galleries there. We are nine museums and galleries and the archives across Tyneside. Just give you a an indication of the spread. TWAM has a collection that spans over 250 years of history, meaning that a number of objects are linked with Britain's colonial past. Since 2019 TWAM has been committed to acknowledging and addressing the injustice of colonial legacies by platforming other voices and perspectives, organizational practice and behaviors under review to address fundamental issues about power structures and true community inclusion, as well as its specific work around repatriation. Whilst we deal with what decolonization means to TWAM at a strategic level, work has begun on an operational level to make our problematic colonial past transparent through continuing research stuff development and engagement with our communities. We continue to highlight and embed previously hidden or unknown stories within the collections so as to present more inclusive viewpoint in all narratives.

This comes at a point where TWAM is redrawing its own strategic vision. In this way to amass the opportunity to embed decolonization firmly within

---

[*] Jo Anderson, Adam Goldwater, Kylea Little, Tyne and Wear Archive and Museums, Newcastle UK.

a single strategy for the service, making it core and lived. The ambition is for TWAM to be a radical and sustainable business as much as relevant and inclusive cultural organization. TWAM is a large and successful archive museums service which received ordinarily 1.3 million visits per year across its nine venues, which it manages on behalf of all local authorities Gateshead, Newcastle, North Tyneside and South Tyneside. Along with Newcastle University.

TWAM has a strong reputation for innovative thinking and for quality of access, equalities, inclusion, wellbeing and learning. TWAM has increasingly recognized this entrepreneurial approach. TWAM has a wide network of local, regional, national and international partnerships across the educational community, business and cultural sectors, too.

I'm also manages a county archive Tyne&Wear, where it's quite unique in its governance model and structures. The relationship between the four local authority partners are set out on a 10 year joint agreement which runs until 2027 and the relationship with Newcastle University in respect to the Great North Museum and the Hatton Art Gallery lies outside of this joint agreement within a separate agreement. TWAM recognizes its areas of influence lie in the objects, stories, that collects the interpretation applies to them, the ways in which engages with the communities it serves, and the people it employs to carry out this work.

We in common with many other individuals and organizations feel the need to challenge ourselves and to step outside of our institutional comfort zones. We're in the process of creating Vision, TWAM 3.0, setting out how we would develop over the next four years and how this will ensure that the experience we provide is more interactive and self directed, more community focused and focused on users and their needs, and more public welcoming and flexible. Building on our strengths of partnership work in diversity, children and young people learning, community engagement and outstanding collections, we've developed a Vision for TWAM 3.0 that explicitly recognizes that the heart the next phase of our evolution will be through a program for inspiring and creative work drawing strength and inspiration from the diversity of our venues, collections and audiences to allow us to be a catalyst for creativity, risk and experimentation.

The last 18 months has marked a rebirth for TWAM as the organization emerges from a period of reflection created by the shadow of COVID, and the appointment of a new director with renewed vigor for developing our practice to better engage the communities we serve, and to act as a cultural beacon across the Northeast of England and beyond. It's backed by a strong partnership with the four local authorities and Newcastle University, which despite the pressures of the pandemic have kept their funding commitments in place. What support TWAM 3.0, TWAM cultural and creative vision working together to make sense of the world through compelling stories of heritage, Art, Culture and Science. Strength through diversity of venues, collections, staff, audiences and producers, valuing voices of workers and culture of audience. Consultation, experimentation and agency to shape responses to local issues, seed audience contribution and develop understanding of the need of our many users, working as a catalyst through partnerships to share learning and encourage innovation, and a resilient and enterprising business model with a new governance structure providing challenge and support. The COVID-19 situation provided both a challenge and an opportunity for the ongoing development of TWAM 3.0. The challenge in that we've had to adapt rapidly to a situation in which had restricted direct contact with audiences and users, but an opportunity which allowed us to think in a new and different way about the services we deliver, we will be taking forward this learning over the life of this plan. In addition, the impetus of our developing response to Black Lives Matter has facilitators strong and unified staff focus on issues of quality, and is in itself an expression of the direction of travel of TWAM 3.0. Key initial commitment is to the decolonization of our collections and their interpretation. This will involve a review of our collections and acquisition processes to ensure we're moving towards wider and equitable representation of cultures in the collections we hold the region. Through review of our approaches to interpretation and the stories we tell with them. This work has already commenced at the Great North Museum, Hancock and Discovery Museum, and we're planning our approaches across the wider organization. Delighted to pass on to Kylee Little and Jo Anderson who will be able to tell you more about that specific work.

At great North museum Hancock, our decolonization journey began during a research trip to Canada. I spoke with several curators in Vancouver, who frequently worked with First Nations communities, and it became apparent that the Great North museum Hancock would need a repatriation policy, if we want it to be open and transparent about what our intentions were regarding material from indigenous peoples. The Great North Museum, Hancock had no such policy in place at the time. The museum had once before repatriated Maori human remains. But this had been one single experience and there was no document in place that would guide either the museum or an indigenous community in discussions for any future repatriations. Through creating this policy, we hope that it may encourage any community worldwide to approach us and begin an honest and open dialogue about certain objects within our collection. In early 2020, the director of the Australian Institute of Aboriginal and Torres Strait Islander studies came to the UK to learn about the Aboriginal collections in a number of cultural institutions and discuss possible returns.

The Great North museum Hancock was included in this conversation. And consequently, we conducted a thorough review of our collections, and paid particular attention to the provenance of Australian objects. Despite COVID-19 pause in this project, we've continued to investigate our objects of Australian provenance to discover previously unknown facts. The research conducted on our Australian and Aboriginal objects indicated that the whole world cultures collection was lacking important information, especially regarding provenance. Taking advantage of the COVID-19 shut down, we were able to spend a significant amount of time, researching over 230 objects that we have on display in our world cultures gallery. To gain a better understanding of how these objects came to the UK. Research revealed that perhaps unsurprisingly, many of the objects are firmly linked to the British Empire.

One of the most important discoveries was confirmation that a bronze instrument on display was taken during the destruction of Benin in 1897. Since then, great North museum Hancock has alerted the Nigerian government to the presence of abandoned bronze here in Newcastle, and are open to discussing the repatriation of this object at their convenience. For now, the bronze object is still on display, but we are reinterpreting it. It's new label will now make it very clear that the bronze was stolen and not in a punitive expedition as it's still sometimes called, but during a massacre conducted by British forces. Similar work has also extended into our Egyptology collection. Research on mummified irtyru has revealed that her provenance was not as straightforward as we had previously believed. Her case label not only contained factually wrong information, it was distinctly Eurocentric in nature, and focused heavily on the European men who were involved in taking her remains out of Egypt. This interpretation has since been rewritten to acknowledge Irtyru as a human who once lived in ancient Egypt and the problems inherent in displaying her remains.

Hi, my name is Kylie. I'm keeper of history at Discovery Museum. And I'm here to talk about exchange.

Exchange1.0 was a community led collections for research pilot project led by National Museums Scotland, and the National Maritime Museum.

It was funded by The Arts and Humanities Research Council. It ran from January to July 2022. And the project enabled seven organizations around the UK, including Discovery Museum, which you can see in this slide here, this the atrium, to work with South Asian, African and Caribbean community groups to explore experiences of empire, migration, and life in Britain, through their collections with a view to gathering evidence for best practice guidelines for community led research. The curatorial and communities team at Discovery Museum worked together to release a call after which was disseminated through various networks of our contacts to recruit people for a community steering group. We ended up with nine members in the steering group, you can see them here in the photographs. And they all represented key organizations from around the region. One stipulation of the grant was that the community members had to be renumerated for their time. And this was new for TWAM, and required a lot of detailed conversations about developing that process, which we did successfully. The steering group also created a memorandum of understanding and that guided the spirit of the meetings and the project. The museum team shared information about our collections and the group visited Discovery Museum. Some of them came for the first time, some had been many times. And they fed back that they couldn't see themselves or their lives, or stories represented in the museum galleries or collections. So using all of this information, the steering group decided to create two different projects. One was a women's trail around the permanent galleries at the museum. So they chose 16 contemporary women from the region who had made significant contributions in the fields of academia, health, science, and community activism. The women are all from African, South Asian, or Caribbean diaspora communities. And you can see this, as the start of the trail in the museum, each woman has a panel which features a portrait photograph, and then some texts with the story of their lives on. The group also decided to explore Indian indentureship and its connection to the region. Indentureship was a system by which more than 1 million Indians were transported to labor in European colonies, following the Abolition of the Slave Trade in the early 19th century. Pat, one of the members of our steering group is descended from Indian indentured laborers, who were taken from India to Trinidad and then she herself moved to the northeast of England. We connected this up with the fact that in the museum collection, we have two and half block models of ships built in the Northeast of England, that we use to transport Indian indentured laborers. So you can see on the screen here, Pat's family, bottom left and half block ship model at the top. We shared paths research into her family history combined with the shipbuilding history and the region via an in person talk, which was also broadcast online to the public, And that's the bottom picture on the right. Further, creative output was a spiritual offering on the banks of the river time to honor the journeys of all of our ancestors,

As well as new research and the creative outputs that I've mentioned, this demo group asked us many probing questions about various museum processes from catering suppliers to shop stock, to our freelance contracts, and how we did our communications strategy. They also met our leadership team to discuss how to ensure that this work was embedded in the organization. Exchange 2.0 began in January this year, and will complete in May 2023, as well. So we continue to work with the steering group from the original project. And this phase is all about embedding that work and reaching much wider audiences.

Thank you.

Thanks to Kylie and Jo.

So to conclude the history of TWAM collection spanned over 250 years and this means that a number of our objects inextricably linked with Britain's colonial past and systemic racism. We acknowledge this and are working towards using these collections in an equitable and just way. Many museums were founded during the height of the British Empire. And for us decolonization means acknowledging this and thinking about what this legacy means for us. We know that many of our objects came from former British colonies, but we don't always know how they ended up here. Many were gifts or souvenirs from travel and trade, but some was stolen, taken by force or gifted under duress. So we want to find out as much as we can about the objects in the museum. How did we acquire them? What meaning do they hold? Is the information we already have accurate? We can do this by carrying out historical research, but also reaching out to source communities. We want to find new perspectives that improve our understanding and add to the stories we can tell in the museum, and which make a contribution to acknowledging past wrongs. We also want to build trust for those who feel like their voice in the museum has been silenced. TWAM's mission firmly sets us up in a social context, putting people at the heart of our work. We believe this is increasingly important. Our work over the next couple of years particularly in relation to equalities, has highlighted this. In this plan, this vision of TWAM 3.0, sets our ways in which we can work with individuals and communities supporting health and well being and contributing to regeneration. Different people will see TWAM in different ways. The creative organization, a federation of museums and galleries, a social justice organization, a heritage organization, and an arts organization, the focus for research and impact the tourism asset, the community service, underlying this as its civic purpose. We need to amplify the value of what we're doing, because we believe society needs us now more than ever.

    Thank you.

地方博物馆服务的去殖民化：从战略到社区

乔·安德森　亚当·戈德华特　凯利·利特尔 *

简单做个开场白，我叫亚当·戈德华特（Adam Goldwater），在汉考克大北方博物馆担任博物馆经理。随后，凯利·利特尔（Kylie Little）和乔·安德森（Joanne Anderson）将一同参与演讲。

先对我们的博物馆和美术馆做一个简要介绍。在泰恩赛德，博物馆、美术馆和档案馆加起来共有九家，这里是分布示意图。泰恩威尔档案馆与博物馆（TWAM）中的藏品跨越了250余年的历史，这意味着许多物品与英国的殖民历史有关。自2019年以来，泰恩威尔档案馆与博物馆就致力于为其他声音和观点提供发声平台，借此承认并解决殖民主义遗留的不公正问题，对组织的实践和行为进行审查，以解决有关权力结构和社区真实包容性等基本问题，并落实遗产返还这一具体工作。我们一边在战略层面上阐释去殖民化对泰恩威尔档案馆与博物馆的意义，一边在实操层面上着手工作，通过持续的研究发展和深入的社区互动，使我们难以条分缕析的殖民历史变得清晰透明。我们始终强调藏品背后隐秘的或不为人知的故事，并将其融入藏品叙述中，使得在叙述中呈现更多的包容性观点。

泰恩威尔档案馆与博物馆正在重新制定自己的战略愿景，并借这种方式积累机会，在服务中充分融入去殖民化，使其成为核心和长久的任务。我们的目标是使泰恩威尔档案馆与博物馆成为一个积极、可持续的商业组织，以及有价值的、包容性的文化组织。泰恩威尔档案馆与博物馆是一家成功的大型档案图书馆服务机构，9个场馆通常每年接待游客130万人次。泰恩威尔档案馆与博物馆代表盖茨黑德、纽卡斯尔、北泰恩赛德和南泰恩

---

* 乔·安德森、亚当·戈德华特、凯利·利特尔，英国泰恩威尔郡档案馆与博物馆。

赛德等地方当局管理这9个场馆，还与纽卡斯尔大学有所合作。

泰恩威尔档案馆与博物馆在创新思维、可享服务质量、平等、平等性、包容性、福祉和学习能力方面有着良好的声誉。泰恩威尔档案馆与博物馆已经逐渐认识到企业经营办法的重要性，其合作伙伴分布广泛，包括地方级、区域级、国家级和国际伙伴，横跨教育界、商业和文化领域。

我还在管理泰恩威尔郡档案馆，一个县级档案馆，该馆的治理模式和结构相当独特。四个地方当局通过签署为期10年的联合协议达成伙伴关系，该协议将持续到2027年。除了该联合协议之外，我们还和纽卡斯尔大学就大北方博物馆和哈顿画廊方面的管理签署单独协议。泰恩威尔档案馆与博物馆认识到，只有通过对收集的物品和其故事进行解读、积极参与社区服务的方式，并发动员工执行这项工作，才能发挥其行业内的影响力。

和其他许多个人和组织一样，我们深感挑战自己、走出自身舒适区的必要性。目前，我们正在创建TWAM 3.0的愿景，厘清未来四年该如何发展，以及该如何确保我们提供的体验具有以下特征：更有互动性和自我指导性、更加以社区为中心、更关注用户和他们的需求，以及更加对公众友好和灵活。我们在多样性、儿童和青少年学习、社区参与和杰出藏品等方面建立起自己的伙伴关系优势，并依赖该优势制定TWAM 3.0的愿景。其中，明确强调了我们下一阶段的发展核心是通过鼓舞人心和创造性的工作计划，从我们多样的场馆、藏品和观众中博采众长、汲取灵感，从而在为我们带来风险和试验的同时，也滋生了创造力。

过去18个月，泰恩威尔档案馆与博物馆也迎来新生，新冠疫情的负面影响令我们反思，也带来新的变化。新主管的任命也为工作发展注入了新的活力，帮助我们更好地吸引所服务的社区，并成为英国东北地区乃至其他地方的文化标杆。4个地方当局和纽卡斯尔大学作为靠谱的伙伴，给予我们强有力的支持。尽管疫情下，大家都财政紧张，但他们仍信守承诺，资金到位。支持TWAM 3.0的，是泰恩威尔档案馆与博物馆的文化和创意愿景，通过引人入胜的遗产、艺术、文化和科学的故事，共同理解这个世界，借助场馆、藏品、员工、观众和制作人多样性的优势，重视员工的声音和观众的文化背景，利用磋商、实验和政府机构，对当地问题进行回应，重视类似观众的贡献，并发展我们对用户需求的理解，在伙伴关系中成为催化剂，分享新知、鼓励创新，形成适应性强和有进取心的商业模式，形成新的治理结构，从而迎接挑战和得到支持。对于正在发展的TWAM 3.0，新冠疫情既带来机遇也带来挑战。挑战在于，我们有时无法与观众和用户直接接触，我们得迅速适应这种情况；机遇在于，我们能够以全新的视角思考我们所提供的服务。我们将在本计划落实期间持续思考学习。此外，我们积极响应黑人平权运动，促进全体工作人员对平等问题的思考和关注，这本身就体现了TWAM 3.0的发展方向。一个首要的关键任务是对我们的藏品及其解释进行去殖民化，其中涉及对藏品和收购过程进行审查，以确保我们区域所持有的藏品背后蕴含的文化更加多元，更加平等。我们还会对藏品的解释方式以及我们要讲的故事进行审查。我们已经在汉考克大北方博物馆和发现博物馆开始这项工作，并计划让更多机构参与进来。接下来的时间交给凯利·利特尔和乔·安德森，由他们负责分享这项工作的更多信息。

汉考克大北方博物馆的去殖民化之旅始于对加拿大的研究，我曾与温哥华的几位策展人交谈过，他们常常与第一民族打交道。汉考克大北方博物馆如果需要公开透明地说明我们对原住民物件的意图，就需要落实归还政策。当时，汉考克大北方博物馆尚无相应的政策。此前，博物馆曾归还过毛利人遗骸，但仅归还过一次，目前没有任何指导性文件，好让博物馆或原住民社区就未来的归还问题进行讨论。我们希望，这个政策可以鼓励世界各地的任何社区与我们联系，我们愿开诚布公，与大家就藏品中某些物品的归属进行交流。2020年年初，澳大利亚原住民和托雷斯海峡岛民研究所所长来到了英国，了解多个文化机构中的原住民藏品，并商讨了归还的可能。

汉考克大北方博物馆也加入了此次商讨。因此，我们对藏品进行了彻底的审查，尤其关注澳大利亚物品的来源，尽管这个项目因新冠疫情而暂停，但我们仍在继续调查来自澳大利亚的物品，希望发现既往未知的事实。对澳大利亚和原住民物品展开的研究表明，世界文化藏品往往缺乏重要的信息，尤其是关于出处的信息。新冠疫情导致博物馆闭馆，我们正好有机会花大量的时间研究我们在世界文化展厅中展出的230多件物品，以便更好地了解这些物品如何来到英国。研究结果或许并不让人意外，许多物品都与大英帝国有着密切的联系。

其中一个重大发现是，我们确认了一件青铜乐器展件是在1897年贝宁城毁城时遭到掠夺的。此后，汉考克大北方博物馆便提醒尼日利亚政府，纽卡斯尔存在属于他们的青铜器，并乐意在他们方便的时候讨论该物品的归还问题。现在，该青铜物件仍在展出，但我们对其重新做了解读。新标签清楚说明，该青铜器是在英国军队进行的一次大屠杀中横遭偷窃，摒弃了惩罚性讨伐的说法，尽管该说法仍时有提及。我们还对埃及藏品展开了相似的工作，对木乃伊化的伊尔蒂鲁（Irtyru）女士的研究表明，该物件的出处并不像我们既往认为的那样简单，先不说展品标签本身包含了事实错误，其内容本质也完全是欧洲中心主义的——标签着重描述将伊尔蒂鲁的遗体运出埃及的那些欧洲人。我们重新做了解读，承认伊尔蒂鲁是一个曾生活于古埃及的人类，并且在之前的遗骸展览中存在问题。

大家好，我是凯利。我在发现博物馆担任史料保管员，此刻，我想聊聊交换的问题。

交换1.0是由苏格兰国家博物馆和英国国家海事博物馆领导的一个社区主导的藏品研究试点项目。

该项目由英国艺术与人文研究委员会资助，运行时间为2022年1月至7月。在这个项目中，英国国内的7个组织，包括发现博物馆在内。这7个组织得以与南亚、非洲和加勒比社区团体合作，通过他们的藏品研究帝国、移民和英国生活等知识，以期收集参考依据，用于形成社区主导研究的最佳实践指南。博物馆的策展团队和社区团队共同发布了一项呼吁。随后我们通过各种社会关系网络传播该呼吁，为社区指导小组招募人员。最后，我们共招募到9名指导小组成员，他们都是地方重要组织的代表。拨款的一个前提便是，款项必须拨给付出时间的社区成员。对泰恩威尔档案博物馆来说，这是全新的形式，我们需要讨论很多细节来落实，最后我们还是做到了。指导小组还制定了一份合作备忘录，该备忘录对会议和项目的精神进行了指导说明。博物馆团队分享了藏品的有关信息，指导小组也参观了发现博物馆。有些成员是第一次来访，有些成员已造访多次。他们反馈说，他们在博物馆展厅或藏品中没有看到自己、自己的生活或是故事。因此，在获得相关信息后，指导小组决定创建两个不同的项目，一个是围绕博物馆常设展厅搭建的女性长廊，指导小组为此选择了当地的16位当代女性，她们在学术、卫生、科学和社区活动等领域做出了重大贡献。这些女性都来自非洲、南亚或加勒比地区的侨民社区。在博物馆长廊的起点，每位女性对应一块展板，上附人像照片，以及描写她们生活故事的文字。该小组还决定研究印度契约制及其与当地的相关性。在19世纪初奴隶贸易废除后，契约制作为替代制度造成100多万印度劳动力被运送到欧洲殖民地。帕特（Pat）是指导小组的成员，她是印度契约劳工的后代，她在印度的祖先被运送到特立尼达，随后她自己移居到英国东北地区。在博物馆的藏品中，我们有两个半英国东北部建造的船舶的模型，我们曾使用这种船舶运送印度契约劳工，这也就把契约制和当地地区串联起来。我们将帕特的家族历史和造船历史以及英国东北地区结合起来，并通过面谈的形式分享该研究路径。这段谈话也上传至网上，面向公众传播。另一个创造性的成果是在泰晤士河畔的精神供奉，以纪念祖先所踏过的征程。

除了我提到的新研究和创造性成果，这个小组还向我们提出了许多关于博物馆各种流程的问题，启发我们思考，从餐饮供应到商店库存，再到我们的灵活用工合同，以及我们如何落实沟通策略。他们还会见了我们的领导团队，讨论如何确保这项工作融入组织运作中。交换2.0于2023年1月份开始，并将于2023年5月完成。因此，我们继续与原项目的指导小组合作，而这一阶段就是要把这项工作融入其中，让更多的人了解。

谢谢，谢谢凯利和乔。

我负责总结横跨了250多年的泰恩威尔档案博物馆藏品的历史。250多年意味着我们的一些物品与英国的殖民历史和系统性种族主义有着密不可分的关联。我们承认这一点，并努力以公平公正的方式使用这些藏品。许多博物馆是在大英帝国的鼎盛时期建立的。而对我们来说，去殖民化意味着承认这一点，并思考这种遗产背后的意义。我们知道，我们的许多物品来自前英国殖民地，但很多时候，我们不清楚这些物品是怎样到我们手中的。许多物品是旅行和贸易中的礼物或纪念品，但也有一些是来路不明，或盗窃、或强取豪夺。因此，我们想尽可能了解博物馆物品背后的故事，我们怎样获得？这些物品暗含着什么意义？我们目前掌握的信息是否正确？为了寻找答案，我们当然可以借助历史研究，但也可以深入藏品所属社区。我们希望能找到新的视角，改善我们的理解，并丰富我们在博物馆里可讲述的故事，从而有助于我们承认过去犯下的错误。博物馆会忽略一些人的声音，我们希望能重新建立起他们的信任。为肩负起泰恩威尔档案博物馆的使命，我们需置身于社会背景中，在工作中以人为本，这也将成为越来越重要的事情。我们计划在未来几年展开的工作，特别是与平等有关的工作，已经充分说明了这一点。在这个计划中，TWAM 3.0 的愿景指引我们，在面向个人和社区时，我们应支持社会的健康和福祉，使其不断焕发新生。不同人有看待泰恩威尔档案博物馆的不同视角。泰恩威尔档案博物馆或许是创意组织、博物馆和美术馆联盟、社会公正组织、遗产组织、艺术组织、关注研究和影响的组织、拥有旅游资产的组织、社区服务组织，但本质都是为了造福市民。我们需要让更多人看到我们所从事事业的价值，因为我们相信现在的社会比以往任何时候都更需要我们。

谢谢！

Let's Go Round Again —
The Museum Carousel and Its "Others"

Roshi Naidoo*

Hello, everyone, and thank you very much for inviting me to this very important conference. My paper is called Let's go around again, the museum carousel and its others.

I sit down to write a conference paper on the above subject. I've written this paper before. Well, not exactly this one, but variations on the theme of how institutional cultural policy around decolonization and diversity in the UK museums sector regularly fall short of addressing its own structural racism, favoring instead the performance art of showcasing their latest flagship initiative. They are initiatives which speak to the issues Yes, often very convincingly, but they also deliberately and skillfully evade key questions, such as the positionality of its leaders, policymakers, or curators. The ways in which white supremacy lurks in its funding, outcomes, evaluation, project cycle model, or how the complexities and nuances of black subjectivity, creativity, agency and joy are sacrificed on the altar of neat deliverables, and social media friendly posts.

Aimed primarily at legitimizing the museum is as a force for social good, rather than dismantling power hierarchies. What should I do? Make these points again and update them for 2023 and the current decolonial term? This would be a valid way to approach this, but I'm uneasy and must address why being

---

* Roshi Naidoo, Decolonising Programme Officer, Museums Association UK.

told that this time is different, that the museum carousel at least understands the circular motion of the ways in which it addresses and engages with its others. But do they really understand. This is how I see the dance: When the funding runs out for the project perpetually situated at the edges of museum concerns, and they move on to the next issue. The kind folk could populate the museum wring their hands in frustration, agreeing that this cycle is terrible, and ask but how can we stop it? Museum folks are nice, we know that, they want to change we know that too. And nice people who want to change can't be part of the problem, can they? The activists, outside curators, consultants, academics, etc. say the following: Make changes at the core of museum work. Forensically consider what is being said in these projects and the theoretical ideas behind them. Learn about the cultural politics of race and representation and about intersectionality. Understand the breadth, depth and complexities of our colonial past and present. Consider your positionality and anxious responses when confronted with calls for power shifts, stop funding short term projects and fund structural change. Do your reaching out to communities work in tandem with considering how you recruit for actual paid jobs in the sector. Stop instrumentalizing our artists, historians, creatives etc for your own institutional self aggrandizement. That we may have no interest at all in reforming the museum and may go elsewhere in search of cultural, political and social liberation. It could go on and the list of recommendations reports and interventions spanning decades which attest to this are lying still in filing cabinets of many museums. So there is an answer. But when we furnish them with this, they become like the wise monkeys. And they speak over us to ask the question again, this time formulated within an intellectual and critical paradigm that fits the policies, processes and practices that they've always worked within. Now back in a comfort zone, they will suggest their own answer. We are met with a white noise of Babel and can just pick out the names of strategic reports and government policies, couched in excruciatingly dead sector speak, along with references to communities and phrases such as lived experience, delivered blandly and without context or understanding. The slogan is that museums must decolonize, however, the message also is, but the museum will tell you how to do it. We come back and try again. There's a huge body of work that can help here, we say. But it has to begin with you considering your fragility and the responses you bring to the table whenever we bring this stuff up. Maybe start with this youtube clip. It's only an hour long. But this is already too much and no one is listening.

Museums instead will do the same thing over and over again yet expect a different outcome. Or maybe the outcome they get is actually the desired one. I assume on this roundabout I'm also complicit in keeping it going. In this circuit then I know the role I must play as a wave of interest in all things decolonial and anti racist comes into being it means I can earn a living and someone might look at my apparently fractured CV and understand the thread of continuity that runs through it. I phrase things in sector friendly language, hold my tongue when asked what I think of Project, which is at best just barely acceptable, but at worst is peddling homogenized essentialist myths, grateful that at least as always, it is only a temporary exhibition and will be gone soon. I will accept that museums are on the beginning of a journey, and must be treated with patience and will therefore sit on the knowledge that endless white innocence is a historical trope, which is enacted to maintain power. I will appear unthreatening, to an extent, but not unthreatening enough to be offered a full time senior job in the museum to address the things that I've raised. The things that management has assured me it's so important to them and key to their strategic vision going forward. There is a game being played a set of rules and gambits to observe, and I, too, am part of the problem. As I started my own microcosm of these cyclical events, I know what will happen, I will be applauded and commended for my provocative, thought provoking paper, people will ask me afterwards to discuss things at the break, I will be invited onto an advisory board or to a confidential meeting with a high up somewhere, usually for no fee. Then we will hit a wall and I will go away again till the next time.

So in response to that, and as a small attempt to break the cycle, I'm not going to give a traditional paper of the sort I've always given. Instead, I'm going to present you with three small vignettes of what life working on the ground in the UK museum sector is like, and show how an understanding of what is happening in these interpersonal anxiety ridden multi layered moments may be more helpful than what I have presented to the sector in the past. I've merged and anonymized incidents, but each reflects a plethora of other identical moments. And all examples describe a climate that mitigates against change, despite claims to the contrary.

So, vignette one, the meeting decides that although they recognize that there was a lot of theoretical work in the field of decolonization, that what people in the sector really want is action and guidance on practice, help with the doing not so much of the thinking, self reflection, which is just holding things up. The inference they've never spelt out is that you are a bit too academic and out of touch with the on-the-ground museum folk, who are just keen to work with local communities to reinterpret their collection, change the racist label on an object and open up their doors to more people. Your suggestion with a bit of thinking before this process may be essential to the success of this venture has not gone down well. Besides, there isn't the time or the money. You've suddenly been labeled as over intellectual and weirdly positioned as too white-identified and middle class as a result, despite being a working class person of color, and therefore in opposition to the communities they're working with. They don't need a politics of nuance to be brought to bear on the knee jerk essentialism that accompanies their project. But to express oppositional thinking and awareness of how structures of power confine and define us, is part of the DNA of minoritized groups. And to dismiss this discussion as elitist academic or ivory tower in nature woefully misunderstands the intellectual traditions of resistance that we inhabit. Soon, the self same community is going to tell the museum that they're sick of being used as a resource, and will bring the same critical skills to bear on them to project the relationship breakdown resulting in the shedding of well meaning tears of regret, and bafflement about what went wrong. Rather than learn from this, though, do the reading with self reflection, they will repeat this mistake the next time. This is white supremacy at work, not as visible as a hateful comments on the website, true, but part of the same network of thinking that refuses to see people in all their complexity, and as having value and identity outside of racism structures, and totally unaware of the histories of agency and resistance that people of color inhabit.

Vignette Two: the museum consults the community about the gallery reinterpretation and makes changes based on this other people from what the museum understands as the same community points out that the new display is rubbish. No one in the museum has thought about what expertise was actually needed for the refit. And that not everyone who is a person of color will think the same thing or have the same response to the artifacts on display. There has been no respect paid to the expertise on colonial history, or the politics of representation. But we did really extensive consultation, they were taught, the subtext and the silence in the meeting is you can't please these people. This then becomes an issue of racial infighting, not an issue of white supremacy at work again.

Vignette Three: a senior museum person signed up to all the diversity decolonial and anti racist initiatives, confides that in the current museum climate, there is nothing that speaks to him as a straight white man. He also complains that ethnic minorities haven't applied for post so how can museums be berated for not recruiting more widely, it is a familiar moment in both your years in museum work and in life in general, you're being asked to actually reinforce this to shrug and agree that identity politics has gone too far. Or to telegraph your sympathy through silence. You have two moves here. One is to do just this and deal with, "why didn't I say" later. The other is to speak. The fiction in the sector is that these moments are difficult conversations can always be embarked on, they can't, and I really admire those who have the tenacity and or use their privileged position to do this. My experience of this moment is that once I say for example, kindly, usually, that:A. whiteness is an identity politics, albeit rendered invisible, and that you need to understand your anxieties or B. what else is decolonization about? If not about understanding the workings of straight white men or C. Why does other people expressing their agency in subjectivity oppress you? or D. Where is your sense of solidarity or even curiosity? A familiar pattern of attack, both in content and effect will ensue, No matter how nice the person in question is. Before I've got the first words out, and it becomes clear, I'm not agreeing, I'm spoken over immediately. I'm accused of misunderstanding. The hurts party is now the man who I have unfairly labeled as racist even though I have not by not understanding what was being said. A long list of mitigation engulfs me. And even though each confirms the view that white fragility is at play, I cannot speak again, and small, fractured parts of sentences emerge from my mouth and disappear into the air.

There is no listening, no desire to learn, no humility in these moments that so many, many of us deal, the psychic damage done to us is not an issue. And the fact that this is a scene that I've played over and over again, can't be discussed. This is not simply a recollection of one incident, but of many, and all from people who are not culture warriors or rabid fanatical right wingers attacking the museum's through concerted political campaigns. It comes from nice liberal kind people who would be welcoming to a black person in a museum and would bend over backwards to accommodate their needs or to discuss an issue of the provenance of an artifact with them. People who are keen to do decolonial work with the local community. But this mismatch of such people enacting decolonization work merely procedural, without doing the most important decolonization work, which happens between their ears, is one of the keys to unlocking this problem.

So, in conclusion, if my readings of the sector here have any validity, then there are various ways in which we can interpret these patterns. We can see this as evidence of the endurance of the bedrock contradictions of enlightenment ideology, which historically has always been able to hold together the notion of freedom for all while oppressing the majority, are we being managed as troubling others in ways which may both give voice to us but also seek to contain and limit those voices is the museum attempting to manage a fear of its own engulfment and loss of authority through hysterical reactions to the fact that we are not coming for inclusion, but for power, and museums hiding behind institutional speak as a means of avoiding that messy emotional labor that comes with genuine decolonial work which confronts those deep circuits of economic, social, political and cultural power and white authority in particular.

Recently, I went see the procession at Tate Britain in London, a piece of work by the sculptor and contemporary artists Hew Locke, the spectacular, vibrant, colorful, detailed, thought provoking large scale installation set between the classical pillars of the galleries foyer, echoed with the centuries of labor, misery and resistance that lives in that structure, and in the built environment of our colonial cities. Perhaps this is just a thread that can't be pulled on.

Thank you very much and we look forward to hearing your questions.

让我们再绕一圈吧：
博物馆的旋转木马与它的"其他部分"

罗希·奈杜 [*]

大家好，感谢主办方邀请我参加这次重要的会议，我的文章题目是《让我们再绕一圈吧：博物馆的旋转木马与它的"其他部分"》。

当我坐下来准备这次会议的文章时，我发现我之前写过，当然并不是这一篇，而是写过很多与这次主题相关的文章，这些文章都讨论了英国文化政策在博物馆的去殖民化和多样性的问题上的失败，在制度层面无法解决自身结构性种族歧视的问题，并且转而沦为鼓吹其标志性项目的一场表演。这些项目确实在应对相关的问题，而且往往也令人信服，但它们也有意地、富有技巧地回避了关键的问题，例如领导者、政策制定者和策展人的立场，在经费支持、产出、评估、项目周期模型中潜藏的白人至上主义问题，或者是种族问题的复杂性与实质问题，以及黑人的主体性、创造力、能动性、愉悦感，如何让位给了制作简洁直白的内容以及便于社交网络传播的帖子的需求。

这样的结果主要的作用是合理化博物馆的存在，将其描述为服务于社会公共利益的机构，而不会去挑战权力结构。我该做什么呢？是再次重申自己的观点，更新成2023版，加一些去殖民化热点词汇吗？这样当然也是非常合理的解释该主题的方式，但我对此感到不安，也希望能说明我的原因。我被告知这次将会是不一样的，博物馆里的旋转木马至少从与同类的观察接触中知道自己在绕圈。但他们真的理解吗？以下是我所观察到的过程：当这些永远存在于博物馆边缘的项目耗尽经费，移向下一个问

---

[*] 罗希·奈杜，英国博物馆协会去殖民化项目主管。

题时，博物馆人总是怀着善意、沮丧地抱着双手，并赞同地说"这种循环太糟糕了"，并且询问"那我们要怎样才能打破这种循环呢？"我们都知道，博物馆人是充满善意的。我们也知道，博物馆人希望能改进。充满善意的、希望改进的人不可能是问题的一部分，不是吗？活动家、馆外策展人、咨询师、学者等等，都会说出以下言论：将变革置于博物馆工作的核心，以循证的方式吸纳这个项目中的理念和理论，了解种族问题中的文化政治、代表性问题，以及交叉性概念，理解历史上和当下的殖民主义问题的宽度、深度和复杂程度，反思自身的立场以及遇到呼吁权力变革时充满焦虑的回应，停止资助短期项目并改为资助结构性的变革，做好社区外展工作并认真考虑行业内带薪全职工作的雇佣方式，停止将艺术家、历史学家、创作者作为获取机构夸耀的工具人。有些人认为他们对于博物馆变革毫无兴趣，而去别处追求文化、政治、社会解放。还有无数诸如此类的观点，而见证了这些观点的过去几十年以来的建议书、报告、干预项目都静静地躺在博物馆的档案柜里。所以答案是存在的，但当我们将答案置于循环中，人们就成了复读机，提问的声音盖过了回答，并将提问置于一直沿用的符合政策、流程、实践的学术和批判范式中，而回到了舒适区后，他们也自然而然有了自己的答案。我们会遇到引经据典的白噪音，并且他们都有关于"战略报告""政府政策"的关键词。伴随着死气沉沉的业内术语，提及社区参与和生命体验等术语，但这些单调的引用总是缺乏语境或理解。我们的口号是"博物馆必须去殖民化"，但潜台词是"博物馆会告诉你怎么做"。然后我们又回到了开端，但这次的起点是反思自身的脆弱性，以及每次我们提起这个主题时你能带来的回应。或许你可以先看看这个视频，只有一小时长，但这已经太长了，没人在听。

博物馆总是一次又一次做着相同的事情，但却期待着不一样的结果，又或许这样的结果本就是博物馆所希望获得的。我想在这个循环中我本人也是共谋者，我知道这场循环中我要扮演的角色。随着所有与去殖民化和反种族歧视相关的话题又迎来一波高涨的兴趣，这意味着我又可以重拾营生，又有人或许会来浏览我看起来断断续续的履历，然后在履历中找到一丝贯穿性。我可以熟练地将内容转化为业内熟悉的语言，并在别人问我对于项目的看法时知道适时地沉默。这些项目在最好的情况下只能说是可以接受，而最糟糕的就是助长同质化的本质主义思想，同时暗自庆幸，至少这只是一场临展，马上就结束了。我可以接受博物馆还在旅途的开端，而且我们必须耐心地对待此事，并且闭口不谈永无止境的"白人无辜"的历史形象是用来维持其权力的手段。在一定程度上，我会表现得没有威胁性，但威胁程度并没有低到能够获得一份博物馆全职的管理层的职位来解决我提出的问题。尽管博物馆的管理层向我保证这些问题是非常重要的，是他们实现战略愿景的关键。这是一场博弈，而从中就能看到规则和技巧，并且我也构成了问题的一部分。随着我总结了这些循环的缩影，我可以预见事情的发展。人们会称赞我充满挑战性、引人深思的论文，会在会议间隙来提问和讨论。我会被邀请参加某个咨询会或是某些高层人士的闭门会议。这些通常都是无薪的职务。然后我们会遇到某个困难，然后我就退出，直到下一波兴趣的到来。

因此，作为一个打破这种循环的小小尝试，我在今天的演讲中不会作和以往相似的论文，我会改为讲述在英国博物馆界工作时的三场小插曲，并希望展示这些人际间充满焦虑的、多层次的现实场景，可能会比我过去向业界展现的成果更有帮助。我融合了一些事件并且让人物保持匿名状态，但每个插曲都对应着一系列相似的场景，而所有的案例都在描绘一种阻碍变革的环境，尽管人们总是宣称支持变革。

插曲一：会议决定，尽管他们意识到在去殖民化的领域有许多理论工作，但业内人士真正需要的是行动和指导实践，多帮助实践而不是只会耽误事情的思考或反思，这背后他们从不明说的潜台词是，"你太过学术了，不够接地气，无法触及实践中的博物馆人"，而他们只是迫切希望能够和本土社区一起重新阐释他们的藏品，改一改文物上种族歧视的标签，并且迎来更多观众。你关于开展工作前多思考的建议或许对于项目确实很重要，但开展起来都是困难重重的，而且我们也没有做这些的时间或者经费。于是你突然就被贴上了过于学院派、站位过于接近白人中产精英的标签。尽管你是一个工薪阶层的有色人种，却因此被置于他们希望开展合作的社区的对立面。他们项目的完成只需要膝跳反应般的本质主义，而不需要富有复杂内涵的权力关系分析。但是，对抗性思考的表达和对于权力结构如何限制或定义我们的意识，这本身就是边缘群体DNA中的一部分。而将这些讨论视为象牙塔里的精英主义学院派并不予重视，恶意地误解了少数群体本就继承着的抗争性学术传统。然后，同一社区会告诉博物馆他们不再愿意做博物馆的资源，并对项目进行相同的批判，造成关系的破裂，继而带来了悔恨和带着善意的泪水，以及对于到底哪里做错了的疑问，但他们并不会从中学到需要带着反思去阅读文献，他们还会重复上一次的错误。这便是白人至上主义的运行机制，这可能并不如网站上的仇恨言论般显而易见。但两者都属于同一种拒绝看见他者复杂性的思考模式。这种思考模式也无法看到种族歧视结构以外的价值和身份，也完全无法意识到有色人种所拥有的具备能动性和反抗性的历史传统。

插曲二：博物馆向社群咨询了对艺术品的重新阐释并做出了相应的改变。博物馆认为来自同一个社群的其他人指出，这个展览太糟糕了。博物馆的工作人员中没有人认真地思考过到底什么样的专业知识才能满足重新调整的需求，也没人意识到，有色人种中并不是每个人都有一样的想法或者对展览和文物会有一样的反应。展览并没能尊重殖民主义历史的专业性或是代表性中的权力结构。他们会说："但我们做了充分的咨询啊。"会议室中的沉默和这话的潜台词是"你永远无法令这些人感到满意"。于是问题就变成了种族内部斗争，不再是白人至上主义的问题了。

插曲三：一位博物馆高层人士报名参加了所有的多样性、反种族歧视、去殖民化项目，然后私下吐露：在当下的博物馆环境中，他感觉没有什么事和他这位正直的白人男子有关系了。他还会抱怨为什么没有少数族裔来应聘他博物馆的岗位，所以人们怎么可以指责他的博物馆招聘范围不够广呢。这个场景在你的博物馆职业生涯和人生中都似曾相识。他实际是在要求你强化他的观点，耸耸肩并且赞同地说"是啊，种族政治太过分了"，或者用沉默来表达你的同情。你有两个选项。一是选择沉默，然后事后再去消化"我应该说些什么"的情绪；另一个选项是发声。业内对于这一场景的叙事是，这是开启困难对话的时刻。但这并不能开启对话，而我也尊敬那些有毅力或能够利用自身优势去开启对话的人。我在这种场景中的体验是，一旦我开口，友善地说出以下几种回应：A. 虽然白人身份常常在讨论中隐身，但也是种族政治的一部分，你需要自己消化你的焦虑情绪；B. 去殖民化关注的居然还能是理解白人男子思维方式以外的东西吗？C. 为什么别人表达自己的主体性，发挥能动性就构成了对你的压迫呢？D. 你的团结意识和好奇心去哪了？随之而来的便是一系列熟悉的攻击，既在内容层面也在目标效果层面，无论被攻击者是多么的友善。即使在我还没能说出几个词，但能看出来我并不赞同他的观点。他就会抢先发言，指责我误解了他的意思。于是受害人就变成了被无端地错误地视为种族主义者的白人男性，即使我并没有这么说。但因为误解了他说的话，我就陷入了一连串的需要缓和关系的举动中。即使每个瞬间都验证了白人脆弱性的存在，我也无话可说了，只有一些零星的破碎的语句从我唇中挤出，消失在空气中。

这些场景中没有倾听，没有学习的欲望，没有谦虚，而我们中许多人都要反复地面对这些场景。这些对我们造成的精神损伤不值一提，而这些场景在我脑中反复播放，却无法被讨论。这不是对某次事件的回忆，而是有太多这样的场景了。所有的参与者都并不是要处心积虑攻击博物馆的文化战争斗士或者狂热的右翼分子，而是来自抱着善意的、彬彬有礼的，非常欢迎黑人来到博物馆中的自由主义者。他们会不遗余力地满足少数族裔的需求，或与他们讨论文物的来源问题。他们是愿意和本土社区一起开展去殖民化工作的，但这之间的差距就在于这些人只希望做程序性的去殖民化工作，而不愿意做发生在头脑中的最重要的去殖民化工作，而这是解决问题的关键。

因此，总而言之，如果我对业界的描述有任何部分能够成立，那我们有许多种阐释这些规律的方式。我们可以从中看出启蒙主义理念中持久的基础性的矛盾之处。这些理念在历史上一边高举着"人人自由"的大旗，一边又压迫着大部分的人。我们是否处在一种作为扰乱者的他者的处境，这赋予了我们发声的机会，但同时又限制和束缚了我们的声音。博物馆是否在尝试控制自身对于被吞噬和失去权威的恐惧。因而在面对我们并没有在实现包容性这一事实时出现歇斯底里的反应，而博物馆躲在专业术语之后，来逃避复杂混乱的情绪工作。但这样的情绪工作是真诚的去殖民化事业中必然出现的，因为需要对抗那么多根植的经济、社会、政治和文化权力，尤其是其中的白人权威。

最近，我去了伦敦的泰特美术馆，看到了当代雕塑家、艺术家休·洛克（Hew Locke）的一件作品。这件宏伟的、充满活力的、多彩的、富有细节、引人深思的大型装置艺术，位于美术馆大厅的古典主义支柱之间、在其结构中回响着几个世纪以来的劳动、悲剧与抗争，被放置于这一殖民城市的环境中，或许这团乱麻并无线头可寻。

非常感谢，我期待听到你们的提问。

Asia's Difficult Heritage-making between Nationalism and Transnationalism: Colonial Prisons in South Korea, China and Taiwan, China

Hyun Kyung Lee*

    Hello everyone! I am Hyun Kyung Lee, and work as an Assistant Professor at Critical Global Studies Institute at Sogang University in Seoul, South Korea.

    I am so honoured and pleased to participate in the ICOM-IMREC Decolonialisation Expert Seminar "Museums, Decolonialisation, Restitution: A Global Conversation". In particular, I would like to express my great gratitude to Dr. Carol Scott for her generosity and warm support as well as Dr. Inkyung Chang who recommended me to this meaningful event, and is going to give me comments as a discussant. Today, I would like to give you my paper "Asia's Difficult Heritage-making between nationalism and transnationalism with the three-colonial prison-turned-museums in China, South Korea, and Taiwan, China".

    I have been working on Asia's difficult heritage for the last ten years, and published two monographs *Difficult Heritage in Nation Building* by focusing on Japanese colonial architectural heritage in South Korea, and *Heritage, Memory, and Punishment* with the case of colonial prisons in East Asia. As an editor and chapter contributor, I participated in the book project, and the edited volume "Frontiers of Memory in the Asia-Pacific: Difficult Heritage

---

* Hyun Kyung Lee, Assistant Professor, Critical Global Studies Institute, Sogang University South Korea.

and the Transnational Politics of Post-colonial Nationalism" published in 2022. By discussing whether Asia's difficult heritage is either a troublemaker or peacemaker, I have examined colonial heritage and Cold War heritage in East Asia, difficult heritage interpretation and peace-building processes at UNESCO, and transnational difficult heritage networking in Asia.

Then, what is difficult heritage?

Difficult heritage can be understood in two different contexts: first: places associated with traumatic historic events and second, places have diverse perspectives and interpretations due to traumatic historic events, and they lead to political dissonance and memory conflicts that affect the formation of identity. Such as the Auschwitz Concentration Camp in Poland and The Hiroshima Atomic Bomb Dome in Japan.

Asia's difficult heritage has been dealt with in the context of nationalism. However, I relocate difficult heritage in between nationalism and transnationalism, reflecting my second book project. I have chosen colonial prisons in Asia as difficult heritage. I would like to perceive colonial prisons as modern prisons in the context of world penal history, colonial products in the context of colonialism, and difficult heritage in the context of post-colonial heritage management. Therefore, I have taken three cases from the colonial prisons in Asia: Lushun Russo-Japanese Prison in China, Seodaemun Prison in South Korea, and Chiayi Old Prison in Taiwan, China. Three of them were constructed by Japanese imperial authorities. First, I will examine the birth of three colonial prisons during the colonial period. Next, I will investigate how the difficult past has been heritagised in three different places. Then, on the basis of different perceptions on the Japanese colonial period, I will analyse how three colonial prisons have transformed into three museums during the post-colonial period. Hence, this is a transnational comparative study of de-commissioned, post-colonial prisons in Seoul, Lushun, Chiayi in order to understand the role of difficult heritage between nationalism and transnationalism.

Shall we start with three questions in order to understand why East Asia's colonial prisons are both modern and colonial products and how western penal reforms were linked to East Asia's colonial prisons? First, by examining the Western penal reform in the 18th Century, we consider how the changing thinking of punishment embodied in the architectural style and structure of modern prisons? Second, what did Meiji Japan learn from the Western penal system and practices during Meiji Japan's penal reform in the late 19th Century? Third, how were Japan's learnings employed in East Asia's colonial prison's design and structure during the early 20th Century? The Western penal reform brought about sensational changes of punishment that consequently affected the concept of the prison. Before the penal reform, people were punished through torture that means inflicting pain was the main focus. Hence, the prison functioned as a short detention that was simply to hold inmates securely.

But after the penal reform, the definition of punishment was changed to deprivation of the liberty of movement for education. The one penal reformer group, penal reformer John Howard and the quakers argued that education was needed in order to reconcile the broken relationship with God as they believed that human beings' wrongdoing stemmed from the broken relationship with God. In order to help people strengthen the one-to-one relationship with God, solitary confinement was emphasised and the Pennsylvania system was adopted. The other penal reformer group Cesare Beccaria and Jeremy Benthan argued that education was needed in order to reach restorative justice for the society. By emphasising the discipline, labour in silence was considered to be the most important punishment and it was adopted to the Auburn system in New York. Both groups agreed to facilitate easier surveillance and a programme of correction. Considering all the values of the punishment, Jeremy Bentham created the Panopticon structure that can be applied to prison, factory, and mental hospital. As you can see the image in the middle of the slide, one warden is able to watch over many inmates (more than ten). Hence, the Panopticon provided an efficient management system.

After Japan joined the imperialism as a late comer, Meiji Japan made an effort to create Imperial Japan's penal reform system that could be employed to both the nation and its colonies. Meiji Japan sent Japanese scholars to the British colonies of Hong Kong (China) and Singapore, and to Europe, and they learned about modern prison's system, architectural designs. Ohara Shige Kana and Yamashita Keijiro are two main figures in Meiji Japan's penal reform. You can see some examples that Meiji penal reforms were applied to Japanese modern prisons, such as Nara Prison in Japan (radial structure that would be a variation of panopticon structure and red bricks) Kanazawa Prison in Japan (red brick and radial structure like Nara case). Then how about Japanese colonial prisons? They were similar in structure and designs to Nara and Kanazawa prisons combining Pennsylvania system (solitary confinement), Auburn system (labour), and Pentonville structure (panopticon). The Japanese colonial prison aimed to not only "correct" colonial prisoners into obedient and dutiful subjects to an imperial community, but also exhibit and project a positive image of imperial Japan to Western countries in order to prove how Japan's colonial rule was civilised.

Let me walk you through each case. The first case is Seodaemun Prison in Seoul. Seodaemun Prison was constructed in 1907 and opened in 1908, and used as a colonial prison until liberation from Japan in 1945. It is known that many Korean independent activists were imprisoned. After liberation, it was still reused as a prison during the post-colonial period. Many political prisoners related to the democracy movement were imprisoned in this prison. When this was moved to Uiwang city in 1987 due to its deterioration, this site was converted into Seodaemun Prison history hall and independence park to commemorate Korean independence activists.

The second case is the Lushun Russo-Japanese Prison. The Lushun Russo-Japanese Prison witnessed how the Sino-Japanese War and the Russo-Japanese

War contributed to the colonisation of Dalian-Lushun, and by extension to the colonisation of Korea, in the first half of the twentieth century. Lushun Prison was built and managed by Russian authorities between 1902 and 1906, and after the defeat of the Russian Empire in 1905, Japan took control over Lushun and the Japanese colonial administration started to use the Lushun Prison and renamed it as "Prison Agency, Kanto Administration". Could you please see the photo at the lower left hand side of the slide? The white buildings were the parts constructed by the Russian authorities and the red buildings were the parts built by the Japanese authorities. From 1945 to 1955, this area was occupied by the Ryojun Naval Base and this prison site was used as housing from 1955 to 1970. Due to the 1969 Zhenbao Island Incident, the Chinese Communist Party decided to use the defunct prison as evidence of war crimes and as material propaganda to mobilise and organise both anti-Russian and anti-Japanese sentiment. After the restoration process during 1970 and 1971, from 1971 this prison site was used as the Lushun Russo-Japanese Prison Museum.

The third case is the Chiayi Prison in Chiayi. The Chiayi Prison was constructed in 1919, and it was used as a colonial prison in 1945. It was reused as a prison from 1945 to 1994, and subsequently used as the staff housing from 1994 to 2005. As you can see the photo in the middle of the slide, Chiayi is famous for the Alishan Mountain, and the Alishan Railway. In particular, Alishan Railway that was constructed by the Japanese authorities has been considered to be a proud industrial heritage in Taiwan, and it is one of the most important tourist attractions. Considering such tourism, this museum was preserved and reopened as a museum of penal affairs managed by the Ministry of Justice from 2005. This museum does not particularly narrate colonial history, but provides a general story of penal affairs that are different from Seodaemun Prison and Lushun Prison.

The current use and interpretation of three colonial prisons are closely depending on how each place perceives the Japanese imperial period after the end of the Second World War, and how each of them builds up their current international relationship with Japan. As both South Korea and China mainly build up the anti-Japanese colonialism in their official narratives, both museums narrate to strengthen the official narratives. For example, Seodaemun Prison and Lushun Prison carried out a transnational UNESCO World Heritage Nomination Project from 2015 to 2017 by sharing the stories of An Jung-Geun who was the Korean independence activist and was imprisoned in Lushun Prison. However, the changing political climate between Japan, South Korea, China, and US—such as issues surrounding the TAHHD (Terminal High Altitude Area Defence) anti-ballistic missile defence system—ultimately led to the breakdown of collaboration between South Korea and China. This shows the international relationship deeply affected such transnational heritage-making processes. The former Chiayi Prison is also used for the educational purposes, to help students understand penal system and the law, but is not closely tied up with the other two cases. China Taiwan's position on their colonial history is ambiguous in relation to the wide spectrum of pro-Japanese and anti-Japanese sentiments, and the Taiwan (China) case is not used to generate patriotic anti-Japanese sentiments. This shows that while Asia definitely shares certain colonial experiences and material cultures, each Asian region has its own distinctive perspectives and responses to their colonial legacies.

As seen in three cases, if we examine the colonial prisons by focusing on only colonial pasts, each prison history can be trapped into the rigid political frame of nationalism. In order to overcome this, it is also important to understand them in the transnational context. We tend to comprehend them as educational materials, but we need to relocate them in the shared material culture as modern and colonial products.

Such difficult heritage sites are easily politicised and diplomatised, and these prisons-turned-museum sites are abused to preach for each nation's political purposes. In order to achieve a genuinely shared memory, rather than a common memory made up of assorted aggregates, communication is essential for opening up the process of remembering to a multitude of voices, instead of indoctrination. By pointing to the transnational shared nature of these penal heritage museums, we hope that penal heritage, as heritage shared across borders, can be constantly revisited and remade, in ways that open up communication about human pain and difficult memories, in the service of conciliation rather than rivalry.

That is all that I have prepared. Any comments and feedback are more than welcome. In addition, I would love to learn more about global perspectives on museums, decolonialisation, and restitution from all of you. Thank you.

在民族主义和跨国主义之间产生的亚洲黑暗遗产：以中国、韩国和中国台湾地区的三个殖民地监狱改造而成的博物馆为例

李玄卿 *

大家好！我是李玄卿，是韩国首尔西江大学全球批判性研究院的助理教授。

非常荣幸和开心能够参加本次国际博物馆协会研究与交流中心组织的"博物馆、去殖民化、文物返还：全球对话"专家研讨会。我要特别感谢卡罗尔·斯科特博士给予我慷慨且热情的支持，感谢张仁卿博士推荐我参加这个有意义的活动并在讨论中给了我很多建议。今天，我想要和大家分享我的一篇文章：《在民族主义和跨国主义之间产生的亚洲黑暗遗产：以中国、韩国和中国台湾地区的三个殖民监狱改造而成的博物馆为例》。

在过去的十年里，我一直从事亚洲黑暗遗产的研究并出版了两本专著，其中《国家建设中的黑暗遗产》一书关注的是韩国日据时期的建筑遗产，《遗产、记忆与惩罚》一书则以东亚的殖民监狱为案例开展研究。此外，我参与了2022年出版的《亚太记忆的边界：黑暗遗产与后殖民民族主义的跨国政治》一书的编辑和章节撰稿。为了探究亚洲的黑暗遗产所担任的角色是一个麻烦制造者，还是和平创造者，我研究了东亚的殖民遗产和冷战遗产、联合国教科文组织的黑暗遗产阐释与和平建设进程，以及亚洲的跨国黑暗遗产网络。

那么，什么是黑暗遗产？

在两种不同的背景下，黑暗遗产有着不同的解释：第一种解释是与创

---

* 李玄卿，韩国西江大学全球批判性研究院助理教授。

伤性历史事件相关的地方；第二种解释是某一地点在创伤性历史事件的影响下产生了不同的观点和解释，这些差异导致了影响身份形成的政治矛盾与记忆冲突。例如，位于波兰的奥斯威辛集中营和日本广岛的原爆圆顶塔。

亚洲的黑暗遗产一直以来都与民族主义相关联，而在我的第二本书中，我将黑暗遗产置于民族主义和跨国主义之间。我选择了亚洲的几个殖民监狱作为黑暗遗产的案例进行研究，在文中，我既将殖民地监狱视为世界刑罚史背景下的现代监狱，也将其视为后殖民时期遗产管理背景下的黑暗遗产。因此，我选择了日本帝国主义在其殖民地建造的三个监狱作为案例，它们分别是：旅顺日俄监狱（中国大陆）、西大门刑务所（韩国首尔）和嘉义旧监狱（中国台湾地区）。首先，我将讨论这三个殖民监狱的诞生以及这些"艰难的过去"是如何被遗产化的。接下来，基于对日本殖民时代的不同看法，我将分析这些殖民监狱在后殖民时代是如何转变为博物馆的。本研究以位于首尔、旅顺和嘉义的三个已于后殖民时代被撤销的殖民监狱为对象，通过它们之间的比较研究以了解黑暗遗产在民族主义和跨国主义之间的角色。

为了了解东亚的殖民地监狱为什么被视为现代社会和殖民时期的产物，以及西方的刑罚改革是如何与东亚的殖民地监狱相关联的，我们可以从以下三个问题着手：首先，在18世纪西方刑罚改革中，现代监狱的建筑风格和结构如何体现不断变化的刑罚思想？其次，在19世纪末日本明治时期刑罚改革中，日本从西方的刑罚制度和实践中习得了什么？最后，20世纪初，东亚殖民地监狱的设计和建造是如何借鉴日本经验的？西方的刑罚改革引发了惩罚手段的急遽变化，继而影响了监狱的概念。刑罚改革之前，人们以对肉体施加痛苦的酷刑作为惩罚方式，因此监狱的功能只是为犯人的短暂关押提供保障。

然而在刑罚改革之后，惩罚的定义被转变为以教育为目的剥夺行动自由。以约翰·霍华德（John Howard）为代表的贵格会认为，人类的错误行为源于其自身与上帝的关系发生破裂，因此需要通过教育以调和这种关系。为了帮助人们加强与上帝间一对一的关系，他们提出了"单独监禁"这一形式，并被宾夕法尼亚监狱系统所采用。以切萨雷·贝卡里亚（Cesare Beccaria）和杰里米·边沁（Jeremy Benthan）为代表的另一个刑罚改革团体则认为，教育是为了实现社会正义的恢复性司法。他们强调纪律，认为劳役是最有用的惩罚方式。这一观点被纽约的奥本监狱系统采用。这两个刑法改革团体都认为应该优化监督和刑罚方式。考虑到惩罚手段的重要性，杰里米·边沁提出了一套适用于监狱、工厂和精神病院的全景敞视机制。在这种机制下，一位典狱长可以同时看管10个以上的犯人。因此，全景敞视成了一个高效的管理方式。

日本成为帝国主义中的后发国家后，致力于建立适用于本国及其殖民地的刑罚改革制度。因此，明治时期，日本向当时作为英国殖民地的中国香港地区和新加坡以及欧洲派去了学者，以学习其现代的监狱制度和建筑设计。大原加奈森和山下启次郎是日本明治时期推动刑罚改革的两位代表人物。你可以看到一些关于日本明治时期刑罚改革下的现代监狱案例，比如奈良监狱的建筑设计采用了红砖建造的放射状结构，这种结构由全景敞视结构变化而来。金泽监狱的结构也与奈良监狱类似。那么，日本殖民地的监狱是怎样的？它们在结构和设计上与奈良监狱和金泽监狱相似，结合了宾夕法尼亚监狱制度中的单独监禁、奥本监狱制度中的劳役要求，以及本顿维尔监狱中的全景敞视结构。日本殖民地监狱的目的不仅仅是为了将殖民地囚犯"纠正"为对日本帝国主义归顺和服从的臣民，同时也要向西方列国彰显和投射日本帝国的殖民统治是多么的文明。

让我们来分别看一下这些案例。第一个案例是位于韩国首尔的西大门刑务所。西大门刑务所建造于1907年并于次年作为殖民监狱启用，直到1945年朝鲜告别了日本的殖民主义统治后，作为殖民监狱停止使用。据悉，许多独立活动人士在朝鲜解放后被监禁，因此西大门刑务所在后殖民时期仍被作为监狱重新启用，并且关押了许多与民主运动有关的政治犯。1987年，由于该地的环境恶化，监狱搬迁至义王市，而原建筑为了纪念韩国独立运动家而被改造为西大门刑务所历史馆。

第二个案例是位于中国辽宁省的旅顺日俄监狱。旅顺日俄监狱见证了20世纪上半叶经甲午战争和日俄战争后导致大连、旅顺殖民化的过程，以及对韩国殖民化的影响。旅顺日俄监狱在1902年至1906年由俄国当局建造和管理。1905年俄国战败后，日本控制了旅顺地区，日本殖民当局开始使用该监狱，并将其更名为"关东都督府监狱本属"。其中，白色建筑是俄当局建造的部分，红色建筑则是日本当局建造的部分。1945年至1955年，这一区域被用作旅顺港海军基地。1955年至1970年，该监狱旧址被用作住房。在1969年珍宝岛事件的影响下，这座已经废弃的监狱成为日俄两国入侵罪行的证据。经过两年的修复，旅顺日俄监狱旧址被作为旅顺日俄监狱博物馆开始使用。

第三个案例是位于中国台湾地区的嘉义监狱。嘉义监狱建造于1919年，至1945年间都被作为殖民地监狱使用。1945年至1994年，嘉义监狱被重新启用，随后在1994年至2005年被用作员工宿舍。嘉义因阿里山和阿里山铁路而闻名，特别是由日本当局兴建的阿里山铁路一直被认为是中国台湾地区引以为荣的工业遗产。考虑到当地的旅游业，嘉义监狱被保留下来并作为司法部管理的狱政博物馆，于2005年重新开放。与西大门刑务所和旅顺日俄监狱不同的是，嘉义监狱并没有特别强调中国台湾地区在历史上曾被当作殖民地的故事。

现如今，这三座殖民地监狱的使用和阐释都与二战后当地如何看待日本帝国主义时期，以及当地与日本建立的国际关系密切相关。韩国和中国大陆在其官方叙事中都进行了反对日本殖民主义的建构，因此两个案例中的博物馆叙事都加强了官方话语。例如，西大门刑务所和旅顺日俄监狱于2015年至2017年间开展了联合国教科文组织世界遗产名录的跨国联合申报，描述了韩国独立活动家安重根被囚禁在旅顺俄日监狱的故事。然而，日本、韩国、中国和美国之间不断变化的政治局势——例如围绕萨德反导弹系统（THAAD）产生的一系列问题，最终导致了该项目合作的破裂。这也表明，国际关系深刻影响着跨国的遗产化进程。嘉义监狱旧址也被用作教育目的，以帮助学生了解刑法制度和法律。但与其他两个案例不同的是，中国台湾地区对于其殖民历史的立场在"亲日"与"反日"之间模糊不清，因此该监狱并没有用于建构反日的爱国情绪。这一案例表明，虽然亚洲地区共享着某些殖民地经历与物质文化，但对其殖民遗产都有着自己独特的观点和反应。

从这三个案例中可以看出，如果我们只关注过去的殖民经历以研究殖民监狱，这些监狱的历史就会被纳入民族主义框架。因此，为了避免这一点，在跨国背景下理解这些监狱就变得非常重要。虽然我们关注这些黑暗遗产可以作为教育的素材，但同时我们也需要将其视为殖民地的产物，是共同物质文化记忆的一部分。

黑暗遗产有时候会成为具有外交含义的话题，相应地，由殖民监狱遗址改造而成的博物馆也有可能受到这种形势变化的影响。为了保留全面的群体记忆，向大众开放记忆过程的关键是交流。通过分析这些监狱遗址博物馆的特点，我们希望能够讨论它们作为跨国遗产可以不断地被重新审视和重塑，从而打开人类之间关于痛苦和灾难记忆的交流，以便调解相互的关系而非增加敌视。

以上就是我的全部内容，欢迎各位提出任何意见和反馈。我很愿意向大家学习更多在全球视角下，关于博物馆、去殖民化和文物返还的内容。谢谢大家。

Justice, Re-orientation and Empowering African Source Communities by Decolonising Museum Spaces

Samba Yonga[*]

The history of knowledge production in Zambia and many parts of Africa has been impacted by the colonial experience that has disrupted, dislocated and de-contextualised indigenous knowledge systems and artefacts (Lajul). As is well known, part of this happened through separating artefacts from their source communities, thereby rendering misrepresented meanings which have caused generations of memory loss and knowledge asymmetries that till present-day have not been adequately addressed. These inaccurate rendered meanings continue to be the source of knowledge for museums and knowledge institutions with little consideration for the communities of origin in Africa (Arowosegbe).

In the past few years, Western ethnographic museums and institutions of knowledge have centred conversations around their problematic collections of indigenous artefacts and knowledge from source communities in Africa, in an attempt to correct the asymmetries created as a result of the dislocation and de-contextualisation.

Great as this effort has been there remains a reduced engagement and lack of acknowledgement of the source communities and how they can contribute to the process of reorientation of museums and institutions of knowledge

---

[*] Samba Yonga, Co founder of Women's History Museum of Zambia.

(Moiloa).

The colonial legacy, largely responsible for the dislocation of artefacts and indigenous knowledge systems, did not only de-contextualise artefacts when they removed them from their place of origin but also impacted the source communities and left them to deal with the grief, loss and gradual invalidation of their knowledge. This is a common phenomenon in the Global South (Hernandez). As part of the continuous quest for respectful forms of practice of museums and knowledge production (Castro) this presentation interrogates how this can be done to ensure an equitable and inclusive process.

Generations of this separation has now manifested into source communities that have not only lost the value of their knowledge but also lost the agency to communicate that they are valid knowledge producers and keepers. In many cases, they have also lost the ability to produce this knowledge.

Museums have served as identity formation institutions that have largely legitimised Eurocentric cultural hierarchical systems (Castro). The by-product of this in Africa or Zambia, where I am from, has led to de-legitimised and invalidated indigenous knowledge systems in source communities that are not necessarily given a voice.

I would like to share examples that show the impact of artefact dislocation on a source community. I want to start with the story of an artefact in a museum.

This artefact is currently in the National Museums of World Cultures In Stockholm, Sweden, and in its current state is producing knowledge without the connection of the source.

This separation means there is a lack of representation and cultural context that the artefact does not contain when exhibited outside its original source community. This situation has perpetuated what Dr. Inés de Castro refers to as stereotypes and fixed attributions that may not be accurate in relation to the artefacts and continue to be validated as knowledge (Castro).

The impact of this separation has caused a disruption of narratives, arrested development of knowledge production of source communities, distorted knowledge production by non-indigenous scholars and a manifestation of splintered communities and populations in the communities of origin.

The initial phenomenon to consider is the separation of artefacts and knowledge from the community and how in real terms contact with Western epistemologies has had an impact on the lives of source communities or communities of origin.

The case of the Luvale costume

The Likumbi Lya Mize is a rich traditional ceremony of the Luvale, Cokwe and Lucazi people in the north-western part of Zambia and parts of Congo and Angola where male initiates graduate from their coming-of-age ceremony. One of the most significant parts is the procession of the Makishi, a majestic parade of masked figures who are the embodiment of ancestors that appear during the very important coming-of-age ritual and ceremony of initiate boys called *Mukanda* (Wele). The ancestors come to life through the Makishi and bring their knowledge from the past to the present and give these teachings to the initiates as a rite of passage.

The Makishis many lessons and rituals teach the boys values and life skills that relate to life skills and being a good and responsible person in society; how to look after a homestead, being in harmony with nature, how to extract wealth from nature with care, how to care and till the land, how to be responsible leaders in their communities. If we examine some of the teachings closely, today they could be likened to environmental conservation, responsible mineral extraction, organic food production, nutrition, responsible agriculture, technology of blacksmithing and even meditation and mindfulness.

And yet, 100 years ago when this knowledge was removed and systematically oppressed within the communities, without care or a sense of responsibility, this community was denied the opportunity to produce and validate knowledge systems that today are valued practices across the world.

In the National Museum of World Cultures in Stockholm, this costume of the Makishi had none of that context and nuance I just shared. When the masked costume and its elements were removed from the community and brought into the museum it was separated from the knowledge and made invalid both for the community and for the museum. The significance and actual knowledge transmission gets lost in a void that is unable to be unlocked because there is no direct reference to the source communities that holds this knowledge.

For over 100 years this has been happening repeatedly in the museum space. Making the value of the object for both the museum and the community almost irrelevant except for the fact that it is an object of curiosity.

These distortions also impact how the narratives and how they end up being disseminated and recorded as knowledge. This disadvantages those who are not in the position to manage this process of producing this knowledge.

The arrested development of knowledge production of source communities brings the question of who manages the production of knowledge in our own countries and how this situation has impacted the status quo. The Universities, Museums and institutions in Zambia and many African countries use Western frameworks of knowledge which excludes practices like the Mukanda right-of-passage ceremony as a way of learning or producing knowledge or even transmitting it. The *privilege* of education for many African scholars and museology experts restricts their learning to theories, themes and subjects that are mostly far removed from indigenous studies, so this does not give the knowledge the chance to develop.

This brings to attention the fact that knowledge of indigenous people or systems of source communities in the museums in the West is not robust—the Makishi artefact of the Luvale is from a matrilineal society which means historically, they gave women significant positions of leadership including having positions like female Kings, women owning land and women were seen as equals (White) and yet now in our current state of perception of our culture we have had development organisations from the West come in and teach us how we need to "include" women and "manage" the cultural norm where Zambians perceive women as not being leaders because of our "tradition" ... which tradition? The one that had women leaders but was erased and violently opposed?

Or is it a reference to the patriarchy introduced by the colonisers. It is well documented that in the 1900s the colonising efforts in Zambia, as in many African countries during colonisation, had it as policy to remove or undermine the female chiefs and leaders since it did not fall within their governing policy at the time and curiously up to this day, even after years of independence, the impact of the coloniality of gender is felt (Saungweme) and unfortunately our own museums and knowledge institutions have perpetuated this narrative. This is not uncommon in many Zambian and other African societies.

As a result of some of these observations made, there remains a splintered community that is facing the deep grief, loss and an arrested development that limits the communities rights to revitalise their knowledge (Hernandez) and continues to minimise the value of the knowledge that even the communities now firmly believe that the Western framework of knowledge is better than the local knowledge.

Much has been talked about on what is needed to correct this situation and there are some African scholars and knowledge keepers doing this work already.

There are interventions by African scholars and experts in the Western and African museum landscape that are working towards pushing a fresh ideology around source communities and indigenous knowledge systems in Africa.

Even as the reorientation and restitution process continues we need to see more African scholars engage in more African-centred research and academic documentation. This contribution should be in a way that does not see experts influenced with trending theories and discourse that is largely dictated by the Global North. The nature of academic publishing, as it is, does not allow space for diverse discourse looking into what Dr. Livingstone Muchefa in Zimbabwe describes as *community intellectual voices,* is vital for this discourse.

Another intervention is creating agency for African source communities—reviving and validating obscured indigenous knowledge systems and consolidating the restitution process through the use of source communities that still have the legitimate knowledge that has survived and complementing it with various technologies to provide immediacy to the process of correction.

Provenance research conducted by the institution that this author co-founded, with the communities of origin for the objects that are in the National Museums of World Cultures has birthed a project called "Shared Histories-Empowering Women's Narratives" (Women's History Museum of Zambia) and one of the main outputs for this project was creating a digital repatriation platform where a portion of the 800+ Zambian artefacts, documents and images that are in the museum in Sweden are transferred to this platform. During this process of development we felt that it was important for us to return to the source communities and verify the objects with the community knowledge keepers. We did not know what would happen as some of these objects had not been seen for 100 years by the communities. We were delighted to find elders who were able to not only identify the objects but to also provide additional context and learning and this meta data is now being added to the objects in the museum.

A final one but not exhaustive at all is recognising the power of language by using indigenous language when coding and decoding indigenous knowledge systems and artefacts. Often meaning and value is lost through translation and we need to restore that level of meaning-making through accurate decoding of language. This can only be done with African experts and source communities.

We often refer to this loss of context as a *dismembering*, because parts of the indigenous knowledge has been dismembered and the broken pieces are presented as a whole, the real value of the knowledge can be restored through a process of re-stitching the pieces of knowledge that have been dismantled through a reconfiguration of the knowledge with the origin communities.

The work to undo the legacy of distorted knowledge production in African indigenous spaces is a vital and necessary rendering of museums and knowledge production that is happening in order to build a legacy museum-making that attempts to be inclusive, representative, equitable, diverse and validating for all.

Bibliography

Arowosegbe, Jeremiah O. "African Scholars, African Studies and Knowledge Production on Africa." *JSTOR* (2016).

Castro, Inés de. "The Linden-Museum of the Future." Leonhard Emmerling, Latika Gupta, Luiza Proença, Memory Biwa. *Museum Futures*. Berlin: Turia Kant, 2021. 319–338.

Hernandez, Jessica. *Fresh Banana Leaves — Healing Indigenous Landscapes Through Indigenous Science*. North Atlantic Books, 2022.

—. *Fresh Banana Leaves Healing Indigenous Landscapes Through Indigenoous Science*. North Atlantic Books, 2022.

Lajul, Wilfred. "Reconstructing African Fractured Epistemologies for African Development." *Synthesis Philosophica* (2018): 51–76.

Moiloa, Molemo. "nto>ntu: Reimagining Relational Infrastructures of Museums in Africa." Leonard Emmerling, Latika Gupta, Luiza Proença, Memory Biwa. *Museum Futures*. Berlin: Turia Kant, 2021. 357–364.

Saungweme, Furaha Joy Sekai. "A Critique of Africa's Post-Colonial Freedoms Through a Feminist Lens: Challenging Patriarchy and Assessing the Gains." *https://za.boell.org/en/2021/07/07/critique-africas-post-colonial-freedoms-through-feminist-lens-*

challenging-patriarchy. Cape Town: Henrich Böll Stiftung, 7 July 2021. Article on website.

Wele, Patrick. *Likumbi Lya Mize and Other Traditional Ceremonies*. Lusaka: Zambia Educational Publishing House, 1993.

White, CMN. *A Preliminary Survey of the Luvale Rural Economy*. Manchester: Manchester University Press, 1968.

Women's History Museum of Zambia. *www.whmzambia.org*. 22 May 2022. 22 May 2022.

博物馆去殖民化视角下非洲原住民社区
社会公正、重新定位与赋权

桑巴·杨格*

赞比亚和许多非洲其他地区被殖民的经历使得本土知识体系与文物①遭到严重破坏,脱离了当地原生环境,这也影响了此后他们知识生成的历史。众所周知,这一现象出现的部分原因就是文物脱离了原有时空背景下的原生语境,进而被歪曲理解产生了错误的含义,并造成了几代人的记忆缺失和知识错位,且至今仍未得到充分解决。然而,目前的博物馆和一些知识机构却一直很少考虑到非洲作为文物原生社区的语境,继续将歪曲事实的释义看作是其知识来源。

在过去几年中,为解决因错位和去语境化而导致的失衡,西方一些民族志博物馆(ethnographic museums)和知识机构围绕其收藏的源自非洲当地的有争议性的文物展开了对话。

尽管做出了巨大努力,但目前文物的原生社区及其在博物馆和知识机构重新定位的发展过程中参与度仍然很低,而且缺乏认可度。

殖民遗产是造成当地文物和原住民知识体系错位的重要原因。殖民掠夺时,文物不仅失去了其原生语境,还对其本土社区造成了影响,使当地社区承受着文物损失与悲痛,并不得不去面对本土认知逐渐丧失影响力的

---

* 桑巴·杨格,赞比亚妇女历史博物馆联合创始人。
① 这里翻译所用"文物"一词对应的是英文单词"artefacts",表示的是历史过往中人们创造的或与创造活动有关的物质文化和精神文化的遗存(下同)。见李晓东:《文物学》,学苑出版社2005年版,第4页。

问题。这在发展中国家①其实是一个普遍现象。不断寻求转变这一现象的良好方式已经成为博物馆实践和知识生成中的一个部分,本次演讲将探讨如何才能做到这一点,以确保能够有一个公平和包容的进程。

这种世代相传的分离现象(指文物脱离原生语境)现在已经表现为本土社区不仅失去了其知识的价值效用,还失去了为他们发声、传达他们是有效的知识创造者和保护者的机构。而且在大多数情况下,他们也失去了知识生成的能力。

凭借博物馆作为构建身份认知机构的特点,以欧洲为中心的文化等级制度很大程度上得以合法化。而在非洲或赞比亚,也就是我的家乡,这种做法的副作用会导致那些不一定拥有发言权的原住民所处的本土社区失去原有知识体系的合法性与价值意义。

我想与大家分享一些案例,说明文物流失对其原生社区的影响,先从博物馆中一件文物的故事说起。

这件文物目前收藏在瑞典斯德哥尔摩的国立世界文化博物馆(National Museums of World Cultures)中,其目前的状态是在脱离原生环境的情况下去塑造知识。

这种分离意味着缺乏表征性和文化背景,因为文物在其来源社区之外展出的时候并不包含其原生社区语境的内容。这种情况正如伊内斯·卡斯特罗博士(Dr. Inés de Castro)所说的那样,"关于文物的一些刻板印象和固定属性并不准确,但它们却依旧能够被认定为知识"。

文物与原生语境分离的影响会造成叙事的中断、文物原生社区知识生成的发展停滞、非原住民学者认知形成的扭曲,并带来文物原生环境中社区与人口分裂的表现。

首先要考虑的现象是文物和源自本土社区的知识的分离,以及与西方认识论的实际接触会对文物原生环境及其原生社区的生活带来怎样的影响。

---

① 原文中这里使用的"Global South"并不是仅仅指地理意义上的南半球,而是指发展中国家。因为发展中国家的地理位置大多位于南半球和北半球的南部,发达国家多在北半球的北部,故以南、北分别指代之。

卢瓦勒人（Luvale）①服饰的案例

Likumbi Lya Mize②是赞比亚西北部以及刚果和安哥拉部分地区的卢瓦勒人、乔奎人（Cokwe）和卢查齐人（Lucazi）的一个内容丰富的传统仪式，男性通过这个仪式表示迎来成年。这个仪式中最重要的部分是马基西舞会（Makishi）③。"马基西"是一个由象征着祖先化身的蒙面人组成的盛大游行队伍，会出现在非常重要的未成年男孩的成年仪式——"穆坎达"（Mukanda）上（Wele）。祖先通过马基西舞会"复活"，将他们的知识从过去带到现在，并将这些知识传授给后代年轻人，并以此作为一种成年仪式。

马基西中的许多课程和仪式教导男孩们价值观和生活技能，这些技能都与帮助他们生活和在社会中成为一个有责任感的好人有关：如何照看家园、与大自然和谐相处、如何小心谨慎地从大自然中获取财富、如何保护和耕种土地、如何成为社区中负责任的领导者。如果我们仔细研究其中的一些教育内容，以今天的视角可以将其比作环境保护、矿产科学开采、有机食品生产、营养、科学农业、金属锻造技术，甚至包括冥想和正念。

然而，100年前当这些知识在社区内被移除并受到系统性压迫时，由于缺少关注和责任意识，这个社群被剥夺了生成和验证知识体系的机会，而这些知识体系如今已成为全世界的重要实践。

在斯德哥尔摩的国立世界文化博物馆中，"马基西"服饰已经没有了

---

① 卢瓦勒（Luvale）是赞比亚西北部和安哥拉东南操班图语的民族。卢瓦勒人和赞比亚西北部其他民族有明显不同之处——卢瓦勒人有强固的家系与氏族结构。
② Likumbi Lya Mize仪式是在赞比亚西北部卢瓦勒人的传统节日。从历史上看，这个节日标志着那些因为"Mukanda"（男性割礼）而隐居社会的男孩们重新进入社会（即成年礼）。
③ 马基西是男性成年礼仪式上跳的一种面具舞，以面具和装饰的夸张为特色。通常男孩长到12岁，在形式上要完成从男孩到男人的转变，需要离家"修炼"一个月，其间由长者教会他在部落中生存的技能以及性教育。一个月"出关"时，与部落的人一起跳马基西舞，面具人物代表部落逝去的祖先，通过这种形式帮助男孩的成长。近年来，随着社会的进步，面具舞的原本功能性的意义正在逐渐淡化，更多地出现在旅游场所，作为当地民族文化展现在世人面前。2005年，马基西舞被联合国教科文组织列为"人类口述和非物质文化遗产"。

我刚才分享的那种语境和细节。当这套面具服饰及其元素从原生社区中移出并被放入博物馆时，它就已经与原有的知识语境分离了，对原生社区和博物馆来说也都是无效的。因为没有那些拥有知识语境的本土社区作为参照，（文物的）意义和实际知识的传递被遗失在一个无解的空间里。

一百多年来，这种情况其实在博物馆中反复出现。很多文物除了满足猎奇这一事实之外，对博物馆和原生社区的价值几乎微乎其微。

这些歪曲的事实也影响了叙事的方式，以及它们最终如何被当作知识进行传播和记录为知识。而这会对那些无法掌控这一知识生成过程的人造成障碍。

文物原生社区知识生成的发展停滞带来了这样一个问题：在我们国家，谁来管控知识的生成？这种情况又对现状造成了怎样的影响？赞比亚和非洲许多其他国家的大学、博物馆以及相关机构都在使用西方的知识框架作为一种学习或知识生成甚至是知识传播的方式，但却将"穆坎达"成年仪式这样的本土实情排除在外。许多非洲学者和博物馆学专家特殊的教育经历将他们的学习限制在了理论、主题思想和学科上，而这些内容大多与土著研究相去甚远，因此这种模式并没有给（当地）认知提供发展的机会。

这也让我们关注到一个事实，即西方博物馆中关于原住民或原住民社区体系的知识并不丰富——卢瓦勒人的马基西舞会中使用的面具来自母系氏族，这意味着，在历史上妇女被赋予了重要的领导地位，包括女王职位、妇女拥有土地，妇女被视为平等的。然而目前，在对自己文化有所感知的现实状况下，西方的发展组织来到我们这里，教我们如何去"包容"妇女，还因为所谓的赞比亚人认为妇女不能成为领导者的"传统"而要来"管理"（我们的）文化规范……哪个传统？是那个有妇女领袖却被抹杀和暴力反对的传统么？还是指殖民者引入的父权制呢？有充分证据证明，赞比亚和许多其他非洲国家一样在20世纪受到殖民统治，在此期间，由于不符合当时的统治政策，殖民者对女性酋长和领导人提出了清除或者削弱的政策。而令人奇怪的是，时至今日，即使在独立多年之后，人们依旧能感受到性别殖民主义的影响，而且不幸的是，我们自己的博物馆和知识机构也延续了这种说法。这种情况在赞比亚和其他非洲社会并不少见。

根据上述观察结果，这些破碎的社区依旧面临着文物损失的沉痛与发展停滞的问题，这限制了社区重振本土知识的权利，并进一步忽略了本土认知的价值意义，甚至当地社区现在也坚信西方的知识框架比当地知识更好。

人们已经针对如何改变这一现象展开了诸多探讨，一些非洲学者和知识保存者也正在做这项工作。

非洲一些专家学者已经在西方和非洲的博物馆领域采取了一些干预措施，正极力围绕非洲本土的社区与知识体系助推形成一种新的意识形态。

即使本土社区新定位和文物返还的进程正在持续推进，我们也需要看到更多非洲学者参与到更多的以非洲为中心的研究和学术论文当中去。这种学术贡献不应使专家们受到发达国家占据主导的理论趋势和话语的影响。学术出版的性质决定了它无法为多样化的讨论提供空间，而根据津巴布韦利文斯敦·穆切法（Livingstone Muchefa）博士的研究，他将这种多元的讨论看作是"本土社区认知的声音"，认为这种声音对全球话语至关重要。

另一项干预措施是为非洲的文物本土社区创建机构——恢复并证实被掩盖的本土知识系统，通过利用仍然拥有合理科学知识的本土社区来巩固归文物返还的进程，并以各种技术辅以补充，为及时纠正进程提供帮助。

笔者与他人共同创办的机构——赞比亚妇女历史博物馆——联合（文物）本土社区为收藏在国立世界文化博物馆中的源自非洲社区的——物品举办了一个名为"历史共享——强化妇女话语权"（Shared Histories—Empowering Women's Narratives）的项目，该项目的主要成果之一是创建了一个数字文物返还平台，将瑞典的博物馆所收藏的 800 多件赞比亚文物、文件和图像当中的一部分转移到了该平台中。在项目开发的过程中，我们认为有必要回到文物的本土社区，与当地社区的知识保护者一起证实这些物件。我们不知道会发生什么，因为其中一些物品已经有上百年没有出现在本土社区中了。我们很高兴找到了本地的先辈长者，他们不仅可以识别物品，还能提供更多的文物背景和知识，现在这些元数据正被添加到收藏在博物馆的物品中。

最后一点但并非详尽无遗的干预措施就是认识到语言的力量，即通过使用本土语言对原住民的知识认知体系和文物进行编码和解码。翻译往往会失去原本内容的意义和价值，我们需要通过准确的语言解码来尽可能恢复内容创作的原意。而这只有非洲专家和本土社区才能做到。

我们通常把这种语境的丧失称为肢解，因为本土知识的一部分已被肢解，但这些破碎的碎片却不得不被当作一个整体来呈现。而将已经被肢解的知识碎片与原生社区的知识进行重组后，再将其重新缝合，通过这一过程，我们可以恢复知识的真正价值。

消除非洲原住民空间中那些遗留的被歪曲生成的知识，对于博物馆和知识生成是一种十分重要且必要的认知渲染，这种氛围渲染是为了建立一种试图对所有人都具有包容性、代表性、公平性、多样性和有效性的博物馆遗产。

参考文献

Arowosegbe, Jeremiah O. "African Scholars, African Studies and Knowledge Production on Africa." *JSTOR* (2016).

Castro, Inés de. "The Linden-Museum of the Future." Leonhard Emmerling, Latika Gupta, Luiza Proença, Memory Biwa. *Museum Futures*. Berlin: Turia Kant, 2021. 319-338.

Hernandez, Jessica. *Fresh Banana Leaves—Healing Indigenous Landscapes Through Indigenous Science*. North Atlantic Books, 2022.

—. *Fresh Banana Leaves Healing Indigenous Landscapes Through Indigenoous Science*. North Atlantic Books, 2022.

Lajul, Wilfred. "Reconstructing African Fractured Epistemologies for African Development." *Synthesis Philosophica* (2018): 51-76.

Moiloa, Molemo. "nto>ntu: Reimagining Relational Infrastructures of Museums in Africa." Leonard Emmerling, Latika Gupta, Luiza Proença, Memory Biwa. *Museum Futures*. Berlin: Turia Kant, 2021. 357-364.

Saungweme, Furaha Joy Sekai. "A Critique of Africa's Post-Colonial Freedoms Through a Feminist Lens: Challenging Patriarchy and Assessing the Gains." *https://za.boell.org/en/2021/07/07/critique-africas-post-colonial-freedoms-through-feminist-lens-challenging-patriarchy*. Cape Town: Henrich Böll Stiftung, 7 July 2021. Article on website.

Wele, Patrick. *Likumbi Lya Mize and Other Traditional Ceremonies*. Lusaka: Zambia Educational Publishing House, 1993.

White, CMN. *A Preliminary Survey of the Luvale Rural Economy*. Manchester: Manchester University Press, 1968.

Women's History Museum of Zambia. *www.whmzambia.org*. 22 May 2022. 22 May 2022.

The Role of International Soft Law in Return of Cultural Objects Removed in Colonial Contexts

Yunxia Wang[*]

Abstract: The return of cultural objects removed in colonial contexts is a serious problem left over by history. The existing international conventions dealing with disputes over the return/restitution of cultural objects cannot be the legal basis due to their lack of retroactive effect. International soft laws such as the Washington Principles and the ICOM Recommendations have played a great role in dealing with disputes over the restitution of Jewish looted arts during World War II, and have accumulated experience for resolutions of similar problems left over by history. The new approaches for the return of colonial cultural objects in France and Germany have greatly contributed to the international community's reflection on the necessity and feasibility of the return of cultural objects from colonial contexts. However, it is not enough to rely on policies and actions taken by governments or museums of countries concerned. A declaration or recommendation should be issued by important international organizations such as ICOM in due course to establish a unified framework for the return of colonial cultural objects, so as to provide a legal basis for proper resolution on the issue among countries concerned.

Key words: International Soft Law; Colonial Contexts; Restitution; Cultural Objects

---

[*] Yunxia Wang, Professor of Renmin University of China, UNESCO Chair on Cultural Heritage Law.

Cultural object[1] is the unique expression of a specific country or a specific ethnic group for its way of life, and is important witnesses to the history of that country or nation. The illegal removal of cultural objects not only destroys the normal trading order, but also causes the rapid loss of cultural resources in the country of origin, resulting in a serious inequity in the possession of cultural resources between the country of origin and the country of destination. Therefore, for more than half a century, the international community has gradually established a special legal mechanism to combat the illegal trafficking of cultural properties and promote the return of cultural properties to their countries of origin. However, the return of colonial cultural objects is a complicated problem left over from history. Since the end of World War II, more and more colonies and protectorates have emerged from the state of war and gained independence. The demand for the return of cultural objects has gradually increased, but relevant parties have not been able to reach consensus on key issues. In recent years, with the deepening reflection on colonial domination, it has become a major issue to actively respond to the demand for the return of colonial cultural objects that the international community needs to face together.

"Restitution", "Repatriation" or "Return"

The colonial cultural objects mentioned in this article refer to the illegal removal of cultural objects in colonial contexts, which involves plundering during war time or occupation, or confiscation and expropriation, as well as forced/unfair trade and involuntary gifts based on colonial domination and impact. As to the requests for recovery of cultural objects, we come across

---

[1] In the Chinese legal context, "cultural object" is roughly equivalent to "tangible cultural heritage", which is close to the internationally accepted meaning of "cultural property". In this paper, the term "cultural property" or "cultural object" is used interchangeably, respecting the original expression in the relevant international legal documents.

three similar terms, i.e., "restitution", "repatriation" and "return". In dealing with colonial cultural objects requests, the terminology is quite confusing. The significant Savoy-Sarr Report used the term of "restitution"[1], the Practical Guide for Museums in England used both "restitution" and "repatriation"[2], while the Guidelines for German Museums used the term of "return" in the section of recommendations.[3] The choice of terminology is indicative of the position and caution of the drafters of the report and guidelines, as well as the lack of sufficient consensus in this area.

It is necessary to conduct a semantic analysis of the three terms in order to determine the premise for discussing.

"Restitution" is an old and rigorous legal term that presupposes the unlawful deprivation of property belonging to the right holder by someone. As a result of legal redress, the offender must return the original property or restore its original state, that is, restore the condition before the damage occurred. "Restitution" includes the return of the original property to its rightful owner, or compensation with equivalents or monetary compensation. Specific to the field of cultural property, the aim of "restitution" is to restore, as far as possible, the previous legal status of the cultural property. The aim is either attained directly, through unconditional return of cultural property identified as goods looted or stolen, or sometimes indirectly, by way of restitution by equivalent, where goods similar to those taken are submitted.[4] Therefore, the term "restitution" is usually

---

[1] Sarr, Felwine and Savoy, Bénédicte. "The Restitution of African Cultural Heritage: Toward a New Relational Ethics." www.about-africa.de/images/sonstiges/2018/sarr_savoy_en.pdf. Accessed 16 May 2023.

[2] IAL. "Restitution and Repatriation: A Practical Guide for Museums in England." www.artscouncil.org.uk/supporting-arts-museums-and-libraries/supporting-collections-and-cultural-property/restitution-and. Accessed 8 May 2023.

[3] "Guidelines for German Museums Care of Collections from Colonial Contexts." www.museumsbund.de/wp-content/uploads/2021/03/mb-leitfaden-en-web.pdf. Accessed 8 May 2023.

[4] Kowalski, Wojciech. "Types of Claims for Recovery of Lost Cultural Property." *Museum International*, vol. 57, no. 4, 2005, p. 97.

used for requests for the return of cultural property looted in wartime or stolen in peacetime.

"Repatriation" means to send someone or something back to the land where it came from. Applied to cultural property/heritage field, it generally concerns the problem of indigenous claims for human remains and cultural objects within the nation state. For example, those so called "settler colonial nation states" including Australia, Canada, New Zealand and the United States of America enacted acts to repatriate human remains and specific categories of objects to the descendants of the cultures from which the material was originally taken. Therefore, the term "repatriation" is usually connected with a minority group's ceremonial practices, contemporary identity, and "cultural survival" within larger processes of national narratives and reconciliation within settler-colonial nation states. [1]

Comparatively speaking, "return" is a fairly neutral term, though perhaps focusing on action by the requested State or institution.[2] It generally refers to cultural property that is to be returned to the country of origin, without a specific judgment as to whether removal from that country was illegal or not at the time it occurred.[3] It is thus a broader and less controversial term than "restitution" and "repatriation" that covers all types of requests for recovery of cultural objects.

In 1978, in order to help its member states to address pleas for return of cultural properties, the Intergovernmental Committee for Promoting the Return of Cultural Property to its Countries of Origin or its Restitution in Case of

---

[1] See Skrydstrup, Martin. "Theorizing Repatriation." *Journal of European Ethnology*, vol. 39, no. 2, pp. 57–58.
[2] Prott, Lyndel V. "Note on Terminology", *Witness to History: A Compendium of Documents and Writings on the Return of Cultural Objects*, UNESCO Publishing, 2009, p. xxi.
[3] Carducci, Guido. "'Repatriation', 'Restitution' and 'Return' of Cultural Property: International Law and Practice." *UTIMUT: Past Heritage, Future Partnerships: Discussions on Repatriation in the 21st Century*, edited by Mille Gabriel and Jens Dahl, Copenhagen, 2008, Document No. 122, p. 128.

Illicit Appropriation drafted The Guidelines for the Use of the Standard Form Concerning Request for Return or Restitution. Point A.9 in the Guidelines explains: "The term 'return' should apply to cases where objects left their countries of origin prior to the crystallization of national and international law on the protection of cultural property. Such transfers of ownership were often made from a colonized territory to the territory of the colonial power or from a territory under foreign occupation. In many cases, they were the result of an exchange, gift or sale and did not therefore infringe any laws existing at the time. In some cases, however, the legitimacy of the transfer can be questioned."[1] Accordingly, the term "return" is the most appropriate one for recovery of cultural objects taken in colonial contexts, although there is still a lot of terminology confusion in different documents and publications.

The Difficulty and Legitimacy of the Issue of the Return of Colonial Cultural Objects

The return of colonial cultural objects refers to the return of illegally transferred cultural objects in a colonial context, both in relation to looting during war or occupation, but also in relation to unfair trade, involuntary gifts or confiscation and expropriation, the difficulty of this issue is not only due to the lack of retroactivity of existing international legal documents, but also due to the lack of reflection on colonialism by relevant countries, and the lack of sufficient recognition of the demand for the return of colonial cultural objects.

Firstly, the existing international conventions are not retroactive and cannot be directly applied to the claims for the return of colonial cultural objects. The relevant conventions on the return issue that have been introduced by the international community since the mid-20th century mainly apply to requests

---

[1] See Kowalski, Wojciech. "Types of Claims for Recovery of Lost Cultural Property." *Museum International,* vol. 57, no. 4, 2005, p. 96.

for the return of cultural properties transferred during wartime and stolen or illegally exported during peacetime. The UNESCO Convention for the Protection of Cultural Property in the Event of Armed Conflict 1954 (hereinafter referred to as "the Hague Convention") prohibits theft, misappropriation, plundering and any forms of destruction of the cultural property of another State Party in the event of armed conflict and requires States Parties to take all necessary steps to prosecute and impose penalties or sanctions on any person who violates the Convention, regardless of nationality.[1] The UNESCO Convention on Convention on the Means of Prohibiting and Preventing the Illicit Import, Export and Transfer of Ownership of Cultural Property 1970 (hereinafter referred to as "the 1970 Convention") requests state parties to take necessary measures to prevent museums and similar institutions from acquiring cultural property originating in another State Party which has been illegally exported in the States concerned, to prohibit the import of cultural property stolen from museums and public monuments or similar institutions of another State Party, and to take appropriate measures to return such cultural property to the State Party of origin.[2] The UNIDROIT Convention Concerning Stolen or Illegally Exported Cultural Objects 1995 (hereafter referred to as "1995 Convention") provided that the possessor of a cultural object which has been stolen (including illegally excavated) shall return it to its rightful owner, regardless of whether it has been acquired in good faith. The current possessor may receive fair and reasonable compensation provided that he exercised the duty of due diligence when acquiring the object at the return of the cultural

---

[1] See UNESCO. "Convention for the Protection of Cultural Property in the Event of Armed Conflict", 1954, Article 4 and 28. en.unesco.org/sites/default/files/1954_Convention_EN_2020.pdf. Accessed 1 February 2023.

[2] See UNESCO. "Convention on the Means of Prohibiting and Preventing the Illicit Import, Export and Transfer of Ownership of Cultural Property", 1970, Article 7. www.unesco.org/en/legal-affairs/convention-means-prohibiting-and-preventing-illicit-import-export-and-transfer-ownership-cultural. Accessed 1 February 2023.

objects.① The principles contained in the Hague Convention regarding respect for cultural property in occupied territories and the prohibition of wanton destruction of cultural property in armed conflicts have been repeatedly confirmed by relevant non contracting parties and international organizations, and to some extent, it has the nature of customary international law.② The 1970 Convention and 1995 Convention have played positive roles in combating the illegal traffic of cultural properties and promoting their return to the countries of origin or rightful holders, and many European countries have amended their civil codes or cultural heritage laws by introducing the duty of due diligence and longer limitations.③ However, since these Conventions do not have retroactive effect, it is difficult for them to play a direct role in disputes over the return of colonial cultural objects.

Secondly, the return of colonial cultural objects is a historical problem left unresolved for a long time. Among the many complex factors, one of the main reasons is that the issue of returning cultural objects did not appear in most peace agreements. Starting from the late 15th century, with the opening of new shipping routes from Europe to the Indian Ocean and the Americas, European countries began large-scale colonization campaign in the Americas, Africa, and Asia, plundering countless cultural treasures and transporting them back to Europe to fill their museums. Although many colonies got rid of the colonial domination after the two World Wars, due to their ultimate demand for political

---

① See UNIDROIT. "UNIDROIT Convention on Stolen or Illegally Exported Cultural Objects", 1995, Article 3 and 4. www.unidroit.org/instruments/cultural-property/1995-convention/. Accessed 1 February 2023.
② See Meyer, David A. "The 1954 Hague Convention and Its Emergence into Customary International Law." *Boston University International Law Journal*, vol. 11, no. 2, 1993, p. 356; Also Birov, Victoria A. "Prize and Plunder: The Pillage of Works of Art and the International Law of War." *NYU Journal of International Law and Politics*, Vol. 30, no. 1, 1997, p. 208.
③ Switzerland, the Netherlands, Belgium and other countries have introduced the duty of due diligence for buyers of cultural objects. See Frigo, Manlio. "The Impact of the UNIDROIT Convention on International Case Law and Practice: An Appraisal." *Uniform Law Review*, vol. 20, no. 4, 2015, pp. 631-632.

independence, with very few exceptions[①], the return of cultural relics usually did not appear in peace agreements with the colonial powers, making it a long-standing historical legacy that could not be resolved between the former colonial powers and the former colonies.

Thirdly, there is insufficient reflection by the colonialists on the history of colonialism. Many European and American museums are reluctant to respond to the demand for return on the stand of "cultural property internationalism" defined by Prof. John Henry Merryman.[②] They believe that most of the collections from colonies are legally acquired, such as those purchased or donated by collectors, or given voluntarily by colonial people, or distributed based on "cooperation agreements". They completely ignore the colonial plundering history behind these collections, on the contrary, emphasize their contributions to the protection and exhibition of these cultural relics. The Declaration on the Importance and Value of the Universal Museum can be said to be the most representative to this idea. On 10 December 2002, the declaration signed by the directors of 18 world-renowned museums caused global shock, which emphasizing:

Calls to repatriate objects that have belonged to museum collections for many years have become an important issue for museums ... To narrow the focus

---

① The 1919 Treaty of Versailles may be a typical example. Articles 245, 246 and 247 provided for the return of special cultural objects, such as archives, historical souvenirs and works of art removed from France during the war of 1870–1871 and World War I, the original Koran removed from Medina by the Turkish authorities and is stated to have been presented to the ex-Emperor Willem II, and the skull of the Sultan Mkwawa, which were taken from German East Africa by the Germans, must be returned or handed over to the countries concerned within six months. Article 247 required Germany to provide manuscripts, ancient books, books, maps and collections of the same type and value to the University of Reuven as compensation for the damages caused by the bombing of the library in Leuven, Belgium, in accordance with the principle of "Restitution in Kind". www.files.ethz.ch/isn/125327/1416_Treaty_Versailles.pdf. Accessed 1 February 2023.

② See Merryman, John H. "Two Ways of Thinking about Cultural Property." *Thinking about Elgin Marbles: Critical Essays on Cultural Property, Art and Law*, edited by John Henry Merryman, Kluwer Law International, 2009, pp. 66–67.

of museums whose collections are diverse and multifaceted would therefore be a disservice to all visitors.[1]

Although there are many difficulties on the issue of colonial cultural objects, the return appeal does have its legitimacy. In fact, On the one hand, the return of cultural objects helps to restore the sacred link between sovereignty and cultural heritage. Cultural heritage is the symbol of a state or nation, and to occupy and conquer a state or nation is to control its cultural heritage. As Prof. Ana F. Vrdoljak said:

In the colonial relationship, the possession of these cultural objects was central to the collective imaginings of the occupier and the occupied. For colonial occupiers, these objects represented the possession of people, territories and resources within an empire. Their centralization and public display reinforced and projected a national imperial imagining. Conversely, for colonized peoples, the removal of these cultural objects represented the dispossession of their lands, autonomy and identity.[2]

Thus, the independence of the colonies was necessarily accompanied by claims for the return of the cultural objects that constituted the most important cultural heritage of the state, which also helped to promote the restoration of relations between former colonies and former colony powers. On the other hand, the return of cultural objects can help to correct the bad effects of historical injustices. Colonial domination is often accompanied by genocide and ethnic cleansing taking the plunder of cultural objects as a regular tool, as the famous Chinese saying goes, "To destroy a state must first go to its history." The return of cultural objects can compensate for the infringement of historical injustice to

---

[1] See "Declaration on the importance and value of universal museums." www.hermitagemuseum. org/wps/portal/hermitage/news/news-item/news/1999_2013/hm11_1_93/?lng. Accessed 9 May 2023.

[2] Vrdoljak, Ana F. "International Law, Museums and the Return of Cultural Objects." *Witness to History: A Compendium of Documents and Writings on the Return of Cultural Objects*, edited by Lyndel V. Prott, UNESCO Publishing, 2009, p. 194.

the victim to a certain extent, and it also shows the colonist's self-reflection on historical injustice.

Role of International Soft Law in Handling Requests of Cultural Objects Caused by Illegally Transferred in History

The so-called "international soft law" is the opposite concept of "international hard law". From a legal point of view, binding legal norms are regarded as hard law, while non-binding norms are regarded as soft law. Therefore, conventions, treaties and protocols in force are classified as hard law, while all international legal documents that are not designed to be binding, including resolutions of the United Nations General Assembly, codes of practice, joint statements and declarations, can be classified as soft law.[①] Since hard law norms set clear rights and obligations for contracting parties and have strong binding force, it will be a long period of game and trade-off in their drafting, adoption, signature and ratification, and full of various disputes and variables in their implementation process. However, soft law can play a greater role in the international dispute settlement because of its flexibility, guidance and non-coercion. This is particularly evident in the field of cultural heritage protection, especially on the issue of promoting the return of illegally transferred cultural relics that have occurred in history. The international community has adopted many non-binding resolutions, recommendations, model laws, guidelines, principles, declarations and so on, which provide a basis for consultations among relevant countries. Representative soft law documents include:

Relevant Resolutions of the United Nations on Combat of Illicit Trafficking in Cultural Objects.

[①] He Zhipeng. "International Soft Law in the Era of De-globalization." *Journal of Wuhan University (Social Sceince)*, vol. 70, no. 4, 2017, p. 55. (in Chinese)

As an important international organization dedicated to promoting international security, economic development, social progress, democracy, freedom and permanent peace, the United Nations has continuously called on all member states to strengthen cooperation since the 1970's to combat illicit trafficking in cultural property illegally transferred due to occupation of war and colonization, theft and smuggling, and facilitate their return to the countries of origin. Some resolutions explicitly mentioned the importance of the return of colonial objects. The Resolution 3187 deplores the wholesale removal of works of art from one country to another as a result of colonial or foreign occupation, recognizes the special obligations in this connection of those countries which had access to such valuable objects, and calls upon all the States concerned to prohibit the expropriation of works of art from territories still under colonial or alien domination.① Subsequent the Resolution 3391, 31/40 and 32/18 reaffirms the contents of Resolution 3187 and calls on those States concerned which have not yet done so to proceed to the restitution of works of art, monuments, museum pieces, manuscripts and documents to their countries of origin, such restitution being calculated to strengthen international understanding and co-operation.② While these resolutions do not make it mandatory for member states to return colonial cultural objects, they welcome all voluntary forms of restitution of illegally transferred cultural property, repeatedly recognize the mechanisms of international cooperation in existing international conventions

---

① See UN. General Assembly. "Restitution of works of art to countries victims of appropriation", U.N. Doc. A/RES/3187, 1973. digitallibrary.un.org/record/190996/files/A_RES_3187%28XXVIII%29-EN.pdf. Accessed 4 February 2023.

② See UN. General Assembly. "Restitution of works of art to countries victims of expropriation", U.N. Doc. A/RES/3391, 1975. digitallibrary.un.org/record/189355/files/A_RES_3391%28XXX%29-EN. pdf; UN. General Assembly. "Protection and restitution of works of art as part of the preservation and further development of cultural values", U.N. Doc. A/RES/31/40, 1976. documents-dds-ny.un.org/doc/RESOLUTION/GEN/NR0/302/23/PDF/NR030223.pdf?OpenElement; UN. General Assembly. "Restitution of works of art to countries victims of expropriation", U.N. Doc. A/RES/32/18, 1977. documents-dds-ny.un.org/doc/RESOLUTION/GEN/NR0/312/53/IMG/NR031253.pdf?OpenElement. Accessed 22 May 2023.

to combat illicit trafficking in cultural property. It has significantly enhanced the control and combating of illicit trafficking in cultural property by member states, and raised their attention to the issue of the return of cultural objects that had been illegally removed in history. Echoing these resolutions, resolutions issued by UNESCO, Human Rights Council and other UN bodies condemning the wanton destruction of cultural heritage and protecting cultural rights also uphold the existing rules of international law to combat illicit trafficking in cultural property and promote the return of cultural property to its countries of origin.[1]

Principles and Declarations on the Restitution of Cultural Properties Looted during World War II.

During World War II, cultural properties in occupied countries were extensively destroyed and looted, or illegally detained and transferred as spoils of war by the occupying authorities. Due to the huge loopholes in the postwar mechanism for handling the restitution of cultural properties, and the prolonged Cold War between the East and West, the restitution of illegally transferred cultural properties during World War II has become a heavy historical legacy issue.[2] Since the 1990s, European and American countries, as well as relevant international organizations, have resumed dialogue on the issue of Nazi plundering of Jewish assets, especially the restitution of artworks, which was not completely resolved in the postwar era, in order to promote the restitution operations in related countries. The Washington

---

[1] For example, the Resolution on Cultural Rights and the Protection of Cultural Heritage adopted by the Human Rights Council on 22 March 2018 reaffirmed the relevant contents of the General Assembly resolutions and closely links the promotion of the return of illicit traffic in cultural property to countries of origin with the maintenance of cultural rights, peace and development. For the resolution, see documents-dds-ny.un.org/doc/UNDOC/GEN/G18/258/79/PDF/G1825879.pdf?OpenElement. Accessed 15 May 2023.

[2] For a detailed study of this topic, see Wang Yunxia, Hu Shanchen and Li Yuan. *The Road Home for Looted Cultural Relics: Legal and Ethical Issues in the Restitution of looted Cultural Relics during World War II*. Chapters 1 and 2, The Commercial Press, 2021. (in Chinese)

Principles on Nazi-Confiscated Art (hereafter referred as "The Washington Principles")[①], endorsed by the 44 governments participants in the Washington Conference on Holocaust-Era Assets 1998, ICOM Recommendations concerning the Return of Works of Art Belonging to Jewish Owners 1999[②], and Resolution 1205 (1999) of the Parliamentary Assembly of the Council of Europe on Looted Jewish Cultural Property[③] are important examples. These principles, recommendations and resolutions encourage governments and public institutions to provide greater assistance and wider cooperation in addressing Nazis looted cultural properties and to return works of art originally belonging to Jews to their original owners or their descendants. Driven by these soft law documents, many countries in Europe and America have introduced special laws and policies, established specialized commissions or government bodies to handle disputes over the restitution of artworks looted during the Holocaust, and made special institutional arrangements for the restitution. The UK Holocaust (Return of Cultural Objects) Act 2009 empowers the trustees of named national institutions in Britain to de-accession any artefacts or cultural objects currently held in their collections which were stolen by or on behalf of the Nazi regime between 1933 and 1945, so that these artefacts can be returned to the lawful owners or their heirs.[④] The US Holocaust Expropriated Art Recovery Act of 2016 not only has retroactivity, but also breaks the statute of limitations for general requests for the return

---

① See "Washington Conference Principles on Nazi-Confiscated Art." www.lootedartcommission.com/Washington-principles. Accessed 5 Feb 2023. As a follow-up to the Washington Conference, government representatives of relevant countries held the Vilnius Forum in 2000 and the Tresin Conference in 2009, issuing the Vilnius Forum Declaration and the Tresin Declaration respectively.
② See "ICOM Recommendations concerning the Return of Works of Art Belonging to Jewish Owners." www.lootedartcommission.com/OXSHQE36019. Accessed 5 Feb 2023.
③ See "Resolution 1205 (1999) of the Parliamentary Assembly on looted Jewish cultural property." www.lootedart.com/MG7Q7P50270. Accessed 6 Feb 2023.
④ See "Holocaust (Return of Cultural Objects) Act 2009." www.lootedart.com/NQ2TYV515471. Accessed 16 May 2023.

of cultural relics, allowing people who lost art between 1933 and 1945 due to Nazi persecution to bring lawsuits and other legal actions within six years of the time after the whereabouts of art has discovered.① In the practice of restitution, soft law documents such as the Washington Principles have also played an important role, which have not only been invoked as ratio decidendi for judgments, but also become an important basis for negotiation in the alternative dispute resolution mechanism.②

Although these soft law documents only address the restitution of cultural properties looted by the Nazis during World War II, they do provide an important reference for the solution of the return of colonial cultural objects. First of all, the illegal transfer of cultural properties that occurred during World War II has a similar historical background and pattern of behavior to the illegal removal of colonial cultural objects, both are associated with war, military occupation or threat of force, and both involve the illegal deprivation of the rights of the original owners; Moreover, in many countries and regions, the belligerents of World War II also were colonial powers, such as Japan, which began to colonize the Korean Peninsula as early as 1905, resulting in the extremely complicated issue of the return of illegally removed cultural objects of the Korean Peninsula. Secondly, the return of cultural properties illegally transferred connected to World War II is a problem left over by history that needs to be solved by breaking the existing legal rules. Since the international community can promote countries to amend the existing legal rules through a series of soft law documents, it is not impossible to solve the problem of the return of colonial cultural objects in a similar way.

---

① See Blakemore, Erin. "Reclaiming Nazi-Looted Art Is About to Get Easier." www.smithsonianmag.com/smart-news/new-law-will-make-it-easier-reclaim-nazi-looted-art-180961394/. Accessed 6 Feb 2023.
② ArThemis run by the Art Law Center at University of Geneva collects a number of cases mentioning the role of soft law documents such as the Washington Principles. For detailed information, see plone.unige.ch/art-adr/nazi-looted-art-spoliation-nazie. Accessed 16 May 2023.

A Declaration or Recommendation to Promote the Returen of Colonial Cultural Objects is Expected

For over half a century, the return of colonial cultural objects has been carried out successively among relevant countries, but these actions are carried out on a case-by-case basis and lack unified policies and measures. In November 2017, visiting Burkina Faso, French President Emmanuel Macron announced a stunning decision: France will return all items held in public collections removed from sub-Saharan Africa during the colonial era to Africa. France's new approach can be said to have had a butterfly effect on a global scale, sparking a new wave of the return of colonial cultural objects. One year later, the panel of experts appointed by the President of France published the famous "Sarr-Savoy Report" titled as *The Restitution of African Cultural Heritage, Toward a New Relational Ethic*, which provides a detailed review of the historical context of the plundering of cultural objects during colonial occupation and demonstrates the necessity for restitution. The report recommends that French public museums conduct detailed investigations and make inventories of African artefacts on a case-by-case basis, develop different return plans and measures according to different context. It analyzes the existing legal obstacles for restitution and suggests to modify some rules, especially "the principle of inalienability of public collections", so as to facilitate the smooth restitution.[1] As a first step, the French parliament passed a bill to approve the return of 27 artefacts to Benin and Senegal, which were looted by French troops from the royal palace of Appomey in 1892. Germany followed closely and announced measures to return cultural objects looted or illegally obtained in colonial context. In July 2018, the German Museums Association published

---

[1] See "The Restitution of African Cultural Heritage. Toward a New Relational Ethics." www.about-africa.de/images/sonstiges/2018/sarr_savoy_en.pdf. Accessed 16 May 2023.

the Guidelines on Dealing with Collections from Colonial Contexts, which provides guidance for German museums to verify the origin of collections with a colonial background and possible paths for their return.[①] On 13 March, 2019, the German cultural administrative authorities at federal and local level jointly issued the Framework Principles for dealing with collections from colonial contexts calling on public and private cultural heritage institutions and scientific or academic institutions to conduct thorough provenance research to collections from colonial contexts, and ensure that the country of origin or the community concerned can obtain such information timely. It suggests that human remains from colonial contexts are to be returned in priority, and requests for the return of artefacts from colonial contexts are to be processed promptly, closely cooperated with the country of origin or the community concerned.[②]

The return approaches of France and Germany have also received positive responses from other European and American countries, such as the Netherlands, the United States, and the United Kingdom, which have returned some cultural objects illegally obtained from Africa in the colonial era. The practice in France, Germany and other countries has accumulated experience for the return of colonial cultural objects on a larger scale. However, it should also be noted that the policies of certain countries or the voluntary actions of museums are not enough. The implementation of these policies strongly depends on the leadership's governing philosophy, which is easy to cause questions from the political opposition and lacks coherence and stability. The voluntary returning measures taken by museums collecting cultural objects from colonial

---

[①] See German Museums Association. "Guidelines on Dealing with Collections from Colonial Contexts." www.museumsbund.de/publikationen/guidelines-on-dealing-with-collections-from-colonial-contexts-2/. Accessed 17 May 2023.

[②] See "Framework Principles for dealing with collections from colonial contexts." www.auswaertiges-amt.de/blob/2210152/b2731f8b59210c77c68177cdcd3d03de/190412-stm-m-sammlungsgut-kolonial-kontext-en-data.pdf. Accessed 17 May 2023.

contexts will not only make it difficult to overcome legal obstacles to the disposal of collections, but also cause public concerns about the function and development of museums. Perhaps it is time for an influential international body to consider a declaration or recommendation that would provide framework guidelines for the return of colonial objects worldwide.

In my opinion, the most appropriate international body is the ICOM. The ICOM, at the request of UNESCO back in 1977, set up an ad hoc Committee for the Return of Cultural Property to "Study on the principles, conditions and means for the restitution or return of cultural property in view of reconstituting dispersed heritages"[①]. The Committee published a significant report in title of Return of Cultural Property to their Countries of Origin: Bangladesh, Mali, Western Samoa—A Preliminary Survey of Three National Situations. It was acclaimed by Prof. Lyndel. V. Protas "the first effort of an international organization to try to assess the losses of badly affected developing countries in three quite different regions of the world. This document is therefore both of historic significance, and, for the countries concerned, of continuing current relevance."[②] Although the work was not sustained, it laid an important foundation for the drafting of a declaration or proposal on the return of colonial cultural relics.

Based on the experience of previous soft law documents on the restitution of cultural properties looted during World War II and the policies of returning cultural relics in colonial contexts in France and Germany, this declaration or recommendation would at least clarify the following points:

Firstly, clarify the scope of return. It is immoral to continue to collect and preserve objects that have been illegally transferred in relation to the context

---

① ICOM ad hoc Committee for the Return of Cultural Property. "Return of Cultural Property to their Countries of Origin: Bangladesh, Mali, Western Samoa —A Preliminary Survey of Three National Situations." *Witness to History: A Compendium of Documents and Writings on the Return of Cultural Objects*, edited by Lyndel. V. Prott, UNESCO Publishing, 2009, p. 183.

② Ibid, p. 182.

of colonial domination, whether based on military plunder, confiscation and requisition during occupation, or forced/unfair trade and donation under military threat, as long as they are not based on the express consent of their original owners. The request for return to countries of origin or communities concerned is encouraged to handle through friendly consultation.

Secondly, different disposal suggestions could be adopted according to the mode or character of removal in colonial contexts. Human remains should be returned in priority; Priority of return should also be given to cultural objects acquired as a result of military plunder and occupation, or confiscation and requisition; Objects acquired through scientific expeditions and unfair purchases or donations are encouraged to return unless there are enough evidences that the removal had the explicit consent of their original owners.

Thirdly, it is recommended that relevant countries consider appropriate modifications to existing legal rules, such as limiting the scope of application of the principle of inalienability of public collection or state-owned property, extending the statute of limitations for requests for the return of cultural objects, and excluding the application of good faith acquisition, in order to facilitate legal actions by descendants of those whose cultural objects had been illegally removed.

Finally, for cultural objects that cannot be returned in the sense of ownership due to legal obstacles, changes in boundaries or uncertainty of descendants, cooperation in establishing museums and cultural activity centers, long-term lease, cooperative exhibitions, and digital achievement sharing can be adopted to help the people affected by colonial domination realize their right to access and enjoy cultural heritage.

Conclusion

The illegal removal of colonial cultural objects is a historical injustice, and no matter what we do today, history cannot be changed. But if we can face up to the wrongs of historical injustice and correct the unjust consequences it has caused, we can open up a new future of cooperation and development in the era of decolonization. Correcting historical injustice not only requires the joint efforts of all sectors of society, but also requires innovation in legal tools.

References

Blakemore, Erin. "Reclaiming Nazi-Looted Art Is About to Get Easier." www.smithsonianmag.com/smart-news/new-law-will-make-it-easier-reclaim-nazi-looted-art-180961394/. Accessed 6 Feb 2023.

Birov, Victoria A. "Prize and Plunder: The Pillage of Works of Art and the International Law of War." *NYU Journal of International Law and Politics*, vol. 30, no. 1, 1997, p. 208.

Carducci, Guido. " 'Repatriation', 'Restitution' and 'Return' of Cultural Property: International Law and Practice." *UTIMUT: Past Heritage, Future Partnerships: Discussions on Repatriation in the 21st Century*, edited by Mille Gabriel and Jens Dahl, Copenhagen, 2008, Document No. 122, p. 128.

"Declaration on the importance and value of universal museums." www.hermitagemuseum.org/wps/portal/hermitage/news/news-item/news/1999_2013 /hm11_1_93/?lng. Accessed 9 May 2023.

Frigo, Manlio. "The Impact of the UNIDROIT Convention on International Case Law and Practice: An Appraisal." *Uniform Law Review*, vol. 20, no. 4, 2015, pp. 631–632.

"Framework Principles for dealing with collections from colonial contexts." www.auswaertiges-amt.de/blob/2210152/b2731f8b59210c77c68177cdcd3d03de/190412-stm-m-sammlungsgut-kolonial-kontext-en-data.pdf. Accessed 17 May 2023.

German Museums Association. "Guidelines on Dealing with Collections from Colonial Contexts." www.museumsbund.de/publikationen/guidelines-on-dealing-with-collections-from-colonial-contexts-2/. Accessed 17 May 2023.

"Guidelines for German Museums Care of Collections from Colonial Contexts." www.

museumsbund.de/wp-content/uploads/2021/03/mb-leitfaden-en-web.pdf. Accessed 8 May 2023.

He Zhipeng. "International Soft Law in the Era of De-globalization." *Journal of Wuhan University (Social Sceince)*, vol. 70, no. 4, p. 55.

"Holocaust (Return of Cultural Objects) Act 2009." www.lootedart.com/NQ2TYV515471. Accessed 16 May 2023.

IAL. "Restitution and Repatriation: A Practical Guide for Museums in England." www.artscouncil.org.uk/supporting-arts-museums-and-libraries/supporting-collections-and-cultural-property/restitution-and. Accessed 8 May 2023.

ICOM ad hoc Committee for the Return of Cultural Property. "Return of Cultural Property to their Countries of Origin: Bangladesh, Mali, Western Samoa—A Preliminary Survey of Three National Situations." *Witness to History: A Compendium of Documents and Writings on the Return of Cultural Objects*, edited by Lyndel. V. Prott, UNESCO Publishing, 2009, p. 183.

"ICOM Recommendations concerning the Return of Works of Art Belonging to Jewish Owners." www.lootedartcommission.com/OXSHQE36019. Accessed 5 Feb 2023.

Kowalski, Wojciech. "Types of Claims for Recovery of Lost Cultural Property." *Museum International*, vol. 57, no. 4, 2005, p. 97.

Merryman, John H. "Two Ways of Thinking about Cultural Property." *Thinking about Elgin Marbles: Critical Essays on Cultural Property, Art and Law*, edited by John Henry Merryman, Kluwer Law International, 2009, pp. 66–67.

Meyer, David A. "The 1954 Hague Convention and Its Emergence into Customary International Law." *Boston University International Law Journal*, vol. 11, no. 2, 1993, p. 356.

Prott, Lyndel V. Note on Terminology, *Witness to History: A Compendium of Documents and Writings on the Return of Cultural Objects*, UNESCO Publishing, 2009, p. xxi.

"Resolution 1205 (1999) of the Parliamentary Assembly on looted Jewish cultural property." www.lootedart.com/MG7Q7P50270. Accessed 6 Feb 2023.

Sarr, Felwine. and Savoy, Bénédicte. "The Restitution of African Cultural Heritage: Toward a New Relational Ethics." www.about-africa.de/images/sonstiges/2018/sarr_savoy_en.pdf. Accessed 16 May 2023.

Skrydstrup, Martin. "Theorizing Repatriation." *Journal of European Ethnology*, vol. 39, no. 2, pp. 57–58.

"The Restitution of African Cultural Heritage. Toward a New Relational Ethics." www.about-africa.de/images/sonstiges/2018/sarr_savoy_en.pdf. Accessed 16 May 2023.

UNESCO. "Convention for the Protection of Cultural Property in the Event of Armed Conflict", 1954. en.unesco.org/sites/default/files/1954_Convention_EN_2020.pdf. Accessed 22 May 2023.

UNESCO. "Convention on the Means of Prohibiting and Preventing the Illicit Import, Export and Transfer of Ownership of Cultural Property", 1970. www.unesco.org/en/legal-affairs/convention-means-prohibiting-and-preventing-illicit-import-export-and-transfer-ownership-cultural. Accessed 22 May 2023.

UN. General Assembly. "Protection and restitution of works of art as part of the preservation and further development of cultural values", U.N. Doc. A/RES/31/40, 1976. documents-dds-ny.un.org/doc/RESOLUTION/GEN/NR0/302/23/PDF/NR0302 23.pdf?OpenElement. Accessed 22 May 2023.

UN. General Assembly. "Restitution of works of art to countries victims of appropriation", U.N. Doc. A/RES/3187, 1973. digitallibrary.un.org/record/190996/files/A_RES_3187%28XXVIII%29-EN.pdf. Accessed 22 May 2023.

UN. General Assembly. "Restitution of works of art to countries victims of expropriation", U.N. Doc. A/RES/3391, 1975. digitallibrary.un.org/record/189355/files/A_RES_3391%28XXX%29-EN.pdf. Accessed 22 May 2023.

UN. General Assembly. "Restitution of works of art to countries victims of expropriation", U.N. Doc. A/RES/32/18, 1977. documents-dds-ny.un.org/doc/RESOLUTION/GEN/NR0/312/53/IMG/NR031253.pdf?OpenElement. Accessed 22 May 2023.

UNIDROIT. "UNIDROIT Convention on Stolen or Illegally Exported Cultural Objects", 1995. www.unidroit.org/instruments/cultural-property/1995-convention/. Accessed 22 May 2023.

Vrdoljak, Ana F. "International Law, Museums and the Return of Cultural Objects." *Witness to History: A Compendium of Documents and Writings on the Return of Cultural Objects*, edited by Lyndel V. Prott, UNESCO Publishing, 2009, p. 194.

Wang Yunxia, Hu Shanchen and Li Yuan. *The Road Home for Looted Cultural Relics: Legal and Ethical Issues in the Restitution of looted Cultural Relics during World*

War II. Chapters 1 and 2, The Commercial Press, 2021.

"Washington Conference Principles on Nazi-Confiscated Art." www.lootedartcommission.com/ Washington-principles. Accessed 5 Feb 2023.

重视国际软法在殖民地文物返还问题上的作用

王云霞 *

摘要： 殖民地时期被非法转移文物的返还是一个重要的历史遗留问题，既涉及对历史非正义行为的理性反思，也影响到相关国家之间的现实政治关系和长远社会发展。处理文物返还纠纷的现有国际公约由于缺乏溯及既往的效力，无法解决殖民地文物返还问题。《华盛顿原则》和国际博物馆协会《关于将犹太人艺术品返还其所有人的建议》等国际软法文件在处理二战期间犹太人被掠艺术品返还纠纷中已经发挥了巨大的作用，为类似历史遗留问题的解决积累了经验。法德等国殖民地文物返还政策探索了新的返还路径，并极大地促进了国际社会对殖民地文物返还必要性和可行性的思考。但仅仅依赖相关国家政府或博物馆自身的行动是不够的，应当由联合国教科文组织（UNESCO）或国际博协等重要的国际机构适时发布宣言，来建立殖民地文物返还的统一框架，为相关国家之间妥善解决殖民地文物返还提供依据。

关键词： 国际软法；殖民地时期；文物返还；文物

文物[①]是特定国家、特定民族对于其生活方式的独特表达，是该国家、民族历史的重要见证。文物的非法转移不仅破坏了文物的正常交易秩序，也引起文物原属国文化资源的急剧流失，造成原属国与流入国之间文化资源占有状况的严重不公平。因此，半个多世纪以来，国际社会逐步建立专门法律机制来打击文物的非法贩运，促进文物返还给原属国。然而，殖民

---

* 王云霞，中国人民大学法学院教授，联合国教科文组织"文化遗产法教席"主持人。
① 在中国法律语境中，"文物"大致相当于"物质文化遗产"，与国际通行的"文化财产"含义接近。本文提及相关国际法律文件时，尊其原有表达交替使用"文化财产"或"文物"一词。

地文物返还问题是一个复杂的历史遗留问题。自20世纪中叶以来，众多殖民地、被保护国获得独立，越来越多的国家摆脱了战乱状态，文物返还诉求逐渐增多，但相关各方一直未能在关键问题上达成共识。近年来，随着对殖民统治的反思日渐加深，如何积极应对殖民地文物返还诉求，成为国际社会需要共同面对的一个重大问题。

一、殖民地文物返还问题的复杂性和正当性

殖民地文物返还，指的是殖民背景下非法转移文物的返还，既涉及战争或占领期间的掠夺，也包括不公平的交易、不自愿的赠与或没收、征用等行为。该问题的复杂性不仅由于现有的国际法律文件缺乏针对性，更由于相关国家对殖民主义反思不足，对原属国的文物返还诉求缺乏足够的认同。

首先，既有的国际公约缺乏溯及力，无法直接适用于殖民地文物的返还诉求。国际社会自20世纪中叶以来陆续出台的相关文物返还公约主要适用于战争时期转移文物，以及和平时期被盗或非法出口文物的返还诉求。如1954年联合国教科文组织《关于发生武装冲突时保护文化财产的公约》（简称《海牙公约》）禁止在武装冲突情况下对另一缔约国文化财产进行盗窃、盗用、掠夺和任何形式的破坏行为，要求缔约各国对违反该公约的任何人，不论其国籍，采取一切必要步骤进行追诉并施以刑罚或予以制裁。[①]其第一议定书进一步要求缔约各方采取措施，防止在武装冲突期间从其所占领土内出口文化财产，并在敌对行为终止时，将已出口的位于其领土内的文化财产返还给被占领土的主管当局，且此项财产不得作为战争赔偿而予以留置。[②]该公约是世界上第一个专门针对文化财产保护的国际公约。虽然公约文本并未直接涉及文化财产的非法贩运及其返还问题，但其关于尊重被占领土上的文化财产、禁止武装冲突中肆意破坏文化

[①] 参见《海牙公约》第4条、第28条，公约中文版全文可在中华人民共和国条约数据库获得：http://treaty.mfa.gov.cn/web/detail1.jsp?objid=1531876071649，2023年2月1日访问。
[②] 参见《海牙公约》第一议定书第1条，https://www.unesco.org/en/legal-affairs/protocol-convention-protection-cultural-property-event-armed-conflict，2023年2月1日访问。

财产等规则被某些非缔约国和相关国际组织反复确认，在某种程度上已具有习惯国际法性质①，对于殖民地文物返还纠纷也具有参考价值。1970年联合国教科文组织《关于禁止和防止非法进出口文化财产和非法转让其所有权的方法的公约》（以下简称《1970年公约》）则是国际社会直面文化财产的非法贩运及其后果的首个多边条约。它要求缔约国采取必要措施，防止本国博物馆及类似机构获取来自另一缔约国的文化财产，禁止进口从另一缔约国的博物馆和公共纪念馆或类似机构中窃取的文化财产，并根据原主缔约国的要求，采取适当措施收回并返还此类文化财产；还要求缔约国通过一切适当手段，防止可能引起非法进出口的文化财产的所有权转让，并使非法出口的文化财产尽早归还其合法所有者。②该公约为缔约国之间处理非法转移文物的返还诉求提供了基本依据，也为相关缔约国之间缔结关于打击文物非法贩运和促进文物返还双边协议，以及有关区域多边合作提供了框架。由于该公约主要针对缔约国之间关于打击文物非法贩运的责任和文物返还国际合作进行规制，未能回应私法领域的文物返还请求，1995年，国际统一私法协会（UNIDROIT）受联合国教科文组织的委托，通过了《关于被盗或非法出口文物公约》（以下简称《1995年公约》），为私法领域统一有关文物返还规则奠定了重要基础。该公约规定：被盗（包括盗掘）文物占有人应当将文物返还给合法所有者，无论其是否为善意占有均应返还，但只要现占有人能够证明自己在获取该文物时尽到了审慎义务，可在返还文物时获得合理补偿；非法出口文物的原属国可以请求文物所在地国归还从其领土非法出口的文物，原属国只要能够证明文物的非法出口损害了其文化或宗教方面的利益，或该文物对于原属国具有重要的文化意义，所在地国法院或主管当局应命令归还该文

---

① 许多学者撰文讨论过《海牙公约》相关规则的习惯国际法性质，如David A. Meyer, The 1954 Hague Convention and Its Emergence into Customary International Law, 11 B.U. INT'L. L.J. (1993), P356；Victoria A. Birov, Prize and Plunder: The Pillage of Works of Art and the International Law of War, 30 N.Y.U. J. INT'L L. & POL. (1997), P208；钟慧：《武装冲突中的文化遗产的非法掠夺及其返还——试论一项新的国际习惯规则》，载《国际关系与国际法学刊》第8卷，第131—158页。

② 参见1970年公约第7条、第13条，公约中文版全文可在中华人民共和国条约数据库获得：http://treaty.mfa.gov.cn/tykfiles/20180718/1531876060956.pdf，2023年2月1日访问。

物。①虽然《1995年公约》的成员国较少，但其对欧盟相关法律和政策产生了较大影响，对于某些非缔约国的文物返还法律制度也产生了一定的影响，不少欧洲国家都修改了民法典或文化遗产法中相关审慎义务和诉讼时效等规定。②《1970年公约》和《1995年公约》规定的文物返还机制对于公约在缔约国生效后发生的非法转移文物的返还具有积极意义，但由于公约不具有溯及既往的效力，对于殖民地非法转移文物的返还纠纷则很难直接发挥作用。

其次，殖民地文物返还是一个长期得不到解决的历史遗留问题。在众多复杂因素中，一个最主要的原因是文物返还问题并未出现在大多数和平协议中。从15世纪末开始，随着欧洲通往印度洋和美洲的新航道的开辟，欧洲国家开始了对美洲、非洲和亚洲的大规模殖民活动，掠夺了无数殖民地文化瑰宝，并将它们运回欧洲，填满本国的博物馆。虽然第二次世界大战以后，许多殖民地摆脱了宗主国的殖民统治，但由于这些殖民地的最终诉求主要是政治独立，除了极少数情况外③，文物返还通常没有出现在与宗主国的和平协议中，使文物返还成为横亘在前宗主国与前殖民地之间长期得不到解决的历史遗留问题。

造成殖民地文物返还困难的另一个深层原因是殖民主义者对于殖民主义历史的反思不足。不少欧美博物馆认为大部分来自殖民地的藏品是合法的，比如是其出资购买或收藏者捐赠的，或者是殖民地人民"自愿"赠送的，或者基于"合作协议"分配得到的，不仅完全忽视这些藏品背后的殖

---

① 参见1995年公约第3条和第5条，公约中文版可在中华人民共和国条约数据库获得：http://treaty.mfa.gov.cn/tykfiles/20180718/1531876070902.pdf，2023年2月1日访问。

② 如瑞士、荷兰、比利时等国均引入了文物购买人的审慎义务，See Manlio Frigo, The Impact of the UNIDROIT Convention on International Case Law and Practice: An Appraisal, 20 Unif. L. Rev. 631-632 (2015).

③ 1919年《凡尔赛条约》也许是个例外，该条约第245、246和247条对一些特殊文物的归还做了规定，如1870—1871年普法战争期间和一战中从法国转移走的档案、历史纪念物和艺术品，被土耳其作为礼物赠送给德皇威廉二世的《古兰经》原始刻本，被德国人从德属东非带走的苏丹姆克瓦头盖骨等重要文物需在6个月内归还或移交给有关国家。第247条还要求德国对轰炸比利时鲁文图书馆造成的损失按照"同类归还"（Restitution in Kind）原则，向鲁文大学提供相同种类、相同价值的手稿、古籍、图书、地图和藏品等作为补偿。参见 Treaty of Versailles, Art. 238, 245, 246 & 247. 网址 https://www.files.ethz.ch/isn/125327/1416_Treaty_Versailles.pdf，2023年2月1日访问。

民掠夺历史,反而还强调其对于保护和展出这些文物的贡献,以此为由拒绝殖民地的返还诉求。①

事实上,殖民地时期非法转移文物的返还有其正当性。一方面,文物返还有助于恢复殖民地与宗主国之间在主权和文化遗产上的关系。"对于殖民占领者而言,这些文物代表着对一个王国中民众、领土和资源的占有。它们的集中和公开展示突出了国家性的帝国想象。与之相反,对于被殖民的民族而言,这些文物的迁移反映了土地、自治权和身份的丧失。"②因此,返还这些文物有助于修复殖民地与宗主国之间的正常关系。另一方面,文物返还有助于纠正历史非正义行为带来的恶劣影响。殖民主义统治往往伴随着种族灭绝和种族清洗,而对文物的掠夺则是种族灭绝和清洗的一个重要工具,所谓"灭人之国,必先去其史"。返还文物能够在一定程度上弥补历史非正义行为对受害者的侵害,同时也表明侵害者自身对历史非正义行为的反省。此外,返还文物还与去殖民化后更广泛的民族自决权联系在一起。文物是一个民族保存、复兴、发展其集体文化身份能力的基础,归还土地、祖先遗骸、文化遗产和资源的过程,有助于维护已经获得独立的前殖民地的民族自决权。③

二、国际软法在解决历史上非法转移文物返还问题上具有特殊的重要性

所谓"国际软法"是与"国际硬法"相对的概念。从法理上看,具有

---

① 《关于环球博物馆重要性和价值的声明》可以说是其中最典型的代表。2002年12月10日,一份由18个世界知名博物馆馆长签署的声明引起全球震惊,该声明强调:"那些几十年前甚至几百年前就存放于欧美各博物馆的物品和纪念物与今天的情形不同。多年来,由购买、捐赠和分配获得的物品,已经成为收藏它们的博物馆的一部分,因而也成为所在国家文化遗产的一部分。……(返还)将缩小博物馆藏品的多样性和丰富性,因而对观众是一种损害。"参见 Declaration on the importance and value of universal museums,网址:https://www.hermitagemuseum.org/wps/portal/hermitage/news/news-item/news/1999_2013/hm11_1_93/?lng 2023年2月1日访问。
② [澳]安娜·弗尔多利亚克:《国际法、博物馆和文物归还》,转引自[澳]林德尔·V.普罗特主编:《历史的见证》,国家文物局博物馆与社会文物司译,译林出版社2010年版,第169页。
③ 同上。

约束力的法律规范被视为硬法,而不具有约束力的规范则被视为软法。软法所涵盖的范围很广,除了生效的公约、条约、议定书外,所有设计上不具有约束力的国际法律文件,包括联合国大会的决议、实践准则、联合声明和宣言等均可被归入其中。① 由于硬法规范对相关缔约方设置了明确的权利和义务,具有较强的约束力,其起草、通过、签署和批准各个环节都需经过长时间的博弈和权衡才能完成,其实施过程也常常会出现各种争议和变数,在国际纠纷解决机制中,软法反而因其灵活性、引导性和非强制性能够发挥更大的作用。这一点在文化遗产保护领域表现得非常突出,尤其是在促进历史上发生的非法转移文物返还问题上,国际社会通过了许多不具有约束力的决议、建议、准则、示范法、原则、宣言等软法文件,为相关国家之间进行磋商提供了依据。其中比较有代表性的软法文件包括如下。

(一)联合国系统打击文物非法贩运的相关决议

作为致力于促进国际安全、经济发展、社会进步、民主自由和永久和平的重要国际组织,联合国从20世纪70年代开始,就不断呼吁各国加强合作,打击文化财产的非法贩运,返还因战争、殖民及盗窃、走私等原因非法转移的文化财产。联合国大会在20世纪70年代基本上每年均将该主题列入讨论议题,通过一个正式的《归还各国被掠夺艺术品》或《文化财产应送回或归还原主国》的决议,提请成员国政府加入联合国教科文组织《1970年公约》及其他相关文化遗产保护公约,积极打击文化财产的非法贩运,解决非法转移文化财产的返还问题。20世纪八九十年代,联合国大会通过涉及该主题决议的频率从每年一次,改为每两年一次。进入21世纪以后,联大会议通过此类决议的频率改为每三年一次。② 这些决议虽然没有直接针对殖民地文物返还问题进行规定,但其重新确认和肯定既有的国

---

① 参见何志鹏:《逆全球化潮流与国际软法的趋势》,载《武汉大学学报(哲学社会科学版)》2017年第4期,第55页。
② 参见联大会议2021年第76/16号《文化财产返还或归还原主国决议》开头部分,https://documents-dds-ny.un.org/doc/UNDOC/GEN/N21/375/03/PDF/N2137503.pdf?OpenElement,2023年2月4日访问。

际公约有关打击文化财产非法贩运的国际合作机制，欢迎一切自愿形式归还非法转移文化财产的举措，呼吁成员国制定相关法律和政策，加强对相关利害方的职业道德准则培训和公众教育，极大地提升了成员国对非法贩运文化财产行为的管控和打击力度，也提高了各国对历史上发生的非法转移文化财产返还问题的关注。此外，联合国教科文组织、人权理事会等机构出台的关于谴责肆意破坏文化遗产、保护文化权利方面的决议①，也维护了打击文化财产非法贩运、促进文化财产返还原属国的既有国际法规则。

（二）政府间国际会议和国际组织有关二战文物返还的原则和宣言

二战期间，许多国家的文物遭到大规模破坏和掠夺，或被占领当局当作战利品非法留置和转移。由于战后处理文物返还机制存在巨大漏洞，更由于东、西方世界的长期冷战，二战期间被非法转移文物的返还成为一个沉重的历史遗留问题。② 欧美国家和相关国际组织从20世纪90年代开始，对二战后未能彻底解决的纳粹掠夺犹太资产，尤其是艺术品及其他文化财产的返还问题重新展开对话和沟通，以推动各国展开返还行动。1998年"大屠杀时期资产返还问题"华盛顿国际会议签署的《关于遭纳粹没收艺术品的华盛顿原则》（以下简称《华盛顿原则》）③、1999年国际博物馆协会《关于将犹太人艺术品返还其所有人的建议》④以及欧洲委员会第1205号《有关被掠犹太文化财产的决议》⑤就是其中的重要代表。这些原则、建议

---

① 如人权理事会人权2018年3月22日通过的《文化权利和文化遗产保护决议》重申了联大会议决议的相关内容，并将促进非法贩运文化财产返还原属国与维护文化权利及其和平、发展紧密结合起来，https://documents-dds-ny.un.org/doc/UNDOC/GEN/G18/099/80/PDF/G1809980.pdf?OpenElement，2023年2月4日访问。
② 关于该主题的详细研究，可参见王云霞、胡姗辰、李源：《被掠文物回家路——"二战"被掠文物返还的法律与道德问题》，商务印书馆2021年版，第一、二章。
③ 参见华盛顿会议"关于处理纳粹所掠艺术品的原则"，网址：https://www.lootedartcommission.com/Washington-principles，2023年2月5日访问。作为华盛顿会议的后续行动，相关国家政府代表又于2000年召开维尔纽斯论坛和2009年召开特雷辛会议，分别发布了《维尔纽斯论坛宣言》和《特雷辛宣言》。
④ 参见《国际博协关于归还犹太人艺术品的建议》，网址：https://www.lootedartcommission.com/OXSHQE36019，2023年2月5日访问。
⑤ 参见 Resolution 1205 (1999) of the Parliamentary Assembly on Looted Jewish Cultural Property，网址：https://www.lootedart.com/MG7Q7P50270，2023年2月6日访问。

和决议鼓励各国政府和公共机构为解决被纳粹掠夺文物的返还提供更多的帮助和更广泛的合作，将原属于犹太人或其他合法所有者的艺术品归还给原所有权人或其后裔。在这些软法文件的推动下，欧美许多国家纷纷出台特别法律和政策，成立专门受理大屠杀时期被掠艺术品返还纠纷的机构，对被掠艺术品返还做出特别制度安排。比如英国2009年通过的《大屠杀（归还文物）法》（2019年修正），规定博物馆可以从藏品中撤出任何被纳粹政权窃取的文物，以便将这些文物归还给合法所有者或其继承人。[1]美国2016年通过的《大屠杀期间掠夺艺术品返还法》，则不仅赋予该法以溯及力，还突破了一般文物返还请求的诉讼时效，赋予被纳粹剥夺艺术品后人在发现其下落后6年的诉讼时效，以方便其通过诉讼恢复对艺术品的相关权利。[2]在返还实践中，《华盛顿原则》等软法文件也发挥了重要作用，不仅在相关法院判决中被作为判决理由援引，在可替代性纠纷解决机制中也成为双方谈判协商的重要依据。[3]

虽然这些软法文件只是针对二战时期被纳粹掠夺艺术品的返还，并未涉及殖民地文物返还问题，但为殖民地文物返还文物的解决提供了重要的参考。首先，二战期间发生的文物掠夺或非法转移与殖民地文物掠夺或非法转移具有相似的历史背景和行为模式，都与战争、军事占领或武力威胁相关联，都涉及对原所有人权利的非法剥夺；而且在不少国家和地区，二战交战国也存在殖民统治行为，如日本早在1905年即开始对朝鲜半岛实行殖民统治，导致朝鲜半岛被掠文物的返还问题异常复杂。其次，二战文物返还同样是一个需要突破现有法律规则去解决的历史遗留问题，既然国际社会可以通过一系列软法文件来促进各国改变现有法律规则，那么，用类似的方法解决殖民地文物返还问题也不是不可能的。

---

[1] 参见 *Holocaust (Return of Cultural Objects) Act 2009*，网址：https://www.lootedart.com/NQ2TYV515471，2023年2月6日访问。

[2] 参见 Erin Blakemore, Reclaiming Nazi-Looted Art Is about to Get Easier，网址：https://www.smithsonianmag.com/smart-news/new-law-will-make-it-easier-reclaim-nazi-looted-art-180961394/，2023年2月6日访问。

[3] 详情可参见日内瓦大学艺术法中心的文物返还数据库（ArThemis）：https://plone.unige.ch/art-adr/nazi-looted-art-spoliation-nazie，有不少案例提及《华盛顿原则》等软法文件发挥的作用。

三、促进殖民地文物返还宣言或建议的出台值得期待

半个多世纪以来,殖民地文物返还行动在相关国家之间一直在陆续进行,但这些行动都是以个案方式进行的,缺乏统一的政策和措施。2017年11月,正在布基纳法索访问的法国总统马克龙宣布了一项震惊世界的决定:法国将立刻返还国家博物馆系统所藏的殖民时代从撒哈拉以南非洲移走的所有文物。这项决定可以说在全球范围内产生了蝴蝶效应,掀起了殖民地文物返还的新浪潮。法国总统任命的专家小组发表了著名的《非洲文化遗产的返还:走向一种新的伦理关系》(即"马克龙报告"),对殖民地文物掠夺及其返还请求的历史背景进行了详细梳理,论证了返还殖民地文物的必要性。报告建议法国各国家博物馆对非洲文物的来源按照不同情况进行详细调查、列出清单,区分情况制定不同的返还计划和措施,还对返还可能涉及的法律障碍以及如何克服障碍提出了建议。[1]作为返还行动的第一步,法国政府随即启动了将一批1892年法国军队从阿波美皇家宫殿掠夺的文物返还给贝宁和塞内加尔的程序。德国紧随其后,也宣布将采取措施,归还其从殖民地掠夺或非法获取的文物。德国博物馆协会于2018年7月公布了《殖民背景下的收藏文物处置指南》,为德国博物馆查证具有殖民背景的文物来源以及归还的可能路径提供指导。[2]2019年3月13日,德国政府相关部门发布了《殖民背景下文物收藏处置框架原则》,号召公私文物收藏机构、科研机构对其收藏和拥有的殖民背景文物的来源进行彻底研究查证,并保证原属国及相关社区能够及时获知这些信息;还根据不同类型文物提出具体的处置要求,殖民背景下的文物返还请求应及时处理,并通过与原属国或相关社区的双边协议

---

[1] 参见 The Restitution of African Cultural Heritage. Toward a New Relational Ethics,网址:https://www.about-africa.de/images/sonstiges/2018/sarr_savoy_en.pdf,2023年2月7日访问。

[2] German Museums Association, Guidelines on Dealing with Collections from Colonial Contexts,网址:https://www.museumsbund.de/publikationen/guidelines-on-dealing-with-collections-from-colonial-contexts-2/,2023年2月7日访问。

实现返还。①

　　法德两国的返还行动也得到其他一些欧美国家的积极响应，荷兰、美国、英国等国均返还了某些殖民时期从非洲非法获得的文物。法德等国殖民地文物返还政策为殖民地文物返还奠定了重要基础，为更大范围内开展殖民地文物返还行动积累了经验。但是，也应该看到，仅靠某些国家的政策或博物馆的自觉行动是不够的。这些政策的实施强烈依赖领导者的执政理念，容易引起政治反对派的质疑，缺乏连贯性和稳定性。而收藏殖民地文物的博物馆自发采取的促进返还措施，不仅很难逾越藏品处置方面的法律障碍，也会引起各界对于博物馆定位及其发展的担心。也许，是时候由具有影响力的国际组织来考虑出台一项宣言或建议，为全球范围内殖民地文物返还提供框架性指引了。

　　鉴于殖民地文物返还问题的复杂性，我认为，可以借鉴以往二战文物返还软法文件和法德殖民地文物返还政策的某些经验，由联合国教科文组织或国际博协出台一项关于促进殖民地文物返还的宣言或建议。该宣言或建议至少应明确以下要点。

　　首先，明确返还的对象。凡是与殖民统治背景相关的被非法转移文物，无论是基于军事掠夺，还是占领时期被没收和征用，或者在军事威胁下被迫交易和捐赠的文物，只要不是基于原所有人的明确同意，继续收藏和保有都是不道德的，鼓励通过友好协商，返还其原属国或来源社区。

　　其次，对殖民地非法转移文物分类采取不同的处置建议：属于人体遗骸的文物必须尽快返还；基于军事掠夺或被没收和征用获得的文物应该优先返还；通过科学探险以及通过不公平购买或捐赠等途径获得的文物也应该尽量返还，除非有证据表明，它们得到了管理者或原所有人的明确同意。

　　再次，建议相关国家考虑适当变通现有的法律规则，如限制公共收藏品或国家财产不可让与规则的适用范围，延长有关文物返还请求的诉讼时

---

① *Framework Principles for Dealing with Collections from Colonial Contexts*，网址：https://www.auswaertiges-amt.de/blob/2210152/b2731f8b59210c77c68177cdcd3d03de/190412-stm-m-sammlungsgut-kolonial-kontext-en-data.pdf，2023年2月7日访问。

效，对善意取得制度进行限制等，以方便被非法转移文物的后人采取法律行动恢复其权利。

最后，对于确实存在法律障碍无法实现所有权意义上返还的文物，或者因疆界变更、后人无法确定等原因无法返还的文物，可以采用合作建立博物馆、文化活动中心、长期租赁、合作展览、数字化成果共享等方式，帮助受殖民统治影响的国家和社区实现其接近和享受文化遗产的权利。

总之，殖民地文物的非法转移是一种历史非正义行为，无论今天做什么都无法改变历史。但如果我们能够正视历史非正义行为的错误，纠正其造成的不公正后果，就能够在去殖民化时代开启合作与发展的新未来。而纠正历史非正义行为，不仅需要社会各界的共同努力，也需要法律工具的创新。

On Coloniality and Restitution from a Latin American Perspective

Américo Castilla[*]

As a former attorney at law, I confess that legal instruments are only the beginning, at times necessary beginnings, of an effort to formalize or encourage certain social behaviours, or rather impose social conducts which society, in all its complexity, sniffs, like dogs do, to find out if they were passed in the benefit of the same species or if they are rather the expression of conflicting or adverse interests.

UNESCO has been prolific in dictating guidelines and procedures in benefit of the conservation and fair management of cultural and natural heritage. I won't now quote that background legislation as other eminent jurists will foreseeably do it, but you may be reassured that in Latin America we have also done our part. The UNESCOs Conventions have been ratified by almost all countries of the region, and most recently two important convenings converged in México: the MondiaCult World Conference of Cultural Ministers[①], and the Ibero-American Museums 10th Conference[②] of all Spanish and Portuguese speaking countries of the world, and they both referred to the theme we are now discussing. MondiaCult on chapter 10 (vi), recommends: "expanding efforts to promote the protection, return and restitution of cultural property, including

---

[*] Américo Castilla, Academic Director, TyPA Lab on Museum Management, Argentina.
[①] https://www.unesco.org/sites/default/files/medias/fichiers/2022/09/6.MONDIACULT_EN_DRAFT%20FINAL%20DECLARATION_FINAL_1.pdf.
[②] http://www.ibermuseos.org/wp-content/uploads/2022/10/10eim-declaracion-es-1.pdf.

in consultation with the populations concerned and with their free, prior and informed consent"[1], and the Ibero-American convening, in chapters 3 and 9, recommends the: "Incorporation of the decolonial perspective in the institutions and museum processes" and the: "Emphasis on the solidarity values of ancestral knowledge and practices."

Even if the World Conference resolution goes more in detail into the processes of restitution, the Ibero-American Conference final statement goes to the chore of the mandate of the 18 countries involved when recommending: "incorporating the decolonial perspective in the institutions and museum processes". In other words, first we all need to understand the nature of the problem, and the reasons to impulse actions to revert the conscious or unconscious acceptance of centuries of imposition of a racist frame of power still in operation.

What is that decolonial perspective as seen from Latin America, and which have been the practical examples of the efforts, not always successful, to critically revert the scenario? Rita Segato[2], an Argentine anthropologist who has worked widely in Latin America over themes of coloniality and violence against women, says: "Coloniality not only organizes the world economically in a proto-global market, but also organizes our subjectivity. Dictating how to think, feel, and be

---

[1] Chapter 17 of the MondiaCult Resolution further recommends: We call for an open and inclusive international dialogue for the return and restitution of cultural property, including illegally exported property, to countries of origin under UNESCO's aegis, as well as those outside the scope of the UNESCO 1970 Convention, as an ethical imperative to foster the right of peoples and communities to the enjoyment of their cultural heritage, and in light of the increasing claims from the countries concerned, with a view to strengthen social cohesion and intergenerational transmission of cultural heritage; and we encourage UNESCO to promote the effective implementation of existing legal frameworks or policies for the return of cultural property to its countries of Origin or its restitution in case of illicit appropriation, through proactive mediation by the UNESCO Intergovernmental Committee for Promoting the Return of Cultural Property, and to assist countries in the conservation and management of cultural property in situ, through capacity building and the promotion of educational and culturally sensitive approaches, notably in museums and cultural institutions. We also call on UNESCO, as the leading UN.

[2] Segato, Rita. *The Critique of Coloniality*. Routledge, UK, 2022.

in the world. The coloniality of power, of knowledge, of feeling, is the cognitive empire of Eurocentrism, given by the moral superiority of the European, which gives rise to modernity as a claim to universal knowledge". I think that this thought of Rita's condenses a lot of what we are talking about, because our work as museum leaders begins precisely at that point. In investigating how coloniality has been formed, how it has been constituted, that is, how in those processes of constitution, it has removed alternative knowledge. The modernity machinery, from the 16th century to the present time was constituted by cornering all existing knowledge, and not only that of the great civilizations, but of all cultural groups that preceded it. And the museum, as in many cases the church and the university, fulfilled a fundamental task in the founding of that Western civilization and the destitution of other civilizations and of that other knowledge. Investigating then goes beyond tracing the genealogy of the museum from the cabinets of curiosities to today and its drifts from Europe to the Americas. Investigating is uncovering, removing the veil, its function in this operation of constitution/removal. So how do we set free from that code?

How do we rethink it? According to Walter Mignolo[1], it is necessary to restore a terminology that the colonial code dismissed, given that in the West, the code "epistemology" dismissed the notion of "gnoseology", and "aesthetics" dismissed "aesthesis". A gnoseological reconstruction of epistemology and aesthesis of aesthetics are therefore among our current preoccupations. In other words, rather than trying to decolonize the museum, we should focus on decolonizing the idea we have of what the museum institution is, and on how to undertake decolonial tasks that contribute to restoring knowledge and building future knowledge according to different frames of values based on solidarity, and accepting nature as part of, and not alien of our own existence.

Is a meteorite a cultural good? According to the Mocovi first nation

---

[1] Mignolo, Walter D. Delinking. The rhetoric of modernity, the logic of coloniality and the grammar of de-coloniality. *Cultural Studies*, n. 21(2-3), p. 449-514, 2007.

people of Argentina it certainly is[①], as the one that grounded in their territory is believed to bring harmony to one of the most discriminated communities, renews fertility and transmits heavenly powers to those who dance around it. A field of meteorites at "Campo del Cielo" (Heavenly Field) in the province of Chaco, Argentina, where one of the biggest meteorites in the world has fallen, is in such way invested with cultural attributes as to have been claimed by Latin American artists to be taken to the 2022 Documenta Biennial at Kassel, Germany, to represent their culture (its monumental weight could have been one of the impediments, not to mention the local first nations opposition to its removal from a sacred space).

The unfair market transactions and spoliations of goods despite their strong spiritual meaning for its owners, have a long history, mainly of artistic, historical, paleontological, and ethnographic or archaeological pieces. As we now see, also meteorites may be added to that list. They all require some type of predominance of power by the acquirer or spoiler, whether economic, political, military, or social. It is at that point that the colonial frame of power persists. Unless in the case of voluntary donation of cultural goods as part of a community's social phenomena, as studied by the anthropologist Marcel Mauss[②], those forced appropriations disregard the powerful social and ceremonial value attached to those pieces and are labeled at fancy museums according to a colonial aesthetic pattern. To prevent those transactions, some countries of Latin America declare them as State ownership and require the public registration of those cultural goods possessed by civil citizens, who can only transmit them by inheritance, but not buy, sell, import, or export them.[③]

---

① https://meteoritoelchaco.wordpress.com/2012/10/09/la-nacion-oculta-en-el-meteorito/.

② Mauss, Marcel. *Essai sur le don. Forme et raison de l'échange dans les societés archaiques* (*L'Année Sociologique* 1923–1924).

③ The author, as Secretary of Heritage of Argentina, had the privilege of putting into effect the Law 25.743/2003. https://www.argentina.gob.ar/normativa/nacional/ley-25743-86356, the Committee for the Prevention of Illicit Traffic of Cultural Goods, and its public campaign.

In Argentina, a very strong campaign against the illicit traffic of cultural goods was well received and was widely exhibited in airports and control posts all over the country. Illegal imports of archaeological goods from Perú, Bolivia and Ecuador were legally seized by the Argentine government and offered back to the countries to which they belong. In this case, restitution was not previously claimed by the Andean countries but on the contrary, they were unexpected recipients of the offer of extraordinary collections which they had considered lost. The looting of fossils destined to commercial markets such as the annual fossil market in Tucson, Arizona, USA, determined the Argentine government to build a case at the Arizona Court of Justice to restitute a whole lift-van full of scientific and cultural evidence illegally smuggled from paleontological sites, mainly of Patagonia, where they are part of its cultural landscape.

Even if the States legislate and campaign, there is a question remaining. How do the descendants of the first nations communities, or mestizo cultures, react to the persistence of colonial behavior and which are their actual and legitimate demands? And furthermore, how do current citizens of all origins who inhabit our countries react to rooted colonial mandates? An interesting case, linked to sacred ceremonial sacrifices done at very high altitudes of the Andes mountains performed by the Incas around the 15 Century, is now subject to contemporary discussions and not only among archaeologists or indigenous groups, but by all those concerned with climate change and social urgencies. The Inca Trail, declared World Heritage Landscape by UNESCO in 2014, points out specific human actions such as the exceptional burial rituals performed by offering the lives of Inca youngsters of noble linage in mountain peaks over 5,000 and up to 6,700 meters high, mostly at the South of their large empire, or Tihuantisuyu, probably as a tribute to the water provision for their sustainability. Those mummified corpses, originally considered messengers to the superior forces of nature, were found by archaeologists in recent decades, wrapped together with material representations of the Inca Empire — golden llamas, figures of men, Amazonian feather tufts, carved ocean valves and illustrated textiles—and brought down to urban museums or universities for further studies and exhibitions. The unconsented indigenous inhabitants of the region are now blaming these practices for the desertification of their land and claim the human remains and objects to be taken back to their sacred sites. Much is still to be learned about those ecosystems and cosmovision in terms of harmony. Also, the example of the Kallawaya herbal knowledge of Bolivia, also declared as Intangible Cultural Heritage by UNESCO in 2003, speaks of a mouth-to-mouth transmission of indigenous medical healing that have cured generations of people and required safeguarding from undiscriminated medical labs business. The materialization of these legal or safeguarding provisions in Latin America is far from reaching the whole of the 50 million indigenous peoples, holders of a knowledge that needs to be reconstituted.

In short, the word restitution involves values of respect to diversity, equity, and justice that, when violated, may affect communities within their own national context or victimized by the "collapse of global biodiversity, or the power of an economic system dependent on the fallacy of endless growth, consumption, and debt"[①]. Also, colonial mandates may be rooted in such a way within a particular society, conveying racism and injustice many centuries after foreign political domination seems over. Museums are not totally aware of the fact that they were created as important components of those hegemonic roles, and there is no such thing as a post-colonial period as if it were only a neutral field of study. There is a colonial condition, called coloniality as first described by the Peruvian sociologist Anibal Quijano[②], which still today cancels knowledge and promotes racism, and museums have the opportunity and responsibility to promote a unique discussion, helped by their polysemic and, in

---

① Janes, Robert. The Value of Museums in averting societal collapse. *Curator Magazine*, 2022.
② Quijano, Aníbal. Coloniality of Power, Eurocentrism and Latin America. *Nepantla: Views from South*, n. 1, v. 3, pp. 533-580, 2000.

the best of cases, polyphonic collections.

Universality of laws are now in crisis, as also is endless global growth. The initiative for restitution is not limited to material goods — and we have given examples of how objects are not "cultural" according to their colonial periodical classification (artistic, historical, or ethnographic), and rather respond to the feelings, use and adscriptions awarded by diverse peoples — but must be accompanied by the most important of restitutions, that of the production of knowledge unfairly cancelled. Legal dispositions may only be legitimate if they respond to a mature discussion and necessary efforts for consent among diverse ways of understanding this extraordinary and unequal planet.

论殖民性——拉丁美洲视角下的殖民性与返还问题

亚美利卡·卡斯蒂洛 *

对一名曾经做过律师的人来说，我认为将一些行为写入法律条文有时只是将某些特定的社会行为正式化或程序化的起点，更确切地说，是一种在复杂的社会中规训和探查的手段，通过这种方式确认这些行为是否对同一物种有利，或者它们是否是利益冲突时矛盾的体现。但即便是处于这些潜在的纷繁矛盾之中，联合国教科文组织在制定指导方针和程序方面也卓有成效。

为了加强文化和自然遗产的保护并对其进行公平管理，联合国教科文组织做出了很多努力。在此我不再赘述文化遗产保护立法的背景，因为可能其他法学专家还会提到这点。但是你可以相信，拉丁美洲在文化遗产保护方面已经尽心尽力。联合国教科文组织制定的各项公约已经得到了南美洲近乎所有国家与地区的认可与批准。最近，在墨西哥召开了两次会议①，这两次会议特别提到了我们现在正在进行的讨论，其中之一是MondiaCult世界文化部长会议。另一个是全体西语系国家的第十届伊比利亚美洲博物馆会议。②这两个会议都在谈论我们现在的主题。比如：MondiaCult世界文化部长会议在第十章的第五部分提到："促进文化财产的保护和返还，包括与相关群体协商，尊重他们的自由并征得他们的事先知情权和同意。"③

---

* 亚美利卡·卡斯蒂洛，阿根廷艺术理论与实践基金会实验中心博物馆管理研究院学术主管。

① https://www.unesco.org/sites/default/files/medias/fichiers/2022/09/6.MONDIACULT_EN_DRAFT%20FINAL%20DECLARATION_FINAL_1.pdf.

② http://www.ibermuseos.org/wp-content/uploads/2022/10/10eim-declaracion-es-1.pdf.

③ Chapter 17 of the MondiaCult Resolution further recommends: We call for an open and inclusive international dialogue for the return and restitution of cultural property, including illegally exported property, to countries of origin under UNESCO's aegis, as well as those outside the scope of the UNESCO 1970 Convention, as an ethical imperative to foster the right of peoples and（转下页）

第十届伊比利亚美洲博物馆会议在其第三章和第九章也提到:"建议将非殖民主义观点纳入相关机构和博物馆的发展进程中。"同时也"强调这种一以贯之的知识与实践的团结价值观。"

虽然这个世界性会议的决议更加详细地讨论了文化遗产返还的过程,但这并不意味着我们对于这些内容有了更深的认知。会议的最后声明触及了18个相关国家的核心任务。该任务是在建议将去殖民主义视角纳入相关机构和博物馆的发展进程时提出的。换言之,我们首先需要了解问题的本质以及我们必须采取行动来扭转几个世纪以来仍在运作的种族主义权力框架的理由。

那么从拉丁美洲文化圈的视角看,什么是去殖民化呢?又有哪些实际的事例表明,批判性地扭转殖民化情况的努力并不总是成功的呢?阿根廷人类学家丽塔·塞加托[①](Rita Segato)在拉丁美洲广泛从事殖民主义和针对妇女的暴力问题研究。她认为:"殖民主义不仅在经济上把世界组织成一个全球市场原型,同时也塑造了我们的主体性,塑造了我们如何思考、感受并融入这个世界的方式。权力、知识和情感的殖民性是通过赋予欧洲人的道德优越性而构成的欧洲中心主义的认知帝国主义,这将现代性视为了普适的认知。"我认为这一观点浓缩了很多我们现在正在讨论的内容。因为我们作为博物馆领导者的工作正是从这一点开始的:研究殖民性是如何形成的。研究它的构成,它的建构机制中,殖民性如何取代了丰富多样

(接上页) communities to the enjoyment of their cultural heritage, and in light of the increasing claims from the countries concerned, with a view to strengthen social cohesion and intergenerational transmission of cultural heritage; and we encourage UNESCO to promote the effective implementation of existing legal frameworks or policies for the return of cultural property to its countries of Origin or its restitution in case of illicit appropriation, through proactive mediation by the UNESCO Intergovernmental Committee for Promoting the Return of Cultural Property, and to assist countries in the conservation and management of cultural property in situ, through capacity building and the promotion of educational and culturally sensitive approaches, notably in museums and cultural institutions. We also call on UNESCO, as the leading UN agency in the fight against illicit traffic in cultural proprieties, to propose concrete measures and initiatives to combat this increasing phenomenon and encourage art market actors, museums and private collectors; and to adopt an updated text of the International Code of Ethics for Traders in Cultural Property.

① Segato, Rita. *The Critique of Coloniality*. Routledge, UK, 2022.

的文化信息。从16世纪到现在，现代性机制是通过攫取所有现有的信息知识而构成的，不仅是伟大文明的知识信息，而且是在它之前的所有文化群体的知识。博物馆在许多情况下，像教会和大学一样，在西方文明的建立过程中完成了一项基本任务。对所有文明和所有文化信息进行研究，不仅可以追溯人类的收藏形式从最初的珍奇柜到今天的博物馆，也包括了收藏文化从欧洲漂流到美洲的考察。研究调查让神秘与未知之事展现于世，拂去尘埃，展露真相。那么我们要如何跳出程序的限制，如何进行重新思考？

沃尔特·米尼奥洛[①]（Walter Mignolo）是阿根廷裔的伟大思想家，在美国杜克大学工作，他说我们需要重建博物馆学的认识论。与其试图将博物馆去殖民化，我们更应该专注于将自己的想法去殖民化。我们也应该对于博物馆机构的性质有一个清晰的认知。我们应该弄清楚如何开展有助于恢复多样认知的去殖民化工作，根据不同的价值观框架，以和谐与团结为基础，建立我们未来的认知体系，我们也要接受自然，把它视为我们自身存在的一部分。

陨石是文化物品吗？阿根廷麦科维原住民的答案是肯定的。[②]因为陨石根植于他们生活的土地，被认为能给备受歧视的社区带来和谐，以团结为纽带，陨石将上天的力量传递给那些在它周围跳舞的人。在阿根廷查科省，一块由陨石组成的黄色陨石场，曾是世界上最大的陨石之一，它以这种方式被赋予了文化属性。拉丁美洲当代艺术家们在2022年德国卡塞尔文献双年展上宣布，陨石代表了拉丁美洲的文化（但是陨石巨大的重量将成为一个障碍，不仅如此，原住民反对将其从他们神圣的土地上移走）。

这种对所有者具有强烈精神意义的物品的不公平市场交易和商品掠夺有着悠久的历史。其交易及掠夺对象主要是艺术、历史、古生物、民族志或考古类的物件。正如我们现在看到的，陨石也可能被交易与掠夺，这些交易都需要某种类型的优势力量，即：收购方或掠夺者在经济、政治、军

[①] Mignolo, Walter D. Delinking. The rhetoric of modernity, the logic of coloniality and the grammar of decoloniality. *Cultural Studies*, n. 21 (2-3), pp. 449-514, 2007.

[②] https://meteoritoelchaco.wordpress.com/2012/10/09/la-nacion-oculta-en-el-meteorito/.

事或社会方面拥有某种类型的优势权力。正因为这一现象，殖民权力的框架继续存在。除非自愿捐赠文化物品作为我们社区社会现象的一部分。正如人类学家马塞尔·莫斯①（Marcel Mauss）所研究的那样，这些强行占有的行为无视了这些作品所具有的强大的社会和纪念价值，并在花哨的博物馆里按照殖民主义的审美模式被贴上标签。为了防止这种交易，一些拉丁美洲国家宣布艺术品以及文化遗产为国家所有。同时，要求对主权公民所拥有的文化产品进行公开登记，公民只能通过继承来拥有它们，而不能对其进行购买、出售、进口或出口行为。②在阿根廷，一场声势浩大的打击非法贩运文物的运动受到好评，并在全国各地的机场检查站广泛传播，并产生了正面反响。而这种宣传活动，劝退了炫耀私人考古和古生物相关收藏的人。从秘鲁、玻利维亚和厄瓜多尔非法进口的考古文化遗产等相关物品被阿根廷政府合法没收，并且被返还给它们原本所属的国家。在这种情况下，安第斯国家之前并没有要求返还，相反，他们意外地收到了之前认为已经丢失的特别藏品。掠夺的化石注定要进入商业市场，例如美国亚利桑那州图森市的年度化石市场。阿根廷政府决定向亚利桑那州法院提起诉讼，要求返还从古生物学遗址（主要是巴塔哥尼亚地区）非法走私来的一整套科学和文化遗产，它们是巴塔哥尼亚文化景观的一部分。

即使各州进行立法和宣传，但仍然存在一个问题。原住民公民或混血文化的后代对持续的殖民行为有什么样的反应？哪些是他们实际且合法的需求？此外，居住在我们国家的所有民族的公民如何对根深蒂固的殖民主义作出反应？有一个与在安第斯山脉高海拔地区举行的神圣祭祀仪式有关的有趣案例。15世纪左右印加人的神圣祭祀仪式，现在成为当代讨论的主题，对其产生关注的不仅是考古学家或原住民人群，也包括关心气候变化和社会热点的人们。印加古道，2014年被联合国教科文组织评为世界遗产景观，这包括了特定的人类行为，比如特殊的丧葬仪式，在海拔超过

---

① Mauss, Marcel. Essai sur le don. Forme et raison de l'échange dans les sociétés archaiques (L'Année Sociologique 1923–1924).
② The author, as Secretary of Heritage of Argentina, had the privilege of putting into effect the Law 25.743/2003. https://www.argentina.gob.ar/normativa/nacional/ley-25743-86356, the Committee for the Prevention of Illicit Traffic of Cultural Goods, and its public campaign.

5 000米、高达6 700米的山峰上，献祭印加贵族血统年轻人的习俗。这些山峰大多位于他们庞大帝国的南部，或者位于Tihuantisuyu，可能是为了献祭给当地水资源的持续供应。那些木乃伊化的尸骸最初被认为是超自然力量的信使，他们是考古学家在近几十年间发现的，与印加帝国的其他物质遗存一起被包裹起来：金羊驼、人像、亚马逊羽毛丛、精美的雕刻和绘图纺织品，它们被带到城市博物馆以及大学中进行进一步的研究和展览。本地的印加后裔原住民现在正在谴责这些未经允许就带走文物的行为，他们认为这导致了本地土地的沙漠化，并要求将人类遗骸和印加遗物送回圣地。关于生态系统与宇宙观的和谐理论，仍存在着许多未知。除此之外，玻利维亚的卡拉瓦亚草药知识也是一个很好的事例。在2003年，它被联合国教科文组织评为非物质文化遗产口口相传的本土医学治疗方法，已经使一代又一代的人受益。受益者则要求对其进行保护，确保不受到医疗实验室的业务歧视。这一法律或保障条款在拉丁美洲的落实还远远不够，拉丁美洲的5 000万原住民甚至更多人的认知体系需要重构。

简而言之，"返还"这个词包含了尊重多样、平等和公平正义的价值观。这些价值观若受到侵犯可能会影响到各自国家的相关人群。"全球生物多样性的崩溃，或者依赖无休止增长、消费和债务谬论的经济体系的力量"[1]也会使相关人群受到影响。此外，殖民主义可能以这种方式根植于特定社会。在殖民国家的政治统治似乎结束后的许多个世纪里，依旧在制造着种族主义和不公。博物馆并没有完全意识到，它们是作为这些霸权角色的重要组成部分而创建的。同时也不存在所谓的后殖民时期，似乎它只是一个中立的研究领域。秘鲁社会学家阿尼巴尔·奎杰罗[2]（Aníbal Quijano）首先提出了一种被称为殖民性的殖民状态，这种殖民状况至今仍在消除知识，滋长种族主义，而博物馆有机会和责任推动一场由多元文化所引领的独特讨论。在最好的情况下，通过汇集博物馆中的多元藏品，进行多元文化的表达。

---

[1] Janes, Robert. The Value of Museums in averting societal collapse. *Curator Magazine*, 2022.
[2] Quijano, Aníbal. Coloniality of Power, Eurocentrism and Latin America. *Nepantla: Views from South*, n. 1, v. 3, pp. 533–580, 2000.

法律的普适性和无尽的全球性增长现在正处于危机之中。返还的倡议并不局限于物质物品，我们已经举例说明，在殖民时期不属于"文化"的物品，它们未来将可能是艺术的、历史的、民族的，在不同民族中有着不同的情感、功能和赞誉。这种意识是伴随文化遗产返还的最重要的部分。因此，要彻底扭转不平等的殖民认知对于社会价值观的侵蚀。只有经过成熟的讨论和必要的努力，在理解这个非凡而不平等的世界里的各种方式下达成一致，法律处置才可能是合法的。

Examining the Museum Decolonisation and "Semi-colonial"

Yong Duan Ruiqi Zhang Xi Zheng[*]

Abstract: The loss of cultural objects is a common international phenomenon that has accompanied colonisation and globalisation over the last three centuries. Colonies lost a large number of representative cultural objects in the context of an unjust international political and economic order, and there is still serious illegal smuggling of objects. With the gradual independence and development of some countries over the last hundred years, the conflict between those countries which lost artifacts and those which received them has become more acute. The *Declaration on the Importance and Value of Universal Museums* published in 2002 by 18 museums from seven countries, represented a position taken by some large European and American museums against the restitution of cultural objects. However, in the last decade, with the joint and continuous efforts of the international communities, UNESCO and ICOM, the countries represented by France, Germany and the Netherlands, from the government to the academics and public, have gradually shown a new attitude and willingness to return cultural objects with a colonial background, and there are more and more promising cases and trends. It is worth noting that after 1840, China was embroiled in internal and external wars, and its society was in what scholars call a "semi-colonial" state, with a lack of government authority

---

[*] Yong Duan, Vice Chancellor of Shanghai University, Shanghai, China. Ruiqi Zhang, Researcher and Deputy Secretary General Research Center for Chinese Relics Overseas, Shanghai, China. Xi Zheng, a teacher at Middle School Affiliated to East China University of Science and Technology, Shanghai, China.

and socio-economic depression, during which time many valuable and precious cultural objects were also illegally lost, one of which is the Tang Dynasty Honglujing Stone. Lost cultural objects from similar war-torn and semi-colonial contexts should also be brought to the attention of the international community in order to better achieve fair justice in terms of cultural objects that balances history and reality through international understanding and cooperation.

Key words: Loss of Cultural Objects; Restitution; Decolonisation; Semi-colony

Cultural heritage is a testament to human civilisation, a bridge that connects the past, present and future of human society. The cultural heritage of different regions and ethnic groups is not only the material carrier of the history and culture, but also the intermediary for mutual understanding and communication. Unfortunately, due to complex political and economic factors, especially in the large-scale colonial activities of European and American powers, there has been a problem of illegal outflow of a large number of cultural objects.

The international loss of cultural property is a widespread phenomenon that has accompanied colonisation and globalisation for almost three centuries. The loss of sovereignty of the colonies has led to the loss of a large number of representative cultural relics under an unjust international political and economic order. According to the survey by the Senegalese scholar Felwine Sarr and the French art historian Bénédicte Savoy, more than 90% of Africa's (sub-Saharan) material cultural heritage is scattered in European and American museums.[1] About 40% of the collections in the Dutch Nationaal Museum van Wereldculturen have a colonial

---

[1] Felwine Sarr and Bénédicte Savoy, *Rapport sur la restitution du patrimoine culturel africain: Vers une nouvelle éthique relationnelle*, Ministère de la Culture and Université Paris Nanterre, 2018-11, http://restitutionreport2018.com/sarr_savoy_fr.pdf.

background.① In 1997 and 1998, ICOM adopted the theme of "The fight against illicit traffic of cultural property" for International Museum Day. This is the only time since the creation and launch of International Museum Day in 1992 that the same theme has been used for two consecutive years, an indication of the importance that the international museum community attaches to illicit trafficking of cultural goods. According to UNESCO statistics, the illegal trade in cultural heritage is still the third largest illegal trade after drugs and arms smuggling. It is clear that the loss of artifacts is both a historical problem and a current problem.

Over the past decade, the relentless pursuit of the countries that have lost artifacts and the concerted efforts of the international community have brought cultural objects with a colonial background, collected in countries that have received them, to the forefront of international attention. Current research on the issue of cultural objects restitution focuses mainly on the decolonisation of museums, the study of illicitly trafficked cultural property, and related legal and ethical issues. Some scholars interpret the cultural heritage issues in terms of emotional value and resonance②, accusing some countries of treating colonial cultural objects as "spoils of war" while projecting the dominant position of the white man in their museums.③

1. Hard line of the *Universal Declaration* and the Change of Position in the Last Decade

In the 1970s and 1990s, the international discussions on issues such as the

---

① The Nationaal Museum Van Wereldculturen was founded in 2014 by the Tropenmuseum in Amsterdam, the Afrika Museum in Behr-Dahl and the Museum Volkenkunde in Leiden. There are around 450,000 objects in the collection, around 40% of which from colonial context. See: Catherine Hickley. *The Netherlands: Museums confront the country's colonial past*. https://en.unesco.org/courier/2020-4/netherlands-museums-confront-countrys-colonial-past.

② Smith, L. S. 2020. *Emotional Heritage: Visitor Engagement at Museums and Heritage Sites*. London: Routledge. Tolia-Kelly, D., E. Waterton, and S. Watson, (eds.) 2017. *Heritage, Affect, and Emotion: Politics, Practices, and Infrastructures*. London: Routledge.

③ Dan Hicks, *The Brutish museums: the Benin Bronzes, colonial violence and cultural restitution*. London: Pluto Press. 2020.

protection of cultural property and the fight against cultural heritage crime led to the generation of the UNESCO *Convention on the Means of Prohibiting and Preventing the Illicit Import, Export, and Transfer of Ownership of Cultural Property* (1970 Convention for short)[1] and the UNIDROIT *Convention on Stolen or Illegally Exported Cultural Objects* (1995 Convention for short)[2], which played an important role in promoting a new order in international cultural exchange. However, their role in the practice of restitution of cultural objects is limited by their limitations in terms of time (no retroactive effect to pre-signature cases), space (small number of collecting countries that are parties to the Convention) and object (limited to harm to special interests).

The ongoing recovery of repatriation of the so-called "Elgin Marbles"[3] by Greece led to the publication of the *Declaration on the Importance and Value of Universal Museums*[4] (2002, Universal Declaration for short), initiated

---

[1] UNESCO. *Convention on the Means of Prohibiting and Preventing the Illicit Import, Export and Transfer of Ownership of Cultural Property*. 1970−11−14. https://en.unesco.org/about-us/legal-affairs/convention-means-prohibiting-and-preventing-illicit-import-export-and.

[2] UNIDROIT. *Convention on Stolen or Illegally Exported Cultural Objects*. 1995−06−24. https://www.unidroit.org/instruments/cultural-property/1995-convention/.

[3] The Elgin Marbles were originally part of the Parthenon Temple in Athens, Greece. They were bought by Lord Elgin from the Ottoman rulers occupying Greece and shipped back to England. They were eventually collected by the British Museum. The Greek government and public have asked for their return, but this has been refused. For an introduction to the Elgin Marbles, see: https://www.britishmuseum.org/about-us/british-museum-story/contested-objects-collection/parthenon-sculptures.

[4] The Bizot Group, also known as the International Group of Organizers of Major Exhibitions, is organized by Irène Bizot, the director of the Réunion des Musées Nationaux, founded in 1992 as an international group of museums that regularly organizes meetings of the world's major museum directors. The conference aims to promote exchanges between museums, including the exchange of exhibits and exhibitions, and dialogue on policies and strategies related to the development of museum. see: Emmanuel Koblenz, "Wink. The 'Groupe Bizot': a cartellisation of the major museum institutions?", *Business and History*, vol. 3, no 76, 2014, pp. 143– 145 ; Kostas Arvanitis (2016). *Museums and Restitution: New Practices, New Approaches*. Routledge.

by the Bizot Group[1] and signed by the directors of 18 museums from seven European and American countries, namely the Art Institute of Chicago, the Museum of Fine Arts in Boston, the Museum of Modern Art in New York, the Cleveland Museum of Art, the Philadelphia Museum of Art, J. Paul Getty Museum in Los Angeles, the Solomon R. Guggenheim Museum in New York, the Los Angeles County Museum of Art, the Whitney Museum of American Art in New York, the Metropolitan Museum of Art, the Bavarian State Museum in Munich, the State Museums in Berlin, the Galleria degli Uffizi in Florence, the Prado Museum in Spain, the Thyssen-Bornemisza Museum in Madrid, the Rijksmuseum in Amsterdam, the State Hermitage Museum in St. Petersburg, and the Louvre Museum in Paris. This statement is a strong expression of the Universal Museum's rejection of the return of artifacts that are the common cultural property of all humanity. Although not a signatory, the British Museum later issued a statement in support of the Declaration.[2] Upon its release, the international community and the museum field were stunned and criticised by various voices from the International Council of Museums (ICOM) and national museum organisations including China. Some scholars believe that the essence of this statement is to exempt the "universal museum" from relics claims.[3] Some also question whether the statement implies an endorsement of colonialism, as museums are tools for preserving, expanding and reproducing memories, and the display of colonial artifacts in museums is actually a continuation of violence and trauma[4], playing an even more prominent role.[5]

---

[1] Yong Duan. "The Universal Museum and Cultural Heritage", *Chinese Museum*, vol. 4, 2007, pp. 56–62.

[2] Lyndel V. Prott. *Witnesses to History: A Compendium of Documents and Writings on the Return of Cultural Objects*. Paris: UNESCO press, 2009, p. 118.

[3] Geoffrey Lewis. The universal museum: a special case?. *ICOM*, 2004 (01), p. 3.

[4] Dan Hicks, *The Brutish Museums: The Benin Bronzes, Colonial Violence and Cultural Restitution*. London: Pluto Press. 2020, pp. 181–182.

[5] Nicholas Thomas, *Entangled Objects: Exchange, Material Culture, and Colonialism in the Pacific*, Cambridge MA: Harvard University Press, 1991.

It was then that the authors began their formal research into the subject of lost cultural objects.

The Universal Declaration became a symbol of the hard line of refusing to return artifacts to their countries of origin, but it was actually an elegy reflecting back to the traditional dominant thinking. It has also stimulated extensive attention, thinking and research by the international community on the issue of illicit trafficking of artifacts, and has continually placed European and American museums that collect such artifacts under constant moral scrutiny. Under the pressure of repatriation from the countries of origin, the spirit of international conventions and public opinion in Europe and America, colonial background artifacts with both historical and realistic significance have become a hot research topic in the past decade, and countries such as France, Germany and the Netherlands have gradually changed their attitude towards colonial contexts artifacts.

In a 2017 speech in Burkina Faso, French President Emmanuel Macron pledged to return African artifacts looted by France.[1] The following year, the French government released a report on the return of the African cultural objects, written by Felvine Sarr and Bénédicte Savoy, which indicates that permanent restitution would eventually be achieved.[2] From the original principle that "public property cannot be transferred"[3] to the publication of the new government report and the recent restitution actions, France

---

[1] Anna Codrea-Rado. Emmanuel Macron Says Return of African Artifacts Is a Top Priority. *The New York Times*, 2017-11-29. https://www.nytimes.com/2017/11/29/arts/emmanuel-macron-africa.html.

[2] For the French version of the report, see: Felwine Sarr and Bénédicte Savoy, *Rapport sur la restitution du patrimoine culturel africain: Vers une nouvelle éthique relationnelle*, Ministère de la Culture and Université Paris Nanterre, November 2018, http://restitutionreport2018.com/sarr_savoy_fr.pdf. English version, see: Felwine Sarr and Benedicte Savoy. *The Restitution of African Cultural Heritage. Toward a New Relational* (2018-11). Ethics.

[3] This principle, based on the *Ordinance of Moulins* of 1566, states that royal properties are inalienable and non-transferable, and has been used by France to refuse any form of restitution of colonial objects.

has directly challenged the Universal Declaration and forced governments and museums in various countries to reconsider the issue of restitution and return, creating a positive chain effect. While the German authority has taken a positive stance in dealing with Nazi-looted artifacts from the 1930s and 1940s, actively assuming historical responsibility, but they have paid less attention to colonial background artifacts. With the publication of the new French government report and the promotion of local scholars, the German Museums Association published the *Guidelines on Dealing with Collections from Colonial Contexts* in 2018①, which were updated with a second edition in 2019, supplementing expert opinions and reflecting the intention to strengthen exchange and cooperation with the places of origin of the artifacts. In the same year, commissioners for culture from 16 German states signed the *Framework Principles for Dealing with Collections from Colonial Contexts*②, committing to implement repatriation procedures in their capacity as governments. In 2019, the Nationaal Museum Van Wereldculturen of the Netherlands released the document entitled "Return of Cultural Objects: Principles and Process".③ The document aims to address the historical issues with the collections of its member museums, to adopt a transparent approach

---

① Working Group on behalf of the Board of the German Museums Association. *Guidelines on Dealing with Collections from Colonial Contexts*. Berlin: German Museums Association Press, 2018.

② *Framework Principles for Dealing with Collections from Colonial Contexts Agreed by the Federal Government Commissioner for Culture and the Media, the Federal Foreign Office Minister of State for International Cultural Policy, the Cultural Affairs Ministers of the Länder and the Municipal Umbrella Organisations*. 2019-03-13. https://www.auswaertiges-amt.de/blob/2210152/b2731f8b59210c77c68177cdcd3d03de/190412-stm-m-sammlungsgut-kolonial-kontext-en-data.pdf.

③ For information on the attitude of Dutch museums deal with colonial objects: Catherine Hickley. *The Netherlands: Museums confront the country's colonial past*. https://en.unesco.org/courier/2020-4/netherlands-museums-confront-countrys-colonial-past. Full text of the principles and process, see: Nationaal Museum van Wereldculturen, *Return of Cultural Objects: Principles and Process*. 2019-03-07. https://www.volkenkunde.nl/sites/default/files/2019-05/Claims%20for%20Return%20of%20Cultural%20Objects%20N MVW%20Principles%20and%20Process.pdf.

to the handling and evaluation of repatriation requests, and to bring about changes in relevant policies in the Netherlands. The document was endorsed by Taco Dibbets, director of the Rijksmuseum in Amsterdam.[1] In the same year, the Netherlands established a commission on colonial collections, which was mandated by the government to publish a research report on colonial collections entitled "Report Advisory Committee on the National Policy Framework for Colonial Collections" in 2020.[2] The Dutch government announced that in 2021 that it would unconditionally return artifacts illegally taken from the Dutch colonies; the artifacts stolen from former colonies of other countries, or artifacts of special cultural, historical, or religious significance to a country, which may also be returned.[3]

The British authority and museums have long been strongly opposed to the repatriation of lost artifacts to their original countries. With the change in attitude of other major European museum powers, Britain has had to re-examine and reconsider this issue. The British Museum, in 2019, expressed its agreement with the idea of transparent attention to the provenance of objects and establishing a new relationship between Europe and Africa, but also stated that the return of artifacts from its collection is not part of this new relationship.[4] The UK's Culture Secretary, Jeremy Wright, also made it clear that the UK would not introduce legislation to force national museums to repatriate artifacts,

---

[1] Daniel Boffey. Rijksmuseum laments Dutch failure to return stolen colonial art. *The Guardian*, 2019-03-13. https://www.theguardian.com/world/2019/mar/13/rijksmuseum-laments-dutch-failure-to-return-stolen-colonial-art.

[2] Sofia Lovegrove. *Report on National Policy Framework for Colonial Collections: "Recognition of Injustice and Willingness to Rectify It"*. 2020-10-08. https://dutchculture.nl/en/news/Report-Advisory-Committee-National-Policy-Framework-Colonial-Collections.

[3] Sarah Cascone. *The Dutch Government Just Promised to Return Any Stolen Colonial-Era Objects in Its Collections Back to Their Countries of Origin*. 2020-02-04. https://news.artnet.com/art-world/netherlands-restitution-guidelines-1941734.

[4] Lanre Bakare. British Museum 'has head in sand' over return of artefacts. *The Guardian*, 2019-06-21. https://www.theguardian.com/culture/2019/jun/21/british-museum-head-in-sand-return-artefacts-colonial.

and that discussions with other countries should focus on "cultural cooperation" and "long-term loans".① As part of a general trend of "decolonisation" research and action by European governments and British institutions, the UK authority finally began to change its intransigent stance and legally returned 72 Benin bronzes at the end of 2022. This marks a positive trend in the international community for the return of objects from colonial background.

The return of the Benin Bronzes can be seen as the latest case of political change between countries.② Annette Weiner has described the Benin Bronzes as "inalienable possessions".③ Inalienable possessions are objects that have spiritual, historical and ritual value to the community of owners and should not be taken out of context because of their cultural status.④ Dan Hicks, Professor of Contemporary Archaeology at Oxford University and curator at the Pitt Rivers Museum, focuses on the story of the Benin Bronzes in his book *The Brutish Museums: The Benin Bronzes, Colonial Violence and Cultural Restitution*, exploring their imperial and colonial history and describing the violence and wars that have taken place on African soil as "World Wars Zero"⑤. He condemns the unified rhetoric of institutions such as the British Museum when dealing

---

① David Sanderson. Minister rules out return of treasures. 2019-04-22. https://www.thetimes.co.uk/article/minister-rules-out-return-of-treasures-2jlf3qh63.

② The Benin Bronzes are thousands of metal plaques and sculptures depicting scenes from court life and ceremonies. Originally adorning the pillars and beams of the royal palace of the Kingdom of Benin, they are among the largest and most impressive works of sculpture in Africa. In 1897, a British military expedition looted much of the cultural objects, including the bronzes mentioned in the article. Of these, 200 pieces Benin bronzes are in the collection of the British Museum, while the rest are scattered among various museums and private collectors in Europe.

③ Annette B. Weiner, *Inalienable Possessions: The Paradox of Keeping-While-Giving*. Berkeley: University of California Press, 1992.

④ Winani Thebele. Book Review: The Brutish Museums: The Benin Bronzes, Colonial Violence and Cultural Restitution, by Dan Hicks, *The Art Bulletin*, 2022, 104 (1), pp. 185-188, DOI: 10.1080/00043079.2022.1991765.

⑤ Dan Hicks, *The Brutish museums: The Benin Bronzes, Colonial Violence and Cultural Restitution*. London: Pluto Press. 2020.

with issues related to colonial artifacts, and even proclaims the universality of museums.① Hicks believes that museums are not just time capsules, they are weapons in themselves, and that keeping artifacts in colonial museums is a continuation of war and violence, so he calls for the restitution of all artifacts and for museums to truly decolonise by removing the colonial imprint.② Nigeria has been calling for their restitution since the 1960s, and in the summer of 2021, Germany returned 440 pieces; in November 2022, the Horniman Museum in London agreed to return 72 pieces from its collection (with 6 to be returned to Nigeria and the rest to remain in London on loan for display). After more than 60 years of pursuing, this marks a milestone victory. Like the Elgin Marbles of Greece, the Benin Bronzes are one of the classic cases of lost artifacts, as well as a starting point for further academic research.

2. The Loss and Return of Chinese Cultural Relics

According to the authors' latest research, about 15 million Chinese cultural relics have so far been imported into overseas public and private collections, covering all kinds of cultural relics such as ceramics, bronzes, jades, paintings, silks, and oracle bones. Most of them are mainly collected in major museums in the United States, Europe and Japan.③ It should be acknowledged that the vast majority of these are artworks, commodities and souvenirs exchanged through legitimate communication. However, about 10%, or 1.5 million pieces, are illegally looted, mainly from the three disasters which represented by the

---

① Dan Hicks, *The Brutish museums: The Benin Bronzes, Colonial Violence and Cultural Restitution*. London: Pluto Press. 2020, pp. 34–36.
② Hilary Morgan V. Leathem. Book Review: The Brutish museums: the Benin Bronzes, colonial violence and cultural restitution, *International Journal of Heritage Studies*, 27 (12), 2021, pp. 1343–1344, DOI: 10.1080/13527258.2021.1960888.
③ Yong Duan and Chen Li. *Investigation and Research of Lost Cultural Relics in the Qing Palace*. Nanjing: Yilin Press, 2016.

burning and plundering of the Old Summer Palace by the Anglo-French Allied forces in the 19th century, the dispersal of the Dunhuang manuscripts and the smuggling of the Longmen Grottoes in the first half of the 20th century, and the illegal excavation and smuggling of objects from some regions in the 1990s. As a result, China has become one of the world's leading countries in the looting of cultural relics. The ICOM published the Red List of Endangered Chinese Cultural Relics in 2010 to help prevent the theft, looting, and smuggling of Chinese cultural relics.

The Chinese government has signed international conventions such as the 1970 Convention and the 1995 Convention. To compensate for the limitations of international conventions in terms of retroactivity and binding force, the Chinese government has also initiated cooperation by signing bilateral agreements with related countries. So far, more than 20 governments, including Peru, India, Italy, the Philippines, Greece, Chile, Cyprus, Venezuela, the United States, Turkey, Ethiopia, Australia, etc., have signed agreements or memoranda of understanding with China to prevent theft, looting, and illegal import and export of cultural relics.[1]

As for the illegally looted cultural relics, they should of course be returned through restitution in accordance with the spirit of international conventions. However, due to various complex reasons, there are mainly three ways to return lost Chinese relics so far, including purchase, donation and restitution.[2]

---

[1] Zhengxin Huo, Hao Liu, Meng Yu. *The Battle over the Lost Cultural Treasures: An Empirical Study on the International Recovery of Cultural Treasures in Modern Times*. Beijing: China University of Political Science and Law Press. 2018, p. 479.

[2] With regard to the introduction of related cases in this section, see: Jinghui Li and Xiaoming Yang. Huainan Weng (ed.). *The Return: A Chronicle of the Return of Chinese Cultural Relics Abroad*. Encyclopedia of China Publishing House. 2022; National Cultural Heritage Administration (ed.). *The Journey Back Home: An Exhibition of Chinese Artifacts Repatriated from Overseas, for the 70th Anniversary of the Founding of the People's Republic of China*. Cultural Relics Press. 2019; Yong Duan and Chen Li. *Investigation and Research of Lost Cultural Relics in the Qing Palace*. Nanjing: Yilin Press, 2016; and some related news or reports.

Purchasing refers mainly to the expedient measure adopted by the Chinese government, domestic institutions and individuals in certain circumstances to promote the return of cultural relics that are difficult to recover by legal or diplomatic means. It must be recognised that there are obvious drawbacks to the approach of buying back stolen cultural relics. It is like buying back one's own stolen property, which not only causes secondary emotional trauma to the country of origin, but also encourages new illegal trade in cultural relics. For example,

In the 1950s, the Chinese government bought from Hong Kong a number of precious paintings and calligraphies that had been originally been collected by the imperial court over the dynasties, such as Wang Xianzhi's *Mid-Autumn Lettering* (中秋帖), Wang Xun's *Bo Yuan Lettering* (伯远帖), Han Huang's *Five Oxen* (五牛图), Dong Yuan's *Xiaoxiang Tu* (潇湘图), Gu Hongzhong's *Han Xizai Night Banquet* (韩熙载夜宴图), and Zhao Ji's *Auspicious Dragon and Rock* (祥龙石图).

In 1952, the Chinese government purchased more than 50,000 precious coin relics, including gold, silver and copper coins, banknotes and banknote plates, etc.

In 2000, the China Poly Group purchased the bronze statues of monkey heads, ox heads and tiger heads originally from the Yuanmingyuan Garden from the Christie's and Sotheby's Hong Kong.

In 2000, the Shanghai Library of China bought the Weng's Book Collection of Changshu (常熟翁氏藏书).

In 2003, the Shanghai Museum purchased the four volumes of the finest copy of the "Chun Hua Ge Tie" (淳化阁帖) of the Northern Song Dynasty (960−1127).

In 2003, Ms. Wing-Chun Cheung, an entrepreneur from Hong Kong China, purchased and donated the olive-shaped vase made during the Yongzheng period.

In 2003, Mr. Stanley Ho, an entrepreneur from Macao China, purchased and donated the bronze statue of the pig's head originally from Yuanmingyuan Garden.

From 2004 to 2005, China's National Cultural Heritage Administration purchased 7 Buddha statues originally from the Longmen Grottoes in Henan Province.

In 2006, China's National Cultural Heritage Administration purchased the bronze tripod of *Zilong*, originally from Henan Province.

In 2007, Mr. Stanley Ho procured the Bronze of Horse Head originally from Yuanmingyuan Garden and returned it back in 2019.

In 2008, Mr. Peng Xu, an entrepreneur from Mainland China, purchased and donated the Buddha head originally from Cave 10 of Tianlong Mountain Grottoes.

In 2014, the Hunan Museum received social sponsorship to purchase the "King of Square Vessels" (body) from abroad.

In 2020, Mr. Liang Jin, an entrepreneur from Zhejiang Province, purchased and donated two volumes of the *Yongle Dadian* (永乐大典).

Donation refers to the return of stolen Chinese cultural relics by overseas Chinese, international friends, foreign governments and museums as a benevolent gift or friendly diplomatic gesture. This kind of buy-and-return arrangement is currently the most popular method of repatriating cultural relics. For example,

In 1925, the director of the Oriental Art Institute of the Metropolitan Museum of Art in the United States returned to the Palace Museum in China a court porcelain from the Temple of Heaven in Beijing that had been acquired by the Eight-Nation Alliance.

Between 1951 and 1958, the Soviet government returned 64 volumes of the *Yongle Dadian* (永乐大典) on three occasions, that had been stolen during the War of the Eight-Nation Alliance.

In 1955, the East German government returned 3 volumes of the *Yongle Dadian* and 10 Boxer flags to China.

From 1959 to 1964, Mr. Chuen Yeung, a collector of Hong Kong China, donated over 5,000 artefacts, including ceramics, bronzes, jades, lacquer and bamboo wares, etc.

From 1963 to 1972, Mr. Baozhang Hou, a pathologist living abroad have donated more than 2,000 artefacts from his family collection, including ceramics, bronzes, paintings and calligraphy, etc.

In 1975, Dr. Ambrose Harting, an Englishman, donated bronze cranes and other artefacts lost from the Qing Yi Yuan (formerly the Summer Palace) in 1860.

In 1984, Mr. Yip Yee, a collector from Hong Kong China, bequeathed his 81 rhinoceros horn artefacts to the National Palace Museum.

In 1993, Mr. Maurice R. Greenberg of the U.S. donated 10 bronze windows originally from the Summer Palace.

In 2000, Mr Wanli Zhuang, a Chinese collector living in the Philippines, bequeathed to the Shanghai Museum 232 pieces of lost paintings and calligraphy that he had collected throughout his life.

In 2000, Mr. Robert Hatfield Ellsworth, an American collector, donated one of the painted relief warrior stones originally from the Wang Chuzhi tomb in Hebei Province.

In 2001, National Gallery of Canada donated a relief statue of Luohan originally found in the Longmen Grottoes.

In 2005, the British government of Portsmouth donated the Da Gu bell to Tianjin China.

In 2005, Swedish Museum of East Asia donated horse figurines made in the Han Dynasty (206 BC–220 AD).

In 2006, Association for the Protection of Chinese Art in Europe donated a bronze tripod from the Warring States period (475–221 BC).

In 2006, Mr. Shixing Fan donated artefacts originally from Hanyang Mausoleum.

In 2009, Mr. Jirong Fan and Ms. Yingying Hu donated 9 pieces of bronzes.

In 2011, Mr. Yim Kwok, a collector from Hong Kong China, donated 2 golden bird-shaped pieces and a group of the goldware originally from the Qingong Tomb in Dabaozi, Gansu Province.

In 2012 and 2014, Mr. Qiyong Cao and Mrs. Luobizhen Cao, collectors from Hong Kong China, donated their collection of 168 lacquer wares to the Zhejiang Museum.

In 2013, the French Pinault family donated two bronzes: rabbit and mouse heads, which they had bought at the Christie's auction house in Paris.

In 2015, Weng's descendants donated the *Diary of Weng Tonghe* and other documents.

In 2016, Chung Tai Temple in Taiwan China donated the pagoda body of the Dengyu stone pagoda, originally from Shanxi Province.

In 2018, an anonymous overseas buyer donated the bronze called "Hu-Ying" made in the Western Zhou (1027–771 BC) and originally collected in the Yuan Ming Yuan (Old Summer Palace).

In 2020, a Chinese in Japan donated a Buddha head from the Tianlongshan Grottoes, back to the Grottoes in Taiyuan.

Recovery is the way to resolve disputes over the ownership of lost cultural property in accordance with international conventions and national laws. They are the most consistent with the relevant international conventions and ethical principles, but also the most difficult because of their limitations. For example,

In 1998, after three years of diplomatic negotiations, litigation and out-of-court settlements, China's National Cultural Heritage Administration recovered more than 3,400 ceramic figurines, porcelain pieces, and bronze mirrors from Britain.

In 2000, China's National Cultural Heritage Administration recovered one of the painted relief warrior stones originally from the Wang Chuzhi tomb in Hebei Province, which had been smuggled to the U.S..

In 2008, China's National Cultural Heritage Administration negotiated the return of a Northern Dynasties (386-581) Bodhisattva stone statue which has been stolen in 1994 from the site of Longhua Temple in Shandong Province from the Miho Museum in Japan.

In 2010, after 6 years of investigation and return negotiations, the Shaanxi Provincial Bureau of Cultural Relics successfully recovered and returned the Tang Dynasty Wu Huifei Stone Stele, that had been stolen and smuggled to the U.S..

In 2015, after four years of tracking, sanctioning, and negotiation, China's National Cultural Heritage Administration successfully recovered the goldware stolen from the Qingong Tomb in Dabaozi, Gansu Province.

In 2019, China's National Cultural Heritage Administration urgently teamed up with several departments, such as public security and foreign affairs, to recover the stolen 8 bronze vessels of Zengbokefu from Hubei; and with the help of the Japanese government, they were successfully recovered in five months.

It is particularly noteworthy that some of the cultural objects repatriated were actively seized and returned by foreign authorities in accordance with international conventions and bilateral agreements. All of these artifacts were successfully returned to China following the appropriate procedures. Such cases demonstrate the importance of good international relations and international consensus in combating and recovering illicit trafficking in cultural relics. For example,

In 2008, the Danish government returned 156 pieces of ceramic burial objects originally from graves in Shaanxi, Shanxi, and Sichuan provinces, which had been seized by Danish customs in 2006.

In 2011, the U.S. government returned more than 10 precious Chinese cultural relics and 22 dinosaur eggs that had been seized;

In 2015, the U.S. Department of Homeland Security transferred the smuggled 22 pre-Tang dynasty artefacts and a fossil of Liaoning Anchiornis huxleyi.

In 2019, the Italian customs returned 796 pieces seized in 2007.

In 2019, the U.S. Federal Bureau of Investigation returned the 361 pieces of smuggled Chinese cultural relics seized in 2014.

In 2021, the U.S. government returned 12 seized artefacts, including 5 bronze Buddha statues and a gilded crystal offering pagoda inlaid with gemstones.

In 2023, the U.S. government returned 2 seized carved stones to China, dating from the Northern Dynasties (386 −581) to the Tang Dynasty (618 − 907).

According to China's official statistics, over the past 70 years from 1949 to 2019, China has successfully facilitated the return of more than 300 batches of cultural relics totalling 150000 pieces through various means.

3. "Semi-colony" in the Context of the Loss of Chinese Cultural Relics

The term "colonial background artifacts" is taken from the *Guidelines on Dealing with Collections from Colonial Contexts* published by the German Museums Association in 2018, which covers collections from the formal colonial ruling context, the informal colonial ruling context and those that reflect colonialism.

The restitution of colonial artifacts can be said to break through the limitations of the above-mentioned international conventions in terms of retroactivity and binding force, which represents the victory of human moral principles, which in turn can promote the progress and improvement of the law. Compared with the differences or even contradictions between the laws of different countries, the human society clearly has a strong consistency on the moral level, and the basic moral principles are truly universal, which should also become the consensus basis for the restitution of illegally trafficked cultural relics at the international level.

China has been in a state of internal and external turmoil since 1840, and society has been in a state of what the academic world calls "semi-colony". The government lacks authority, the social and economic conditions are grim, and large amounts of cultural heritage have been plundered, stolen, and lost, with many similarities to colonial societies, which are said to be in the background of "informal colonial rule".

The Tang Dynasty Honglujing Stone (鸿胪井刻石), which was lost to Japan in 1908, is used to illustrate this point.

The Tang Dynasty Honglujing Stone was carved in 714 AD. Cui Xin, the minister called Hongluqin (鸿胪卿) in the Tang Dynasty, was ordered by Emperor Xuanzong of the Tang Dynasty to confer the title of King of Bohai State in Liaodong. On his way back, he dug two wells at the Golden Mountain (黄金山) of today's Lvshun to commemorate, known as "Honglu Well" (鸿胪井), and inscribed: The Minister Cui Xin, dug these two wells to commemorate the inauguration of the Mohe nation in the second year of the Kaiyuan reign on 18th May ("敕持节宣劳靺鞨使鸿胪卿崔忻井两口永为记验开元二年五月十八日"). This inscription can be corroborated and supplemented by historical documents and is of great historical value.

After the Boxer Rebellion in 1900, the Eight-Nation Alliance entered Beijing, China, and Russia further invaded part of north-eastern China. In 1904–1905 the Russo-Japanese War broke out, and Japan eventually won and occupied part of the region, including Lvshun. In 1908, the Japanese naval commander stationed in Lvshun took the Honglujing Stone back to Japan as a "spoil of war" and presented it to the emperor. Since then, it has been displayed in the courtyard of the Imperial Palace in Tokyo. It can be seen that the Hongcujing Stone is a lost cultural relic that was illegally plundered by the occupier in the context of the Chinese government's loss of sovereignty, which should be recovered according to the spirit of international conventions and ethical principles. Moreover, the Stone is currently only in the private collection of the Japanese royal family, not the public property of Japan, so the legal relationship for its return is relatively simple.

Chinese scholars have conducted long-term research on the Honglujing Stone, and there is a "Tang Honglujing Stone Research Association" which has accumulated a wealth of archival material. The "Honglujing Stone Memorial Hall" has been built in Dalian to disseminate knowledge about the stone to the public. To make claims of restitution, Chinese people have also travelled to Japan many times since the 1990s. On 6th May 2022, the Research Centre of Chinese Relics Overseas of Shanghai University hosted the "Tang Honglujing Stone Restitution Symposium" to share the latest news and research of the programme.

These legitimate demands have also been supported by Japanese enlightened people. Japanese lawyer Ichinose Keiichiro founded the "Association for the Promotion of the Return of Chinese Cultural Relics" in Japan in 2021, with the participation of some Japanese university professors and lawyers, with the aim of demanding that the Japanese government proactively return the Chinese cultural relics looted in Japan during the First Sino-Japanese War, the Russo-Japanese War, and Japan's full-scale invasion of China. Ichinose Keiichiro believes that as long as these lost Chinese cultural relics from the colonial context remain in Japan, "true friendship between Japan and China cannot be discussed". On 20th April 2022, the Advancement Association held an "Emergency Meeting to Demand the Return of Plundered Chinese Cultural Relics" at the Japanese House of Representatives, demanding that the Tang Dynasty Honglujing Stone at the Tokyo Imperial Palace and the three Chinese stone lions at Yasukuni Shrine and the Yamagata Memorial Museum be returned as soon as possible.[①] The authors hope and believe that with the understanding and cooperation between the Chinese and Japanese governments and the public, the Honglujing Stone will surely return to its homeland in the near future.

In 2019, the 40th session of the General Conference of the United Nations Educational, Scientific and Cultural Organization (UNESCO) declared 14 November as the "International Day against Illicit Trafficking in Cultural Property". The following year, UNESCO Director General Audrey Azoulay, in her speech on the occasion of International Day against Illicit Trafficking in Cultural Property, said: "UNESCO therefore calls upon everyone to realize that stealing, selling or buying a looted work is tantamount to participating in pillaging peoples' heritage and robbing their memories."[②] On 14 November 2021, Shanghai University hosted the First China Forum on the International Day against Illicit Trafficking in Cultural Property, together with the special exhibition "International Responsibility for Human Heritage". Director of Culture and Emergencies of UNESCO, as well as many Chinese and overseas experts and scholars delivered speeches offline or online.

Two years later, it is our great honour and pleasure to host this international symposium on "Museums, Decolonisation and Restitution: a global conversation" at Shanghai University. We are delighted to have this opportunity to exchange and discuss with my colleagues at home and abroad. The authors also call upon the international community to pay due attention to the lost cultural relics from the war-torn and "semi-colonial" backgrounds, while promoting the restitution of cultural objects from colonial background.

---

① The three stone lions were removed from the Sanxue Temple in Haicheng, Liaoning Province.
② Audrey Azoulay, *Message on the occasion of International Day against Illicit Trafficking in Cultural Propert*. 2020 -11 -14. For English version, see: https://en.unesco.org/sites/default/files/en-14-nov.pdf; For Chinese version, see: https://zh.unesco.org/sites/default/files/ch-14-nov.pdf.

To jointly promote fair justice that takes into account both history and reality by strengthening exchanges, enhancing understanding, building mutual trust, and carrying out cooperation, on the premise of recognising the universal value of cultural relics, adhering to the moral standards of object circulation, facing up to the history, and tacitly recognising the limitations of the law, with an attitude of mutual understanding and cooperation.

博物馆去殖民化与"半殖民地"问题

段 勇 张睿锜 郑 希*

摘要：国际间文物流失是近三百年伴随着殖民化和全球化而产生的普遍现象。丧失主权的殖民地在不公正的国际政治经济秩序下流失了大量具有代表性的文物，且至今仍存在严重的文物非法走私。随着现代一百年来民族国家的逐步独立和发展，文物流失国与文物流入国的矛盾日益尖锐。2002年来自7个国家的18家博物馆发表《关于普适性博物馆的价值及重要性的宣言》代表了欧美文物流入国拒绝归还流失文物的传统立场。然而，近十年来，在国际社会各方及联合国教科文组织、国际博协等共同且持续的努力下，以法国、德国、荷兰为代表的国家从政府、学界到博物馆界，对于殖民背景文物逐步表现出新的立场和意愿，国际文物返还出现了越来越多的可喜案例和趋势。值得注意的是，中国在1840年以后长期陷于内外战乱，社会也处于学术界所称的"半殖民地"状态，政府缺乏权威，社会经济萧条，在此期间同样非法流失了大量珍贵文物，唐代的鸿胪井刻石就是其中之一。这种类似战乱背景和"半殖民地"背景的流失文物也同样应该引起国际社会的关注，以便更好地通过国际间的谅解与合作来实现兼顾历史与现实的公平正义。

关键词：文物流失；文物返还；去殖民化；半殖民地

文化遗产是人类文明的见证，是连接人类社会过去、现在和未来的桥梁。不同地域和族群的文化遗产，不仅是该地区和族群历史、文化的物质载体，也成为不同地域和族群相互认识、交流的媒介。遗憾的是，由于复

---

* 段勇，上海大学党委副书记；张睿锜，中国海外文物研究中心研究员兼副秘书长；郑希，华东理工大学附属中学教师。

杂的政治、经济等原因，特别是在欧美列强的大规模殖民活动中，存在大量文化遗产非法流失的问题。

国际间文物流失是近三百年伴随着殖民化和全球化而产生的普遍现象，丧失主权的殖民地在不公正的国际政治经济秩序下流失了大量具有代表性的文物。根据塞内加尔学者费雯·萨尔（Felwine Sarr）和法国艺术史学家贝尼迪克特·萨瓦（Bénédicte Savoy）的调查，撒哈拉沙漠以南非洲有超过90%的物质文化遗产流散于欧洲和美国的博物馆中。① 荷兰国家世界文化博物馆（Nationaal Museum Van Wereldculturen）的藏品中约40%具有殖民背景。② 1997年和1998年，国际博物馆协会连续两年将国际博物馆日的主题定为"与文物的非法贩运和交易行为作斗争"（The fight against illicit traffic of cultural property），这是自1992年创立并发布国际博物馆日活动主题以来，唯一出现两年使用同一主题的情况，足以见得国际博物馆界对非法贩运文化财产行为的重视程度。而据联合国教科文组织统计数据，文化遗产的非法贩运目前仍是仅次于毒品走私和武器走私的第三大非法贸易。由此可见，文物流失既是历史问题，也是现实问题。

经过文物流失国的不懈追索和国际社会的共同努力，过去十年，文物流入国收藏的殖民背景文物越来越成为国际关注的热点问题。目前，关于文物返还问题的研究也主要集中在博物馆去殖民化以及与之相关的非法流失文物的调查、法律和道德问题的探讨等方面。有学者从情感价值和情感共鸣角度解读文化遗产相关问题③，斥责一些国家一边回应殖民地国家的文物只是"战利品"，一边在其博物馆展示中投射白人的

---

① Felwine Sarr and Bénédicte Savoy, *Rapport sur la restitution du patrimoine culturel africain: Vers une nouvelle éthique relationnelle*, Ministère de la Culture and Université Paris Nanterre, November 2018, http://restitutionreport2018.com/sarr_savoy_fr.pdf.

② 该馆成立于2014年，由阿姆斯特丹的热带博物馆（Tropenmuseum）、贝赫-达尔的非洲博物馆（Afrika Museum）以及莱顿的莱登民族学博物馆（Museum Volkenkunde）组成。共有约450 000件藏品，其中约40%的藏品有殖民背景。参见：Catherine Hickley. *The Netherlands: Museums confront the country's colonial past*. https://en.unesco.org/courier/2020-4/netherlands-museums-confront-countrys-colonial-past.

③ Smith, L. S. 2020. *Emotional Heritage: Visitor Engagement at Museums and Heritage Sites*. London: Routledge. Tolia-Kelly, D., E. Waterton, and S. Watson, (eds). 2017. *Heritage, Affect, and Emotion: Politics, Practices, and Infrastructures*. London: Routledge.

统治地位。①

一、《普适宣言》的强硬立场和近十年的立场转变

20世纪70年代和90年代，国际社会在针对保护文化财产和打击文物犯罪等问题的讨论中，产生了联合国教科文组织《关于禁止和防止非法进出口文化财产和非法转让其所有权的方法的公约》(*Convention on the Means of Prohibiting and Preventing the Illicit Import, Export and Transfer of Ownership of Cultural Property*，简称《1970年公约》)②和国际统一私法协会《关于盗窃或非法出口文物的公约》(*Convention on Stolen or Illegally Exported Cultural Objects*，简称《1995年公约》)③，在推动形成国际文物交流新秩序方面发挥了重要作用。但是它们也存在适用时间（对签约前的案例不具有溯及力）、适用空间（文物流入国缔约数量少）、适用对象（仅限于损害特殊利益）等局限性，因此在文物追索返还实践中作用比较有限。

希腊对于所谓"埃尔金大理石雕"（Elgin Marbles）④的持续追索引发了以比佐集团（Bizot Group）⑤为核心的欧美7个国家的18家博物馆馆长联合

---

① Dan Hicks, *The Brutish Museums: The Benin Bronzes, Colonial Violence and Cultural Restitution*. London: Pluto Press. 2020.
② 联合国教科文组织：《关于禁止和防止非法进出口文化财产和非法转让其所有权的方法的公约》，1970年11月14日，https://en.unesco.org/about-us/legal-affairs/convention-means-prohibiting-and-preventing-illicit-import-export-and。
③ 国际统一私法协会：《关于盗窃或非法出口文物的公约》，1995年6月24日，https://www.unidroit.org/instruments/cultural-property/1995-convention/。
④ 埃尔金大理石雕原属于希腊雅典帕特农神庙石雕的一部分，被埃尔金勋爵从当时占领希腊的奥斯曼土耳其统治者手中购买并运回英国，最后被大英博物馆买入。希腊政府和民众一直向大英博物馆提出返还埃尔金大理石雕的请求，但均遭到了拒绝。关于埃尔金大理石雕的介绍参见：https://www.britishmuseum.org/about-us/british-museum-story/contested-objects-collection/parthenon-sculptures。
⑤ 比佐集团（Bizot Group），也称为国际大型展览组织者集团（The International Group of Organizers of Major Exhibitions）是由国家级博物馆联合会（Réunion des musées nationaux）负责人伊莲娜·比佐（Irène Bizot）成立于1992年的国际博物馆团体，定期举行世界大博物馆馆长会议。该会议旨在促进博物馆之间的交流，包括展品和展览交换，并就博物馆行业发展的相关政策和战略进行对话。参见：Emmanuel Koblenz, "Wink. The 'Groupe Bizot': a cartellisation of the major museum institutions?", *Business and History*, vol. 3, no 76, 2014, pp.143 −145; Kostas Arvanitis (2016). *Museums and Restitution: New Practices, New Approaches*. Routledge.

签署并发布了《关于普适性博物馆的价值及重要性的宣言》(Declaration on the Importance and Value of Universal Museums, 2002年), 简称《普适宣言》①, 包括美国的芝加哥艺术博物馆、波士顿美术博物馆、纽约现代艺术博物馆、克里夫兰艺术博物馆、费城艺术博物馆、盖蒂艺术博物馆、古根海姆博物馆、洛杉矶艺术博物馆、惠特尼美国艺术博物馆、大都会艺术博物馆,德国的慕尼黑巴伐利亚国立博物馆、柏林国家博物馆,意大利佛罗伦萨的乌菲齐博物馆,西班牙普拉多博物馆、提森·博里米萨博物馆,荷兰的阿姆斯特丹国立博物馆,俄罗斯圣彼得堡艾尔米塔什博物馆,法国的卢浮宫博物馆。该宣言表明了"普适性博物馆"以文物作为全人类的共同文化财产为由拒绝归还的强硬立场。大英博物馆虽然没在该宣言的签署者之列,但其随后发表了对宣言的支持声明。②此宣言一经发布,引起了国际社会和博物馆行业的哗然和批驳,国际博协和包括中国在内的各国博物馆组织均以多种形式发声。有学者认为,这一声明的实质是为比佐集团为核心的"普适博物馆"在面对文物追索时取得豁免权。③也有学者怀疑该声明背后透露着对殖民主义的支持,因为"博物馆是记忆保留、扩展和重复的工具",博物馆展示殖民地文物的行为其实是暴力和创伤的延续④,在这些历史展示中发挥更加明显的作用。⑤笔者也是从那时开始正式研究流失文物问题的。

《普适宣言》表面上成为文物流入国拒绝归还文物的强硬立场的标志,实际上是传统强权思维回光返照的挽歌。它进一步激发了国际社会对于非法流失文物问题的广泛关注、思考、研究,并将收藏相关文物的欧美博物馆持续置于道德聚光灯的烤灼之下。在文物流失国的追索、国际公约精神

---

① 段勇:《博物馆与文化遗产的"普世"问题探析——兼论我国处理非法流失文物的对策》,《中国博物馆》2007年第4期,第56—62页。
② Lyndel V. Prott. *Witnesses to History: A Compendium of Documents and Writings on the Return of Cultural Objects*. Paris: UNESCO press, 2009, p.118.
③ Geoffrey Lewis. The universal museum: a special case?. *ICOM*, 2004 (01), p.3.
④ Dan Hicks, *The Brutish Museums: The Benin Bronzes, Colonial Violence and Cultural Restitution*. London: Pluto Press. 2020, pp.181-182.
⑤ Nicholas Thomas, *Entangled Objects: Exchange, Material Culture, and Colonialism in the Pacific*, Cambridge MA: Harvard University Press, 1991.

的普及和欧美社会舆论的施压下，在过去十年里，兼具历史和现实意义的殖民背景文物终于成为国际文物流失的研究热点，以法国、德国、荷兰为代表的国家对待殖民背景文物的处理态度都逐渐发生了转变。

法国总统埃马纽埃尔·马克龙（Emmanuel Macron）2017年在布基纳法索的演讲中承诺法国将归还被掠夺的非洲文物。①次年，法国政府发布了由费雯·萨尔和贝尼迪克特·萨瓦撰写的《非洲文化遗产的归还报告》（*Rapport sur la restitution du patrimoine culturel africain*），该报告表明要最终实现永久归还（permanent restitutions）。②法国从奉行"公共物品不可转让"的原则③，到政府新报告的发布和近年来实质性归还行动的开展，直接挑战了《普适宣言》，迫使各国政府和博物馆重新考虑文物返还问题，产生了积极的连锁效应。德国政府在处理20世纪三四十年代的纳粹掠夺文物问题上一直持积极态度，主动承担历史责任，但对殖民背景文物关注较少。在法国政府新报告和本国学者的推动下，德国博物馆协会于2018年公布了《殖民背景藏品处理指南》④，2019年更新到第二版，补充了专家观点，体现了其期望加强与文物原属地交流合作的意愿。同年，德国16个州的文化部部长签署了《处理殖民背景藏品的框架原则》⑤，以政府身份承

---

① Anna Codrea-Rado. Emmanuel Macron Says Return of African Artifacts Is a Top Priority. *The New York Times*, 2017-11-29. https://www.nytimes.com/2017/11/29/arts/emmanuel-macron-africa.html.

② 关于该报告的法文版，参见：Felwine Sarr and Bénédicte Savoy, *Rapport sur la restitution du patrimoine culturel africain: Vers une nouvelle éthique relationnelle*, Ministère de la Culture and Université Paris Nanterre, November 2018, http://restitutionreport2018.com/sarr_savoy_fr.pdf。英文版见：Felwine Sarr and Benedicte Savoy. *The Restitution of African Cultural Heritage. Toward a New Relational* (2018-11). Ethics. http://restitutionreport2018.com/sarr_savoy_en.pdf。

③ 该原则建立于1566年颁布的《穆兰敕令》，规定皇家遗产是不可剥夺和不可转让的，法国曾以此为依据拒绝任何形式的殖民地文物返还。

④ Working Group on behalf of the Board of the German Museums Association. *Guidelines on Dealing with Collections from Colonial Contexts*. Berlin: German Museums Association Press, 2018.

⑤ *Framework Principles for Dealing with Collections from Colonial Contexts Agreed by the Federal Government Commissioner for Culture and the Media, the Federal Foreign Office Minister of State for International Cultural Policy, the Cultural Affairs Ministers of the Länder and the Municipal Umbrella Organisations*. (2019-03-13). https://www.auswaertiges-amt.de/blob/2210152/b2731f8b59210c77c68177cdcd3d03de/190412-stm-m-sammlungsgut-kolonial-kontext-en-data.pdf.

诺将制定返还程序。2019年，荷兰国家世界文化博物馆发布了《文物返还：原则和程序》。①该文件旨在处理该机构下属博物馆藏品的历史性问题，采取透明方式处理和评估关于文物追索的请求，并希望促成荷兰相关政策的变化。该文件得到了阿姆斯特丹国立博物馆（Rijksmuseum）馆长塔科·迪贝茨（Taco Dibbets）的声援。②同年，荷兰成立了殖民收藏委员会（Commissie Nationaal kader koloniale collecties），受政府委托于次年发布了一份关于殖民藏品问题的调查报告《殖民收藏国家政策框架咨询委员会报告》（*Report Advisory Committee on the National Policy Framework for Colonial Collections*）。③2021年荷兰政府宣布，将无条件返还明确是从荷兰殖民地非法所得文物；对其他国家前殖民地被盗文物，或对一个国家具有特殊文化、历史或宗教意义的文物，也有可能返还。④

英国政府和博物馆对于流失文物返还原属国的态度曾经是坚决反对的，近年迫于文物原属国的追索压力及欧洲其他博物馆大国态度的转变，英国也不得不逐步重新审视这一问题。大英博物馆于2019年表示赞成关于"透明地关注文物出处"和"建立欧洲与非洲之间新关系"的观点，但也表示返还英国收藏的文物不包含在新关系之中。⑤英国文化部长杰里

---

① 有关荷兰博物馆对殖民时期文物的态度参见：Catherine Hickley. *The Netherlands: Museums confront the country's colonial past*. https://en.unesco.org/courier/2020-4/netherlands-museums-confront-countrys-colonial-past.《文物返还：原则和程序》全文可参见：Nationaal Museum van Wereldculturen, *Return of Cultural Objects: Principles and Process*, 2019-03-07, https://www.volkenkunde.nl/sites/default/files/2019-05/Claims%20for%20Return%20of%20Cultural%20Objects%20NMVW%20Principles%20and%20Process.pdf.

② Daniel Boffey. *Rijksmuseum laments Dutch failure to return stolen colonial art*. The Guardian, 2019-03-13. https://www.theguardian.com/world/2019/mar/13/rijksmuseum-laments-dutch-failure-to-return-stolen-colonial-art.

③ Sofia Lovegrove. *Report on National Policy Framework for Colonial Collections: "Recognition of Injustice and Willingness to Rectify It"*. 2020-10-08. https://dutchculture.nl/en/news/Report-Advisory-Committee-National-Policy-Framework-Colonial-Collections.

④ Sarah Cascone. *The Dutch Government Just Promised to Return Any Stolen Colonial-Era Objects in Its Collections Back to Their Countries of Origin*. 2020-02-04. https://news.artnet.com/art-world/netherlands-restitution-guidelines-1941734.

⑤ Lanre Bakare. *British Museum 'has head in sand' over return of artefacts*. The Guardian, 2019-06-21. https://www.theguardian.com/culture/2019/jun/21/british-museum-head-in-sand-return-artefacts-colonial.

米·赖特（Jeremy Wright）也明确表示英国将不会出台主要立法来强制国家博物馆归还文物，与其他国家的讨论应集中在"文化合作"和"长期租借上"。①如今在欧洲其他国家政府以及英国相关机构进行"去殖民化"研究和行动的整体趋势下，英国终于在去年开始改变其强硬的拒绝态度，于2022年年底在法律意义上归还了72件贝宁青铜器（Benin Bronzes）。这标志着国际社会基本形成了殖民地文物返还的有利趋势。

贝宁青铜器的返还堪称各国政策转变的最新案例。②安妮特·韦纳（Annette Weiner）将贝宁青铜器定位为"不可剥夺的财产"（inalienable possessions）。③不可剥夺的财产是对所有者社区具有精神、历史和仪式价值的物品，不应因其文化地位而断章取义。④牛津大学当代考古学教授、皮特里斯博物馆（Pitt Rivers Museum）策展人丹·希克斯（Dan Hicks）在其《残暴的博物馆：贝宁青铜器、殖民暴力和文化归还》（*The Brutish Museums: The Benin Bronzes, Colonial Violence and Cultural Restitution*）一书中聚焦贝宁青铜器的流失过程和非洲文化遗产被迫迁离非洲大陆的历史，探讨其背后的帝国和殖民历史，形象地称非洲土地上发生的暴力和战争为"零次世界大战"。⑤他谴责了大英博物馆等机构在面对殖民地文物相关问题时的统一口径，甚至标榜博物馆的普适性。⑥希克斯认为"博物馆不仅是时间胶囊，其本身就是一件武器"，如果让文物继续留在殖民国家的博物馆里就是对战争和暴力的延续，因此他号召"归还一切"，通过消

---

① David Sanderson. Minister rules out return of treasures. 2019-04-22. https://www.thetimes.co.uk/article/minister-rules-out-return-of-treasures-2jlf3qh63.
② 贝宁青铜器是数千多块金属牌匾和雕塑，内容有表现宫廷生活、庆典仪式等场景，原装饰于贝宁王国皇宫的立柱和横梁上，是非洲雕塑艺术中最具规模和震撼力的艺术品之一。1897年，英国在一次军事远征中掠夺了包含文中提及的青铜器在内的大量文化遗产。其中，200件贝宁青铜器被大英博物馆收藏，其余散藏于欧洲多个博物馆和私人藏家。
③ Annette B. Weiner, *Inalienable Possessions: The Paradox of Keeping-While-Giving*. Berkeley: University of California Press, 1992.
④ Winani Thebele. Book Review: The Brutish Museums: The Benin Bronzes, Colonial Violence and Cultural Restitution, by Dan Hicks, *The Art Bulletin*, 2022, 104 (1), pp.185-188, DOI: 10.1080/00043079.2022.1991765.
⑤ Dan Hicks, *The Brutish Museums: The Benin Bronzes, Colonial Violence and Cultural Restitution*. London: Pluto Press. 2020.
⑥ Ibid., pp.34-36.

除殖民印象，让博物馆真正做到去殖民化。①尼日利亚自20世纪60年代便一再呼吁各国归还，直到2021年夏天，德国博物馆归还了440件；2022年11月，英国伦敦霍尼曼博物馆同意将该馆收藏的72件青铜器文物归还尼方，其中有6件将返回尼日利亚，其余将以租借的形式继续在伦敦展出。长达60多年的追索，至此取得阶段性胜利。贝宁青铜器成为与希腊埃尔金大理石雕一样备受关注的流失文物经典案例，也成为学术界延伸研究的出发点。

二、中国文物的流失与回归途径

据笔者最新研究，迄今为止进入海外公私收藏领域的中国文物总数约有1 500万件，涵盖了陶瓷、青铜器、玉器、书画、丝绸、甲骨等所有文物种类，主要收藏于美国、欧洲与日本的大型博物馆。②应该承认，其中绝大多数属于正当交流的艺术品、商品、纪念品等。但是也有大约10%，即150万件为非法流失文物，主要源于19世纪以英法联军焚毁劫掠圆明园为代表、20世纪前半叶以敦煌文书流散和龙门石窟盗凿为代表、20世纪90年代部分地区地下文物被非法盗掘并走私出境为代表的三次文物流失高潮。中国也因此成为国际上最主要的文物流失国之一。国际博物馆协会曾于2010年编制《中国濒危文物红色目录》以帮助防止盗窃、盗掘和走私贩运中国文物。

中国政府已签署加入了联合国教科文组织《1970年公约》和国际统一私法协会《1995年公约》等国际公约。同时，为了弥补国际公约在溯及力和约束力方面的局限性，中国政府还通过与相关国家签署双边协议的方式展开合作，迄今已先后与秘鲁、印度、意大利、菲律宾、希腊、智利、塞浦路斯、委内瑞拉、美国、土耳其、埃塞俄比亚、澳大利亚等二十余个国

---

① Hilary Morgan V. Leathem. Book Review: The Brutish museums: the Benin Bronzes, colonial violence and cultural restitution, *International Journal of Heritage Studies*, 27 (12), 2021, pp.1343-1344, DOI: 10.1080/13527258.2021.1960888.

② 段勇、李晨：《国宝星散复寻踪——清宫散佚文物调查研究》，译林出版社2016年版。

家政府签署了防止盗窃、盗掘和非法进出境文物的协定或谅解备忘录。①

对于非法流失文物，原则上当然都应该依照国际公约精神通过追索促成返还。但是由于各种复杂的原因，迄今为止中国流失文物的回归途径主要有三种，即购回、捐回和追索。②

购回主要指中国政府、国内机构和个人在特定情况下针对一些难以通过法律追索或外交手段回归的文物采用商业购买的权宜之计促成回归。但是，必须认识到，对于非法流失文物，这种购买回来的方式存在明显弊病，类似于花钱买回自己的被盗家产，既是对流失国民众的二次情感伤害，也容易助长新的文物非法流失。通过购回促成文物回归的案例，例如：

20世纪50年代，中国政府购回了包括王献之《中秋帖》、王珣《伯远帖》、韩滉《五牛图》、董源《潇湘图》、顾闳中《韩熙载夜宴图》、赵佶《祥龙石图》等皇家宫廷收藏过的历代珍贵书画；

1952年，中国文化部文物局购回5万余枚珍贵钱币文物，包括金币、银币、铜币、纸币、钞版等；

2000年，中国保利集团购回圆明园猴首、牛首、虎首铜像；

2000年，上海图书馆购回常熟翁氏藏书；

2003年，上海博物馆购回北宋祖刻最善本《淳化阁帖》四卷；

2003年，中国香港企业家张永珍女士购回清雍正橄榄瓶；

2003年，中国澳门企业家何鸿燊先生购回圆明园猪首铜像；

2004年至2005年，中国国家文物局购回龙门石窟古阳洞高树龛北魏释尊佛首等7件佛教造像；

2006年，中国国家文物局购回河南辉县商代子龙鼎；

2007年，中国澳门企业家何鸿燊先生购得圆明园马首铜像，并于2019

---

① 霍政欣、刘浩、余萌：《流失文物争夺战——当代跨国文物追索的实证研究》，中国政法大学出版社2018年版，第479页。
② 关于本节中涉及的中国海外文物回归案例和相关文物介绍，参见：李竞辉、杨晓明著，翁淮南编：《归来：中国海外文物回归纪实》，中国大百科全书出版社2022年版；国家文物局编：《回归之路：新中国成立70周年流失文物回归成果展》，文物出版社2019年版；段勇，李晨：《国宝星散复寻踪——清宫散佚文物调查研究》，南京译林出版社2016年版；以及相关新闻报道等。因所涉资料众多，挂漏之处，请方家指正补充。

年捐回；

2008年，中国大陆企业家许鹏先生购回天龙山石窟10号窟佛首；

2014年，湖南省博物馆购回商代青铜重器皿方罍器身；

2020年，浙江籍企业家金亮先生购回2册《永乐大典》。

捐回是指海外华人华侨、国际友好人士、外国政府和博物馆将其所藏或所购中国流失文物以善意捐赠或友好外交的方式促成回归。这种介于购买和追索之间的方式是目前最通行的文物回归途径。通过捐赠促成文物回归的案例，例如：

1925年，美国大都会艺术博物馆东方艺术所所长向中国归还一件八国联军时期从天坛掠走的宫廷瓷器；

1951年至1958年，苏联政府先后3次向中国归还64册八国联军时掠走的《永乐大典》；

1955年，德意志民主共和国返还3册《永乐大典》和10面义和团旗帜；

1959年至1964年，移居中国香港的文物收藏家杨铨先生捐赠5 000余件文物，包括陶瓷、铜器、玉石器、漆木竹器、文具等；

1963年至1972年，寓居海外的病理学专家侯宝璋先生及其家属数次择其家藏2 000余件文物捐赠给国家，涵盖陶瓷、铜器、书画等门类；

1975年，英国安布罗斯·哈丁博士（Ambrose Harting）赠还1860年流失自清漪园（颐和园前身）的清代铜鹤等文物；

1984年，中国香港收藏家叶义先生将其毕生珍藏81件犀角文物遗赠故宫博物院；

1993年，美国保险公司董事长莫里斯·格林伯格先生（Maurice R. Greenberg）捐赠颐和园宝云阁铜窗10扇；

2000年，旅居菲律宾的华人收藏家庄万里先生将一生搜集的失散海外的书画作品232件遗赠上海博物馆；

2000年，美国收藏家安思远先生（Robert Hatfield Ellsworth，1929—2014）捐赠河北曲阳王处直墓甬道彩绘浮雕武士石刻之一；

2001年，加拿大国家美术馆捐赠龙门石窟看经寺浮雕罗汉像；

2005年，英国朴次茅斯市政府捐赠返还天津大沽古钟；

2005年，瑞典东亚博物馆捐赠返还汉代陶马俑；

2006年，欧洲保护中华艺术协会（Association for the Protection of Chinese Art in Europe）捐赠一件战国青铜鼎；

2006年，美籍华人范世兴先生等人捐赠汉阳陵文物；

2009年，华人收藏家范季融和胡盈莹夫妇捐赠9件秦公晋侯青铜器；

2011年，中国香港收藏家郭炎先生捐赠甘肃大堡子山秦公墓地两件鸷鸟形金饰片和一组金饰片；

2012年和2014年，中国香港收藏家曹其镛先生和曹罗碧珍女士两次将毕生收藏珍贵漆器168件捐赠浙江省博物馆；

2013年，法国皮诺家族捐赠他们从巴黎佳士得拍卖行中购得的圆明园鼠首、兔首铜像；

2015年，翁氏后人捐赠《翁同龢日记》等文献；

2016年，中国台湾中台禅寺捐赠山西榆社县邓峪石塔塔身；

2018年，境外买家将圆明园西周青铜"虎鎣"捐赠给中国；

2020年，日本华人捐赠天龙山石窟佛首返回太原。

追索返还是按照国际公约、各涉事国家法律来解决流失文物归属纠纷的方式，是最符合相关国际公约精神和伦理道德原则的一种回归方式，但也是受制于公约局限性而难度最大的一种方式。例如：

1998年中国国家文物局通过3年外交交涉、法律诉讼和庭外和解，一次性从英国追索回陶俑、瓷器、铜镜等文物共3 400余件；

2000年，中国国家文物局从美国成功追索河北曲阳王处直墓甬道彩绘浮雕武士石刻之一；

2008年，中国国家文物局交涉日本美秀博物馆归还1994年被盗的山东省龙华寺遗址北朝菩萨石立像；

2010年陕西省文物局经过6年调查取证和追索谈判，成功追回被盗掘走私到美国的唐代贞顺皇后武惠妃石椁和壁画；

2015年，中国国家文物局经过4年的追索、制裁、谈判，成功从法国追回甘肃大堡子秦公墓地被盗掘的金饰片；

2019年，中国国家文物局紧急会同公安、外交等多部门联合追索湖北被盗的8件曾伯克父青铜组器，在日本政府的配合协助下，仅历时5个月便成功将其从日本追回。

特别值得一提的是，有些流失文物回归是外国政府机构按照国际公约精神和双边协议内容主动查扣返还的。这些文物按照相应的程序被成功送回中国。此类案例呈现了良好国际关系和国际共识在打击和追索非法流失文物问题上的重要性。例如：

2008年，丹麦哥本哈根市将2006年查扣的156件来自陕西、山西和四川的、包括夏商至元明时期的珍贵文物归还中国；

2011年，美国政府将收缴的10余件佛像、陶瓷器等珍贵文物和22枚恐龙蛋归还中国；

2015年，美国国土安全部移交中国国家文物局22件唐代以前的文物和1件中国辽宁的赫氏近鸟龙化石；

2019年，意大利海关将2007年查获的796件从中国非法盗掘走私的出土文物归还中国；

2019年，美国联邦调查局于2014年查获的361件走私入境的中国文物，均通过履行相关程序后顺利回到中国；

2021年，美国查获的5件金铜佛造像和1件铜鎏金水晶嵌宝石供养塔等共计12件文物艺术品返还中国；

2023年，美国将查没的2件北朝至唐代围屏石榻返还中国。

据中国官方统计，从1949年至2019年的70年间，中国通过各种途径，成功促成了300余批次、共15万件流失文物回归祖国。

三、从中国文物流失的背景谈"半殖民地"问题

"殖民背景文物"一词来自德国博物馆协会于2018年发布的《殖民背景藏品处理指南》（*Guidelines on Dealing with Collections from Colonial Contexts*），包括正式殖民统治背景的藏品、非正式殖民统治背景的藏品以及反映殖民主义的藏品。

殖民背景文物的追索返还，可以说突破了前述国际公约在溯及力和约束力方面的局限性，是人类道德原则的胜利，而道德原则的胜利又能促进法律的进一步完善。相对于各国法律之间存在的差异甚至矛盾，人类社会在道德层面显然具有更强一致性，基本道德原则才是真正具有普适性的，而这也理应成为国际间非法流失文物返还的共识基础。

中国在1840年以后长期陷于内外战乱，社会也处于学术界所称的"半殖民地"状态，政府缺乏权威，社会经济萧条，大量文化遗产被掠夺、盗窃和流失，与殖民地社会有很多相似的地方，或者说处于"非正式殖民统治背景"。

笔者仅以中国1908年流失到日本的唐代鸿胪井刻石为案例来说明这一问题。

公元714年，中国唐朝的鸿胪卿崔忻奉唐玄宗之命从首都长安赴辽东册封渤海国王、返程途中在今旅顺黄金山下凿井纪念，称"鸿胪井"，并刻石纪事："敕持节宣劳靺鞨使鸿胪卿崔忻井两口永为记验开元二年五月十八日"，能够与历史文献互证和补充，具有极高的历史价值。

1900年义和团事件后，八国联军进入中国北京，俄罗斯进一步乘人之危侵占了中国东北部分地区。1904—1905年，日本与俄罗斯爆发日俄战争，日本最终击败俄罗斯并占领了包括旅顺在内的部分地区。1908年驻守旅顺的日本海军指挥官将鸿胪井刻石作为所谓的"战利品"掠往日本，进献给天皇，此后至今陈设于日本东京皇宫庭院内。可见，鸿胪井刻石是在当时中国政府丧失对该地区的主权控制力情况下，被占领者非法掠夺的流失文物，理应根据国际公约精神和伦理道德原则追索。而且该刻石目前仅属于日本皇室私人收藏，未成为日本的公共财产，返还的法律关系相对简单。

中国学者对鸿胪井刻石进行了长期研究，民间有"中华唐鸿胪井刻石研究会"，积累了丰富的档案资料，大连建有"鸿胪井刻石纪念馆"，对公众传播鸿胪井刻石的知识，中国民间人士还从20世纪90年代起多次赴日本提出追索要求。2022年5月6日，上海大学中国海外文物研究中心主办了"唐鸿胪井刻石追索返还研讨会"。

这些正当要求也得到了日本有识之士的同情和支持，日本律师一濑敬一郎 2021 年在日本发起成立了"中国文物返还运动推进会",一些日本大学教授和律师参加,旨在要求日本政府主动归还甲午战争、日俄战争、日本全面侵华战争期间掠夺至日本的中国文物。一濑敬一郎认为只要这些殖民背景下的中国流失文物还留在日本,"真正的日中友好就无从谈起"。2022 年 4 月 20 日,该推进会在日本众议院举行了"要求返还日掳中国文物紧急集会",要求尽快归还现存于东京皇宫的唐鸿胪井刻石和现存于靖国神社及山县有朋纪念馆的三尊中国石狮。[①] 笔者希望并相信,在中日两国政府和民间的谅解与合作下,唐鸿胪井刻石一定能在不远的将来回归故土。

2019 年,联合国教科文组织大会第四十届会议将每年的 11 月 14 日确定为"打击非法贩运文化财产国际日"(International Day against Illicit Trafficking in Cultural Property)。次年的国际日上,教科文组织总干事奥德雷·阿祖莱在"打击非法贩运文化遗产 50 年"的致辞中呼吁:偷窃、出售或购买被掠夺的艺术品,就是在参与对各地人民以及历史记忆的掠夺。[②] 2021 年 11 月 14 日,上海大学承办了首届"打击非法贩运文化财产国际日"中国主场论坛,并配套举办了"人类遗产·国际责任——首届'打击非法贩运文化财产国际日'主题展",联合国教科文组织应急局局长以及众多中外专家学者均线下或线上参会致辞、演讲。

时隔两年,在上海大学举办本次"博物馆、去殖民化、文物返还:全球对话"国际研讨会,笔者深感荣幸和欣喜,很高兴有机会与国内外同仁交流讨论,也在此呼吁国际社会,在推进殖民背景文物返还的同时,对类似战乱背景和"半殖民地"背景的流失文物也同样予以足够关注。我们主张通过加强交流、增进了解、建立互信、开展合作,在承认文物的普适价值、坚持流通的道德标准、正视历史的传承经历、默认法律的局限作用的前提下,以彼此谅解与相互合作的态度来共同推进兼顾历史与现实的公平正义。

[①] 三尊石狮原属辽宁海城三学寺。
[②] 奥德雷·阿祖莱:《打击非法贩运文化财产国际日致辞》,2020 年 11 月 14 日。中文版参见:https://zh.unesco.org/sites/default/files/ch-14-nov.pdf;英文版参见:https://en.unesco.org/sites/default/files/en-14-nov.pdf。

Digitally Distributing Authority and Care: Hinemihi o te Ao Tawhito and Her Return[1]

Haidy Geismar[*]

Introduction

In this short essay I reflect on my participation in a project linking Māori communities in London and Aotearoa New Zealand to the National Trust (henceforth NT), the largest heritage charity and membership organization in the United Kingdom. Te Maru o Hinemini (henceforth Te Maru), meaning the embrace of Hinemihi, was first founded as a "Friends group" of the National Trust, comprising a group of scholars, cultural stakeholders, and practitioners committed to opening up dialogue about the appropriate protocols of care for the Māori meeting house Hinemihi o te Ao Tawhito, sited in the grounds of Clandon Park, a NT property in Surrey. Over time, calls for Hinemihi's return to New Zealand have intensified and, after a catastrophic fire in 2015 that almost completely destroyed the main house at Clandon, a formal request was made for her return by the New Zealand Government via Heritage New Zealand Pouhere Taonga on behalf of Hinemihi's descendants.

In the wake of the fire and the Covid −19 Pandemic, both of which closed Clandon to the public, this international negotiation has moved online.

---

[*] Haidy Geismar, Professor of Anthropology, co-director Digital Anthropology Programme, UCL.
[1] Acknowledgments: I would like to thank my colleagues in Te Maru o Hinemihi for supporting and giving constructive feedback and criticism. I would particularly like to thank Samantha Callaghan for reading a previous draft. Any mistakes are my own responsibility.

Managed by a heritage consultant based in Italy, and linking Te Maru, now an independent organization, and the NT, to descendants of Hinemihi, with a group (Ngā Kohinga Whakairo o Hinemihi) specially formed in New Zealand to make carvings for a new house for the NT in exchange for Hinemihi's return. The three groups have met regularly over Zoom for several years now to negotiate the protocols and structure of this return, changing practice at the NT, and opening up a third space for the negotiation of new relations of care and accountability. Workshops and resources on cultural protocols have been shared, and new languages have been learned on both sides of the globe. Put in the context of my earlier work which has explored the capacity of digital technologies to remediate both material collections and immaterial forms of knowledge and practice (Geismar, 2018), I explore here some of the themes that have emerged during our intensive online work and explore the changes that this has precipitated within the NT. These discussions have taken place within what has been a febrile moment for restitution and repatriation within the UK characterized by the current government laying down a mandate for "retain and explain" to arm's length national collections (Dowdon, 2020) and the Head of the NT receiving death threats for publishing an inventory of properties connected to slavery and colonialism [Huxtable et al. (National Trust), 2020]. In this politicised environment, I focus on the ways in which our project has enabled a less polarized, yet still effective pathway towards restitution, and how digital communications have enabled new kinds of conversation and a new language of care to emerge.

Te Maru o Hinemihi

In 2014, shortly after I had moved back to England from the USA, I was invited to join the group Te Maru o Hinemihi, a friends group of the National Trust founded to advocate for the care and conservation of the Māori meeting house (whare tupuna) Hinemihi.[1] Brought to England by the former Governor General of New Zealand, Lord Onslow, Hinemihi o te Ao Tawhito was famous for having protected her whānau (family) during the volcanic eruption of Mount Tarawera in 1886, and for being carved by some of Rotorua's most celebrated carvers (Gallup, 1998, and Hooper-Greenhill, 1998, 2000). After her purchase, Lord Onslow re-erected Hinemihi's carvings on a series of new wooden structures moving around the grounds of his family home, Clandon Park. From boathouse to garden house, Hinemihi eventually ended up on the lawn in gardens designed by the renowned landscaper Capability Brown, tucked under a large tree facing the main house. The only meeting house in the UK, and the only to be kept outside of a museum (in Europe and North America), over the years, Hinemihi has hosted christenings, marriages, and memorial services, and become a site of pilgrimage for Māori visiting from home. She has been a home away from home for Māori and wider Pasifika communities in the UK and Europe, hosting yearly feasts and fundraisers for the community, and hosting and supporting Ngāti Rānana (the London Māori club), Te Kohanga Reo o Rānana (the Māori language nest) and Māori dance and kapa haka performance groups (e. g. Manaia), as well as other Pasifika performers including Beats of Polynesia.

During Te Maru's early period a long-term conversation arose about the management and care of Hinemihi, between diaspora community members and the NT, stewarded by Dean Sully, a conservator at University College London (see Sully 2008), working closely with Jim Schuster, a descendant of

---

[1] The initial membership of Te Maru comprised: Alan Gallop, author and researchers, Esther Jessop (one of the founding members of Ngāti Ranana), Maina Tapiata-Thompson (Ngāti Hinemihi), Jim and Cathy Schuster (a descendant of Tene Waitere, and heritage consultants and cultural experts in carving and weaving based in Rotorua), Rosanna Raymond (Pasifika Artist), Dean Sully (conservator), Regan O'Callaghan (Ngāti Hinemihi), Anthony Hoete (Māori architect then based in London), Maia Nuku (curator) and Peter Rice (a financial advisor) Later additions included myself, Samantha Callaghan, Kiwiroa Marshall, Natasha Vaite, Donna Scott, Freddy Whorrall, Laura Pomana-Jackson, and Matthew Jessop.

Tene Waitere, one of Hinemihi's carvers, who is also a heritage consultant in Rotorua. Initially, Te Maru was formed as a Friends organization to make use of the opportunities and affordances of this structure to advocate from within the NT. Early members represented cultural communities (Māori and Pasifika) as well as bringing together different forms of expertise with the idea that they would influence the workings of the Trust from within. Over time, Te Maru became the organization that coordinated with the NT to develop a conversation about Hinemihi's care. Sully, working with NT conservators, established a conservation plan for Hinemihi which included yearly cultural care days, with involvement of volunteers from New Zealand and the diaspora and conservation students from the Institute of Archaeology at UCL.

On the surface this conversation seemed to reinforce dichotomous cultures of care: our discussions often faltered on ontologically distinct understandings of Hinemihi as an entity—the NT viewing her as an object to be managed, preserved, and maintained, and Te Maru bringing together perspectives guided by the understanding of Hinemihi as an important ancestress in carved form, imbued with spirituality (wairua) and power/prestige (mana) and enmeshed within the family relations of connection (whakapapa), that necessitate the responsibilities of care and guardianship. Hooper-Greenhill (2000) describes the multiple and contrasting worlds and cosmologies that Hinemihi inhabits, from the world of art, conservation through to a Māori worldview. Here, I am interested in how these perspectives have been joined together in a new way that overcomes simplistic binaries.

From 2012 onwards, Te Maru moved away from the remit of friends group (to support and sustain from within the structure of the NT) eventually restructuring as a CIC (community interest group), finally in 2023 becoming a CIC (Community Interest Charity). By 2014, a high turnover of staff at the NT and a lack of continuity in a collaborative vision for Hinemihi had resulted in a sense of disconnection between Te Maru and the NT, and a perpetuation of dichotomous roles between indigenous and cultural stakeholders and the mainstream heritage organizations. At this time led by then Chairperson, Anthony Hoete, Te Maru developed a scaffold of 5 "Rs" to frame the discussion they were bringing to the NT, moving from the minimal to the maximal in terms of the vision for Hinemihi's future (see Sully, Raymond and Hoete 2014). [1] The fifth option, to relocate, or repatriate, was increasingly supported by communities from within New Zealand who were often disappointed at Hinemihi's condition when they visited Clandon Park. Sited under a large tree, at risk of falling branches, and exposed to the wind and rain, Hinemihi's carvings were looking worn and faded, and her structure, along with the plain earth floor inside, was increasingly considered unfit for purpose by cultural communities who wanted to be able to be kept warm in winter, stay the night under her eaves, and be able to wash and cook as part of keeping themselves and Hinemihi culturally alive.

In 2015 a New Zealand Land Trust Delegation from New Zealand arrived to discuss Hinemihi's future, leaving behind a koha or gift for the NT and the beginnings of a draft memorandum of understanding that focused on plans to extend Hinemihi's footprint to become a full marae—enabling Māori principles of hospitality with the proposed addition of kitchen and washing facilities to feed and shelter visiting groups. (Sully et al., 2014). These plans intensified after 2015 in the wake of a devastating fire that almost entirely destroyed Clandon Park House. One of the worst fires that the NT has ever experienced left Hinemihi standing safely in the garden, but several of her treasures kept in the house were lost as was the documentation that detailed her purchase.

It was also at this time that the discussion about repatriation recommenced. The fire at Clandon prompted a rethink for the NT which increasingly recentered Hinemihi as not just an "object" in the garden, but as the "other

---

[1] These were R1: repair; R2: restore; R3: reprogramme; R4: redevelop: reprogramme + whare manaaki; R5: relocate.

house", bravely standing, facing the ruins of Clandon as an equal. The emerging plans to reactivate Hinemihi not simply as a treasured artefact but as a living cultural and spiritual centre also changed Te Maru's identity for Hinemihi's people back home in Aotearoa New Zealand, with Te Maru being recognized firstly as a "pukenga group" (a group of experts, gathered to support Hinemihi and her people) and then as the third party in a three-way negotiation between Ngāti Hinemihi and the NT for Hinemihi's return. Gradually, a proposal for an exchange emerged—Hinemihi would return to Aotearoa New Zealand and in return her people would provide carvings for a new whare at Clandon Park.

This period of discussion was also marked by several museological shifts, both globally and nationally, in the curation of Māori taonga, or treasures. Since the curation of *Te Māori*, a travelling exhibition that opened in 1985 at the Metropolitan Museum of Art, moving around the USA before returning to New Zealand, there has been a developing institutionalisation of Māori cultural protocols of care in global museum practice (see Geismar, 2013, chapter 6). This is reflected in the ways in which other meeting houses in museum (for instance Ruatepupuke II in Chicago and Rauru in Hamburg) are cared for, increasingly activated within dynamic cultural relationships and with growing input from Māori people.[①] These include the scheduling of dawn opening and closing ceremonies of singing and incantation to bookend cultural events; the understanding that cultural authorities and elders needed to be included as advisors and participants in projects (and budgeted for accordingly); and the respectful curation of exhibits incorporating cultural protocols into displays. However, the performative or exhibitionary aspects of incorporating Māori protocols into international museum practice has sometimes exceeded the ways in which these

---

① The best example of this is probably the activation of the waka, canoe, in Leiden university which is crewed by a team of Leiden university students, schooled through an ongoing exchange in traditional protocols and knowledge of Māori canoeing practice and protocol, and which has invested in an ongoing cultural exchange each year to celebrate and maintain the waka.

protocols have been internalised into other aspects of practice for instance in care, collections management, and ongoing investment in community engagement. The discussion about alternative practices of care seems to hinge much more on the condition of the ownership of objects. However, the growing number of exchanges between Māori communities and museums holding Māori treasures, the growth of the international repatriation movement, and growing historical research and accountability into the entangled colonial histories of British museums and collections have all ushered in a new culture of care and accountability (Henare, 2005; Clifford, 2013; Salmond, 2013; Sarr and Savoy, 2019).

By 2016, the NT had filed a listed building request with Guildford County Council to remove Hinemihi's carvings for conservation. Their removal, supported by Jim Schuster and Dean Sully, working closely with NT Conservator Emily Nisbet-Hawkins, deconsecrated the wooden structure, and Hinemihi was removed, initially stored in a fine art storage facility in Salisbury, then moved to the NT conservation facility at Knole, and subsequently to Fishbourne Roman Palace where she remains today awaiting the return home. A new organization was formed in New Zealand, Ngā Kohinga Whakairo o Hinemihi Trust, commenced work on plans to carve replacement carvings for a new whare in exchange for the return of Hinemihi. Working together Te Maru, Ngā Kohinga and the NT, a series of Tri-rōpū hui (three partner meetings) was implemented, with the collective meeting regularly online and in person since 2019, the process managed by a heritage consultant based in Rome, Sarah Court, who had previously worked on a heritage impact assessment for Hinemihi.

Into the digital

I have only begun to touch on the complex interactions that have emerged to support the agreement to return Hinemihi to New Zealand in exchange for carvings for a new meeting house that will continue to support the Māori and

Pasifika diaspora communities, as well as drawing on a Māori ethos to support other community engagement under her eaves. In the rest of this paper I want to focus on the specific affordances of digital media, not just as practical tools, but as aesthetic and affective frames that establish alternative practices, epistemologies and working relationships, and which have facilitated a new way of working for the NT.

In an earlier book, *Museum Object Lessons for the Digital Age* (2018), I explored the ways in which museum practices of digitization, from digital cataloguing, 3D scanning, as well as new forms of digital communication and representation, both amplify existing representational conventions and politics in museums but also contain the capacity to import alternative cultural protocols and practices of care, collections management and display. In the case of the Hinemihi project, much of which has intensified since the onset of the Covid-19 Pandemic, almost all our work has become virtual. In some ways this is not new, the primary register of heritage management is already virtual—taking place in the form of meetings, the production of policies, the filling in of planning documents, and the dissemination of information and text (see Riles, 2000). The argument of my book was that digital media both contained a myriad of potential affordances but were easily co-opted into broader ideologies around the power of technology. Whilst digital media may amplify aspirational discourses of accessibility and openness for example, this does not, in fact, make most museum collections more accessible or open. The argument I want to make here is twofold: one, to caution against a kind of digital fetishism which assumes that digital technologies bring completely new ways of being and working into heritage regimes and relations, and two, to combat a parallel strand of technological determinism that forgets to foreground the social worlds and relations that digital technologies and practices not only construct but also inhabit (Geismar, 2020). In the case of the negotiations around Hinemihi, digital communications allowed for a closing of distance between New Zealand and the UK. They also allowed for increased participation in the daily round of meetings and other bureaucracies that underpin heritage practices and decision making. However, they were also enabled by a series of perspectival shifts within the NT that themselves were critically engaged with the polemical publics and counter-publics produced within and through social media and which quietly sought, through careful and considered dialogue and practice to resist the polarization and politics that was being both carefully and harshly implemented/amplified over the course of our project. I want to argue that a primary affordance of the digital is, notwithstanding the emphasis on binary code, to collapse rigid distinctions. Digital technologies enables co-presence to collapse geographic borders and barriers, to unite different knowledge systems and hierarchies, and perform multiple ontologies.

Our digital space can therefore be seen as a form of quiet resistance or rebellion against a highly polarizing virtual public sphere that emerged after the publication of the NT's *Interim Report into Connections between Colonialism and Properties now in the Care of the National Trust* in 2020.[1] The online publication and dissemination of this report resulted in a wave of, often highly negative, media coverage and social media reaction focused on resisting what was described as "woke" cultural movements towards the past. This resulted in the formation of a new group "Restore Trust", the challenging of the charitable status of the NT in Parliament (arguing that the NT had betrayed its charter by becoming "political" through the publication of the report) and the authors of the report, and NT Director Hilary Grady receiving death threats and other violent criticisms over social media (see Geismar 2023 for a short summary of this). The controversy of the report, which simply tabulated which properties were connected to slavery and colonialism, was used to fuel populist criticism of "woke" political correctness and manufacture a sense of "culture wars" which was exploited by factions of the tabloid press and polarized further through

---

[1] https://www.nationaltrust.org.uk/who-we-are/research/addressing-our-histories-of-colonialism-and-historic-slavery, last accessed 27 January 2023.

social media, especially twitter. It is not an understatement to say that social media has fuelled a powerful sense of mistrust, anxiety, and antagonism around vital questions about our shared inheritance of the legacies of colonialism and the global relations that continue to play out in its image.

At the same time, digital communication tools were facilitating a quiet revolution within the NT. Starting each meeting with a Māori blessing and welcome, and ending with a closing chant, after a few months, several NT employees were taking Māori language lessons. Scheduling meetings in the early morning or late at night (out of normal working hours), enabled us to include Māori communities who in turn responded to the conversation by creating and delivering workshops and learning sessions to teach people at the NT about the design, culture and language of traditional Māori architecture, carving, and customs associated with whare tupuna (ancestral houses). When a large delegation from New Zealand was able to come to England, relationships of accountability, respect and personal connection had already been forged. The NT committed time and labour, within an increasingly fraught financial environment to supporting this new community. It was recognized that cultural work, social labour, and commitment was needed in order to manage the successful return of Hinemihi. Often this was done with a backdrop of media blackouts, and confidentiality, imbued with fear that there could be possible backlashes within the media.

Locally, the fire at Clandon park also opened up an alternative perspective on materiality, shifting perceptions of conservation and care. In her book *Curating Decay*, Caitlin DeSilvey explores numerous heritage projects that work within a material environment of dissolution and impermanence (DeSilvey, 2017, Geismar et al., 2022). After much discussion it has been decided not to restore Clandon Park to its former state but to re-develop the burnt ruins as a monument to the material processes of making the English country house. The exposed brickwork and roof beams, all that the fire left behind, are to be used as indexes of the myriad hands of craftspeople and labourers that built the house, or as the NT puts it "showcasing the many hands that made the house". [1] In this context of a renewed attention to materiality comes also a renewed engagement with the possibilities of seeing Hinemihi beyond the remit of the NT's traditional heritage regime. The destruction of the main house has also opened up a conversation about "the other house" and her value and meaning at Clandon. The engagement with Hinemihi's communities and a renewed attention to the terms of this engagement, with a re-centering of Māori language, has brought the Māori concept of "face to face" *kanohi ki te kanohi*, as a framework for understanding the past, and future, relationship between the two houses.

Conclusions

To briefly conclude, whilst digital technologies have facilitated this project, which could not have happened without the affordances of communications technologies including the bridging of time and space through the facilitation of co-presence, digital practices were also enabled by the bringing together of a range of cultural norms around heritage management and protocols of care, that are slowly, in the UK, shifting in response to a global conversation. It has been a big shift for the NT to organize meetings that acknowledge not just the time zone in New Zealand but Māori practices of consensus decision making and consultation, and to acknowledge the emotional as well as practical registers that are required to keep Hinemihi alive and activate her ongoing presence and ancestral authority. The opening up of concepts of community to include not just Maori and Pasifika diaspora, who are present in the UK in such small numbers as to barely register in national museum discourse in the UK, is also a quiet instantiation of the growing recognition that colonial histories and relations need

---

[1] https://www.nationaltrust.org.uk/visit/surrey/clandon-park/the-project-at-clandon-park.

not just to be acknowledged in the past but also in the present. The Hinemihi project is the first international repatriation that the NT has participated in, and its digital pathways are quietly buzzing with new possibilities for engagement, with the formulation of new publics beyond the shores of the United Kingdom, and new practices of care and accountability.

References

Clifford, James. 2013. *Returns: Becoming Indigenous in the Twenty-First Century*. Cambridge, Massachusetts: Harvard University Press.

DeSilvey, Caitlin. 2017. *Curated Decay: Heritage beyond Saving*. Minneapolis: University of Minnesota Press.

Dowden, Oliver. 2020. 'Letter from Culture Secretary on HM Government Position on Contested Heritage'. https://www.gov.uk/government/publications/letter-from-culture-secretary-on-hm-government-position-on-contested-heritage. Last accessed, 15 May 2023.

Gallop, Alan. 1998. *The House with the Golden Eyes: Unlocking the Secret History of 'Hinemihi', the Maori Meeting House from Te Wairoa (New Zealand) and Clandon Park (Surrey, England)*. Sunbury on Thames: Running Horse Books.

Geismar, Haidy. 2013. *Treasured Possesions: Indigenous Interventions into Cultural and Intellectual Property*. Durham, N.C.: Duke University Press.

———. 2018. *Museum Object Lessons for the Digital Age*. UCL Press. http://www.jstor.org/stable/j.ctv1xz0wz.

———. 2020. 'The New Instrumentalism'. In *Lineages and Advancements in Material Culture Studies*, edited by Timothy Carroll, Antonia Walford, and Shireen Walton, 75–88. London: Routledge.

———. 2023. 'Richard Bell's Embassy: Reshaping the Contenporary Art Museum'. *Tate Papers* 35. https://www.tate.org.uk/research/tate-papers/35/richard-bells-embassy-reshaping-the-contemporary-art-museum.

Geismar, Haidy, Ton Otto, and Cameron David Warner. 2022. *Impermanence: Exploring Continuous Change across Cultures*. London: UCL Press.

Henare, Amiria. 2005. *Museums, Anthropology and Imperial Exchange*. Cambridge; New

York: Cambridge University Press.

Hooper-Greenhill, Eilean. 2000. 'Speaking for Herself? Hinemihi and Her Discourses'. In *Museums and the Interpretation of Visual Culture*, 76–102. London: Routledge.

———. 1998. 'Perspectives on Hinemihi: A Maori Meeting House'. In *Colonialism and the Object: Empire, Material Culture, and the Museum*, edited by Tim Barringer and Tom Flynn, 129–143. London: Routledge.

Huxtable, Sally-Anne, Corinne Fowler, Christo Kefalas, and Emma Slocombe. 2020. 'Interim Report on the Connections between Colonialism and Properties Now in the Care of the National Trust, Including Links with Historic Slavery'. National Trust. https://nt.global.ssl.fastly.net/documents/colionialism-and-historic-slavery-report.pdf. Last accessed 15 May 2023.

Riles, Annelise. 2000. *The Network inside Out*. Ann Arbor: University of Michigan Press.

Salmond, Amiria Manutahi. 2013. 'Transforming Translations (Part I): "The Owner of These Bones"'. *HAU: Journal of Ethnographic Theory* 3 (3): 1–32. https://doi.org/10.14318/hau3.3.001.

Sarr, Felwine, and Bénédicte Savoy. 2019. 'Rapport sur la restitution du patrimoine culturel africain. Vers une nouvelle éthique relationnelle [The restitution of African Cultural Heritage: Towards a new relational ethics]'. 2018–26. www.restitutionreport2018.com. Last accessed 15 May 2023.

Sully, Dean, ed. 2008. *Decolonizing Conservation: Caring for Maori Meeting Houses Outside New Zealand*. 1 edition. Walnut Creek, Calif: Routledge.

Sully, Dean, Rosanna Raymond, and Anthony Hoete. 2014. 'Locating Hinemihi's People'. *Journal of Material Culture* 19 (2): 209–229. https://doi.org/10.1177/1359183513514316.

Wijesuriya, Gamini. 2007. 'Conserving Living Taonga: The Concept of Continuity'. In *Decolonising Conservation: The Care for Maori Meeting Houses Outside New Zealand*, edited by Dean Sully, 59–71. London: Taylor & Francis.

以数字方式传播权威和关怀：
Hinemihi o te Ao Tawhito 和她的回归①

海蒂·盖斯马[*]

前言

我想回顾一下我曾参与的一个项目，该项目将伦敦和新西兰的毛利人社区与国民信托（National Trust, NT，英国国家名胜古迹信托，以下简称国民信托）Te Maru o Hinemihi 联系起来，意味着"拥抱 Hinemihi"最初是由一群学者、文化利益相关者和实践者所组成的国民信托友好团体，他们致力于为克兰登公园中的毛利会堂——国民信托财产"Hinemihi"的合理保护展开对话。随着时间的推移，2015年的一场火灾几乎完全摧毁了主要房屋后，要求 Hinemihi 回到新西兰的呼声越来越高。火灾发生后，新西兰政府代表毛利人的后代正式要求英国返还 Hinemihi。

大火和新冠病毒大流行都导致克兰登对公众关闭，在这两场灾难之后，这一国际谈判已转移到网上进行。在意大利的一位遗产顾问的管理下，Te Maru（现在是一个独立的组织）和国民信托 Hinemihi 的后裔联系在一起，新西兰专门成立了一个小组（Ngā Kohinga Whakairo o Hinemihi），为国民信托的新房子制作雕刻品，以换取 Hinemihi 的回归。几年来，这三个团体定期举行视频会议，商讨回归的协议和结构，改变国民信托的做法，为商讨新的关爱和责任关系开辟第三空间。我们分享了有关文化

---

[*] 海蒂·盖斯马，英国伦敦大学学院人类学教授，数字人类学项目联合主管。
① 致谢：我要感谢 Te Maru o Hinemihi 的同事们给予的支持和建设性的反馈与批评。我尤其要感谢萨曼莎-卡拉汉（Samantha Callaghan）阅读了我之前的草稿。任何错误均由我本人负责。

协议的研讨会和资源,并在地球两端学习了新的语言。我早前的工作探索了数字技术对物质藏品以及非物质形式的知识和实践进行补救的能力(Geismar, 2018),结合这一工作,我在此探讨了在我们密集的在线工作中出现的一些主题,并探讨了这在国民信托内部引发的变化。这些讨论是在英国国内归还和送回文物的热潮中进行的,其特点是现任政府规定了"保留和解释"国家收藏品的任务(Dowdon 2020),以及国民信托基金负责人因公布与奴隶制和殖民主义有关的财产清单而受到死亡威胁〔Huxtable et al. (National Trust) 2020〕。在这种政治化的环境中,我将重点放在我们的项目如何使归还的途径不那么两极分化,但仍然有效,以及数字通信如何使新型对话和新的关爱语言得以出现。

Te Maru o Hinemihi

2014年,就在我从美国搬回英国后不久,我受邀加入了Te Maru o Hinemihi组织,这是国民信托的一个友好团体,成立的目的是倡导对毛利会堂(whare tupuna)Hinemihi的关爱和保护。Hinemihi o te Ao Tawhito由前新西兰总督翁斯洛勋爵带到英国,因在1886年塔拉韦拉火山爆发时保护了她的家人而闻名,并由罗托鲁瓦最著名的雕刻家雕刻而成(Gallup, 1998; Hooper-Greenhill, 1998, 2000)。翁斯洛勋爵在买下Hinemihi后,在其家族住宅克兰登公园周围的一系列新木结构上重新竖立了Hinemihi的雕刻。从船屋到花园洋房,Hinemihi最终被安置在著名园林设计师兰斯洛特·布朗设计的花园草坪上,坐落在一棵面向主屋的大树下。作为英国唯一的一座会堂,也是欧洲和北美唯一一座保存在博物馆之外的会堂,多年来,Hinemihi会堂举办过洗礼、婚礼和追悼会,并成为毛利人回家探亲的朝圣之地。她一直是英国和欧洲的毛利人和更广泛的太平洋岛民社区的家外之家,每年为社区举办盛宴和筹款活动,并接待和支持Ngāti Rānana(伦敦毛利人俱乐部)、Te Kohanga Reo o Rānana(毛利语巢穴)、毛利舞蹈和卡帕哈卡表演团体(如Manaia)以及包括波利尼西亚节拍(Beats of Polynesia)在内的其他太平洋岛民表演者。

在Te Maru的早期阶段，散居社区成员与国民信托之间就管理和保护Hinemihi的问题展开了长期对话，对话由伦敦大学学院保护学家迪恩·苏利（Dean Sully, Sully, 2008）负责，他与Hinemihi雕刻师之一特内·怀特雷（Tene Waitere）的后裔吉姆·舒斯特（Jim Schuster）密切合作，吉姆·舒斯特也是罗托鲁瓦的遗产顾问。Te Maru最初是作为一个朋友组织成立的，目的是利用这一组织结构的机会和能力，在国民信托内进行宣传。早期成员代表文化社区（毛利人和太平洋岛民），并汇集了不同形式的专业知识，他们的想法是从内部影响信托基金的运作。随着时间的推移，Te Maru成了与国民信托进行协调的组织，就Hinemihi的保护问题展开对话。苏利与国民信托的保护人员合作，为Hinemihi制定了一项保护计划，其中包括每年一次的文化保护日，新西兰和散居国外的志愿者以及伦敦大学洛杉矶分校考古研究所的保护专业学生也参与其中。

从表面上看，这种对话似乎强化了二元对立的关爱文化：我们的讨论经常在对作为实体的Hinemihi的不同本体论理解上出现偏差——国民信托将其视为需要管理、保存和维护的对象，而Te Maru则将Hinemihi视为雕刻形式的重要祖先，充满灵性（wairua）和权力/声望（mana），并与家庭关系（whakapapa）紧密相连，因此有必要承担照顾和监护的责任。胡珀-格林希尔（Hooper-Greenhill, 2000）描述了Hinemihi所处的多重对比世界和宇宙观，从艺术世界、自然保护到毛利人的世界观。在这里，我感兴趣的是如何以一种新的方式将这些观点结合在一起，从而克服简单的二元对立。

从2012年起，Te Maru脱离了朋友团体的职权范围（在国民信托的结构内提供支持和维持），最终重组为社区利益团体（CIC），并于2023年成为社区利益慈善机构（CIC）。到2014年，由于国民信托的人员更替频繁，以及对Hinemihi的合作愿景缺乏连续性，Te Maru与国民信托之间产生了脱节感，土著和文化利益相关者与主流遗产组织之间的二元对立角色长期存在。此时，在时任主席安东尼·霍特（Anthony Hoete）的领导下，Te Maru制定了一个5个"R"的方案，为他们在国民信托进行的讨论提供框架，从最低限度到最高限度来展望Hinemihi的未来（见Sully, Raymond &

Hoete, 2014）。①第五个方案是搬迁或遣返，这一方案得到了越来越多新西兰国内社区的支持，他们在参观克兰登公园时经常会对Hinemihi的状况感到失望。Hinemihi位于一棵大树下，有树枝倒下的危险，而且暴露在风雨中，她的雕刻看起来已经破旧褪色，她的结构以及内部的普通土层越来越被文化社区认为不适合使用，他们希望能够在冬天取暖，在她的屋檐下过夜，并且能够洗衣做饭，作为保持自己和Hinemihi文化活力的一部分。

2015年，一个新西兰土地信托代表团来到这里，讨论Hinemihi的未来，并为国民信托留下了一份礼物（Koha），以及一份谅解备忘录草案的雏形，该备忘录的重点是扩大Hinemihi占地面积的计划，使其成为一个完整的毛利会堂（marae），建议增加厨房和洗涤设施，为来访团体提供食物和住所（Sully et al., 2014）。2015年，一场毁灭性的大火几乎完全烧毁了克兰登公园大楼，此后，这些计划得到了加强。这是国民信托有史以来经历的最严重的火灾之一，虽然Hinemihi安全地屹立在花园里，但她保存在房子里的几件珍宝以及详细记录购买她的文件都损毁了。

也正是从那时起，关于归还的讨论重新开始。克兰登的大火引发了国民信托的重新思考，它越来越多地不仅将Hinemihi作为花园中的"物件"，而是作为"另一座房子"，勇敢地屹立在那里，与克兰登废墟平起平坐。在新西兰奥特亚罗亚（Aotearoa New Zealand），Te Maru的身份也发生了变化。Te Maru首先被视为"pukenga小组"（一个专家小组，聚集在一起支持Hinemihi和她的人民），然后被视为Ngāti Hinemihi和国民信托就Hinemihi回归问题进行的三方谈判中的第三方。渐渐地，一个交换建议出现了——Hinemihi将返回新西兰奥特亚罗亚，而作为回报，她的族人将为克兰登公园的一个新毛利人房屋提供雕刻品。

在这一讨论期间，全球和国内的博物馆学在毛利珍品（taonga）的策展方面也发生了一些变化。自1985年在大都会艺术博物馆开幕的巡回展览"毛利人"（Te Māori）在美国各地巡回展出后，又回到了新西兰，在全球博物馆实践中，对毛利文化保护规程的制度化正在发展（参见Breismar,

---

① 它们是修复（repair），归还（restore），重新设计（reprogramme），改造（redevelog）和迁至新地点（relocate）。

2013，第6章。）这反映在博物馆中其他会堂［例如芝加哥的鲁特普库克二世（Ruatepupuke II）和汉堡的劳鲁（Rauru）］的管理方式上，这些管理方式在动态的文化关系中越来越活跃，毛利人的投入也越来越多。这些措施包括安排黎明时分的开幕和闭幕仪式，用歌唱和咒语来结束文化活动；认识到文化权威和长老需要作为顾问和参与者参与到项目中来（并相应地编列预算）；以及以尊重的态度策划展览，将文化规程纳入展示中。然而，将毛利人的习俗纳入国际博物馆实践的表演或展览方面，有时超过了将这些习俗内化为其他方面的实践的方式，例如在保护、藏品管理和对社区参与的持续投资方面。关于替代性护理实践的讨论似乎更多地围绕文物所有权的条件展开。然而，毛利社区与收藏毛利珍品的博物馆之间的交流日益增多，国际归还运动的发展，以及对英国博物馆和藏品纠缠不清的殖民历史的历史研究和问责制的不断加强，都带来了一种新的保护和问责文化（Henare, 2005; Clifford, 2013; Salmond, 2013; Sarr & Savoy, 2019）。

到2016年，国民信托向吉尔福德郡议会提交了一份列入保护名录的建筑申请，要求移除Hinemihi的雕刻以便进行保护。在吉姆·舒斯特（Jim Schuster）和迪恩·苏利的支持下，他们与国民信托文物修复员艾米丽-尼斯贝特-霍金斯（Emily Nisbet-Hawkins）密切合作，将木结构的雕刻移走，并将Hinemihi移走，最初存放在索尔兹伯里的一个艺术品储藏设施中，然后搬到位于诺尔（Knole）的国民信托保护设施中，随后又搬到菲什伯恩罗马宫殿（Fishbourne Roman Palace），如今她仍在那里等待回家。新西兰成立了一个新的组织——Ngā Kohinga Whakairo o Hinemihi信托，开始制定计划，雕刻一个新的Whare，以换取Hinemihi的归还。Te Maru、Ngā Kohinga和国民信托共同开展了一系列三方会议（Tri-rōpū hui），自2019年以来定期举行在线和面对面的集体会议，该过程由驻罗马的遗产顾问莎拉·科特（Sarah Court）管理，她之前曾参与过Hinemihi的遗产影响评估工作。

进入数字时代

我刚刚开始触及为支持将Hinemihi归还新西兰的协议而产生的复杂互

动,以换取新会议中心的雕刻,该会议中心将继续支持毛利人和太平洋岛民散居社区,并利用毛利人的精神支持其屋檐下其他社区的参与。在本文的其余部分,我将重点讨论数字媒体的具体优势。数字媒体不仅是实用工具,也是美学和情感框架,它建立了替代性的实践、认识论和工作关系,并促进了国民信托新的工作方式。

在早前出版的《数字时代的博物馆物品课程》(2018)一书中,我探讨了博物馆数字化实践的方式,从数字编目、三维扫描,到新形式的数字通信和表现,既放大了博物馆中现有的表征惯例和政治,也包含了导入替代性文化规程以及护理、藏品管理和展示实践的能力。就Hinemihi项目而言,自新冠疫情爆发以来,我们几乎所有的工作都变成了虚拟的。在某些方面,这并不是什么新鲜事,遗产管理的主要注册方式已经是虚拟的——以会议的形式进行、政策的制定、规划文件的填写以及信息和文本的传播(见Riles,2000)。我在书中提出的观点是,数字媒体既包含无数潜在的能力,但也很容易被更广泛的技术力量意识形态所利用。例如,虽然数字媒体可能会放大可访问性和开放性的理想论调,但事实上,这并不会让大多数博物馆藏品变得更容易访问或更开放。在此,我想提出两方面的论点:其一,警惕一种数字拜物教,这种拜物教认为数字技术为遗产制度和关系带来了全新的存在和工作方式;其二,反对技术决定论的平行分支,这种技术决定论忘记了强调数字技术和实践不仅构建而且还居住在其中的社会世界和关系(Geismar, 2020)。在围绕Hinemihi的谈判中,数字通信拉近了新西兰与英国之间的距离。它们还使人们能够更多地参与日常会议和其他官僚机构,这些都是遗产实践和决策的基础。然而,国民信托内部的一系列视角转变也促成了这些转变,这些转变本身就批判性地参与了在社交媒体中以及通过社交媒体产生的论战性公众和反公众,并通过谨慎而深思熟虑的对话和实践,悄悄地寻求抵制两极分化和政治,而在我们的项目过程中,这种两极分化和政治正在被谨慎而严厉地实施/放大。我想说的是,尽管强调二进制编码,但数字技术的一个主要功能是打破僵化的区分。数字技术使共同在场能够打破地理边界和障碍,将不同的知识体系和等级制度结合起来,并执行多重本体论。

因此，我们的数字空间可以被看作是一种对高度两极化的虚拟公共领域的无声抵抗或反叛，这是在2020年国民信托发表《殖民主义与国民信托托管财产之间的联系》中期报告之后出现的。该报告的在线发布和传播引发了一波非常负面的媒体报道和社交媒体反响，其重点是抵制被称为"觉醒的"面向过去的文化运动。这导致了一个新团体"归还信托"的成立，议会对国民信托的慈善地位提出质疑（认为国民信托通过出版报告变得"政治化"，从而背叛了其章程），报告的作者和国民信托主管希拉里·格雷迪在社交媒体上收到死亡威胁和其他暴力批评（对此事的简短总结见Geismar, 2023）。这份报告只是简单地列出了哪些财产与奴隶制和殖民主义有关，其引发的争议被用来助长民粹主义对"觉醒的"政治正确性的批评，并制造出一种"文化战争"的感觉。这种"文化战争"被小报中的一些派别所利用，并通过社交媒体（尤其是推特）进一步分化。可以毫不夸张地说，社交媒体助长了一种强烈的不信任、焦虑和对立情绪，这些情绪围绕着我们共同继承殖民主义遗产的重要问题，以及以殖民主义形象继续发展的全球关系。

与此同时，数字通信工具也在促进国民信托内部的一场静悄悄的革命。每次会议都以毛利语的祝福和欢迎词开始，以结束语结束，几个月后，几名国民信托员工开始学习毛利语。会议被安排在清晨或深夜（非正常工作时间），使得毛利社区能参与进来，而毛利社区也通过举办工作坊和学习班，向国民信托的员工传授毛利传统建筑的设计、文化和语言、雕刻以及与毛利会堂相关的习俗。当新西兰的一个大型代表团能够来到英国时，双方已经建立了责任、尊重和个人联系的关系。在日益严峻的财政环境下，国民信托投入了大量的时间和人力来支持这个新社区。人们认识到，要使Hinemihi成功回归，就需要文化工作、社会劳动和承诺。这往往是在媒体封锁和保密的背景下进行的，因为人们担心媒体可能会产生反弹。

在当地，克兰登公园的火灾也开启了对物质性的另一种视角，改变了对保护和护理的看法。凯特琳·德西尔维（Caitlin DeSilvey）在她的著作《策展衰败》（*Curating Decay*）中探讨了许多在消解和无常的物质环境中工作的遗产项目（Desilvey, 2017; Geismar et al., 2022）。经过反复讨论后，我们决定不将克兰登公园恢复原状，而是将烧毁的废墟重新开发，作为英国乡村别墅建造过程的物质纪念碑。大火留下的裸露的砖砌结构和屋顶横梁将被用作无数工匠和工人建造房屋的标志，或者正如国民信托所说的那样，"展示建造房屋的无数双手"。在这种重新关注物质性的背景下，我们也重新认识到了超越国民信托传统遗产制度范围来看待Hinemihi的可能性。会堂的毁坏也开启了一场关于"另一座房子"及其在克兰登的价值和意义的对话。与Hinemihi社区的接触以及对这种接触的条件的重新关注，再加上对毛利语言的重新关注，使得毛利人的"面对面"（kanohi ki te kanohi）概念成为理解两座房子之间过去和未来关系的框架。

结语

简而言之，数字技术为本项目提供了便利，如果没有通信技术的支持（包括通过促进共同在场来弥合时间和空间），本项目是不可能开展的。同时，数字实践也得益于一系列围绕遗产管理和保护协议的文化规范的汇集，在英国，这些规范正随着全球对话而慢慢转变。对于国民信托来说，组织会议不仅要考虑新西兰的时区，还要考虑毛利人在决策和协商方面的共识，同时还要考虑让Hinemihi存活下去、激活她的持续存在和祖先的权威所需的情感和实践，这是一个巨大的转变。社区概念的开放不仅包括毛利人和太平洋岛民散居国外者，他们在英国的人数很少，在英国国家博物馆的论述中几乎不被提及，这也悄无声息地体现了人们日益认识到，殖民历史和关系不仅需要在过去得到承认，也需要在现在得到承认。Hinemihi项目是国民信托首次参与的国际性归还项目，其数字途径正悄然迸发出新的参与可能性，在英国海岸之外形成新的公众群体，以及新的关怀和责任实践。

参考文献

Clifford, James. 2013. *Returns: Becoming Indigenous in the Twenty-First Century*. Cambridge, Massachusetts: Harvard University Press.

DeSilvey, Caitlin. 2017. *Curated Decay: Heritage beyond Saving*. Minneapolis: University of Minnesota Press.

Dowden, Oliver. 2020. 'Letter from Culture Secretary on HM Government Position on Contested Heritage'. https://www.gov.uk/government/publications/letter-from-culture-secretary-on-hm-government-position-on-contested-heritage. Last accessed, 15 May 2023.

Gallop, Alan. 1998. *The House with the Golden Eyes: Unlocking the Secret History of 'Hinemihi', the Maori Meeting House from Te Wairoa (New Zealand) and Clandon Park (Surrey, England)*. Sunbury on Thames: Running Horse Books.

Geismar, Haidy. 2013. *Treasured Possesions: Indigenous Interventions into Cultural and Intellectual Property*. Durham, N.C.: Duke University Press.

———. 2018. *Museum Object Lessons for the Digital Age*. UCL Press. http://www.jstor.org/stable/j.ctv1xz0wz.

———. 2020. 'The New Instrumentalism'. In *Lineages and Advancements in Material Culture Studies*, edited by Timothy Carroll, Antonia Walford, and Shireen Walton, 75–88. London: Routledge.

———. 2023. 'Richard Bell's Embassy: Reshaping the Contenporary Art Museum'. *Tate Papers* 35. https://www.tate.org.uk/research/tate-papers/35/richard-bells-embassy-reshaping-the-contemporary-art-museum.

Geismar, Haidy, Ton Otto, and Cameron David Warner. 2022. *Impermanence: Exploring Continuous Change across Cultures*. London: UCL Press.

Henare, Amiria. 2005. *Museums, Anthropology and Imperial Exchange*. Cambridgẽ; New York: Cambridge University Press.

Hooper-Greenhill, Eilean. 2000. 'Speaking for Herself? Hinemihi and Her Discourses'. In *Museums and the Interpretation of Visual Culture*, 76–102. London: Routledge.

———. 1998. 'Perspectives on Hinemihi: A Maori Meeting House'. In *Colonialism and the Object: Empire, Material Culture, and the Museum*, edited by Tim Barringer and Tom Flynn, 129–143. London: Routledge.

Huxtable, Sally-Anne, Corinne Fowler, Christo Kefalas, and Emma Slocombe. 2020. 'Interim Report on the Connections between Colonialism and Properties Now in the Care of the National Trust, Including Links with Historic Slavery'. National Trust. https://nt.global.ssl.fastly.net/documents/colonialism-and-historic-slavery-report.

pdf. Last accessed 15 May 2023.

Riles, Annelise. 2000. *The Network inside Out*. Ann Arbor: University of Michigan Press.

Salmond, Amiria Manutahi. 2013. 'Transforming Translations (Part I): "The Owner of These Bones"'. *HAU: Journal of Ethnographic Theory* 3 (3): 1–32. https://doi.org/10.14318/hau3.3.001.

Sarr, Felwine, and Bénédicte Savoy. 2019. 'Rapport sur la restitution du patrimoine culturel africain. Vers une nouvelle éthique relationnelle [The restitution of African Cultural Heritage: Towards a new relational ethics]'. 2018–26. www.restitutionreport2018.com. Last accessed 15 May 2023.

Sully, Dean, ed. 2008. *Decolonizing Conservation: Caring for Maori Meeting Houses Outside New Zealand*. 1 edition. Walnut Creek, Calif: Routledge.

Sully, Dean, Rosanna Raymond, and Anthony Hoete. 2014. 'Locating Hinemihi's People'. *Journal of Material Culture* 19 (2): 209–229. https://doi.org/10.1177/1359183513514316.

Wijesuriya, Gamini. 2007. 'Conserving Living Taonga: The Concept of Continuity'. In *Decolonising Conservation: The Care for Maori Meeting Houses Outside New Zealand*, edited by Dean Sully, 59–71. London: Taylor & Francis.

How Artist-made Reproductions Can Strengthen Museums and Their Communities: A Case Study

Laura Evans[*]

Abstract: In this paper, the author argues that museums should consider, on a case by case, the repatriation of objects to source communities and the replacement of the original object in the museum's collection with a high-quality reproduction made by artists from the source community. This paper does not focus on other means of reproduction (like 3-D printing) that have become popular in museums. The author focuses on an example of a repatriation case—The Ghost Dance Shirt, formerly at the Kelvingrove Art Gallery & Museum—where the original object was returned to the source community and replaced by a high quality, artist-made reproduction. This paper discusses the benefits of this process and the outcome. Finally, this paper provides suggestions for how museums might recontextualize these contested objects and bring the visitor along with them during the complicated journey of return. A longer version of this paper was published in the June 2020 issue of *The Museum Scholar: Theory & Practice* (Volume 3).

Introduction

In this paper, I will start with a brief examination of the changing views on

---

[*] Laura Evans, Distinguished Teaching Professor, Visual Arts and Design, University of North Texas.

the acceptability of reproductions in art and in museums. I will then advocate for how museums can approach repatriation cases by replacing an original work of art with another original work of art: an artist-made reproduction. I argue that museums should consider, on a case by case, the repatriation of objects to source communities and to replace the original object with a high-quality reproduction made by artists from the source community. A longer version of this paper was published in the June 2020 issue of *The Museum Scholar: Theory & Practice* (Volume 3).

A Brief History of Reproductions

The West's acceptance of reproductions has ebbed and flowed throughout history. Plato espoused that copies were "deteriorated or defective originals"[1] and he attempted to "reorient humans away from the everyday world of mimetic appearance towards a space of originals, ideas, and the Good."[2] In a world where making copies was laborious and arduous, originality was much easier to insist upon.

As humans learned the skills to make reproductions more sustainable and mechanized, they became more in vogue. The invention of the printing press, the casting of sculptures, the lithograph, the camera, the Internet; all of these were technologies that thrust reproductions into the hands and homes of people. Our relationship with reproductions has become more constant but, perhaps, more fraught, or, at least, in terms of museums. Casts of sculptures were once used abundantly and without judgment. At one point, museums were so enamored with casts, that in 1876, a delegation was arranged from European museums for a "cast exchange."[3]

---

[1] Marcus Boon, "Toward a Future of Museum Copying," 254.
[2] Ibid.
[3] Boon, "Toward a Future of Museum Copying."

Copying fell out of fashion as Western society began to place more importance on the sanctity of original intellectual property. With the advent of the 1710 Statute of Anne in Great Britain, otherwise known as the Copyright Act, which is regarded as the birth of modern copyright law, copying was radically curtailed by law.①

With the birth of practical photography in 1839, the schism between copies and originals deepened.② By the 1930s, leading philosophers and academics were articulating this divide. In 1935, Walter Benjamin wrote his seminal text, *The Work of Art in the Age of Mechanical Reproduction*, which is widely cited and clung to in art history and in museums. In it, Benjamin argues that the aura of a work of art—the intangible, inherent quality only found in an original—is lost when it is reproduced by mechanical means.③ An aura cannot be reproduced. Accordingly, a reproduction cannot possibly have the weight and gravitas that an original has. This is the element of Benjamin's argument that museums cling to.

Yet, in other forms of art, the emphasis placed upon the aura of the original is not as weighty. Latour and Lowe④ write about how different forms of art are dependent upon copies as a means of distribution. They point to the performing arts, to literature, and to music. Each of these relies on an original but on an infinite variety of reproductions and, in some cases, variations. As an example of the schism, the authors focus on a play, *King Lear*, where the audience delights in reinterpretations of the original text. New actors, new stagings, new locations for the play invigorate it. We may glean some new information from the play in a restaging of it that we might not have been able to understand from a faithful reproduction of Shakespeare's text. "Why is it so difficult to say the

---

① Boon, "Toward a Future of Museum Copying."
② Walter Benjamin, "Illuminations: Essays and Reflections."
③ Ibid.
④ Bruno Latour and Adam Lowe, "The Migration of the Aura or How to Explore the Original Through its Facsimiles."

same thing and use the same type of judgment for a painting or a sculpture or a building?" ask Latour and Lowe. [1]

An Example of an Artist-Made Reproduction in a Repatriation Case

Why is it so difficult, indeed? I would like to give an example of an original work of art being returned to a source community and being replaced by an original work of art. There are few examples this and even fewer still where a museum replaces an original with a source artist-created reproduction. I would like to share one example of this collaboration: The Ghost Dance Shirt, formerly of the Kelvingrove Museum.

Lou-ann Ika'wega Neel, a repatriation specialist at the Royal British Columbia Museum in Victoria, has suggested indigenous objects in museums be returned to the tribe from where they were removed. Furthermore, she thinks that indigenous artists from these communities should create faithful replicas of the original to take the place of the restituted object in the museum. "These replicas could remain with museums along with much more information, so they can continue to serve as educational tools for people of all cultures. Visitors know that we are not a dead or dying culture. We are still here."[2]

Neel's suggestion was enacted many years earlier, in the 1990s in Glasgow's Kelvingrove Museum. The Kelvingrove was in possession of a Lakota Ghost Shirt, which had been wrongfully taken from a Lakota corpse following The Battle at Wounded Knee.[3] The Wounded Knee Association was made aware of the existence of The Ghost Dance Shirt in the Kelvingrove's

---

[1] Bruno Latour and Adam Lowe, "The Migration of the Aura or How to Explore the Original Through its Facsimiles.", 7.
[2] Kate Brown, "People Across the Globe Want Their Cultural Heritage Back: Canada May Offer a Blueprint For How to Get There," para. 29.
[3] Sam Maddra, "The Wounded Knee Ghost Dance Shirt."

collection in the mid-1990s. Led by Marcella le Beau, a Lakota tribe member and the secretary of the Wounded Knee Association (WKA), the WKA asked for the return of The Ghost Dance Shirt.① The museum, believing the shirt had been acquired in good faith, entered into conversation with the WKA. Through mediated discussions and after Glasgow city residents supported the return of The Ghost Dance Shirt, it was returned to the Lakota in 1998.②

What is remarkable about this story isn't the repatriation of The Ghost Dance Shirt. These repatriations happen, if not frequently enough. What is noteworthy about this case are three things: (1) the Glasgow public was consulted about whether they supported the return of The Ghost Dance Shirt and Glasgowians voted for its return, (2) Marcella Le Beau, who led the WKA in their repatriation claim, made a faithful reproduction of the shirt and gave it to the Kelvingrove where it remains, and (3) the museum displayed the reproduction of the shirt, along with a narrative of the repatriation story.

The faithfully reproduced Ghost Dance Shirt that is currently on display at the Kelvingrove has been described by the House of Commons Culture, Media, and Sport Committee (CMSC) to be "in no doubt ... a better, more educational and more interesting museum display than that with had featured the original shirt."③

Comments by visitors on a board in the exhibition were almost entirely favorable, such as, "all of humanity is connected to each other," and "so glad to see this as a discussion—I knew very little about procedures and cases of repatriation." It would seem that exhibiting the absence of an object can have a powerful impact, no less than that achieved by displaying it.④

Not only has the Kelvingrove gained a richer, more nuanced, transparent,

---

① Sam Maddra, "The Wounded Knee Ghost Dance Shirt."
② Neil Curtis, "'A Welcome and Important Part of Their Role': The Impact of Reparation on Museums in Scotland."
③ House of Commons, Culture, Media and Sport Committee, "Cultural Property Return and Illicit Trade, Seventh Report."
④ Curtis, "A Welcome and Important Part of Their Role," 99.

and moving exhibition of the replicated Ghost Dance Shirt, the relationship with the Lakota tribe has blossomed. Bailie Elizabeth Cameron of the Glasgow City Council said, "We have ended up forging a place in the history of the Lakota, and the Lakota have become part of the history of Glasgow museums."[1] Instead of displaying a static object from a faraway culture, the Kelvingrove is now part of a global, dynamic relationship. What they have lost is the original object but what they have gained is far more worthwhile of a museum in the 21st century.

Likewise, the Lakota have a relationship with Scotland in a way that they didn't have before. In regard to another repatriation case in Scotland, Curtis writes, "... the keeper of the headdress [from the University of Aberdeen's collection] repatriated from Aberdeen bought a kilt jacket to wear when dancing the headdress as a mark of its sojourn in Scotland."[2] In an increasingly globalized world, museums should celebrate the intersections between cultures that can be developed through repatriation.

Conclusions

Steven Conn, a historian, has asked, "Do museums still need objects?" Yes, I believe museums do still need objects. It is, quintessentially, what makes a museum a museum. But, do museums need ALL of their objects? No. Do museums need experiences as much as objects?[3] We continue to move in this direction. Can thoughtfully made artist-created reproductions of repatriated objects create new experiences for visitors that can compete with the experience of seeing the original object? I think so, absolutely.

I will rhetorically ask, does viewing copies somehow lessen the experience of going to a museum? I think when contextualized properly and when so much

---

[1] House of Commons, "Cultural Property Return and Illicit Trade."
[2] Curtis, "A Welcome and Important Part of Their Role," 99.
[3] Hilde Hein, "The Museum In Transition: A Philosophical Primer."

is at stake, artist-made reproductions of items returned to source communities can actually enhance the experience of going to a museum. And, when artists from the source community create new objects, the new object is endowed with an aura that is different than the original, certainly, but important.①

It is key to the success of museums that when replacing originals with artist-made reproductions, that the narrative of the return becomes a part of the object's story.

Latour and Lowe write that when a visual work of art is copied, "... a sense of fakery, counterfeiting or betrayal, has been introduced into the discussion in a way that would seem absurd for a piece of performance art ... It seems almost impossible to say that a facsimile ... is not about falsification but it is a stage in the verification of [the artist's] achievement, a part of its ongoing biography."②

In this vein, it is key to the success of museums that when replacing originals with artist-made reproductions, that the narrative of the return becomes a part of the object's story. This story should be detailed in interpretive materials that surround the reproduced object. Source communities should tell their own stories of loss and what it means for them to be reunited with the objects that were taken from them. Hearing these counternarratives could be a powerful reminder for why museums should support the return of objects to source communities. Furthermore, source communities can tell the stories of creating the artist-made reproduction that remains at the museum. This story of the replacement object could be an opportunity for museum visitors to learn more about the culture where the object originated and the traditional methods of creating this object. Through counternarratives, there are countless opportunities for learning and growing to occur in the museum itself, in the source community, and in the visitor, who benefits from seeing the many layers

---

① Walter Benjamin, "Illuminations: Essays and Reflections."
② Bruno Latour and Adam Lowe, "The Migration of the Aura or How to Explore the Original Through its Facsimiles," 7.

of collaboration between museum and community.

After the opening of the Acropolis Museum in Athens in 2009, *The Guardian* surveyed United Kingdom residents about whether they thought the Elgin Marbles should remain at the British Museum or be returned to Greece. An overwhelming 94.8% of respondents voted for the return of the Elgin Marbles. 5.2% voted for the Marbles to remain in England.[1] This is a staggering difference and signifies something bigger that more museums should be paying attention to. Museum visitors want to have an authentic experience but, maybe more than this, a moral experience that they can feel good about. Museums need to let visitors decide how they feel about reproductions rather than decide how to feel for them. We do not know better than they do about how they will feel about museums that have replaced originals with artist-made reproductions so as to return the originals to their source.

Fouseki has "argued that the reunification discourse is academically-led and does not portray wider public opinion."[2] If museums conducted focus groups, they would probably find that museum visitors feel more strongly about justice and return, than about the authenticity of an object.

Charney writes about museum-going, "we want an authentic encounter as opposed to the experience of gazing at reproductions in books."[3] But, who is "we?" And, who gets to speak for the museum visitor in the case of artist-made reproductions and repatriations? Museum visitors could be as inspired or, even, more inspired by an authentic encounter with an artist-made reproduction than a rote encounter with an original if the original has been returned for moral and ethical reasons. But, we should let visitors speak for themselves. We need more surveys and studies that ask visitors the very important questions of what they

---

[1] Tristram Besterman, "Crossing the Line: Restitution and Cultural Equity."
[2] Kalliopi Fouseki. "Claiming the Parthenon Marbles Back: Whose Claim and On Behalf of Whom?" 174.
[3] Charney, "A Fake of Art," para. 6.

support: a displaced original whose loss is being mourned by the community where it was created, or an artist-made reproduction that highlights the story of return, reunion, and collaboration?

References

Benjamin, Walter. *Illuminations: Essays and Reflections*. New York, NY: Schocken, 1935/1969.

Besterman, Tristram. "Crossing the Line: Restitution and Cultural Equity." In *Museums and Restitution: New Practices, New Approaches*, edited by Louise Tythacott & Kostas Arvanitis, 19–36. Abingdon, England: Routledge, 2016.

Boon, Marcus. "Toward a Future of Museum Copying." In *Museums as Cultures of Copies: The Crafting of Artefacts and Authenticity*, edited by Brita Brenna, Hans Dam Christensen & Olav Hamran, 253–266. Abingdon, England: Routledge Research in Museum Studies, 2018.

Brown, Kate. "People Across the Globe Want Their Cultural Heritage Back: Canada May Offer a Blueprint For How to Get There." *The Guardian*. June 25, 2018. https://news.artnet.com/art-world/canada-restitution-indigenous-culture-1307060.

Charney, Noah. "A Fake of Art." *Aeon*. February 5, 2016. https://aeon.co/essays/is-there-a-place-for-fakery-in-art-galleries-and-museums.

Curtis, Neil. " 'A Welcome and Important Part of Their Role': The Impact of Reparation on Museums in Scotland." In *Museums and Restitution: New Practices, New Approaches*, edited by Louise Tythacott & Kostas Arvanitis, 85–104. Abingdon, England: Routledge, 2016.

Fouseki, Kalliopi. "Claiming the Parthenon Marbles Back: Whose Claim and on Behalf of Whom?" In *Museums and Restitution: New Practices, New Approaches*, edited by Louise Tythacott & Kostas Arvanitis, 163–178. Abingdon, England: Routledge, 2016.

Hein, Hilde. *The Museum In Transition: A Philosophical Primer*. Washington, D.C. : Smithsonian Institution Press, 2010.

House of Commons, Culture, Media and Sport Committee. 2000. "Cultural Property Return and Illicit Trade, Seventh Report." Accessed November 24, 2019. https://

publications.parliament.uk/pa/cm199900/cmselect/cmcumeds/371/37102.htm.

Latour, Bruno and Adam Lowe. "The Migration of the Aura or How to Explore the Original Through its Facsimiles." In *Switching Codes: Thinking through Digital Technology in the Humanities and Arts*, edited by Thomas Bartscherer & Roderick Coover, 1–18. Chicago, Illinois: University of Chicago Press, 2010.

Maddra, Sam. "The Wounded Knee Ghost Dance Shirt." *Journal of Museum Ethnography* 8, 41–58, (1996).

案例研究：艺术家制作的复制品如何作用于博物馆及其社区的发展[①]

劳拉·埃文斯[*]

摘要：在本文中，作者认为博物馆应根据具体情况考虑将文物送回原社区，并用原社区艺术家制作的高质量复制品取代博物馆收藏的原物。本文并不关注博物馆中流行的其他复制手段（如 3D 打印）。作者重点介绍了一个归还案例——原藏于凯尔文格罗夫美术馆和博物馆的"鬼舞衫"，在这个案例中，原作被归还给了原作社区，展品则由艺术家制作的高质量复制品取而代之。本文讨论了这一过程的益处和结果。最后，本文就博物馆如何将这些有争议的物品重新语境化，并在复杂的回归之旅中与参观者同行提出了建议。

前言

这篇文章中，我会先简要介绍艺术界和博物馆对复制品接受程度上的变化，然后我将倡导博物馆如何在个案的基础上用来自艺术品来源社区的艺术家的复制品取代艺术品原作处理遣返案件。

复制品简史

历史上，西方对于复制品的接受程度是波动起伏的：柏拉图认为复制品是"变质的或有缺陷的原作"，他试图"将人类从摹仿外观的日常世

---

[*] 劳拉·埃文斯，美国北得克萨斯州大学视觉艺术与设计学院教授。
[①] 本文原文发表于：June 2020 issue of *The Museum Scholar: Theory & Practice* (Volume 3)。

界转向原创、思想和善的空间",在一个制作复制品费力且不讨好的世界,坚持原创要容易得多。

随着人类掌握了使复制品更具可持续性和机械化的技能,复制品变得越来越流行。印刷机的发明、雕塑的铸造、平版印刷画、照相机、互联网;所有这些技术都将复制品推向了人们的手中和家中。我们与复制品之间的关系变得更加稳定,但或许也更加脆弱,至少在博物馆方面是如此。雕塑的铸件曾一度被大量使用,而且不受任何评判。博物馆一度对铸模如此着迷,以至于在1876年,欧洲博物馆安排了一个代表团进行"铸模交流"。

随着西方社会开始更加重视原创知识产权的神圣不可侵犯性,复制行为逐渐淡出了人们的视野。1710年英国颁布的《安妮法令》(又称《版权法》)被认为是现代版权法的雏形,自此,法律从根本上限制了复制的行为。

随着1839年实用摄影的诞生,复制品和原件之间的分野加深。到了20世纪30年代,主要的哲学家和学者们都在讨论这种分歧。1935年,瓦尔特·本杰明写下了他的开创性作品《机械复制时代的艺术品》,这部作品在艺术史和博物馆中被广泛地引用和讨论。在这本书中,本雅明认为艺术品所蕴含的那种只有在原作中才能找到的无形且固有的"气质",在复制品中已经消失了。当艺术品被机械地复制时,它的气质便消失了。因此,一件复制品不可能具备原作才有的分量和庄重感,这也是本杰明论点中博物馆所倾向的部分。

但在其他的艺术形式中,对原作光环的强调并没有如此重要,拉图尔和洛维分析了不同形式的艺术如何依赖复制作为传播的手段。他们提到了表演艺术、文学和音乐,这些艺术形式中的每一种都依赖于原作,但同时也依赖于无限的复制品,某些情况下,还会依赖于变体。作为分裂的例子,作者将重点放在了《李尔王》一剧上。在这部剧中,观众对原著的重新解读很感兴趣,新的演员、新的舞台、新的地点都使得这部剧充满活力。我们可能会从重新演绎的剧目中获得一些新的信息,而这些信息可能是我们无法从对莎士比亚文本忠实再现的剧目中理解到的。拉图尔和洛维问道:"为什么对一幅画或一件雕塑说同样的话、用同样类型的判断方式,会如此困难?"

文物返还工作中的艺术复制品实例

为什么会这么困难呢?我想举一个例子,一个艺术品的原作被送回了它原本所属于的地方,同时用另一个艺术作品来替代这件原作。这样的例子并不多见,而博物馆用艺术家创作的复制品替代原作的案例就更少了。但我想要分享一个这种合作的例子,那就是"鬼舞衫"(The Ghost Dance Shirt),之前收藏于苏格兰格拉斯哥凯文葛罗夫博物馆(Kelvingrove Museum)。

维多利亚不列颠哥伦比亚皇家博物馆的文物返还专家尼尔(Lou-ann Ika'wega Neel)提议,博物馆应该将原住民的物品返还给它们本来所属的部落。她还认为这些部落的原住民艺术家应该创造出忠实于原作的复制品,用来替代博物馆中被返还的原作的位置。"这些留在博物馆中的复制品可以提供更丰富的信息,这样它们就可以继续作为全人类文化的教育工具,参观者们便会知道,我们并不是一个已经消失或者濒临垂死的文化。我们依然存在。"

尼尔的提议早在20世纪90年代的凯文葛罗夫博物馆便已经被付诸行动。凯文葛罗夫博物馆收藏有一件拉克塔人的"鬼舞衫",是从伤膝河大屠杀[①](The Battle at Wounded Knee)后的一具拉克塔人的尸体上不正当取得的。伤膝河大屠杀协会(WKA)在20世纪90年代中期得知凯文葛罗夫博物馆中这件"鬼舞衫"的存在之后,在拉克塔部落成员、伤膝河大屠杀协会秘书玛塞拉·勒博(Marcella LeBeau Lakota)的带领下,要求返还这件"鬼舞衫"。博物馆认为这件"鬼舞衫"是出于善意而获得的,并与伤膝河大屠杀协会进行了协商。通过协商调解,在格拉斯哥市市民的支持下,"鬼舞衫"于1998年返还给拉克塔部落。

---

① 1890年12月29日的翁迪德尼之战(Wounded Knee Massacre),又名"伤膝河大屠杀",标志着印第安人反抗移民的武装起义(印第安战争 Indian Wars)结束。

这个故事的非凡之处并不是"鬼舞衫"的返还。这种返还时有发生，尽管它并不频繁。在这个案例中，有三点值得注意：第一点，询问了格拉斯哥市公民是否支持"鬼舞衫"的返还，并且得到了他们的投票支持返还；第二点，玛塞拉·勒博在提出了伤膝河大屠杀协会的返还要求的同时，还提议制作了一件鬼舞衫复制品，并把它交给了凯文葛罗夫博物馆，现在复制品还陈列在那里；第三点，博物馆展示了这件复制品，以及对原作返还故事的叙述。

下议院文化、媒体和体育委员会（CMSC）认为，凯文葛罗夫博物馆展示的这件鬼舞衫复制品，"毫无疑问……这是一个比原作更有教育意义、更有趣的博物馆展览"。

参观者在展览的留言板上的评论几乎都是赞美，比如，一条评论写道："所有的人类都是互相联系的。"另一条评论说道："非常开心可以看到这样的讨论，我很少了解到关于文物返还的程序和案例。"似乎看来，展示一件原作的缺席以及复制品出现的故事，可能产生强大的影响，这种影响甚至不亚于展示原作。

凯文葛罗夫博物馆不仅获得了与鬼舞衫有关的更加丰富、细致、透明、动人的展览，他们与拉克塔部落的关系也得到了蓬勃发展。格拉斯哥城市委员会的贝利·卡梅隆（Bailey Elizabeth Cameron）曾说："我们最终在拉克塔人的历史上占据了一席之地，拉克塔人也成了格拉斯哥城市博物馆历史的一部分。"凯文葛罗夫博物馆不再是展示一个来自遥远文化的静态物件，而是成为全球动态关系的一部分。博物馆可能失去的是一件原作，但对于21世纪的博物馆来说，他们之间的关系更有价值和意义。

同时，拉克塔部落与苏格兰的关系也上升到了以前从未有过的地步。关于苏格兰的另一个文物返还案例，柯蒂斯写道："……曾经作为阿伯丁大学所收藏的头饰（贝宁君主青铜头像）被返还给了（来源地的）保管人，保管人购买了一件苏格兰人在跳舞时穿着的套装，作为其在苏格兰逗留的印证。"我认为这两个案例都展示了在这个日益全球化的世界中，博物馆应该为通过文物返还所产生的文化交融而庆祝。

结语

历史学家史蒂芬·康恩（Steven Con）曾发问"博物馆还需要实物吗？"答案是肯定的。我认为博物馆仍然需要实物。本质上来说，这也是博物馆之所以成为博物馆的原因。但是，博物馆需要所有的实物吗？也许并不需要。博物馆对于体验和实物的需求一样多吗？我认为，我们会继续朝着这个方向思考和前进。由艺术家精心制作的文物复制品能否为观众创造新的体验，与观看原始物品的体验相媲美？我想当然可以。

我想反问一句，观看复制品是否会在某种程度上降低参观博物馆的体验？我认为，如果语境恰当并且足够重要的话，艺术家根据原作所制作的复制品，反而会增强博物馆的参观体验。而且，创造复制品的艺术家来自原作的来源部落，他们制作的新作品会被赋予独属于自身的"气质"。这个"气质"与原作完全不同，但它仍然重要。

博物馆的成功关键在于，用艺术家制作的复制品取代原作时，关于返还过程的叙述也已经成了物品故事的一部分。

拉图尔和洛维写道，当一件视觉艺术作品被复制时"……一种伪造、假冒或背叛的感觉被引入了讨论中，这种方式对一件表演艺术作品来说似乎是荒谬的，似乎不可能去说一件摹本……不是伪造的，但是，这是检验艺术家成就的一个阶段，是其正在进行的传记的一部分"。

在这种情况下，博物馆的成功关键在于用艺术家制作的复制品取代原作时，将返还过程的叙述作为物品故事的一部分。这个故事应该在围绕复制品的解释材料中详细说明，原作的来源地区也应该来讲述他们关于失去的故事，以及对他们来说与被掠夺的文物再次相聚意味着什么。通过聆听对方的叙述，我们可能会得到有力的提醒，为什么博物馆应该支持将物品返还给它们的来源地。此外，原作来源地的艺术家可以在博物馆中讲述他们是如何创作复制品的。同时，这个用复制品替代原作的故事可以为博物馆的观众提供一个学习的机会，让他们更多地了解这件物品被创造出来的文化背景，以及制造这件物品的传统方法。通过反向的叙事，博物馆本身拥有无数学习和成长的机会，博物馆会在文物来源地、观众以及自身与文物来源地之间的多层合作中受益。

在2009年雅典卫城博物馆开馆后，《卫报》对英国居民进行了一项调查，这项调查旨在了解他们对于埃尔金大理石雕应该继续留在大英博物馆，还是将其返还给希腊的态度。94.8%的受访者以压倒性的票数支持将埃尔金大理石雕返还，而5.2%的受访者支持将其留在英国。这是一个非常惊人的差异，也意味着应该有更多的博物馆关注这个问题。博物馆观众希望拥有真实的体验，但他们更希望获得良好的道德体验。我认为，博物馆需要让观众自己来决定他们对复制品的看法，而不是由博物馆来为他们做决定。我们不知道观众们会对用艺术家制作的复制品替代原作，并且将原作返还给其来源地的博物馆感受如何。

Fouseki认为，"关于重新统的讨论是学术主导的，并没有反映出更广泛的民意"。如果博物馆聚焦于公众，他们才能发现相较于物品的真实性，博物馆观众对于正义感和文物返还的关注更为强烈。

查尼认为，关于博物馆参观"我们想要的是一种真实的邂逅，而不是凝视着书本上的复制品"。但，"我们"是谁？在使用艺术家创造的复制品和文物返还问题上，谁能代表博物馆观众的声音？博物馆观众在与复制品的现实相遇中受到启发，如果原作是出于伦理和道德的原因被返还的，这种启发甚至可能比在与原作的邂逅中受到的启发更大。但是，我们应该让这些观众为自己发声，我们需要更多的调查和研究以向观众们询问一个非常重要的问题，即：他们支持什么？他们支持的是一个颠沛流离且被创造它的地区所哀悼的原作吗？抑或是支持一个由艺术家制作的复制品所能带来的关于返还、重聚和合作的故事？

参考文献

Benjamin, Walter. *Illuminations: Essays and Reflections.* New York, NY: Schocken, 1935/1969.

Besterman, Tristram. "Crossing the Line: Restitution and Cultural Equity." In *Museums and Restitution: New Practices, New Approaches*, edited by Louise Tythacott &

Kostas Arvanitis, 19–36. Abingdon, England: Routledge, 2016.

Boon, Marcus. "Toward a Future of Museum Copying." In *Museums as Cultures of Copies: The Crafting of Artefacts and Authenticity*, edited by Brita Brenna, Hans Dam Christensen & Olav Hamran, 253–266. Abingdon, England: Routledge Research in Museum Studies, 2018.

Brown, Kate. "People Across the Globe Want Their Cultural Heritage Back: Canada May Offer a Blueprint For How to Get There." *The Guardian.* June 25, 2018. https://news.artnet.com/art-world/canada-restitution-indigenous-culture-1307060.

Charney, Noah. "A Fake of Art." *Aeon.* February 5, 2016. https://aeon.co/essays/is-there-a-place-for-fakery-in-art-galleries-and-museums.

Curtis, Neil. " 'A Welcome and Important Part of Their Role': The Impact of Reparation on Museums in Scotland." In *Museums and Restitution: New Practices, New Approaches*, edited by Louise Tythacott & Kostas Arvanitis, 85–104. Abingdon, England: Routledge, 2016.

Fouseki, Kalliopi. "Claiming the Parthenon Marbles Back: Whose Claim and on Behalf of Whom?" In *Museums and Restitution: New Practices, New Approaches*, edited by Louise Tythacott & Kostas Arvanitis, 163–178. Abingdon, England: Routledge, 2016.

Hein, Hilde. *The Museum In Transition: A Philosophical Primer*. Washington, D.C. : Smithsonian Institution Press, 2010.

House of Commons, Culture, Media and Sport Committee. 2000. "Cultural Property Return and Illicit Trade, Seventh Report." Accessed November 24, 2019. https://publications.parliament.uk/pa/cm199900/cmselect/cmcumeds/371/37102.htm.

Latour, Bruno and Adam Lowe. "The Migration of the Aura or How to Explore the Original Through its Facsimiles." In *Switching Codes: Thinking through Digital Technology in the Humanities and Arts*, edited by Thomas Bartscherer & Roderick Coover, 1–18. Chicago, Illinois: University of Chicago Press, 2010.

Maddra, Sam. "The Wounded Knee Ghost Dance Shirt." *Journal of Museum Ethnography* 8, 41–58, (1996).

The Loss, Return and Convergence of Longmen Grottoes Artefacts

Jiazhen Shi[*]

The construction of the Longmen Grottoes started when Emperor Xiaowen of the Northern Wei dynasty moved the capital to Luoyang (A.D. 493). Among all large-scale Chinese grottoes, the Longmen Grottoes is the only royal-sponsored cave temple by the imperial court in the Northern Wei Dynasty and Tang Dynasty. In the East Hill and the West Hill, there are 2345 numbered niches, nearly 110,000 Buddhist stone statues, 2890 steles and inscriptions, and nearly 80 stupas. At that time, the carving of the Longmen Grottoes was among the country's top priorities. With a team of professionals from relevant industries, the carving represents the top productivity of the Great Tang Dynasty. It is a collection of art in Chinese Buddhist stone carving. Artistic value of the Grand Statue Niche in Fengxiansi Cave, a particular example, surpasses all others of its kind before and since.

On 30 November 2000, the Longmen Grottoes was listed in the World Heritage List by UNESCO. The World Heritage Committee gave the following evaluation: "Grottoes and niches of Longmen contain the largest and most impressive collection of Chinese art of the late Northern Wei and Tang Dynasty. These works, entirely devoted to the Buddhist religion, represent the peak of Chinese stone carving."

---

[*] Jiazhen Shi, Dean of Longmen Grottoes Academy.

1. The misery of the unrest: looted antiquities of Longmen Grottoes

1.1 Background

The late 19th century and the first half of the 20th century saw poverty and wars in China. Scholars from the West and the East, journalists, adventurers and photographers visited China to research and map its historical monuments, sites, architecture, culture and geography. On 30 October 1910, Charles Lang Freer, a famous railroad car manufacturer and art collector from the US, wrote in his diary on his first day in the Longmen Grottoes, "Here, you can see a unique infusion of Greek, Persian, Indian, and Chinese statues and paintings. These works are harmonious and beautiful … They are among the finest historical sites in the world." At the same time, adventurers from the UK, France, the USA, Germany, Japan and Russia looted historical relics in north-western China's Xinjiang and Gansu Province. Scholars from France, Sweden and Japan researched caves, ancient tombs, and ancient buildings in China, particularly in northern China.

In conclusion, the Longmen Grottoes attracted not only academic researchers, and adventurers, but also illegal businessmen, and Chinese degenerates. This results in artificial damage to the Longmen Grottoes and relics dispersed overseas.

1.2 Researches about looted antiquities in the Longmen Grottoes

On November 1965, a research team of three archaeological experts (Wang Hui, Wang Shixiang and Wen Yucheng) from the previous China Academy of Cultural Heritage of the Ministry of Culture and Tourism and the Research Institute of Longmen Cultural Relics (now Longmen Grottoes Academy) has produced findings about 720 marks from the stolen relics in the Longmen Grottoes.

From 1991 to 1992, Wang Zhenguo, a researcher at Longmen Grottoes Academy, researched 96 major caves and found 262 major Buddhist statues, 1063 other kinds of statues, 8 lintels of niches, 10 reliefs of expounding the texts of Buddhism, 2 reliefs of Jataka tales, 1 relief of Buddhist stories, 16 reliefs of donors worshipping the Buddha, 15 steles and inscriptions, 2 incense burners, 2 stupas, 13 heads of animals, 1 bird with golden wings, and 6 unknown stone carvings. These statistics are merely the part of total looted relics of Longmen.

By comparing photos taken by some domestic and foreign researchers in different periods since the first half of the 20th century, the most rampant activities of looting relics in the Longmen Grottoes mainly happened between 1910 and 1936. Among stolen caves, some of the finest and the most representative caves, including the Guyangdong Cave, Lianhuadong Cave (Lotus-flower Cave), Wanfodong Cave (ten-thousand Buddha Cave), and Central Binyang Cave, were severely damaged.

1.3 Investigations of the current situation of dispersed relics

Over years of research by Longmen Grottoes Academy, we find that most looted fine relics were dispersed overseas during the Republic of China (1912–1949). According to the initial statistics, around 200 relics were looted and dispersed to other parts of China or other countries, among which, the US and Japan are the top two.

At present, around 100 Longmen's relics reside in 20 institutions for the collection of cultural relics and private collectors, for example, the Metropolitan Museum of Art, the Nelson-Atkins Museum of Art, the Museum of Fine Arts Boston, the Asian Art Museum of San Francisco, and the Freer Gallery of Art in the US; near 40 relics reside in the Tokyo National Museum, Kyoto National

Museum, Osaka City Museum of Fine Arts, Ohara Museum of Art, and private collectors in Japan. In addition, more than 30 relics reside in the Victoria and Albert Museum (UK), Musée national des arts asiatiques Guimet (France), Museum of Rietberg (Switzerland), and the Royal Ontario Museum (Canada), etc.; over 20 relics reside in relevant institutions in the Chinese mainland, Hong Kong (China), and Taiwan (China).

The statistics listed above are just the tip of the iceberg of current findings about looted and dispersed relics of the Longmen Grottoes. It is difficult to obtain relevant information without published photos, published books, or an exhibition about numerous lost stone-carving relics. In this regard, focus and academic researches need to be continued.

2. Brilliance of the time: repatriation of dispersed relics

2.1 The returning of the statue of Arhats Maha Kasyapa in Kanjingsi Cave

On the south wall of Kanjingsi Cave (Cave for Reading Sutras) in the East Hill, the upper body of the first arhats Maha Kasyapa statue from the western side was stolen in the late 1930s, and disappeared since then. It was transferred to London and Chicago, and then donated to the National Gallery of Canada.

In 2001, the National Gallery of Canada decided to return the statue after discovering and ensuring it was originally from the Longmen Grottoes. On 19 April 2001, the National Gallery of Canada officially return the statue to China at the "the Ceremony of Repatriating Statues from the Canadian Government to the Longmen Grottoes", hosted by the National Cultural Heritage Administration at Cleansing Fragrance (Shufang zhai) in the Palace Museum. The statue was transferred to Henan Museum for a while, then sent back to

Longmen Grottoes Academy for permanent preservation.

2.2 Returning of seven dispersed cultural relics: taking the Buddha head of the niche of Gaoshu in Guyang Cave as an example

Chen Zhejing, an American-born Chinese, is one of the collectors of stolen and dispersed relics in the first half of the twentieth century. At the beginning of the 1990s when Chen cooperated with Longmen Grottoes Research Institute, he expected to find the location of the Buddha's head (Northern Wei dynasty) and Bodhisattva's head (Tang Dynasty) that he collected. Through tough and detailed onsite research about traces of looting relics, Chen, along with researchers at Longmen Grottoes Research Institute, identified their original location, namely, Buddha's head of the niche of Gaoshu in Guyangdong Cave and left standing Bodhisattva's head on the main wall in Huodingdong Cave.

In 2002, Chen selected 16 Buddhist statues from his collections, including relics from the Longmen Grottoes, Yungang Grottoes, and other grottoes to organise a Buddhist Art Exhibition at Beijing Hotel. Buddha's head of the niche of Gaoshu in Guyangdong Cave and left standing Bodhisattva head on the main wall in Huodingdong Cave were among the exhibition. During this exhibition, Chen negotiated with China Cultural Heritage Information and Consulting Center (CCHICC) and Longmen Grottoes Research Institute, and expressed his wishes to return the relics to Longmen Grottoes. The CCHICC reported this issue to the National Cultural Heritage Administration. After requesting instruction from the relevant department, the National Cultural Heritage Administration agreed to use "Special funds for the collection of key national precious cultural relics". The CCHICC organised experts to identify these statues and concluded that they are originally from the Longmen Grottoes, and are treasures indeed.

On 22 October 2005, seven dispersed cultural relics were sent back to Longmen Grottoes and presented at the returning ceremony.

This is the milestone for dispersed Longmen relics, their preservation and development. It represents the determination of the Chinese government to protect the prosperous national cultural heritage. It also witnesses how China fights against poverty and goes forward to the path of prosperity.

3. Longmen Mode: data aggregation and digital reconstruction

3.1 "Digital repatriation" of Longmen Grottoes dispersed relics in Shanghai Museum

When President Xi Jinping visited Dunhuang Academy in 2019, he mentioned the role of high technology, such as digitalisation and information technology, promotes the digital repatriation of dispersed cultural relics, for example, *Dunhuang Documents*, and realises digital sharing for all in the cultural and arts resources in Dunhuang. Over the years, Longmen Grottoes Academy follows takeaways from Xi's speech in Dunhuang, thus making joint efforts with Shanghai Museum to create a new approach for "digitally returning" dispersed cultural relics that originally from Longmen Grottoes. Longmen Grottoes Academy reconstructed dispersed relics to where they were and showcase the completed statues with new technology.

3.2 Reconstruction of dispersed relics

After being sent back to the Longmen Grottoes, the Buddha head of the niche of Gaoshu in Guyangdong Cave was reconstructed by linking 3D printing with the digital model of incomplete statues. Its genuine appearance was restored in the form of a material object.

3.3 Data aggregation for "Queen Wenzhao with her entourage worshipping the Buddha"

Two inscriptions "Emperor Xiaowen and his entourage worshipping the Buddha" and "Queen Wenzhao with her entourage worshipping the Buddha" are located in Central Binyang Cave in the Longmen Grottoes. These two inscriptions illustrate the grand worshipping Buddha ceremony respectively led by Emperor Xiaowen with his officials, and Queen Wenzhao with her attendants. The two inscriptions are both 205 cm in height. Over 40 figures were carved harmoniously on the inscriptions. The work, representing the highest level in inscription carvings, is the earliest themed inscription. Undoubtfully, they are the national cultural relics in the history of Chinese art and Chinese carvings.

In the 1930s, the inscription "Queen Wenzhao with her entourage worshipping the Buddha" was stolen and dispersed overseas. At present, some pieces of the incomplete inscription are collected by the Nelson-Atkins Museum of Art in the US. Since less than 30 percent of pieces were collected from the original inscription, the reconstruction work had to start with positioning and connecting by rubbings, followed by repairing incomplete parts in accordance with the photograph of the inscription. The reconstruction work merely finished two-thirds of the genuine appearance. The lost part is the inscription located at the turning boundary of the walls to the south wall.

Through digitalised technology, the data aggregation project for "Queen Wenzhao with her entourage worshipping the Buddha" achieved digital aggregation of all relevant and current art resources. Based on the approach of digital aggregation and virtue reconstruction, Longmen Grottoes Academy combines methodologies in technology, academics, and arts to "digitally aggregate" the data from "Queen Wenzhao with her entourage worshipping the Buddha" (now resides in the US), the incomplete inscription in the Central Binyang Cave, and over 2,000 pieces preserved by the Academy.

"Data aggregation" plays a role in restoring its genuine appearance, original environment, and prosperous past at that time before the artificial damage.

4. Data aggregation for Longmen Grottoes dispersed cultural relics exhibition

On 14 January 2023, the exhibition "Revive the Glory of Lost Cultural Relics: Digital Reconstruction for Lost Cultural Relics in Longmen Grottoes" was displayed in Luoyang Museum. It is the exhibition that comprehensively showcase the recently proposed development strategy —"friendly cooperation, multiple tracks, data aggregation, and result sharing". With this strategy, research and presentations about digitally reconstructing dispersed cultural relics of Longmen Grottoes, for example, the inscription "Queen Wenzhao with her entourage worshipping the Buddha" will be finished by three-dimensional digital technology.

Since the opening of the exhibition, several reports come from more than 20 social media, including Xinhua New Agency, Guangming Online, CNR, China News Service, China Cultural Relics News (Zhong guo wen wu Bao), ifeng. com, Henan TV, Henan Daily, etc.; as well as from the official website and official Wechat account of the National Cultural Relics Administration, the official website of the People's Government of Henan Province, Culture and Tourism Department of Henan Province, and Henan Provincial Administration of Cultural Heritage.

Currently, the returning of dispersed cultural relics remains challenging due to many complex reasons. In this case, Longmen Grottoes Academy is the pioneer that proposed the idea of "digital returning". Since 2021, the Academy has developed Longmen Mode — "friendly cooperation, multiple tracks, data aggregation, and result sharing" approach. By using new technologies and methods, this approach made great achievements and provided new references to similar challenges in relevant departments and institutions.

龙门石窟文物的流失、回归与聚合

史家珍 *

龙门石窟始凿于公元493年北魏孝文帝迁都洛阳之际，是中国各石窟中唯一由北魏和唐两个朝代皇家直接经营、具有皇家宗庙性质的大型石窟群。龙门东西两山现存编号窟龛2 345个，造像近11万尊，碑刻题记2 890余块，佛塔近80座。它的开凿可以说是当时的国之大者，汇集了当时各方面顶级的专业人员组成的团队，代表了盛唐时期生产力发展的最高水平。它也是中国佛教石刻雕塑艺术的集大成者。特别是奉先寺大卢舍那像龛这一组群雕，其所达到的艺术水平和价值可谓是前无古人、后无来者。

2000年11月30日，龙门石窟被联合国教科文组织列入《世界遗产名录》。世界遗产委员会用"三个最"对龙门石窟给予了极高的评价："龙门地区的石窟和佛龛，展现了中国北魏晚期至唐代最具规模和最为优秀的造型艺术，这些佛教艺术作品，代表了中国石刻艺术的最高峰。"

一、乱世之殇：龙门石窟的盗凿劫掠

（一）流失背景

19世纪末20世纪上半叶的中国，国弱民贫，兵荒马乱，西洋、东洋学人，记者、探险家及其摄影师纷纷来到中国，在广袤的土地上对中国的古迹、遗址、建筑、民俗、地理等进行调查、拍照和测绘。1910年10月30日，美国著名的铁路大王、艺术品鉴藏家弗利尔来到龙门石窟的第一天，在当天的日记中写道："在这里，希腊、波斯、印度与中国的造像和

---

* 史家珍，龙门石窟研究院时任院长。

绘画元素奇特融合，和谐优美……它能与任何存世的古迹相媲美。"随之，英法美德日俄等探险家对中国新疆、甘肃境内古遗址和文物进行了盗凿和劫掠。法国、瑞典和日本学者对中国，特别是北方地区的石窟寺、古墓葬和古建筑进行了调查。

可以说，龙门石窟在吸引众多人员前来调查研究的同时，也引起了诸多外来探险者、不法商人和民族败类对文物的觊觎，致使龙门石窟遭到了疯狂的盗凿和惨烈的破坏，许多精美文物流散海内外。

（二）被盗凿情况调查

1965年11月，经文化部文物博物馆研究所与龙门文物保管所（现龙门石窟研究院）联合组成三人（王辉、王世襄、温玉成）调查小组现场调查，龙门被盗凿痕为720处。

1991—1992年，龙门石窟研究所王振国研究员对龙门石窟96个重点窟龛进行了实地调查，共有主像262尊、其他各类造像1 063尊、龛楣8处、说法图浮雕10幅、本生故事浮雕2幅、佛传故事浮雕1幅、供养人礼佛图16幅、碑刻题记15块、香炉2个、佛塔2座、兽头13铺、金翅鸟1躯、不明雕刻6处被盗凿。这些统计数据仅是龙门石窟文物被盗凿数量的一部分。

据20世纪上半叶国内外考察者不同时段所拍摄的历史老照片比对，盗凿活动在1910—1936年间最为集中和猖獗。而被盗的窟龛中，又以古阳洞、莲花洞、万佛洞、宾阳中洞这几个最为精美最具有代表性的皇家洞窟盗凿最为严重。

（三）流散文物现状调查

经龙门石窟研究院科研人员的多年调查研究，被盗凿的精美文物绝大多数在民国年间流失到了海外。目前初步统计流失海内外的龙门石窟文物约200件，以流落到美国和日本的文物数量最多。

目前已知在美国共有约20家收藏机构及私人收藏者，收藏龙门石窟文物将近100件，包括美国纽约大都会艺术博物馆、堪萨斯州纳尔逊艺术博物馆、波士顿美术馆、旧金山亚洲艺术博物馆、弗利尔美术馆等。在日本，有东京国立博物馆、京都国立博物馆、大阪市立美术馆、仓敷市大原美术馆及私人收藏家等，共收藏龙门石窟文物近40件。此外，英国维多利亚·亚伯特博物馆、法国吉美国立亚洲艺术博物馆、瑞士瑞特保格博物馆、加拿大皇家安大略艺术博物馆等机构收藏有龙门石窟文物30余件。另外在中国大陆、香港地区及台湾地区收藏有龙门石窟造像20余件。

这些仅仅是目前的调查结果，也可以说是龙门石窟被盗凿流失文物的冰山一角，大量流失的石刻文物，因为没有公布图片、没有发表出版或者没有在展览上露过面，我们难以获知相关信息，有待于持续的关注和调查研究。

二、盛世华章：流散文物的回归故里

（一）看经寺摩诃迦叶罗汉像回归

龙门东山看经寺南壁西起第一尊摩诃迦叶罗汉像上半身于20世纪30年代后半期被盗凿，多年不知去向。后辗转于伦敦、芝加哥，被捐赠给加拿大国家美术馆。

2001年，加拿大国家美术馆在发现并确定这件石雕为龙门石窟被盗凿文物后，决定无偿送还中国。同年4月19日，国家文物局在故宫博物院漱芳斋举行了"加拿大政府送还中国龙门石窟雕像交接仪式"。加拿大国家美术馆将其收藏的龙门石窟雕像正式移交中方。次日，该雕像安全抵达河南博物院，经短暂停留即送回龙门石窟研究所永久保存。

（二）古阳洞高树龛佛首等七件流失海外文物回归

美籍华人陈哲敬是20世纪上半叶盗凿流失海外文物的收藏者之一。20世纪90年代初，陈哲敬在和龙门石窟研究所的合作中，希望能找到他所收藏的一件北魏佛头和一件唐代菩萨头像的原有位置。在同研究所科研人员一起对盗凿残迹进行艰苦细致的现场调查后，确认了这两件流失文物原来的位置，即古阳洞北壁高树龛佛首、火顶洞正壁主尊左胁侍菩萨头像。

2002年，陈哲敬从他收藏的佛教造像中挑选了包括龙门、云冈和其他地区在内的16件藏品，在北京饭店举办了佛教艺术展。其中就有龙门古阳洞高树龛佛首和火顶洞正壁主尊左胁侍菩萨头像。其间，通过与中国文物信息咨询中心（CCHICC）、龙门石窟研究所的接触、沟通和协商，陈哲敬希望展品中的文物能够回归龙门。中国文物信息咨询中心随即向国家文物局做了汇报，国家文物局经请示，同意使用财政部设立的"国家重点珍贵文物征集专项经费"予以征集。此后，由中国文物信息咨询中心组织相关专家对拟征集文物进行了严格鉴定，确认其为龙门石窟的文物，且是珍品无疑。

2005年10月22日，"流失海外龙门石窟文物回归庆典"在龙门石窟隆重举行，七件流失海外的龙门文物回归故土。

此次文物回归，在龙门石窟流失文物征集乃至龙门石窟文物保护利用方面都有着里程碑式的意义，充分显示了我国政府保护民族优秀文化遗产的立场和决心，也见证了昔日贫穷落后的中国不断走向繁荣强大的历程。

三、龙门模式：数据聚合与复位合璧

（一）上博藏龙门石窟流散文物的"数字化"回归

2019年，习近平总书记在敦煌研究院座谈时提到，"要通过数字化、信息化等高技术手段，推动流散海外的敦煌遗书等文物的数字化回归，实现敦煌文化艺术资源在全球范围内的数字化共享"。近年来，龙门石窟研究院认真贯彻习近平总书记讲话精神，与上海博物馆合作，开启了龙门石窟流散文物"数字化回归"的新路径，并运用新技术，寻探确认流散文物的原位，实现流散文物与造像遗存的数字复位和完整展示。

（二）流散文物的复位合璧

回归后的古阳洞高树龛佛首即通过3D打印技术与残存造像的数字模型进行重建，以实物的形式再现其历史原貌。

（三）《皇后礼佛图》的数据聚合

帝后礼佛图位于龙门石窟宾阳中洞，分别刻画了北魏孝文帝、文昭皇后带领文武百官、侍从列队礼佛的宏大场景。两块浮雕均高205厘米，雕凿人物达40余人，既浑然一体又变化丰富，是当时最高等级和最高造型艺术水准的浮雕作品，也是最早带有主题性场景构图的浮雕，当属中国美术史、雕塑史中的国宝级文物。

20世纪30年代，《皇后礼佛图》被盗往国外，现以碎块拼接不完整的形式收藏展陈于美国堪萨斯州纳尔逊艺术博物馆。美国堪萨斯州纳尔逊艺术博物馆展出的《皇后礼佛图》，由于所搜集到的浮雕碎块不足原浮雕面积的30%，不得不在将碎块按照拓片定位拼接后，又将缺失部分参考浮雕照片做了造型修复，并且只修复了浮雕的前面三分之二，缺失了随墙壁转折到南壁的三分之一浮雕造型。

《皇后礼佛图》数据聚合项目通过数字化技术实现和完成所有与皇后礼佛图浮雕直接相关的现存造型艺术资料的数字化聚合，并基于数据聚合虚拟造型还原研究方式，结合技术、学术、艺术三大学科领域研究方法，对陈列在美国的《皇后礼佛图》与宾阳中洞浮雕残壁、龙门石窟研究院院藏2 000余块碎块，以"数据聚合"的方式，跨越时空，进行造型还原和环境复原，再现百年前礼佛图未被破坏时的盛景。

四、龙门石窟流散文物数据聚合成果展

2023年1月14日，"复位合璧·华光再现——龙门石窟流散文物数据聚合成果专题展"在洛阳博物馆开展。该展首次集中系统展现近年来龙门石窟研究院秉承"友好合作、多轨并一、数据聚合、成果共享"的理念，将三维数字技术运用于以《皇后礼佛图》为代表的龙门石窟流散文物数字复位研究展示工作所取得的成果。

展览自开展以来，受到了媒体的广泛关注。新华社、光明网、《中国日报》、中央电视台、央广网、中新网、《中国文物报》、凤凰网、河南卫视、《河南日报》等20余家媒体对展览进行了报道。国家文物局官网、官方微信公众号，河南省人民政府，河南省文化和旅游厅，河南省文物局官网等也对展览开幕进行了报道。

当下，流失海外文物的回归之路受诸多复杂因素的影响仍十分艰难。在此背景之下，龙门石窟研究院大力推动"流散海外文物的数字化回归"。2021年以来，我院率先提出"友好合作、多轨并一、数据聚合、成果共享"的流散文物数字化虚拟复原理念，运用新技术、新方式开创海内外流散文物"数据聚合"的"龙门模式"，取得了良好的效果，同时也为相关部门和单位在面对海外流失文物的问题方面提供了新的思路和举措。

Glasgow Museums Repatriation of Objects to the Archaeological Survey of India

Duncan Dornan[*]

In 2022 Glasgow City Council's City Administration Committee approved repatriation of 51 objects to 3 communities.

19 items to be returned to Nigeria, taken in the British punitive raid on Benin City, in 1897.

25 objects to be returned to the Lakota community, some of these objects were taken from the Wounded Knee Massacre site following the battle of December 1890, while others were personal items belonging to named ancestors or are ceremonial artefacts

7 items to be returned to the ownership of the Archaeological Survey of India. 6 of the artefacts were stolen from temples and shrines in different states in Northern India during the 19th century, while the 7th was illegally purchased as a result of theft from the owner. All 7 objects were gifted to Glasgow's museum collection.

Whilst this generated substantial press interest, the process used was first developed in Glasgow in the late 1990s. Following the rejection of a repatriation request from the Lakota, for a group of objects, a further request for the return of the Ghost Shirt was approved by the city in 1998. To support this process a set of criteria were developed, these required the moral and or legal authority

---

[*] Duncan Dornan, Head of Museums and Collections, Glasgow Life, Scotland.

of the claimant to be demonstrated, the identity of the object in question to be confirmed and the future care of the object to be identified as suitable. The fundamental approach was applied to the 2022 repatriation requests, including that from India, though the methodology was adapted as a result of experience. The change specifically removed the item relating to the future care of the object, the rationale for this being that if an object were deemed to be another community's property, then its future use was entirely their business and should not influence the decision-making process.

It is important to emphasise that the formal assessment of a repatriation claim and indeed the claim itself most effectively come as the result of a strong relationship of trust between the museum service and the community representatives making the claim. Given the history of objects in question it may take time for the museums service to establish credibility. Discussions held within a trusting and respectful atmosphere are essential to determining the best outcome for the objects and the community. We must recognise that in some cases physical return of an object may not be the desired course and museum services must respect the wishes of those from whom the objects were taken.

In the case of the Indian objects, ahead of the formal request for repatriation curatorial research was completed, with our partners in India, to confirm the provenance of the objects in question. Once both parties were satisfied about the identification of the items a repatriation request was submitted which was duly approved by the City Council. The next step in the process, ahead of the physical transfer of the objects, was to sign a transfer of title document. In addition to being a necessary legal step, this provided an opportunity for a public ceremony to recognise the history of the objects and to signify a new relationship of equals between both communities. Given the high level of interest in the repatriation in the UK, there was some concern about the public reaction, which was in the event positive. Many Glasgow citizens, of Indian heritage, were invited to the event and expressed pride in the steps taken by their city to right historic wrongs and in the equal relationship which this facilitated. The signing ceremony to transfer title can provide insight into the human, emotional aspects of the process, which is often lost in the business of administration and this most recent event highlighted the care required in managing such events, particularly as the element of the process which is the most public.

The physical move of the objects took place several weeks later, being subject to the normal hurdles of packing and customs controls typical of the movement of museum objects. In this instance we know that new gallery space is being created to exhibit these objects in Delhi, which we expect will be ready by 2024.

In looking back on the experience, it undoubtedly fostered new, positive relationships and demonstrated that the retention of wrongfully removed objects erect barriers which we are not aware of.

英国格拉斯哥多家博物馆向印度考古调查局归还文物

邓肯·多南*

2022年,英国格拉斯哥市议会的城市管理委员会(Glasgow City Council's City Administration Committee)批准将51件物品归还给3个本土社区。

19件物品将被送回尼日利亚,这些物品是1897年英国对贝宁城进行惩罚性袭击时拿走的。

25件物品将归还给拉科塔(Lakota)社区,其中一些物品是1890年12月翁迪德尼之战(Wounded Knee Massacre)后从伤膝河大屠杀遗址取走的[①],另一些则是属于指定祖先的个人物品或礼仪用具。

7件物品将归印度考古调查局所有。其中6件是19世纪期间从印度北部不同邦的寺庙和神社中盗走的,而第7件文物则是在失主失窃后非法购买所得。所有7件文物都被赠予格拉斯哥的博物馆进行收藏。

这项举措在推行的同时也引起了媒体的极大兴趣,但我们所使用的还是20世纪90年代末在格拉斯哥首次开发的返还程序。在拒绝了拉科塔人提出的归还一组文物的请求后,格拉斯哥于1998年再次批准了归还鬼舞衫的请求。为支持这一进程,我们制定了一套标准,要求在证实提出返还需求方在道义和法律上的权威性后,确认有关文物的身份,并确保该文物今后拥有适当的保管方式。这一基本方法仍旧适用于2022年的文物归还申请,包括此次来自印度的申请,但我们也根据经验对方法进行了适当调整。这一修改特别删除了与文物的未来保管有关的内容,理由是如果一件

---

* 邓肯·多南,英国格拉斯哥生活博物馆藏品部主任。
① 1890年12月29日的翁迪德尼之战(Wounded Knee Massacre),又名"伤膝河大屠杀",标志着印第安人反抗移民的武装起义(印第安战争,Indian Wars)结束。——译者注

文物被认为是其他所属社区的财产，那么它的未来用途完全是其所属社区的事，我们不应插手决策过程。

必须强调的是，对文物返还要求的正式评估，乃至归还要求本身，都是博物馆服务部门与提出归还要求的社区代表之间牢固信任关系的结果。鉴于有关文物的历史，博物馆部门可能需要时间来建立信誉。在相互信任和尊重的氛围中展开讨论，对文物和社区取得最佳结果至关重要。我们必须认识到，在某些情况下，实际归还文物可能并不是理想的做法，博物馆服务部门必须尊重文物流失地的意愿。

就印度文物而言，在正式提出返还申请之前，我们与印度的合作伙伴一起完成了策展研究，以确认相关文物的来源。一旦双方都对物品的鉴定结果感到满意，就可以提交物品返还的申请，格拉斯哥的市议会便会给予正式批准。在物品移交之前，下一步工作是签署所有权转让文件。这不仅是一个必要的法律步骤，还提供了一个举行公开仪式的机会，以便确认文物的历史，并标志着两个社区之间建立了新的平等关系。鉴于英国国内对文物返还工作的高度关注，我们对公众的反应产生了一些担忧，不过最终公众的反应是积极的。许多印度裔的格拉斯哥市民应邀参加了这一活动，并对他们的城市为纠正历史错误所采取的措施以及由此而促成的平等关系感到自豪。产权转让签字仪式可以让人们深入感受这一过程中有关人性与情感的因素，而这些方面往往在行政事务中经常会被忽视。最近的这一事件突出了管理此类事件时所需的谨慎，尤其是作为这一过程中最公开的部分。

（在仪式完成的）几周后，这些文物踏上了返还的路程，也经历了博物馆文物搬迁过程中常见的包装和海关检查等障碍。在此期间，我们也得知了印度德里正在建造新的展厅来展出这些文物，预计新展厅将于2024年完工。

回顾这次经历，它无疑促进了新的、积极的联系，并证明，保留因不正当手段而流失的文物会造成我们无法预料的障碍。

Egypt Fights Against Illicit Trafficking— The Government's Efforts to Preserve Cultural Heritage, Combat Illegal Trafficking in Cultural Property, and Recover What Was Stolen

Shaaban AbdelGawad[*]

Abstract: The article presents the Egyptian Government framework to protect the cultural and archaeological heritage. It is examined the 2014 Constitution's three articles to the protection of the Egyptian heritage and Egyptian antiquities in its various ages to preserve the cultural identity and the Law amendment in 1983 to fill the gaps and keep up with community changes. It is further listed the main work of the General Department of Repatriated Antiquities and its co-operations and co-ordinations in national and international context. The role of the National Committee for the Repatriation of Antiquities which reconstituted to overcome obstacles facing the cases of smuggled antiquities is also analysed. 29 thousand of archaeological objects have been repatriated the last ten years due to the Ministry of Antiquities legislative framework which focus on retrieving Egyptian antiquities on display in museums worldwide and to stop the smuggled of the antiquities on a multiple way.

Key words: 2014 Constitution; illegal excavations; trafficking; smuggled antiquities; repatriation; auction houses; Public Prosecution; cultural heritage

---

* Shaaban AbdelGawad, The Head of the Repatriation of Antiquities Department, Ministry of Antiquities, Egypt.

1. Introduction

The issue of antiquities repatriation and the preservation of cultural heritage is part of the national strategy of the Ministry of Antiquities of Egypt. The dominant concern of the Ministry is the active action of its committees and especially the competent department in the formulation of international policy to prevent and combat the illegal trafficking of cultural and archaeological goods. This department, as the most competent State Authority and in accordance with the current legal framework, is intensifying its efforts for collaborations with international agencies within the framework of bilateral relations and multilateral agreements. It works based on the records are kept and further investigates the sales of the auction houses, in order to identify suspiciously trafficked artefacts in collaboration with organizations such as Interpol, and the International Cooperation Office at the Ministry of Justice.

2. National Legislation

2.1 2014 Constitution

The Constitution of 2014 delineated the protection of the Egyptian heritage and Egyptian antiquities in its various ages with the Articles 47–50 of Chapter Two, *Components of Society* in Section Three, *Cultural Components*. These articles commit the Egyptian Government to protect the Egyptian cultural identity with its diverse civilization origins. Furthermore, the State supports the remote areas and the groups most in need, protects the monuments in situ and prohibits to give away any of them as gifts or exchange them. Moreover, the state gives special attention to maintain the components of cultural diversity, from all the Pharaonic, Coptic, Islamic periods and modern architectural, literary and artistic cultural stock. Any attack thereon is a crime punishable by law.

2.2 Law amendments

The Egyptian Law on the Protection of Antiquities No. 117 of 1983 was amended to fill the gaps and keep up with community changes.

The amendments were as follows:

- Amending the Antiquities Protection Law No. 117 of 1983 by Law 3 of 2010 which toughs penalties on acquiring or selling Egyptian artefacts in auction halls abroad. Tough penalties are imposed on individuals caught trying to smuggle artefacts and its executive regulations by Law No. 91 of 2018, for the Egyptian antiquities, in and outside Egypt, and helps the state to seek their restoration.
- Amendment to Law No. 20 of 2020 for illicit trade of antiquities.

3. Addressing illegal excavations and trafficking

Through the Tourism and Antiquities Police, with the aim of seizing smugglers and illegal digging groups inside the Arab Republic of Egypt and confiscating Egyptian artefacts resulting from illegal excavations and stolen ones for the benefit of the Egyptian state.

4. Protecting archaeological sites and securing museums

The Egyptian Ministry of the Interior plays an important role in securing and protecting all archaeological sites and museums throughout the Arab Republic of Egypt. In addition to this, private guards affiliated with the Ministry of Tourism and Antiquities do the same mission, and the Ministry of Tourism and Antiquities' archaeological inspectors perform regular visits to all areas under the Ministry of Tourism and Antiquities and promptly report any encroachment, vandalism, or loss of any artefact, and follow up on whether there are illegal excavations.

5. Confrontation of smuggling operations

- The Central Department of Archaeological Ports was established in 1896 and started with the archaeological unit at Cairo Airport until it reached 40 archaeological units at land, sea, and airports and provided them with qualified archaeologists to work in these ports to examine what is suspected of being archaeological and express an archaeological opinion on it before allowing it to be exported.
- The Department cooperates with all customs and security authorities at air, sea, and land ports to prevent the smuggling of antiquities and cultural property outside the country, as well as activating the international agreements that Egypt signed with other countries and repatriating stolen cultural property to its country of origin if seized.
- The Department cooperates with several entities outside the Ministry, such as the Egyptian National Library and Archives of the Ministry of Culture, the Geological Museum of the Ministry of Environment, Bibliotheca Alexandrina, the National Art Center, and the Scientific Complex.

6. The efforts of the Egyptian state to repatriate the smuggled Egyptian antiquities. They are consisted of two sectors

6.1 The General Department of Repatriated Antiquities which main work is

- Daily follow-up to all the famous auction houses that offer Egyptian antiquities for sale and searching on websites for other unknown galleries to examine the exhibited objects and compare them with the lists of the missing items of the Ministry of Tourism and Antiquities, then inform the Ministry of Foreign Affairs to send its representatives to ensure the authenticity of the documents for these galleries to obtain these Egyptian artefacts. If it is proven that there are objects that are among the lost items of the Ministry or objects that are owned by the auction house without proper bonds, the Department immediately begins to take all necessary measures to demand the return of these objects, whether by amicable, judicial, or diplomatic means.

- Creating a database of the lost items of the Ministry of Tourism and Antiquities, which is updated regularly through continuous follow-up with all sectors and archaeological sites in the Ministry and other relevant authorities, such as the Ministry of Endowments and the Egyptian National Library and Archives, and informing Interpol of the newly missing items to track them internationally.

- Co-operation and co-ordination with the concerned authorities in the country represented (*Antiquities Investigation, Interpol, the International Cooperation Office at the Ministry of Justice, and the Department of Cultural Relations at the Ministry of Foreign Affairs*).

- Co-ordination and follow-up with the authorities of foreign countries in the event of seizing Egyptian artefacts on the borders of a foreign country or what is being circulated by individuals illegally and working to return it to Egypt, whether through diplomatic, judicial, or negotiating methods.

6.2 The National Committee for the Repatriation of Antiquities which reviled

It was formed under the managership of the Minister of Tourism and Antiquities, and representatives from the Ministries of Foreign Affairs, Interior, Justice, the National Security, Tourism, and Antiquities Police, as well as other public figures, to overcome obstacles facing the cases of smuggled antiquities.

Egypt has been successful in repatriating more than 29 thousand archaeological objects during the last ten years.

7. Investigations and tracking of smuggling networks

Co-ordination and co-operation with the investigation authorities in Egypt. The Egyptian Public Prosecution, the Tourism and Antiquities Police, and the Egyptian Ministry of Foreign Affairs cooperated in many cases related to Egyptian antiquities smuggled abroad, whether they were seized or offered for sale, to find out the criminal aspect and track global smuggling networks to limit the illegal trade in Egyptian antiquities.

8. Public awareness efforts and community engagement

The Ministry of Tourism and Antiquities carried out several activities and events related to linking civil society with the Egyptian heritage so that society would be the first to protect it. This role is represented by the Department of Cultural Development and Community Outreach, which is concerned with several files, namely: school students; visitors to libraries, clubs, palaces, cultural, scientific, and artistic centres; university students; women; and people with special needs. Voluntary programmes Care roles, the elderly, and hospitals Partnership programmes With various governmental and cultural institutions, linking the proposed programmes with archaeological openings and discoveries, cultural events, and social events, and providing workshops for workers in the fields of museum education, archaeological awareness, community outreach, and cultural development (participating and supervising the preparation of educational tools and publications directed to the community to raise awareness, holding competitions, community and art exhibitions, educational lectures and seminars, and providing guided tours).

9. International cooperation

• Ensuring the conclusion of bilateral agreements on the protection of cultural and archaeological heritage, which facilitates the procedures for the recovery process with many countries such as Peru, Ecuador, Cuba, Italy, Jordan, Switzerland, China, the USA, Cyprus, Guatemala, Spain, and Saudi Arabia. Other agreements are under-way with some Arab Gulf countries and some European Union countries.

• Continuous communication with organisations sponsoring antiquities, heritage, and human civilization in general, such as UNESCO, ISESCO, ICOM, ICROM, and many others holding regional and international conferences and workshops to combat illegal trafficking in cultural property.

The credit for establishing the General Administration of Recovered Antiquities goes to Mr. Dr. Zahi Hawass, the most famous archaeologist, former Secretary-General of the Supreme Council of Antiquities, and former Minister of Antiquities. When he became Secretary-General of the Supreme Council of Antiquities in 2002, he immediately made the decision to establish the General Administration of Recovered Antiquities. Egypt has been suffering from systematic theft and illegal excavation of its antiquities for many years, whether buried or discovered and displayed in open places that are not subject to strict security. After the proliferation of this phenomenon in the past decade, there was a need to take quick and effective steps to stop this continuous bleeding of our cultural heritage. While it is possible to stop stolen or illegally excavated antiquities inside Egypt or during their smuggling abroad through the management of archaeological checkpoints at the Ministry of Antiquities, once they are actually smuggled out of Egypt, it becomes more difficult due to differences in foreign countries' policies and laws in dealing with such issues compared to Egyptian laws and regulations that criminalise the trafficking, trading, or even possession of antiquities.

From this perspective, the idea of establishing a general administration responsible for tracking lost and smuggled Egyptian antiquities emerged, so that it can communicate with foreign entities and have the necessary flexibility to choose the optimal method of dealing with the recovery of smuggled artefacts, whether through diplomatic means or those that resort to litigation. Thus, the General Administration of Recovered Antiquities was established in 2002, and it was then under the direct supervision of the Secretary-General of the Supreme Council of Antiquities at the time and is currently under the direct supervision of the Minister of Antiquities.

The administration's working mechanism involves updating the list of lost artefacts in real time. The administration receives data on stolen artefacts from archaeological sites, museums, sub-stores, and museums to create a database of stolen artefacts. It also creates a database of the Ministry of Antiquities' lost artefacts that is updated in real-time by continuous follow-up with all sectors and archaeological regions in the ministry and other relevant entities such as the Ministry of Endowments and the Egyptian National Library. The administration also informs Interpol of newly missing artefacts to trace them globally.

The administration also tracks on-line auction sites and sales venues on a daily basis, comparing the artefacts offered for sale to the ministry's lost artefacts and taking immediate action to recover the artefacts that have been proven to have left Egypt by illegal means. In pursuit of this, the administration continuously cooperates with various internal and external entities.

Internally, the entities involved include the Egyptian Antiquities Sector, the Islamic Antiquities Sector, and the Museums Sector to update the lost artefact databases in real-time and inform these sectors of the artefacts that have been detected in auction halls and on-line sites.

9.1 Re-establishment of the National Committee for Retrieving Antiquities

The problem was resolved by the decision of the Prime Minister, No. 1306 for the year 2016, which includes representatives from the ministries of foreign affairs, justice, international cooperation, and interior, in addition to representatives from Egyptian security and regulatory agencies and is headed by the Minister of Antiquities. The goal is to explore all possible means and overcome all obstacles that prevent the retrieval of smuggled Egyptian antiquities abroad through illegal means.

The committee is continuously in contact with organizations concerned with antiquities, heritage, and human civilization in general, such as UNESCO, ISESCO, ICOM, ICROM, and many others. It also works to organize regional and international conferences and workshops.

In terms of legislation, Law No. 117 of 1983 for the Protection of Antiquities and its executive regulations under Law No. 91 of 2018 were amended, and the penalties related to antiquities smuggling and trafficking were tightened. The Ministry of Antiquities also proposed a legislative amendment to the Ministry of Justice's legislative sector to add a paragraph stating that the law applies to anyone who commits a crime outside the Arab Republic of Egypt, in accordance with the provisions of Articles 1, 2, and 3 of the Penal Code.

The ministry is also focused on retrieving Egyptian antiquities on display in museums worldwide. Several pieces have been retrieved from various museums around the world, such as a piece from a panel belonging to King "Nekhtneb II" from the Berlin Museum in Germany, a piece from the panel "Sesh Nefer Tam" from the Macquarie University Museum in Australia, and more recently, the magnificent, gilded coffin belonging to "Nedjemankh" from the Metropolitan Museum in America. The ministry is currently working on retrieving more antiquities from museums around the world.

9.2 Ways to retrieve smuggled antiquities from abroad

Friendly or diplomatic methods: One of the most effective ways to retrieve antiquities is through peaceful negotiations between our embassy abroad and the party possessing Egyptian antiquities. This is particularly successful when negotiating with a government or official entity. However, negotiating with auction houses has a low success rate and only works if there are no ownership documents available at the exhibition hall.

Seizure at international ports and airports: This is done in accordance with the UNESCO Convention on the Prevention of Illicit Import, Export, and Transfer of Ownership of Cultural Property across international borders or through bilateral agreements between Egypt and other countries or markets. These cases sometimes take a long time to prove Egypt's right to these smuggled antiquities, and they are retrieved in accordance with local and international laws in this field. Egypt's General Directorate of Recovered Antiquities negotiates with law enforcement agencies around the world and provides all documents, laws, and evidence that confirms that these antiquities have left Egypt illegally. Egypt has recently succeeded in retrieving hundreds and even thousands of antiquities that were the result of illegal excavations in Egyptian lands.

Co-operation between law enforcement agencies around the world: This method is relatively modern and depends largely on the person responsible for antiquities file retrieval and their relationships with law enforcement agencies around the world. It also depends on their extensive experience and good reputation. Egypt has succeeded in retrieving many smuggled antiquities through direct communication with law enforcement agencies, such as by reviewing export certificates and documentation for pieces crossing borders, whether from Egypt or different countries worldwide. A recent example is the return of the gold coffin of Nedjemankh from the Metropolitan Museum in New

York after lengthy investigations, communication, and negotiations between the General Directorate of Recovered Antiquities and the New York City District Attorney's Office. Many more antiquities are expected to return to Egypt through this method.

9.3 Litigation

When peaceful methods fail to retrieve antiquities, the Ministry of Tourism and Antiquities resorts to legal action by authorising a lawyer to sue the owner of the pieces in their country. However, these attempts often fail, as most of these countries allow trading in antiquities and there are no laws that criminalise it. Therefore, the ruling favours the owner of the pieces, especially if they have ownership documents.

9.4 Pressure on missions operating in Egypt

Recently, the Ministry of Tourism and Antiquities has resorted to pressuring missions operating in Egypt that belong to countries that are markets for Egyptian antiquities and refuse or hesitate to retrieve smuggled pieces. This is done by obstructing their work within Egypt, prompting representatives of these missions to take serious steps with their respective governments to prevent the sale and smuggling of Egyptian antiquities. This method is expected to lead to significant success in future operations.

Egypt has succeeded in retrieving many of its smuggled antiquities between 2002 and the 2011 revolution, including nearly 6,000 diverse pieces of different sizes and shapes, such as the golden sheets for the lower part of the coffin of Akhenaten, which were retrieved from Munich in 2002; the royal mummies of Ramses I, which were retrieved from the Carlos Museum in Atlanta in 2003; and the head of Amenhotep III, which was retrieved from the United States in June 2003, as well as many other antiquities. Since 2011, Egypt has retrieved more than 2,000 diverse pieces of different sizes and shapes, including significant pieces.

10. Suggestions

Some suggestions that may help the international community reduce the smuggling of cultural property and return it to its original homeland are:

i. The owner of the cultural property should create an identity card for the cultural property that accompanies it and carries its picture, date, and movements since leaving its original homeland.

ii. Export certificates for cultural property must be issued by the exporting country and are the most important means of stopping the laundering of stolen artifacts.

iii. Auction houses should make every effort to ensure the accuracy of the pieces offered for sale and verify that they have not left their home country illegally.

iv. Auction houses should create a database for all the antiquities offered for sale and for exhibitors and buyers to facilitate tracking the antiquities that have been sold. Some cases have shown that theft of artefacts can be proven through inventory or scientific excavations, especially in sites that have been subjected to illegal excavations, after several years from the date of theft and smuggling.

v. Many stolen pieces, especially those that are registered, find their way into private collections through the black market and may remain hidden for decades until they are sold later. Therefore, a mechanism must be put in place to monitor private collections and encourage their owners to display the pieces they have.

vi. The sale of antiquities should be prohibited on intermediary websites between the seller and the buyer. The intermediary website cannot verify the legitimacy of the seller's acquisition of these pieces.

Bibliography

Egypt's Constitution of 2014, constituteproject.org.

Hussein Duqeil, Egyptian Antiquities & Legalization of Smuggling in *Institute Journal*, 2019, 5 Septemper.

Ministry of Culture, Supreme Council of Antiquities, Law NO. 117 of 1983 as amended by law NO. 3 of 2010 Promulgating the Antiquities Protection Law. Published in the Official Gazette on February 14, 2010.

State Information Service, your gateway to Egypt, *Sisi okays amendments to Antiquities Protection Law,* on May 23, 2020.

埃及打击非法贩运——政府为保护文化遗产、打击非法贩运文化财产和追索被盗文物所做的努力

沙班·阿卜杜勒·加瓦德 *

  摘要：本文介绍了埃及政府保护考古文化遗产的机制。详述了2014年埃及新宪法中关于保护埃及遗产和不同年代的埃及文物以维护文化特性的三项条款，以及1983年为填补法律空白并跟上社会发展步伐而修订《（埃及）文物保护法》。列举了文物归还司的主要工作，及其与国内和国际的合作和协调。分析了为克服文物走私案所面临的一系列困难而重组的国家文物归还委员会的作用。在过去的十年里，成功追索了29 000件考古文物。文物部出台了追索全球博物馆展出的埃及文物的立法框架，并采取了多种方式阻止文物走私。

  关键词：2014年埃及新宪法；盗掘、贩运、走私文物；归还；拍卖行；公诉机关；文化遗产

一、引言

  文物归还和保护文化遗产是埃及文物部国家战略的一部分。文物部重点关注其下属委员会，特别是主管部门在制定防止和打击非法贩运文化和考古物品的国际政策方面的积极行动。作为国家权威机关，该部门根据现行法律框架，正在加强与国际机构的合作，包括在双边关系和多边协定的框架内开展合作。它根据保存记录开展工作，并进一步调查拍卖行的销售情况，以便与国际刑警组织和司法部国际合作办公室等合作，查明可疑的

---

* 沙班·阿卜杜勒·加瓦德，埃及文物部文物归还司司长。

被贩运文物。

二、国内立法

（一）2014年埃及新宪法

2014年埃及新宪法在第二章《社会构成》（Components of Society）第三节《文化的构成》（Cultural Components）中的第47—50条，规定了保护不同时代的埃及遗产和文物的措施。这些条款要求埃及政府保护具有多样文明起源的埃及文化身份。此外，国家支持边远地区和最需要帮助的群体，保护古迹原址，禁止将任何文物作为礼物赠送或交换。国家特别重视维护文化多样性的组成部分，包括法老时期、科普特时期、伊斯兰时期以及现代建筑、文学和艺术文化。任何破坏文化多样性的行为都应该受到法律的制裁。

（二）《(埃及)文物保护法》修正案

为填补法律空白并跟上社会发展的步伐，1983年对第117号《埃及文物保护法》进行了修订。

修订如下：

1. 根据2010年第3号法律，对1983年第117号《埃及文物保护法》进行了修订，加大对在国外拍卖行收购或出售埃及文物行为的处罚力度。2018年第91号法律对在埃及境内外走私文物的个人施以严厉的惩罚，并确保相关规定得到执行，并帮助国家寻求文物的修复。

2. 通过了2020年20号关于文物非法贸易的法律修正案。

三、解决盗掘和贩运

通过旅游和文物警察，抓获阿拉伯埃及共和国境内缉捕走私者和盗掘团伙，并没收非法所得的埃及文物与被盗文物，以维护埃及的国家利益。

四、保护考古遗址和博物馆安全

埃及内政部在保护阿拉伯埃及共和国境内所有考古遗址和博物馆方面发挥着重要作用。此外，隶属于旅游和文物部的私人警卫也执行着同样的任务，旅游和文物部的考古检查员定期巡查下属区域，及时报告任何侵占、破坏或遗失文物的行为，并跟进是否存在盗掘行为。

五、打击文物走私

中央考古港口部成立于1896年，最初在开罗机场设立考古（发掘）单位，后来发展到陆地、海洋和机场的40个考古单位，并为这些考古单位配备符合资格的考古学家，让他们在这些港口工作，检查疑似考古出土物，并在允许出口前对其发表考古意见。

该部门与海陆空口岸的所有海关和安全部门合作，防止文物和文化财产走私出境，并积极推动埃及与其他国家签署国际协议，倘若文化财产被扣押，将确保其返还给原籍国。

该部门还与文化部以外的多个实体机构展开合作，包括埃及国家图书馆和文化部档案馆、环境部地质博物馆、亚历山大图书馆、国家艺术中心和科学综合体。

六、埃及政府为归还走私埃及文物所做的努力（包括以下两个方面）

（一）文物归还司的主要工作

每天密切关注各大知名拍卖行的埃及文物出售状态，并在网站上搜索其他不知名（小众）画廊，检查其展品情况，并与旅游和文物部发布的遗失物品清单进行比对，通知外交部委派代表确认这些画廊获得的埃及文物的证明的真实性。一旦发现可疑物品与清单相符，或者拍卖行所持物品缺乏适当担保，文物归还司将立即采取一切必要措施，通过友好、司法或外交手段要求归还这些物品。

文物归还司建立和持续更新旅游和文物部遗失物品数据库，与下属所有部门和其他相关单位（如：考古遗址以及捐赠部、埃及国家图书馆和档案馆等）保持紧密联系，定期更新数据，并向国际刑警组织通报新遗失的物品，以便在国际范围内进行追踪。

与代表国家的有关当局（文物调查、国际刑警组织、司法部国际合作办公室和外交部文化关系司）进行合作和协调。

当埃及文物在外国边境被扣押或个人非法流通时，与外国当局协调并采取后续行动，力图通过外交、司法或谈判的手段将文物返还给埃及。

（二）饱受争议中的国家文物归还委员会

在旅游和文物部长、外交部、内政部、司法部、国家安全部、旅游部和文物警察部的代表以及其他公众人物的管理下成立，旨在克服走私文物案件所面临的困难和障碍。

在过去的十年中，埃及已经将超过2.9万件考古物件成功追索回国。

七、调查和追踪走私网络

与埃及调查当局协调和合作。与埃及检察机关、旅游和文物警察局以及外交部在许多埃及文物走私出境的案件中展开合作，无论这些文物是被扣押还是出售，都要查明犯罪行为，追踪全球走私网络，限制埃及文物的非法贸易。

八、提高公众认识和社会参与

为了将市民社会与埃及遗产紧密联系起来，旅游和文物部组织开展了多项活动，推动社会成为保护埃及遗产的首要力量。文化发展和社区外联部主要关注以下群体：在校学生、图书馆、俱乐部、宫殿、文化、科学和艺术中心的游客、大学生、妇女及有特殊需要的人。志愿项目还将老年人纳入考虑范围，与政府和文化机构合作开展各类伙伴方案，同时把提议的方案将考古开放和发现、文化性活动和社会活动联系起来，并为从事博物馆教育、提升考古意识、社区外联和文化发展领域的工作人员提供工作坊（参与和监督面向社区的教育工具和出版物的编写工作，提高认识，举办比赛、社区和艺术展览、教育讲座和研讨会，并提供导游服务）。

九、国际合作

为了便于开展文物的追回工作，埃及与秘鲁、厄瓜多尔、古巴、意大利、约旦、瑞士、中国、美国、塞浦路斯、危地马拉、西班牙和沙特阿拉伯等国缔结了保护文化和考古遗产的双边协定。目前，与一些阿拉伯海湾国家和欧盟国家的协议也在积极推进中。

埃及还与支持文物、遗产和人类文明的组织，如联合国教科文组织、伊斯兰教科文组织（ISESCO）、国际博物馆协会、国际文化财产保存与修复研究中心（ICROM），以及许多举办打击非法贩运文化财产的区域和国际会议及讲习班的其他机构和组织保持紧密联系。

设立文物返还司的功臣是著名的考古学家、最高文物委员会前秘书长和文物局前局长扎西·哈瓦斯（Zahi Hawass）博士。他在2002年出任最高文物委员会秘书长后，立即决定成立文物追索总局。多年来，无论是埃及地下埋藏的还是在没有严格安保的露天场所发现和展示的文物，都遭受着蓄意盗窃和非法挖掘的威胁。这种现象在过去十年中尤为频繁，因此采取快而有效的措施来阻止文化遗产的持续流失变得至关重要。虽然文物部的考古检查站可以在一定程度上阻止埃及境内的文物盗掘和走私，但一旦这些文物走私出境，由于外国处理此类文物的政策和法律与埃及的法规存在差异——埃及将走私、交易甚至拥有文物都定为犯罪行为，这使得追索文物和阻止文化遗产的流失变得更加困难。

从这个角度来看，建立一个负责追踪埃及丢失和走私文物的总局十分必要。它可以与外国的实体机构进行沟通，并具有采取最佳方法（无论是外交途径还是法律诉讼）处理走私文物的追索问题的灵活性。因此，在2002年，埃及成立了文物追索总局，由最高文物委员会秘书长直接领导，目前由文物局局长直接领导。

文物追索局的工作包括实时更新遗失文物清单。管理部门负责接收考古遗址、博物馆和分库被盗文物的数据，建立被盗文物数据库。通过与文物局的所有部门、考古工地区域，以及其他相关实体机构，如捐赠部和埃及国家图书馆，实时更新数据，从而创建一个文物局遗失文物的数据库。此外，我们还向国际刑警组织定期通报更新遗失文物清单，以便在全球范围内进行追踪。

文物追索局还会每天追踪在线拍卖网站和销售场所，将在售文物与该部失踪文物进行比较，一旦发现有匹配的文物就立即采取行动，追回已被证明是通过非法手段离开埃及的文物。为了实现这个目标，文物追索局需要持续与各种内部和外部实体机构开展合作。涉及的内部实体机构包括埃及文物部门、伊斯兰文物部门和博物馆部门，以便于实时更新失踪文物的数据库，并向这些部门通报在拍卖大厅和线上网站发现的文物。

（一）重新设立国家文物追索委员会

2016年第1306号总理决议解决了这一问题，该决议涉及外交部、司法部、国际合作部和内政部的代表，以及埃及安全和监管机构的代表，由文物部部长牵头。我们的目标是寻找一切可能的方法，克服一切障碍，将用非法手段走私到国外的埃及文物追索回国。

该委员会与联合国教科文组织、伊斯兰教科文组织、国际博物馆协会、国际文化财产保存与修复研究中心等与文物、遗产和人类文明相关组织保持联系，还积极组织区域和国际会议和工作坊。

在立法上，1983年第117号《（埃及）文物保护法》及其2018年第91号法律的执行条例得到修订，加重了对走私和贩运文物的处罚。文物部还向司法部门提出一项立法修正案，增加一项规定，根据《（埃及）刑法典》第1、2和3条的规定，该法适用于在阿拉伯埃及共和国境外犯罪的任何人。

文物部还致力于找回在全球博物馆展出的埃及文物。我们已经成功索回了一些文物，如德国柏林博物馆的内克塔内布二世的部分棺板、澳大利亚麦考瑞大学博物馆的Sesh Nefer Tam的部分棺板，以及最近从美国纽约大都会艺术博物馆索回了古埃及祭司Nedjemankh的金棺。该部目前正在努力从全球的博物馆追回更多文物。

（二）从外国追索走私文物的方法

友好或外交途径：通过埃及驻外使馆与持有埃及文物的一方进行和平谈判是追索文物最有效的方法之一。与政府或官方实体谈判成功率较高，但与拍卖行谈判的成功率很低，只有文物出现在展厅且缺少所有权文件（合法来源途径）的情况下才会成功。

在国际港口和机场扣押：以联合国教科文组织《关于禁止和防止非法进出口文化财产和非法转让其所有权的方法的公约》或埃及与其他国家或交易市场之间的双边协议为依据。这些案件有时需要很长时间去证明埃及拥有这些走私文物的权利，根据该领域的当地和国际法律进行索回。埃及文物追索局与全球执法机构进行谈判，并提供所有文件、法律和证据，证实这些文物是非法离开埃及的。最近，埃及成功地索回数百甚至数千件在埃及境内非法挖掘的文物。

全球执法机构之间的合作：这种方法相对现代化，主要取决于负责文物档案检索的人员与世界各地执法机构的关系，以及他们丰富的经验和良好的声誉。埃及通过与执法机构的直接沟通，例如审查从埃及或世界不同国家跨境的文物的出口许可证和文件，成功地追回了许多走私文物。最近的一个案例是，文物追索局在与纽约市地方检察办进行了漫长的调查、沟通和谈判后，美国纽约大都会艺术博物馆归还了古埃及祭司Nedjemankh的金棺。未来，还会有更多的文物通过这种方式回到埃及。

（三）诉讼

当和平的手段无法索回文物时，旅游和文物部会诉诸法律行动，授权律师在文物所有者的国家进行起诉。然而，这些尝试往往以失败告终，因为这些国家大多允许文物交易，且缺少法律条款将文物交易定为刑事犯罪。因此，裁决往往有利于文物所有者，尤其是在他们拥有所有权文件的情况下。

（四）对在埃及开展业务的使团施加压力

最近，旅游和文物部在对埃及开展活动的代表团施加压力，这些代表团来自埃及文物市场的国家（流入国），他们拒绝或犹豫归还走私的埃及文物。具体做法是阻挠这些团体在埃及境内的工作，迫使他们的代表与本国政府共同采取严肃措施，防止进一步出售和走私埃及文物。这种方法有望在未来的行动中取得重大成功。

2002年到2011年，埃及政府已经成功索回了6 000件大小不一、形状各异的走私文物，如2002年从慕尼黑索回的阿肯那顿（Akhenaten）棺下部的金片；2003年从亚特兰大卡洛斯博物馆索回的拉美西斯一世木乃伊；2003年6月从美国索回的阿蒙霍特普三世的头颅等。2011年以来，埃及已经成功索回了2 000多件大小不一、形状各异文物，其中包括一些重要文物。

十、建议

以下是一些建议，可能有助于国际社会遏制文化财产走私并将其返还原主国：

第一，文化财产的所有者应为其制作身份证明，上面印有文化财产的照片、日期和离开故土后的动态。

第二，文化财产的出口许可证必须由出口国签发，这是防止通过被盗文物洗钱的最重要手段。

第三，拍卖行应尽一切努力确保拍卖品的准确性，核实其是否非法离境。

第四，拍卖行应为所有出售的文物以及参展商和买家创建一个数据库，以便跟踪已售出的文物。一些案例表明，清查或科学发掘可以证明文物是被盗掘的，特别是在从被盗和走私之日起数年后被非法发掘的遗址。

第五，许多被盗文物，尤其是曾登记在册的文物，通过黑市进入私人收藏，到后面被出售，可能会隐身几十年。因此，必须建立一种机制来监督私人收藏，并鼓励私人藏家展示他们的藏品。

第六，应禁止买卖双方在中介网站上出售和购买文物，这些平台无法核实卖家买入这些文物时的合法性。

参考文献

Egypt's Constitution of 2014, constituteproject.org.

Hussein Duqeil, Egyptian Antiquities & Legalization of Smuggling in *Institute Journal*, 2019, 5 Septemper.

Ministry of Culture, Supreme Council of Antiquities, Law NO. 117 of 1983 as amended by law NO. 3 of 2010 Promulgating the Antiquities Protection Law. Published in the Official Gazette on February 14, 2010.

State Information Service, your gateway to Egypt, *Sisi okays amendments to Antiquities Protection Law*, on May 23, 202.

The Repatriation of the Ivorian Talking Drum "Djidji Ayokwe": Challenges and Perspectives

Honoré Kouadio Kouassi[*]

Introduction

Art and cultural objects express a diversity of cultural values. In this context, they do have the capacity to promote a collective sense of community in a pluralist world; participate in the building of a dialogue of parity among human cultures and favor intercultural respect and culture of peace.[①] Thus, to defend artistic and cultural objects become a serious mission for the current generation as well as the future ones. A mission of defense of works of arts and cultural objects against every form of illegal possession.

Works of arts and artefacts are almost undeniably significant to human expression and identity. They reflect aspects of the culture of their time or period and place. Regardless of whether it achieves recognition beyond the group responsible for the production, culture makes 'identity' conceivable and converts longing into belonging and solidarity.[②]

Museums preserve cultural heritage, but most of objects in European or American collections present an ethical dilemma. While many objects were obtained

---

[*] Honoré Kouadio Kouassi, Deputy Director-General of the National Higher Institute of Arts, Republic of Cote d'Ivoire.

[①] Hartman, *The Fateful Question of Culture*, (1997), pp. 180, 211.

[②] Opokou, Kwame, *Coordination of African Positions on Restitution Matters*, Modern Ghana, Retrieved 31 July 2019.

through purchase with the permission of the individual maker or community, others, even when legally traded on the art market, may have been taken without consent and in ways that violate cultural traditions (Herman, 2021). This is a particular problem with African art collected during the era of colonization.

The repatriation of African cultural objects from European owned collections to their countries of origin following French President Macron's address of November 2017 in Ouagadougou (Burkina Faso), is a great opportunity to recover African collective identity and memory. This paper articulates the specific case of the "Djidji Ayokwe," an Ivorian talking drum whose formal repatriation process has been initiated by Ivorian Government through the Department of Culture. However, this process cannot be effective without the involvement of museum professionals, local communities, Ivorian and French authorities, sub-regional cooperation, the techniques of preservation, and an appropriate legal framework. From a critical-based approach, we intend to explore the challenges and the perspectives associated with this process. Additionally, the paper investigates the specific context of repatriation as well as the social meaning of the talking drum.

1. Context of the Restitution of Art and Cultural Objects

Since the Djidji Ayokwe was taken away from them, the Bidjan[1] communities, never stopped claiming their property. The 7 villages live separated physically and culturally and yet their sacred drum art of communication gathered them around brotherhood and solidarity years ago. Their requests did not always receive a favorable response from those in authority.

Beyond this, needs to meet, gather and re-build history became more and more persistent within community members. Aspirations, books published on

---

[1] Custodian community of the Djidji Ayokwe.

African cultural arts and the recent announcement by French President Mr. Macron, appeared to be "the suns of"① the cultural heritage reconstructions. It was a great and charitable breath of fresh air.

Macron's declaration in Burkina was the official recognition of the fact that Africa has been for a long time deprived of a part of its history and a significant part of its collective memory to be reconstructed. For most of communities or countries which artefacts were still kept in French Museums, the context was more than appropriate to get involved in the process of returning their cultural arts. In fact, following the announcement and request by the President, Felwine Sarr and Benedicte Savoy wrote a report.

The report presents state of publicly owned French collections of African artworks originating from illegal or irregular possessions or acquisitions. It provides the necessary clarifications for a good understanding of all the contours of the restitution and includes recommendations and measures with relevant action plans. Contexts of identity quest and awareness of memorial duty did welcome the return of cultural heritage project.

International cooperation, joint research and appropriate training, adequate infrastructures for museums in Africa and educational initiatives (Sarr and Savoy 2018) are put forward.

With about 148 Ivorian art collections inventoried in French museums, Côte d'Ivoire is also concerned by this repatriation process that is part of a much general context of return of artefacts to African countries of origin.

President Macron's announcement in November 2017 and the publication of Sarr/Savoy report in November 2018 did steer discussions in many African countries and prompt numerous debates and plans for a " decolonization of museums".

In 2019 (September 10th), the Ivorian Minister in charge of Culture addressed a transmittal letter to his French counterpart, to request the restitution

---

① Term borrowed from Kourouma H in 'Les Soleils des Indépendances'.

of Ivorian collections in French museums.[①]

The first requested object from collections which return is being prepared is the "Djidji Ayokwe"[②], a talking drum inventoried in the Musée du Quai Branly-Jacques Chirac in Paris.

2. Presentation of the "Djidji Ayokwe"

The "Djidji Ayokwe" (panther-lion) is a talking slotted drum that belongs to an Ivorian local phratry called Bidjan that is part of a much larger ethnic group (Ebrie[③]) in Côte d'Ivoire. They live in the South-West and their original name is "Tchaman". The land of Abidjan, the Capital City of Côte d'Ivoire, is their property. Every important political, social and economic event in the capital city is still submitted to a libation ceremony performed by the Head of the Atchan community. The Djidji Ayokwe is at the top of the list of claimed items. It measures 3.50 meters long, weighs 430 kg and is both a musical tool and the symbol of colonial resistance (Ndiaye, 1989).

The Djidji Ayokwe (Picture by *Pulse Cote D'Ivoire*)

The drum alone sums up the entire Bidjan civilization in which the number "4" predominates. The Djidji Ayokwe has four colors. Originally the Bidjan

---

① Cf. Sarr, Felwine ; Savoy, Benedicte (21 November 2018), The Restitution of African Cultural Heritage, Toward a New Relational Ethics (Report). Paris.
② Requested in 2018.
③ Ivorian ethnic group, landowner of the city of Abidjan.

phratry lived in a single city composed of four districts organized in four generation groups. The drum also shows a panther (symbol of the tribe) which conveys ferocity despite its ability to defend a territory. The crocodile drafted on the drum is the symbol of the Bidjans' ancestors.

The upper lip of the drum was more thick and send high-pitched sounds while the lower one sends deep tones. The leopard representation on the drum is the symbol of strength, power and traditional authority.

The drum, a key element of the Bidjan traditional musical art, produces long-distance sounds and sends coded messages to community members. It gives echo to a message of which it is necessary to know how to decipher the codes. Codicity is one of the defining characteristics of the Djidji Ayokwe.

As a communication devise, it did play an important role in fighting against French colonization. With an acoustic reach of more than 20 kilometers, the drum could send indications related to location and military armament of French colonizers to remote Atchan villages. With a subversive role, the artefact operates both as a satellite and a watchman. Pulled out by force in 1916 for impeding colonial activities, the drum was a central art devise for the social

The Bidjan Community (Picture by *ABIDJAN. NET*)

organization of the Atchan group which includes seven villages, all connected to the talking drum. The Djidji Ayokwe was also a sacred artefact maintained by periodic ritual ceremonies. It was the common denominator, vector of social cohesion and arm of defence to the Bidjan community.

The loss of the drum disrupted the social organization of the Bidjan community. The members stopped seeing each other. In the absence of the artefact confiscated by the colonial administration, rituals practices ended and the issue of chieftaincy in some villages arose. The current central leader of the EBRIE highlighted the importance of the role the talking drum has played in maintaining cohesion et solidarity among their different villages. Clavaire Aguego MOBIO said in an interview: "Le Djidji Ayokwe, était le pont de liaison entre les 7 villages qui constituent la communauté Atchan. Grâce à ce tambour, nos parents se réunissaient regulièrement et se parlaient. Quand ils ont perdu ce bien, ils ont été dispersés comme l'avait voulu le colon".[1]

The issue of the restitution of cultural arts is an opportunity to rebuild the cultural heritage and restore the dignity and memory of African people. In this context, Côte d'Ivoire is preparing to live a major historical event with the future return of the Djidji Ayokwe to its community of origin. To this end, several steps and activities have been carried out.

3. Return of the Djidji Ayokwe: Preparation Activities

This section will focus on actions carried out and those planned to be implemented to date within the framework of the return of the Djidji Ayokwe, the very first object requested by Ivorian authorities. There have been general activities on the restitution of cultural heritage and others on the specific return of

---

[1] «Djidji Ayokwe operates as a connecting bridge between the seven villages of the Atchan community. Thanks to it, our grand fathers met on a regular basis to discuss and make important decisions. The loss of the object results in the will of French colonizers that was the disorganization of the group». Translation mine.

the Djidji Ayokwe. In the coming lines, we will focus on Pre-restitution activities.

In 2018, the Economic, Social, Environnemental and Cultural Council (CESEC) of Côte d'Ivoire adopted a draft opinion on the following topic: "Display of the mention Côte d'Ivoire on the labels of every Ivorian art object exhibited in European museums". Many art objects were concerned by the restitution. Thus, following researches works and activities and based on inventories in French museums, the Ivorian Government published a list of 148 objects. A delegation led by the national expert[①] travelled to Paris to work on the effectiveness and conformity of the published list. The report issued from the mission stated that the list is to be updated seeing that not all the works listed are physically available in French museums. Others are in rotating exhibitions in Europe.

Within the framework of sub-regional cooperation, Côte d'Ivoire adopted in 2018 alongside others ECOWAS countries, the regional cultural policy with an action plan on the return of African arts heritage to their countries of origin. The Action Plan provides for support to States in their dealing with requests, sketches of a methodology for inventories of artefacts and strategy of negotiations with the holder countries for the return of cultural objects. Côte d'Ivoire did also ratify the 1995 UNIDROIT Convention on the return of African objects.

In August 2019, Côte d'Ivoire, through the national Department of Culture, officially requested the return of the Djidji Ayokwe to French authorities. In order to allow the Ivorian and French Museum structures to work together in a sustainable perspective on research, a scientific partnership is established between the Musée des Civilisations and the Quai Branly-Jacques Chirac in september 2021. This partnership aims to strengthen the scientific collaboration that will be implemented throughout the whole restitution process.

The Djidji Ayokwe is a sacred object and has suffered significant damages and needs therefore to be restored before return to its community of origin. In

---

① Dr. Memel Kassi Silvie, national expert for restitution.

october 27th, 2022, The Minister of Culture in office[1] with her predecessors, met the Bidjan community in Adjamé[2]. The purpose of this meeting was to involve the community, its elders and traditional Heads in the ongoing return process. It emerged from the meeting that the artefact should go through a ritual of desacralization before restorationv.[3]

In november 7th, 2022, an important delegation including the Minister of culture in office, the national expert for the return of artefacts and ten members of the Bidjan community, initiates of the Djidji Ayokwe, travelled to Paris. Two rituals are performed: the libation of the Quai Branly Museum and the desacralization of the talking drum.

The Bidjan Community Performing a Desacralization Ritual (Picture by *TV5 MONDE*)

---

[1] Mrs. Françoise Remarck, Minister of Culture and Francophonie.
[2] Adjamé is a district of the Capital City Abidjan.
[3] Desacralization was important to allow "lay hands" to restore the Djidji Ayokwe. Restoration was neccesary due to wood degradation. It aims at consolidating the damaged wood to give the drum density and strength for easier handling.

Since January 2023, the restoration of the drum, made by a team of French cultural art restorers is completed and the report of this activity, returned to the Ivorian Department of Culture.

Before restitution scheduled for May 2023[①], the Ivorian Government has planned to renovate the Musée des Civilisations de Côte d'Ivoire. The national committee for cultural art restitution made recommendations for activities to be implemented following the return of the Djidji Ayokwe to its homeland. Thus, artistic and cultural events will be carried out on the whole Ivorian territory. National and foreign experts and scholars meetings, scientific activities to deepen reflections on challenges and perspectives related to the issue of restitution in general and that of the Djidji Ayokwe in particular, will be organized. A national exhibition with a tour will be initiated. In order to allow the object to reconnect with its land of origin, it will first be exhibited within the Bidjan community. Then, it will be exhibited at the Presidency before its final exhibition at the Musée des Civilisations.

In order for the restitution of the Djidji Ayokwe to be an in-depth, long-lasting, sustainable with a real socio-cultural impact and a totally successful activity, several parameters must be taken into account. In other words, the success of restitutions in general should be subject to many multiform challenges to be met courageously. The restitution of the Djidji Ayokwe which is not yet effective to this date, is limited in its process.

4. Limits of a Process and Conditions for a Successful Restitution

The process is not totally inclusive because important actors are missing. In the ongoing process, participants include the Ministry of Culture, the

---

① This date is still provisional because there is a whole legal mechanism related to restitution that must be put in place and which largely depends on the French legislator.

Bidjan community members and the national expert and her staff. The national Chamber of Kings and traditional Chiefs is not formally associated with the process. The returning artefact is primarily a national property. Its return to native land must therefore bring together all the guarantors of Ivorian traditional values from all the cultural areas of the country.

Other national Departments such as The Department of Tourism, The Department of Higher Education and Scientific Research, the Department of Education and even the Department of Communication should be associated in order to contribute each one in its field to enrich and better direct the return of the Djidji Ayokwe. To ensure that knowledge of the Djidji Ayokwe reaches younger Ivorian generations, effective educational initiatives are necessary. Ivorian Scholars, historians and even film makers should organize lectures, discussions and historial documentary films dedicated to the history of the Djidji Ayokwe et the Bidjan community.

TV shows on a regular basis, should organize TV debates on the Djidji Ayokwe. Ministry of Tourism which offers heritage tours, it cannot be outside of a process that is supposed to lead to the return of a cultural object.

The private sector, which provides, in the framework of Public / Private partnership, a punctual financial support for the renovation or building new infrastructures, and provision of technical equipment of museums, must necessarily be a stakeholder in the return of the Djidji Ayokwe. This is the case of Fondation Orange[①], which has recently launched the project of digitalization of the Musée des Civilisations, the most important museum in terms of collections holding.

The issue of training resurfaces as a factor that constitutes another limit to the return of the Djidji Ayokwe. As mentioned in the previous pages, the Djidji Ayokwe was restored by a team of French specialists. At local level, the national

---

[①] Orange Group Foundation specialized in mobile telephony which develops partnerships with cultural infrastructures such as the Musée des Civilisations, Musée des costumes etc.

museum does not have some. What use will restitution be if museum workers are not skilled to restore the artefact if need be? Training local specialists in restoration is necessary to provide appropriate sense and relevance to restitution projects.

We are planning to suggest the restoration as a major in museology be integrated into INSAAC [①] where curators are already trained. First, curators will be initiated to techniques of restoration and then full restorers will be trained to support national museums. Trainings will first be conducted with the technical support of French restoration specialists in the framework of the partnership between the Musée des Civilisations and Quai Branly-Jacques Chirac.

Benin and Senegal have recently requested and received some of their cultural objects. Côte d'Ivoire has launched its process and is preparing too, to receive the Djidji Ayokwe. And yet, it would be more judicious for the issue of restitution to be dealt with within a concerted framework that relies on the instrument of sub-regional cooperation that is ECOWAS for all West African States concerned by the problem of the return of artefacts. As suggested by Felwine Sarr and Benedicte Savoy in their report, True international cultural cooperations is required to ensure the success of the return operation.

Restitutions also raise questions of law and legislation. Cultural objects in French museums are considered French property and inalienable assets. Restitution of Djidji Ayokwe is therefore submitted to a vote by French legislators. The French Government having recognized colonization was at the root of issues related to cultural objects taken from Africans, restitution should be made through political and diplomatic arrangements betweem States.

As mentioned in previous pages, Côte d'Ivoire ratified the Convention of June 24, 1995 (UNIDROIT Convention) on stolen or illicitly exported cultural property. It "promotes understanding between peoples and dissemination of

---

① National Institute of Art and Cultural Action, it is the only one national public art school under the supervision of the Department of Culture.

culture for the well-being of humanity and the progress of civilization"[1]. This legal instrument to support and guide restitutions has not yet been ratified by all holders of African cultural object. This is the case of France.

International Council of Museums (ICOM) has enacted a Code of Ethics that is a reference document for all member museums. The Musée des Civilisations de Côte d'Ivoire is the home museum of the Djidji Ayokwe and as ICOM member, is committed to respecting every single provision of that Code of Ethics which is a set of principles with guidelines for professional practice. In order to take into account local or national realities, this code must be accompanied and reinforced by minimum standards defined by national regulation. Côte d'Ivoire has no such standards. Thus, while the Djidji Ayokwe is returning to its homeland, having a national code of ethics would be a complete legal protection tool for the talking drum and other arts to be returned.

Because of its status of central department, the Musée des Civilisations has only an operating budget essentially devoted to administrative management (salaries, purchase of equipment, invoices and maintenance). As a result, there is no chapter allocated to investment which leaves little room for the management of the collections, namely, acquisition, conservation, restoration, control, security and exhibitions.

Conclusion

The return of African cultural goods to their native lands is an act of highly historical significance because of all the symbolism and issues linked to the restitution. The first issue is the reappropriation of cultural objects that deserve to be reconsidered in light of the long years spent at Quai Branly-Jacques Chirac (France). The second and third issues are the economic and exhibition values

---

[1] Provision from of Uni-Right Agreement (translation mine).

of cultural objects. In other words, value must be given to the cultural arts so as not to depreciate them. And the question of how to bring value to them needs to be asked. Moreover, the issue of restitution cannot do without the question of redefining the museum institution.

This paper provides a general and specific overview of the context of the restitution and introduces the Djidji Ayokwe and its functions. It sums up the preparatory activities related to the upcoming arrival of the talking drum in Côte d'Ivoire, and in a critical perspective, highlights the limits of the process and conditions of successful restitution.

In general terms, the restitution of cultural objects remains a complex issue that should not be settled at the expense of Africa, let alone against social cohesion. It will be necessary to construct measured and unifying discourses around the return and to ensure that these goods participate in the reinforcement of living together.

References

Ashley, S. (2009), *Museums and Globalization: Ideas on Recognition, Restitution, Reconfiguration*, LONDON Debates, SAS.

Louis, Obou. (2015), *L'Univers des Objets Parlants dans la Culture Africaine: Le Masque et le Tambour,* NAC's Journal, of African Cultures and Civilization, PARIS New AF.

Memel, Silvie (2018) «*Le Traffic Illicite des Biens Culturels: Cas des musées de Côte d'Ivoire*», Doctorate Thesis, Abidjan.

Niangoran, B. (1989), «*Les Ebrié et leur organisation politique traditionnelle*» dans les annales de l'Université d4abidjan, Serie F Ethnosociologie.

Ndiaye, F. (1989), «*Ebrié d'Adjamé. Tambour royal ayokwe*», Dans Corps Sculptés, Corps Parés, Corps Masqués, (Exposition), Paris, Galeries Nationales du Grand Palais.

Opokou, K. (2019), *Coordination of African Positions on Restitution Matters*, Modern Ghana, Retrieved, July 2019.

Hannerz, U. (1992), *Cultures and Globalization: Conflicts and Tensions,* New York, Columbia University Press.

Hartman, G. (1997), *The Fateful Question of Culture.* New York, Columbia University Press.

Herman, Alexander (2021), *Restitution: The Return of Cultural Artefacts, Hot Topics in the Art World,* UK, Lund Humphries Publishers.

Sarr, F. (2020), *Restitution of African Artefacts: History, Memory, Traces, Reappropriation, New Ethical Relation (Mimeo).*

Sarr, F.; Savoy B. (2018), *The Restitution of African Cultural Heritage: Toward a New Relational Ethics*, Paris. Available at http//restitutionreport2018. com / Sarr Savoy.

Savoy, B. (2022), *Africa's Struggle for Its Art: History of a Postcolonial Defeat*, Princeton University Press.

科特迪瓦 Bidjan 部落的说话鼓 "Djidji Ayokwe" 的归还：观点与挑战

奥纳瑞・卡瓦迪欧・卡瓦西*

引言

艺术和文物彰显着文化价值观的多样性。在这方面，它们能够在一个多元化的世界中促进集体意识，参与建构人类跨文化平等对话，倡导不同文化之间的相互尊重与文化和平。[①]因此，保护艺术和文物，使其免受任何非法形式的占有，成为人们及其后代的一项严肃使命。

艺术及手工艺品对于人类的表达和身份认同极具重要意义，它们反映了其所处时代或时期、地方文化的各个方面。无论它们是否得到其生产群体之外的认可，文化都使"身份"变得可以想象，并将这种想象具化为一种归属感和团结感。[②]

文化遗产在博物馆中得以保存，但欧洲或美国的大部分收藏都存在伦理问题。许多藏品是在得到制作者个人或社区许可的情况下购得的，然而，也有一些藏品即使来源于艺术市场上的合法交易，但是在未经制作者同意并以违背文化传统的方式被取得的（Herman, 2021）。殖民时代收藏的非洲艺术品尤其存在这个问题。

根据法国总统马克龙于 2017 年 11 月在瓦加杜古（非洲布基纳法索首都）发表的讲话，将欧洲人收藏的非洲文物返还给它们的原属国是一个恢

---

* 奥纳瑞・卡瓦迪欧・卡瓦西，科特迪瓦国家高等艺术研究院副院长。
① Hartman The Fateful question of Culture, (1997) 180 211.
② Opokou, Kwame (21 May 2019), Coordination of African Positions on Restitution Matters, Modern Ghana, Retrieved 31 July 2019.

复非洲集体身份和记忆的重要机会。本文将介绍科特迪瓦Bidjan部落的说话鼓"Djidji Ayokwe"的具体案例，科特迪瓦政府已经通过文化部启动了"Djidji Ayokwe"的正式返还进程。然而，如果没有博物馆专业人员、当地社区、科特迪瓦和法国当局的参与和次区域合作、保护技术以及适当的法律框架，这一进程将无法有效地推动。从批判性的角度出发，我们希望讨论与这一进程相关的挑战和前景。此外，本文还调查了说话鼓"Djidji Ayokwe"归还的特殊背景以及其社会意义。

一、文物及艺术品归还的背景

自从说话鼓"Djidji Ayokwe"被盗走后，Bidjan①长期以来从未停止对它的追索。虽然这7个村落在物理上和文化上都是分离的，但他们神圣的鼓声交流方式在多年前已将他们的兄弟情谊和团结凝聚在一起。然而，他们的请求并没有得到当局的积极回应。

此外，在社区内部，成员们对会面、聚集和重建艺术的需求变得愈加迫切。社区成员强烈的愿望，非洲文化艺术书籍的出版，以及法国总统马克龙先生最近作出的承诺，似乎可以被看作是文化遗产重建的曙光。②

马克龙在布基纳法索发表的讲话正式承认非洲长期以来一直被剥夺了其历史的一部分，其集体记忆的重要部分有待重建。对于那些有许多文物被保存在法国博物馆的社区或国家来说，这一背景下，加入要求归还其流失文物的进程是非常合适的。根据法国总统马克龙的要求，菲尔温·萨尔（Felwine Sarr）和尼迪克特·萨瓦（Benedicte Savoy）撰写了一份报告。

该报告介绍了来自非法或违规购买或取得的法国公共拥有的非洲艺术品的现状，它为充分理解归还的各个方面提供了必要的说明，并包括相关行动计划的建议和措施。在建立身份认同和记忆意识的背景下，文化遗产归还项目"国际合作、共同研究和适当的培训、非洲博物馆的适当基础设施以及教育倡议"（Sarr and Savoy 2018）被提出。

---

① 说话鼓Djidji Ayokwe的所属部落。
② "曙光"一词借用自阿赫马杜·库鲁马的《独立的太阳》。

在法国博物馆中有大约148件科特迪瓦艺术品收藏,因此科特迪瓦也十分关切这一归还过程,这一进程是将文物归还非洲原属国整体进程中的一部分。

马克龙总统于2017年11月发表的讲话以及萨尔和萨瓦于2018年11月出版的报告在许多非洲国家激起了讨论,并引发了许多"博物馆去殖民化"的辩论和计划。

2019年9月10日,科特迪瓦文化部部长致函法国文化部部长,要求归还法国博物馆中的科特迪瓦藏品。[1]

第一件被要求归还的藏品便是"Djidji Ayokwe"[2],这是一种会说话的鼓,收藏于巴黎的凯布朗利博物馆。

二、Djidji Ayokwe 的介绍

Djidji Ayokwe是一种说话鼓,属于科特迪瓦当地一个名为Bidjan的部落,该部落是科特迪瓦Ebrie部族的一部分。他们居住在科特迪瓦的西南部,也曾被称为"Tchaman"。科特迪瓦首都阿比让(Abidjan)也是他们的所在区域,该市的重要政治、社会和经济事件都需要由部落首领进行祭酒仪式。"Djidji Ayokwe"是他们提出要求归还的文物之一,长3.5米,重430千克。它不仅是一种用于通讯的乐器,也是部落抵抗殖民的象征(Ndiaye, 1989)。

图1　Djidji Ayokwe 说话鼓

---

[1] Cf. Sarr, Felwine ; Savoy, Benedicte (21 November 2018), The Restitution of African Cultural Heritage, Toward a New Relational Ethics (Report). Paris.

[2] 于2018年要求归还。

科特迪瓦Bidjan部落的说话鼓"Djidji Ayokwe"的归还：观点与挑战

由四种颜色组成的"Djidji Ayokwe"体现了Bidjan部落文明中以数字"4"为尊的传统。最初，Bidjan部落分为四个区域，分别由四个世代群体组织。这架鼓上还绘有部落的象征——黑豹，象征着强悍的保卫领土的能力，也代表其凶猛性格。鼓上绘制的鳄鱼是Bidjan祖先的象征。

鼓的上鼓面较厚，发出高亢的声音，而下鼓面则发出低沉的声音。鼓上的豹是力量、权力和传统权威的象征。

作为Bidjan传统音乐艺术的关键元素，它可以发出远距离的声音，并向社区成员发送加密信息。秘密性是"Djidji Ayokwe"的重要特征之一。鼓声是信息的载体，而传递信息则必须知道如何对密码进行破译。

作为一种通信工具，它在对抗法国殖民统治方面发挥了重要作用。这架鼓的音响范围超过20千米，可以将与法国殖民者的位置和军事装备有关的信息传送到遥远的Atchan村庄。由于具有极为重要的作用，这架鼓既作为卫星，又承担着守望者的作用。1916年，因阻碍殖民活动，"Djidji Ayokwe"被法国强行武装带走。这架鼓是Atchan部落组织的核心元素，该部落包括七个村庄，所有村庄都与这架说话鼓紧密相连；它也是一件神圣的工艺品，用于定期的部落仪式。它是Bidjan部落凝聚力的基础、载体和部落防卫武器。

图2　Bidjan部落

因此，这架鼓的流失扰乱了Bidjan部落的社会组织，部落成员们无法进行联系。由于法国殖民政府抢夺了这件文物，祭祀仪式无法进行，一些村庄的酋长遇到了麻烦。Ebrie现任首领Clavaire Aguego MOBIO在接受采访时强调了说话鼓在保持不同村庄之间的凝聚力和团结方面发挥的重要作用，他说："Djidji Ayokwe是联系Atchan部落的7个村庄之间的纽带。有了这条纽带，我们的父母才能定期的团聚和交谈。当他们失去这件珍宝时，他们就如殖民者所希望的一样四散了。"①

文物归还问题是重建文化遗产、恢复非洲人尊严和记忆的机会。在这种情况下，科特迪瓦正在为Djidji Ayokwe在未来归还给原属部落而做准备，这将成为一次重大的历史事件。为此，科特迪瓦已经进行了一些行动，并开展了一些相关活动。

三、Djidji Ayokwe的归还：准备活动

本节将重点介绍科特迪瓦当局要求法国归还的第一件文物Djidji Ayokwe的归还框架内已经进行和计划开展的行动。关于文物的归还已经进行了一些一般性活动以及Djidji Ayokwe在归还前的具体活动。接下来，我们将重点介绍后者。

2018年，科特迪瓦经济、社会、环境和文化委员会（CESEC）通过了以下主题的草案意见："在欧洲的博物馆展出的每件科特迪瓦艺术品的标签上都需注明来自科特迪瓦。"许多艺术品都与归还有关。因此，经过研究工作和活动，并根据法国博物馆的清单，科特迪瓦政府公布了一个包含148件文物的清单。由科特迪瓦专家组成的代表团前往巴黎，就已公布清单的有效性和一致性进行研究。代表团报告指出，由于并非所有列出的文物都实际存在于法国博物馆中（有些文物在欧洲进行轮换展览），因此清单需要进行更新。

---

① Le Djidji Ayokwe, était le pont de liaison entre les 7 villages qui constituent la communauté Atchan. Grâce à ce tambour, nos parents se réunissaient regulièrement et se parlaient. Quand ils ont perdu ce bien, ils ont été dispersés comme l'avait voulu le colon. Original mine

在次区域合作框架内，科特迪瓦于2018年与其他西非国家经济共同体（ECOWAS）国家一起通过了地区文化政策，其中包括一项关于将非洲艺术遗产送回原属国的行动计划。该行动计划规定支持各国处理请求、制定文物清单方法以及与文物持有国谈判归还文物的战略。科特迪瓦还批准了1995年国际统一私法协会关于返还非洲文物的公约。

2019年8月，科特迪瓦通过国家文化部正式要求法国当局归还Djidji Ayokwe。为了使科特迪瓦和法国的博物馆机构能够从可持续研究的角度开展合作，文明博物馆（科特迪瓦）和凯布朗利博物馆（法国）于2021年9月建立了科学合作伙伴关系，这一伙伴关系旨在加强整个归还过程中的科学合作。

Djidji Ayokwe受到了严重的破坏，因此在归还之前，尚需要进行修复。2022年10月27日，现任文化部部长①和她的前任部长在Adjamé②会见了Bidjan部落的代表。这次会议的目的是让该部落、其酋长和首领参与正在进行的回归进程。会议认为，文物在归还前应进行一次去神圣化仪式（desacralization）。③

2022年11月7日，一个包括文化部部长、文物归还专家和十名Bidjan部落成员及Djidji Ayokwe信徒在内的重要代表团前往巴黎，他们在巴黎举行了两个仪式：凯布朗利博物馆奠酒仪式以及对说话鼓进行去神圣化仪式。

2023年1月，由法国文物修复人员组成的团队完成了对说话鼓的修复工作，修复报告已交予科特迪瓦文化部。

在2023年5月（计划归还时间）④之前，科特迪瓦政府计划对科特迪瓦文明博物馆进行翻修。国家文化艺术品归还委员会就Djidji Ayokwe归还后

---

① Mrs. Françoise Remarck, Minister of Culture and Francophonie.
② Adjamé是首都阿比让的一个区。
③ Desacralization was important to allow "lay hands" to restore the Djidji Ayokwe. Restoration was neccesary due to wood degradation. It aims at consolidating the damaged wood to give the drum density and strength for easier handling.
④ This date is still provisional because there is a whole legal mechanism related to restitution that must be put in place and which largely depends on the French legislator

图3　Bidjan部落正在举行去神圣化仪式

应实施的活动提出了建议。计划将在科特迪瓦全境开展艺术和文化活动，并组织国内外专家学者会议和科学活动，以深化文物归还问题，特别是与Djidji Ayokwe有关的挑战和前景。此外，国家文化艺术品归还委员会还将举办全国巡回展览。为了使该文物与其原属部落重新建立联系，它将首先在Bidjan部落展出，然后是总统府，最后在文明博物馆进行展览。

为了使Djidji Ayokwe的归还成为一项深入、持久、可持续并具有真正社会文化影响的壮举，有几个方面必须考虑到。换而言之，归还工作的成功与否应取决于能否勇敢地应对多种形式的挑战。迄今为止，Djidji Ayokwe的归还尚未生效，其过程受到限制。

四、进程局限性以及成功归还的必要条件

由于缺少重要的参与方，归还工作并不具有完全的包容性。在目前的进程中，参与者包括文化部、Bidjan部落成员、文物归还专家及相关工作

人员，而部落首领和酋长并没有正式参与到这一进程中。文物是作为国家财产而被归还的，因此，当它返回故土时，必须把科特迪瓦所有文化领域的所有传统价值的保卫者聚集在一起。

其他国家部门，如旅游部、高等教育和科学研究部、教育部，甚至宣传部也应参与进来，在各自的领域为丰富和更好地迎接Djidji Ayokwe的归还做出贡献。为确保科特迪瓦年轻一代了解Djidji Ayokwe，有必要采取一些有效的教育措施。科特迪瓦学者、历史学家甚至电影制片人应组织讲座、讨论和历史纪录片，专门介绍Djidji Ayokwe和Bidjan部落的历史。

电视台应定期组织关于Djidji Ayokwe的电视节目。提供遗产旅游的旅游部，也不能置身于文物归还进程之外。

私营部门在公私伙伴关系的框架内需要为博物馆的翻修或新建基础设施以及技术设备提供必要的经济支持，因此，也必须成为Djidji Ayokwe归还的利益相关者。Fondation Orange基金会[①]近日启动了文明博物馆的数字化项目，该博物馆是科特迪瓦藏品最多的博物馆。

培训问题也是影响Djidji Ayokwe回归的一个方面。如前文所述，Djidji Ayokwe的修复工作是由法国修复专家完成的。然而，如果科特迪瓦国家或地方博物馆的工作人员并不具备必要的文物修复技能，也会对文物的归还造成问题。因此，需要对当地的文物修复专家进行培训，以使他们对修复项目具备适当的认识和相关性。

我们计划建议将修复作为博物馆学的一个课程纳入国家艺术和手工艺品研究所（INSAAC）[②]，因为该研究所已经对馆长进行了培训。首先，将向馆长传授修复技术，然后培训正式修复人员，为国家博物馆提供支持。培训将首先在法国文物修复专家的技术支持下，在文明博物馆与凯布朗利博物馆的伙伴关系框架内进行。

贝宁和塞内加尔最近提出申请并追索了一些文物。科特迪瓦也启动

[①] ORANGE GROUP FOUNDATION specialized in mobile telephony which develops partnerships with cultural infrastructures such as the Musée des Civilisations, Musée des costumes etc.

[②] National Institute of Art and Cultural Action, it is the only one national public art school under the supervision of the Department of Culture.

了Djidji Ayokwe归还的程序，并正在为此做准备。然而，更明智的做法是依靠西非经共体这一分区域合作工具，让所有与文物归还问题有关的西非国家参与进来，在一个协调一致的框架内处理这些归还问题。正如菲尔温·萨尔和尼迪克特·萨瓦在他们的报告中所建议的那样，真正的国际文化合作是确保文物归还行动成功的必要条件。

文物归还还要涉及法律和立法问题。由于法国博物馆中的文物被视为法国财产和不可剥夺的资产，因此，Djidji Ayokwe的归还还需要提交给法国立法委员进行表决。法国政府已经认识到殖民是与从非洲人手中夺取的文物有关的问题的根源，因此应该通过各国之间的政治和外交安排进行归还。

如前文所述，科特迪瓦通过了1995年6月24日关于被盗或非法出口文化财产的公约（《国际统一私法协会公约》）。该公约"促进各国人民之间的了解和文化传播，以增进人类福祉和推动文明进步"[①]。然而，这份支持和指导归还工作的法律文书尚未得到所有非洲文物持有者的批准，包括法国在内。

此外，国际博物馆协会制定了《道德准则》，作为所有成员博物馆的参考文件，而Djidji Ayokwe将要归属的科特迪瓦文明博物馆作为国际博物馆协会的成员之一，它承诺遵守《道德准则》的每一项规定。但考虑到地方或国家的实际情况，该准则必须辅之以国家法规所规定的最低标准并得到加强，而科特迪瓦并没有设定这样的标准。因此，当Djidji Ayokwe返回故土之时，制定国家道德准则将是一个完整的法律保护工具，以保护说话鼓和其他文物的归还。

由于其国家博物馆的地位，文明博物馆的业务预算主要用于行政管理（工资、设备采购、发票和维护），并没有用于投资的部分，也就没有多少资金可用于藏品管理，即购置、保存、修复、控制、安全和展览。

结论

将非洲文化遗产送回其原属国是一项具有重大历史意义的行动，它具

---

① Provision from of Uni-Right Agreement (translation mine).

有象征意义并涉及与归还有关的各种问题。第一个问题是文物的归还，鉴于这些文物在凯布朗利博物馆（法国）度过的漫长岁月，它们需要重新被考虑。第二个和第三个问题分别是文物的经济价值和展览价值。换句话说，必须重视文化艺术，以免使其贬值。因此，如何给他们带来价值的问题需要被提出。此外，文物归还必需对博物馆机构重新进行定义。

本文概述了文物归还的总体背景，并介绍了Djidji Ayokwe及其功能。它总结了与即将抵达科特迪瓦的说话鼓有关的筹备活动，并从批判性角度强调了成功的文化归还进程和所需条件的局限性。

总的来说，文物的归还仍然是一个复杂的问题，不应该以牺牲非洲为代价来解决，更不能损害社会的凝聚力。因此，有必要围绕文物归还问题构建统一的框架，并确保这些文物能重新融入共同的生活。

参考文献

Ashley, S. (2009), *Museums and Globalization: Ideas on Recognition, Restitution, Reconfiguration*, LONDON Debates, SAS.

Louis, Obou. (2015), *L'Univers des Objets Parlants dans la Culture Africaine: Le Masque et le Tambour*, NAC's Journal, of African Cultures and Civilization, PARIS New AF.

Memel, Silvie (2018) *«Le Traffic Illicite des Biens Culturels: Cas des musées de Côte d'Ivoire»*, Doctorate Thesis, Abidjan.

Niangoran, B. (1989), *«Les Ebrié et leur organisation politique traditionnelle»* dans les annales de l'Université d4abidjan, Serie F Ethnosociologie.

Ndiaye, F. (1989), *«Ebrié d'Adjamé. Tambour royal ayokwe»*, Dans Corps Sculptés, Corps Parés, Corps Masqués, (Exposition), Paris, Galeries Nationales du Grand Palais.

Opokou, K. (2019), *Coordination of African Positions on Restitution Matters*, Modern Ghana, Retrieved, July 2019.

Hannerz, U. (1992), *Cultures and Globalization: Conflicts and Tensions*, New York, Columbia University Press.

Hartman, G. (1997), *The Fateful Question of Culture*. New York, Columbia University

Press.

Herman, Alexander (2021), *Restitution: The Return of Cultural Artefacts, Hot Topics in the Art World*, UK, Lund Humphries Publishers.

Sarr, F. (2020), *Restitution of African Artefacts: History, Memory, Traces, Reappropriation*, New Ethical Relation (Mimeo).

Sarr, F.; Savoy B. (2018), *The Restitution of African Cultural Heritage: Toward a New Relational Ethics*, Paris. Available at http//restitutionreport2018.com / Sarr Savoy

Savoy, B. (2022), *Africa's Struggle for Its Art: History of a Postcolonial Defeat*, Princeton University Press.

Repatriation of Ancestral Remains in Australia: Resources for the World

Dr. Michael Pickering[*]

Abstract

Australia has been repatriating remains to its Indigenous people for over 30 years. Over this time, it has had many successful experiences that have allowed the development of refined principles and process to facilitate the return of remains. There have also been issues that have needed addressing.

In the process of repatriation, Australian researchers and Indigenous communities have also revealed and shared new knowledges about both past and present cultures. This knowledge can inform other repatriating agencies, domestically and internationally.

Repatriation activities in Australia have also had outcomes that can inform the 'decolonising museums' debate. The principles and philosophies that have emerged through repatriation of Ancestral Human Remains are also those that can apply to the repatriation of other cultural materials.

Brief Introduction

Australia has been carrying out repatriations of Ancestral Human Remains

---

[*] Dr. Michael Pickering, Honorary Associate Professor, Department of Heritage and Museum Studies, Australian National University; Honorary Associate Professor, Global Station for Indigenous Studies and Cultural Diversity, Hokkaido University, Japan; Partner.Centre for Australian Studies, Cologne University, Germany.

and Secret/sacred objects to Australian Indigenous communities for over 30 years. Over this time, it is conservatively estimated that the remains of approximately 2,500 individuals have been returned to community ownership and control by Australian museums.

It must be acknowledged that the repatriation movement in Australia is the outcome of years of effort by Indigenous Australian activists and advocates. The commitments by Australian governments and collecting institutions is an informed response to this advocacy.

The philosophies, policies, and processes for repatriation of Australian Indigenous Ancestral remains have become refined and increasingly efficient. Australian museums and other Indigenous heritage agencies have, through research and experience and full community engagement, encountered and dealt with the majority of problems and issues likely to confront other agencies engaging in repatriation of Ancestral remains, both domestically and internationally. Particularly in the areas of project governance, where practices and supporting rationales have been developed to ensure that the appropriate communities are identified, engaged, and protected, while at the same time the engaging agency is also protected. Many of the debates, experiences, and outcomes have been reported in scholarly outputs (e.g., Fforde, McKeown and Keeler, 2020; Turnbull, 2017; Turnbull and Pickering, 2010), popular media (see 'Selected media websites' n.d.) and many are easily available on-line (Return, Reconcile, Renew 2021, Pickering, 2020) or through direct contacts with repatriation managers.

Thus, Australian repatriation experiences offer resources for the world. Similarly, there are engagements elsewhere in the world that largely go unreported in accessible forms. In some ways, *this paper is a plea for people to share experiences, positive and negative, that will inform repatriation practitioners internationally.*

It might be argued by some that Australia's experiences in repatriation are specific to the Australian context. Unique due to Australia's remote location, the cultural characteristics of the hundreds of Indigenous cultures that occupy it, and its histories. There have also been international museum colleagues who have denied that their nations lack any Indigenous peoples. Yet they then refer to 'folk minorities' or folk cultures, typically defined by their territorial locations and unique cultural characteristics. In their eyes, this makes Australian experiences irrelevant to their situation.

However, the terms 'Indigenous' and 'folk minority' are, when scrutinised, almost synonymous, referring to small discrete, self-identifying, cultural groups. It is within this broader context that the Australian experience in repatriation is immediately relevant to informing international debates and the development of repatriation processes.

Issues

The majority of Australia's repatriation events have been unproblematic, with well – provenanced remains being returned to Indigenous communities with no issue. Such events are usually a positive experience for the communities, the repatriating agencies and, through supportive media coverage, the wider Australian community. Repatriations are typically seen as good news stories by the general public, generally due to the empathy they share over the principle of respect for the dead, regardless of cultural origins.

It is easy to concentrate attention on the numerous success stories in Australian Indigenous Repatriations. This is often a typical 'tradeshow' approach, common to many Australian conferences and institutional media releases, where museums and government agencies stand up and boast about what a good job they are doing. There is no doubt we have learnt a lot about how to do things through other people's success stories. However, we can also learn a lot, in both scholarly and practical terms, through interrogating the less positive issues that may arise in the repatriation process. Such issues are often concealed. Sometimes through a desire to avoid embarrassment in front of 'the boss' of the museum or agency responsible for the repatriation, but more often to avoid unintentionally arming those opposed to repatriation who would weaponise negative events in order to prevent or delay a future repatriation activity.

Examples of the misuse of such issues include those who argue that more intensive science-based provenancing work, needs to be done—based on a rare episode of poor historical or scientific provenancing. Or those who argue that there are internal community disputes over appropriate authority that must be resolved before remains are returned—often based on a dissenting minority voice in the Indigenous community. There are those who argue biological affiliation to remains is more important than cultural affiliation—despite this being clearly dismissed through numerous legal and scholarly investigations into cultural identity and authority. Often these objections are concealed under the umbrella statement of 'we want to do the right thing.' Finally, there are those who claim the return of remains will 'open the flood gates' to claims on other parts of their collections. This has not happened in Australia, nor has it happened in those international institutions that have decided to return Australian remains.

Despite the numerous successes, there are also day-to-day issues with repatriating remains in Australia. I would identify the silencing of Indigenous activists and advocates through greater government agency interference in repatriation activities, especially with international engagements (Office for the Arts n.d. a). There are gaps in communication between various repatriating agencies, such as museums, heritage agencies, government offices, and universities. There is competition between agencies for control of sectors of repatriation activities, more to ensure their own survival than to better serve Indigenous communities. There are ageing and inflexible grant process that do not accommodate the costs or timeframes of repatriation activities (Office for the Arts n.d, b). There is poor post-return government support for appropriate cultural activities needed for respectful reburial. There are other issues, largely administrative, that interfere with, but do not prevent successful repatriations. But, let's face it, that is business-as-usual for most organisations.

Positive and negative experiences both provide important learning and knowledge resources. Indeed, how difficulties, intellectual and practical, have been approached, moderated, and resolved is probably more valuable to repatriation studies than simple popularist reports of uncomplicated returns.

Outcomes

Despite the issues that can occasionally arise, much has been achieved through repatriation. Of course, the most significant outcome is the unconditional return of Ancestral remains to Australian Indigenous communities. These remains were typically acquired by or for western collecting agencies through illegal and immoral acts such as grave robbing, mutilation of people killed in colonial conflicts, dissection of Indigenous people who died in hospitals, asylums, and prisons, without appropriate consent, and acquisition through purchase or gift in a situation where the relationship between the Indigenous so-called seller or donor and the acquirer was far from equal. Their return is an act of restorative justice.

The 'Australian Government's Policy on Indigenous Repatriation' (2016) explicitly acknowledges the often-disgraceful circumstances of collecting. The sentiments in this policy are shared by state and territory governments, and by the public collecting institutions and heritage agencies under their jurisdiction. These can be summarised as acknowledgements that:

– Australia Indigenous people have the right to the repatriation of their ancestor's remains.

– the original taking of remains was an act of injustice,

– Repatriation is a mechanism for healing and justice in Australian society.

– The return of ancestral remains empowers Aboriginal and Torres Strait Islander peoples to meet their cultural obligations and contribute to the wider Australian society.

The concept of repatriation being, in part, an act addressing past injustices needs little explanation. However, the concept of assisting in 'healing' is less so. To some it might seem mere rhetoric. It is, however, very real in the cultural worlds of Indigenous Australians and can be demonstrated in real outcomes. When remains are returned to their homelands and culturally authorised descendants it is believed that their spirit has also been laid to rest. Lands that were once considered 'sick,' because of the removal of remains, are now considered healed and re-use of the resources of the land can recommence. Victims of the forced removal of children from their parents and lands in the past have recounted how being able to participate in reburials of remains has made them feel that they too, have truly come home. Elders are recognised as having increased authority through achieving returns and managing the culturally appropriate final disposition of remains. Young people are trained and better culturally empowered through their increasing participation in repatriation activities.

Improvements in the social, physical, and mental well-being of communities do occur and are observable. The explicit and formal acknowledgements by Australian Governments, at all levels, that repatriation assists healing is thus an important one.

In addition, there have been other positive outcomes. In a number of cases, an Australian collecting institution's repatriation commitments and activities has resulted in greater social issues-based engagements rather than relatively simple, sterilised exhibition-oriented projects. This has led to increased trust between collecting institutions and Indigenous communities, though this trust must be maintained through continued honest engagements. There are increasing research partnerships between scholars and practitioners of repatriation and those communities that have had remains returned.

These partnerships provide valuable new knowledge that not only informs museum practice, but also provokes consideration as to future directions in museum, academic, and Indigenous interests. Many of the protocols and resources developed in the repatriation of ancestral remains are relevant to those processes that should be applied, not only in the repatriation discussions of other objects and materials, but in engagements with Indigenous communities on other museum collection related matters.

One significant example of repatriation related research emerging from such partnerships is the 'Return, Reconcile, and Renew' (2021) Project, carried out in partnership with three Indigenous cultural blocks, several domestic and international universities and affiliates, a museum, and a major Indigenous representative agency. This research now provides resources for Indigenous and non-Indigenous researchers alike, with a strong focus on providing information to Australian Indigenous communities seeking information about the histories of their own misappropriated ancestors. Initially working with the three Indigenous community partners, the project serves as a model for information management and access that can be applied to other communities seeking information on the whereabouts of their ancestors and is growing in content. The website is also a valuable resource for guidance on governance.

There are also other offshoot studies. Through repatriation stimulated engagements, we are also acquiring new knowledge on contemporary Indigenous societies and their perspectives on the changes in their cultures and histories over time of colonisation. We must remember that 'foreign' societies, Indigenous and non-Indigenous, are not locked in time or space and the legitimate social changes they experience are part of the modern human story, deserving of consideration by progressive museums. We have greater understanding of the significance of cultural heritage to contemporary Australian

Indigenous people. We better understand the legitimacy and attributes of cultural change over time. We have better appreciation of the impacts of cultural beliefs on Indigenous engagements with sensitive collection materials, including human remains, sacred objects, and secular materials (Pickering, 2020).

Australia's repatriation directions have also benefited from Federal and State laws, determinations, and commitments regarding Indigenous social and property rights. One very positive outcome of the legal testing and recognition of Indigenous rights, through Land Rights, Native Title, and heritage legislation, is that mechanisms and criteria for affiliation to lands, beliefs, community identity and culture, have been tested and expanded through various legal processes, usually unrelated to repatriation. These expanded criteria have been objectively proven and can be translated to issues of repatriation, in particular the fact that cultural criteria are as legitimate as biological criteria in assigning rights to Ancestral remains and other cultural heritage.

These legal, and policy precedents can inform international repatriation research, particularly in the areas of how identity and affiliation are defined and how rights may persist in Ancestral remains and cultural heritage. The legal testing of rights challenges the opinions of those who oppose repatriation on the basis that it is driven by sentiment, emotion, politics of convenience, or irrational spiritual beliefs.

Decolonisation and Repatriation

The Decolonisation of museums, and the repatriation of remains and cultural materials, have almost become synonymous. In many public discussions, a final repatriation is represented as the mandatory measure of success for museum decolonisation. However, 'decolonisation' starts with changing institutional culture, not just with the decision to repatriate.

As noted at the beginning, Australian museums had been repatriating ancestral remains for over 30 years, long before decolonisation became the latest buzzword. Repatriations were occurring because they were eventually considered the right thing to do. Retrospectively, 'decolonisation' of the museums was inherent in these changed philosophies and practices but was not the explicit primary motivator.

The increasing profile of the decolonisation debates suggests that museums are engaging more with both decolonisation and, by default, repatriation. Unfortunately, in Australia, this is not always the case. Despite some institutional claims of world leadership in philosophy and practice, it is usually the case that the repatriation practitioners in Australian museums are few and relatively isolated, typically less than 1% of total staffing. They are highly motivated and do their best, but in many ways their work, and the philosophies and scholarship behind their work, is concealed from the rest of the institution. In my own 25 years of experience working in major Australian museums, 'decolonisation' and 'repatriation' were not topics introduced as part of general staff training or discussed on the museum floor. It did not affect the philosophical, theoretical and practices directions of the finance staff, visitor services, facilities managers, public programs, marketing, or administrative staff, amongst others.

Many museums advertise their progressiveness with statements about their engagements with decolonisation or repatriation. New policies and guidelines promising improved recognition of the rights of Indigenous peoples in the management and use of collections are released with much fanfare. However, often these policies and statements progress no further than the nearest highly decorated website or glossy 'policy' (e.g., Janke 2018),

An internal investigation of how these promises are practically implemented can be disappointing. The promises are rarely initiated, rarely penetrate the museum to inform and guide the practices of all staff, and they rarely lead to a real change in the institutional culture.

The repatriation philosophies, policies, and activities of an institution need to be communicated more broadly to both all staff and to the public on a continuing basis, not just when it is convenient to make a media boast. Consideration of 'decolonising' and 'repatriation' debates needs to engage all staff. This does not mean staff taking sides in the debates. It does mean being aware of the debates that are affecting the industry in which they choose to work.

Conclusion

The experiences and evolving philosophies and practices of Australian Museums in repatriation of ancestral remains can and has informed other international museums and heritage agencies policies and practices.

Sharing International Repatriation experiences can inform the 'decolonisation' debate. The 'decolonisation' debate can inform repatriation practices.

And finally, an appreciation of, if not wholehearted support for, the issues involved in repatriation and decolonisation debates and activities must be shared by the entire museums' community, not just by small groups of specialists working in isolation.

References

'Australian Government Policy on Indigenous Repatriation' (2016), Department of Communications and the Arts, https://www.arts.gov.au/sites/default/files/documents/australian_government_policy_on_indigenous_repatriation.pdf, Accessed 1 May 2023.

'Selected media websites' n.d. https://www.bing.com/images/search?q=Australia+aboriginal+repatriation+news&form=HDRSC4&first=1, Accessed 1 May 2023.

Fforde, Cressida., McKeown, C. Timothy., & Keeler, Honor. (eds.) (2020), *The Routledge Companion to Indigenous Repatriation: Return, Reconcile, Renew*. London:

Routledge.

Office for the Arts n.d. a, *Fact Sheet—International Repatriation*, https://www.arts.gov.au/publications/fact-sheet-international-repatriation, Accessed 1 May 2023.

Office for the Arts n.d. b, *Domestic Repatriation*, https://www.arts.gov.au/what-we-do/cultural-heritage/indigenous-repatriation/domestic-repatriation, Accessed 1 May 2023.

Pickering, Michael. (2020), *A Repatriation Handbook: A guide to the repatriation of Australian Aboriginal and Torres Strait Islander Ancestral Remains*. National Museum of Australia. https://www.nma.gov.au/about/publications/repatriation-handbook, Accessed 1 May 2023.

Pickering, Michael. (2020), The Supernatural and Sensitive Indigenous Materials: A Workplace Health and Safety issue? In *Museum Management and Curatorship*. August 2020 Taylor and Francis. UK. https://doi.org/10.1080/09647775.2020.1803113, Accessed 1 May 2023.

Return Reconcile Renew website (2021), https://returnreconcilerenew.info/, Accessed 1 May 2023.

Janke, Terri. (2018), *First Peoples: A Roadmap for Enhancing Indigenous Engagement in Museums and Galleries*, Australian Museums and Galleries Association Incorporated, 2018., Australian Museums and Galleries Association Incorporated, 2018, https://www.amaga-indigenous.org.au/, Accessed 1 May 2023.

Turnbull, Paul. (2017), *Science, Museums and Collecting the Indigenous Dead in Colonial Australia*, Cham: Palgrave Macmillan, 2017.

Turnbull, Paul. and Pickering, Michael. 2010 (eds), *The Long Way Home: The Meaning and Values of Repatriation*. Berghahn Books. New York.

文物返还经验的全球化共享：
以澳大利亚原住民祖先遗骸返还工作为例

迈克尔·皮克林[*]

摘要

三十多年来，澳大利亚一直在为追返原住民遗骸而努力。在此期间，澳大利亚取得了诸多成功经验。为了推进遗骸返还工作，澳大利亚也促进了相关原则与程序的发展与完善。不过，目前还有一些问题需要解决。

在（文物）返还的过程中，澳大利亚的研究人员和原住民社区也揭示并分享了对历史和当今文化的新认知。这些新知识也可为国内外其他从事文物返还工作的机构提供参考。

澳大利亚在文物返还运动中所取得的成果也为"博物馆去殖民化"的研讨提供了参考。在人类祖先遗骸返还过程中形成的原则和理念也可以应用到其他文化材料的追返工作中。

简介

三十多年来，澳大利亚一直在为人类祖先遗骸及（部族）密物/圣物归还至当地原住民社区而努力。保守估计，在此期间，澳大利亚博物馆已将大约2 500具遗骸交还由社区，归属澳大利亚博物馆管理。

必须承认的是，澳大利亚的文物返还运动是澳大利亚当地原住民活动者与倡导者多年努力的成果。澳大利亚政府与收藏机构的承诺也对这一主

---

[*] 迈克尔·皮克林，澳大利亚国立大学文化遗产与博物馆研究系名誉副教授，日本北海道大学原住民研究与文化多样性全球研究站名誉副教授，德国科隆大学澳大利亚研究中心合伙人。

张做出了明智的回应。

　　澳大利亚原住民祖先遗骸返还的理念、政策和程序已日趋完善，效率也越来越高。澳大利亚博物馆和其他的原住民遗产机构通过深入研究、有关经验以及社区的充分参与，已经遇到并解决了国内外其他从事祖先遗骸返还工作的机构可能需要应对的大多数问题与事项。尤其是在项目管理方面，为了确保找出明确的相应社区、做好本土社区参与和保护工作，澳大利亚已经制定了一些做法和支持性依据，同时也为参与返还工作的机构提供保护。（澳大利亚文物返还工作）的许多探讨、经验和成果已经在学术成果（如：Fforde, McKeown and Keeler, 2020; Turnbull, 2017; Turnbull and Pickering, 2010）、大众媒体（详见"Selected media websites"）中进行了报道，并且还有很多内容可以通过线上的方式（Return, Reconcile, Renew 2021, Pickering, 2020）或直接与负责文物返还工作的管理人员联系而轻松获取。

　　因此，澳大利亚文物返还的工经验为全世界提供了可供参考的资源。同样地，世界上其他地方还有很多参与文物返还工作的机构，他们的经验在很大程度上还没有被报道出来，大家也很难了解到他们的工作成果与经验。从某些方面来讲，这篇文章想要呼吁大家为国际上从事文物返还工作的人们，提供正反两方面的经验。

　　一些人可能会觉得，澳大利亚的文物返还经验是在其特定的背景下而特有的。的确，澳大利亚因其"孤岛式"的地理位置、数百种不同的原住民习俗所构成的独特文化特点及其历史而独一无二。而且还有一些国际上的博物馆同行表示，他们国家也有原住民，但他们否认了"原住民"（Indigenous peoples）这一说法，而是用"少数民族"或者"民间文化"来表达其所处位置和独特的文化特征。因此，他们认为澳大利亚的工作经验与他们国家的情况并无关系。

　　然而，"原住民"和"少数民族"这两个词细究起来，基本上可以看作是同义词，都指的是独立的、自我认同的小型文化群体。因此，在这种更为广泛的词义背景下，澳大利亚的文物返还经验为国际研讨与文物返还流程的完善提供了更为直接的参考。

现状与问题

目前，澳大利亚的大部分文物返还项目已经做得较为出色，本土的遗存都在被完好地送还到原住民社区。这对社区、文物返还机构以及通过正向的媒体报道后对更广范围的澳大利亚社会来说都是一次积极的经历。遗骸返还通常是会被公众视为好消息的，因为大多数人都明白"逝者为大"的道理，无关文化习俗。

人们很容易将注意力集中在澳大利亚原住民（祖先遗骸）返还工作中的众多成功案例上。这是一种典型的"展示宣传"方式，在澳大利亚很多会议和机构的媒体发布会上很常见，博物馆和政府机构会在这里夸耀他们工作的成功。毫无疑问，我们从别人的成功经验中学到了很多。但其实，我们通过对文物返还过程中可能出现的一些失败经验进行研究，也能够在学术与实践两方面有所进益。不过，这些问题往往会被隐藏起来：有时是为了避免在博物馆和文物返还机构的"负责人"面前丢脸，但更多时候是为了避免被那些不看好返还工作的人反向利用，那些人会恶意利用返还过程中的失败经验，来阻止或推迟之后的文物返还工作。

对失败案例的不当解读中包括：有些人提出要对缺乏历史或科学证明这一鲜少出现的罕见情况展开更加深入的科学证明工作；还有些人基于原住民社区中少数人的不同意见而提出，在遗骸返还之前，必须先解决好本土社区内部对权力合理性的争议；也有些人认为遗骸的生物联系比文化关系更为重要——尽管这一说法已经被法律和学术界众多的对文化认同和权力的研究所否决。而且人往往是打着"我们想要去做正确的事"的旗号，将自己不当的异议掩饰起来。最后，还有一部分人宣称，遗骸返还相当于打开了文物索要的"闸门"，后续会更进一步去索要其他文物藏品。不过，这种现象在澳大利亚并没有发生过，也没有在那些决定归还澳大利亚原住民祖先遗骸的国际机构中发生过。

尽管我们取得了不少成功经验，但澳大利亚的遗骸返还工作还存在一些日常问题：一是我认为政府机构（尤其是国际参与）在返还工作中的干预，削弱了原住民活动家和倡导者在文物返还工作中的话语权和影响力（详见"Office for the Arts, a"）；二是博物馆、遗产机构、政府和高校等多种从事文物返还工作的机构之间，也存在着沟通上的不足；三是各个机构都竞相争取对文物返还工作中各个部分的控制权，美其名曰是为了更好地服务原住民社区，其实是为了保证机构自身的生存；四是项目拨款程序老化且缺乏灵活性，无法满足文物返还工作的资金成本和时间要求（详见"Office for the Arts, b"）。最后还有，在遗骸归还之后，当地政府在对遗骸进行严肃庄重的重新安葬和为这一仪式准备相应的文化活动等方面，是缺乏支持力度的。当然，还有一些其他问题，主要就是行政问题，虽有这些干扰但并未影响遗骸的成功返还。不过，这对于大多数组织机构来说都是司空见惯的事情，我们还是要面对现实。

其实无论是成功还是失败的经验，都能够给我们提供重要的指引与帮助。事实上，相比起对文物顺利返还进行的简单的大众化报道，如何处理、缓和、解决理论和实践上的困难可能对文物返还研究来说更有意义。

研究发现与成果

尽管偶尔还会出现问题，但文物返还工作还是取得了许多成果。当然，这其中最重要的成果就是将澳大利亚原住民祖先遗骸无条件归还回原住民社区。这些遗骸通常是西方收藏机构通过非法和不道德的行为获取的，如盗墓，或是肢解那些因殖民冲突而丧生的人，抑或是未经允许解剖死在医院、收容所和监狱的原住民，以及在原住民所谓的卖方或捐赠者与收购者之间的关系完全不平等的情况下，以购买或赠予的名义获得的遗骸。因此，归还原住民的祖先遗骸是一种修复正义的行为。

《澳大利亚政府关于原住民遗物返还的政策（2016）》（Australian Government's Policy on Indigenous Repatriation, 2016）明确表示，收藏工作中经常会出现一些不符合伦理道德的"丑闻"。各州和领地政府及其管辖的公共收藏机构和遗产机构也都对此持相同观点。这些观点可以概括为以下几点：

（1）澳大利亚原住民有权要求归还其祖先遗骸；

（2）最初夺走祖先遗骸的行为是不公平的；

（3）遗骸返还是澳大利亚社会进行创伤疗愈和获取公平正义的一种机制；

（4）归还祖先遗骸可以使原住民及托雷斯海峡岛民（Aboriginal and Torres Strait Islander peoples）有能力去履行他们的文化义务，并为澳大利亚社会做出更广泛的贡献。

"文物返还"的概念在某种程度上是一种解决过去不公正问题的行为，其概念无需多言，而帮助原住民"疗愈"他们已经支离破碎的心灵就没有这么简单了。或许对一些人来说，这一说法听起来十分抽象，不切实际。然而，在澳大利亚原住民的文化世界中是真实存在的，而且是可以用实际结果来证明的。当遗骸被送还故乡，并交至其已经通过文化授权的后代手里时，人们相信他们的灵魂才真正得以安息。这片土地曾因遗骸掠夺而"患病"，而现在已经逐渐"痊愈"，可以重新开始对当地的土地资源加以开发利用。过去被迫离开父母与故乡的儿童受害者们也表示，自己能够参与祖先遗骸的重新安葬，让他们真正感觉到自己回家了。通过遗骸返还和管理符合文化要求的遗骸最终处置方式，年长者的权威性得到提高。年轻人也在参与遗骸返还的过程中得到了锻炼，也增强了自身的文化权利。

原住民社区的社会地位和身心健康方面确实有了显而易见的改善。因此，澳大利亚各级政府发表正式声明，遗骸返还对原住民社区的疗愈及改善有重要意义。

此外，我们还有一些另外的积极成果。在许多案例中，澳大利亚收藏机构在文物返还工作中做出的承诺和行为促成了更多以社会热点问题为基础的参与，而不是一些相对简单、完全以展览为导向的项目。这也使得收藏机构与原住民社区之间的信任得以加强，不过这种信任需要持续的诚意接触来维持。而且，理论研究者和实践工作者有关文物返还和拥有返还文物社区的研究合作也日益增多。

这些合作研究提供了宝贵的新认识，不仅为博物馆的实践工作提供了帮助，还引发了对博物馆、学术界和原住民利益的未来发展方向的思考。在返还祖先遗骸的过程中形成的协议与资源都与一些程序有关，这些程序不仅可以在讨论其他文物返还的时候得以应用，而且还可以应用在与原住民社区一起参与其他博物馆藏品相关事宜之时。

与三个原住民文化街区、多所国内外大学及其附属机构、一所博物馆和一所大型的原住民代表机构合作开展的"回归、和解与更新"（Return, Reconcile, and Renew, 2021）项目，就是通过这种合作关系开展文物返还相关研究的重要实例。这项研究现在为当地原住民和非原住民研究员提供资源，重点是为澳大利亚的原住民社区提供信息，帮助他们了解自己祖先曾被盗用的历史。这个项目最初与三个原住民社区合作，被视为是资源管理和获取的典范，其经验可用来帮助其他社区寻找其祖先下落的信息，而且其内容也在不断完善丰富。这个项目的网站也是为管理文物返还工作提供指导的珍贵资源库。

另外，还有其他的一些分支研究。通过促进文物返还工作的顺利开展，我们对当代原住民社会有了新的认知，并了解了他们对其文化和历史在殖民化过程中发生的变化的看法。我们必须记住，"外来"社会，无论是原住民还是非原住民，都不是停滞在当时的时间或空间中的，他们所经历的合理的社会变革也是现代人类故事中的一部分，值得那些追求进取的博物馆去思考。我们更加了解文化遗产对当代澳大利亚原住民的意义。我们更好地理解文化随时间推移而变化的自然道理和属性。我们更为深刻地认识到文化信仰对原住民参与接触敏感藏品素材（包括人类遗骸、祖先圣物、世俗材料等）的重要影响（Pickering, 2020）。

澳大利亚文物返还工作的方针也得益于各联邦和州内关于原住民社会和遗产[①]权利的法律、决议和承诺。通过土地权、原住民土地权和遗产立法对原住民权利进行法律检验和认证后得到的一个非常积极的成果是，关于土地、信仰、社区身份和文化归属的机制和标准，已经通过各种法律程序得到检验和完善。这些程序通常与文物返还工作本体关联不大，但真正改善了原住民社区的发展状况。这些扩充完善的标准已经得到客观证实，并能转化作用于返还工作中，特别是在分配祖先遗骸和其他文化遗产方

[①] 这里原文英语使用为"properties"一词，表示财产，译者根据语境译为"遗产"，如日语语境下会使用"文化财"一词，以财产表示遗产。——译者注

...标准和生物标准同样合法。

...些法律和政策先例可以为国际文物返还研究提供借鉴，特别是在如...界定身份和归属，以及祖先遗骸和文化遗产中的权利如何延续等方面。这种对权利展开的法律检验，对那些以感情、情绪、权宜之计或非理性精神信仰为由而反对遗骸返还工作的观点提出了挑战。

去殖民化与文物返还

博物馆的去殖民化、遗骸和其他文化材料的返还有时候几乎成了同义词。比如在很多公开讨论中，文物的最终返还就被视为是衡量博物馆去殖民化成功与否的强制性标准。然而，"去殖民化"始于制度文化的改变，而不仅仅是文物返还的裁决。

正如开始所说，早在三十多年前，"去殖民化"一词还没有成为新兴热词的时候，澳大利亚博物馆已经在开展祖先遗骸返还的工作了。之所以会出现文物返还的行为，是因为这一工作终究被视为是正确的。回顾过去，博物馆的"去殖民化"是这些理论和实践变化上的内在要求，但并不是一个明确的主要动因。

关于去殖民化的辩论日益受到关注，这表明博物馆正在更多地参与去殖民化活动，并主动参与着文物返还的工作。不幸的是，澳大利亚的情况并非总是如此。尽管一些机构声称自己在理念和实践方面处于世界领先地位，但通常情况下，澳大利亚博物馆中从事文物返还工作的人员数量很少，且相对孤立，基本上不到员工数的1%。他们干劲十足，尽心尽力，但很多时候，他们的工作成果以及背后的理念与学术研究，会被单位其他部门的工作人员所掩盖。我自己在澳大利亚主要博物馆工作的25年中，"非殖民化"和"归还"并没有作为普通员工培训的一部分，也没有在博物馆内讨论过。这并不影响财务人员、游客服务、设施管理人员、公共项目、市场营销或行政人员等的理念、理论和实践方向。

许多博物馆在宣传他们的进步性的时候，都声称自己参与了去殖民化和文物返还的工作。他们大张旗鼓地发布新的政策和指导方针，承诺在藏品的管理和使用方面进一步承认原住民的权利。然而，这些政策和声明往往只停留在最近的装饰华丽的网站或光鲜亮丽的"政策"上（如 Janke, 2018）。

对这些承诺的实际执行情况进行内部调查后可能会令人失望。这些承诺很少是主动的，也很少能渗透到博物馆中，为所有工作人员的实践提供信息和指导，也很少能带来制度文化的真正改变。

从事文物返还工作的机构需要将其返还理念、政策和活动持续地向全体工作人员和公众进行广泛传播，而不仅仅是为了方便只向媒体吹嘘。关于"去殖民化"和"文物返还"的辨析研讨需要所有工作人员的参与，这并不意味着工作人员要在辨析中偏袒某一方，只是说需要他们了解这种辨析研讨对他们所选择的工作会产生影响。

结论

澳大利亚博物馆在祖先遗骸返还方面的经验及其不断发展的理念与实践，能够且已经为其他国际博物馆和遗产机构的政策与做法提供了借鉴。

国际博物馆在归还祖先遗骸和其他文化材料方面的经验及不断演变的理念与实践，也能够且已经为澳大利亚的博物馆和遗产机构的政策与做法提供了借鉴。

分享在国际上从事文物返还工作的经验能够为"去殖民化"的辨析提供信息。

"去殖民化"辨析能够为返还工作实践提供参考。

最后，对文物返还和去殖民化的辨析与行动所涉及的问题的理解，即使不是所有人都全心全意地支持，也必须得到整个博物馆界的认同，而不仅仅是由一小群专家孤立地开展工作。

参考文献

'Australian Government Policy on Indigenous Repatriation' (2016), Department of
    Communications and the Arts https://www.arts.gov.au/sites/default/files/documents/

alian_government_policy_on_indigenous_repatriation.pdf, Accessed 1 May 2023.

selected media websites' n.d. https://www.bing.com/images/search?q=Australia+aboriginal+repatriation+news&form=HDRSC4&first=1, Accessed 1 May 2023.

Fforde, Cressida., McKeown, C. Timothy., & Keeler, Honor. (eds.) (2020), *The Routledge Companion to Indigenous Repatriation: Return, Reconcile, Renew*. London: Routledge.

Office for the Arts n.d. a, *Fact Sheet—International Repatriation* https://www.arts.gov.au/publications/fact-sheet-international-repatriation, Accessed 1 May 2023.

Office for the Arts n.d. b, *Domestic Repatriation* https://www.arts.gov.au/what-we-do/cultural-heritage/indigenous-repatriation/domestic-repatriation, Accessed 1 May 2023.

Pickering, Michael. (2020), *A Repatriation Handbook: A guide to the repatriation of Australian Aboriginal and Torres Strait Islander Ancestral Remains*. National Museum of Australia. https://www.nma.gov.au/about/publications/repatriation-handbook, Accessed 1 May 2023.

Pickering, Michael. (2020), The Supernatural and Sensitive Indigenous Materials: A Workplace Health and Safety issue? In *Museum Management and Curatorship*. August 2020 Taylor and Francis. UK. https://doi.org/10.1080/09647775.2020.1803113, Accessed 1 May 2023.

Return Reconcile Renew website (2021), https://returnreconcilerenew.info/, Accessed 1 May 2023.

Janke, Terri. (2018), *First Peoples: A Roadmap for Enhancing Indigenous Engagement in Museums and Galleries*, Australian Museums and Galleries Association Incorporated, 2018., Australian Museums and Galleries Association Incorporated, 2018, https://www.amaga-indigenous.org.au/, Accessed 1 May 2023.

Turnbull, Paul. (2017), *Science, Museums and Collecting the Indigenous Dead in Colonial Australia*, Cham: Palgrave Macmillan, 2017.

Turnbull, Paul. and Pickering, Michael. 2010 (eds), *The Long Way Home: The Meaning and Values of Repatriation*. Berghahn Books. New York.